4 on

IN SEARCH
OF THE PRIMITIVE

iN SEARCH OF THE PRiMiTiVE

A Critique of Civilization

Stanley Diamond

FOREWORD ERIC R. WOLF

ta

TRANSACTION BOOKS
New Brunswick, New Jersey
Distributed by E.P. Dutton & Company

Library of Congress Catalog Number: 72-82195
ISBN: 0-87855-045-3 (cloth); 0-87855-582-X (paper)

Printed in the United States of America

The author is grateful for permission to reprint portions of this book which originally appeared in the following publications:

"The Politics of Field Work" originally appeared as "Nigerian Discovery" in *Reflections on Community Studies* edited by A. Vidich, M. Stein and J. Bensman (John Wiley, 1964).

"Anthropology in Question" is a revised and expanded version of "Man in Question" from *Reinventing Anthropology* edited by Dell Hymes (Pantheon Books, 1972).

"The Search for the Primitive" is a revised and expanded version of an essay that appeared in *Man's Image in Medicine and Anthropology* edited by Iago Gladston (Library of the New York Academy of Medicine, 1963).

"Plato and the Definition of the Primitive" first appeared in *Culture in History: Essays in Honor of Paul Radin* edited by Stanley Diamond (Columbia University Press, 1960).

"The Uses of the Primitive" was first published in *Primitive Views of the World* edited by Stanley Diamond (Columbia University Press, 1964).

"The Rule of Law versus the Order of Custom" is revised from an essay in *The Rule of Law* edited by Robert Paul Wolff (Simon and Schuster, 1971).

"Job and the Trickster" first appeared as the introduction to a new edition of *The Trickster* by Paul Radin (Schocken Books, 1972).

"What History Is" originally appeared in *Patterns and Process in Culture* by Robert Manners (University of Chicago Press, 1964).

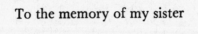

To the memory of my sister

The dream of reason produces monsters.

—Goya

General and abstract ideas are the source of the greatest errors of mankind.

—Rousseau

Shakespeare cared little for the State, the source of all our judgments, apart from its shows and splendours, its turmoils and battles, its flamings-out of the uncivilized heart.

—W.B. Yeats

CONTENTS

FOREWORD

The crisis in the Western world and its imperial hinterland, which is also the crisis of humanity, cannot be confined to social, economic or technological "problems"; it inheres in our definition, our very understanding of man. We live in what we pridefully call civilization, but our laws and machines have taken on a life of their own; they stand against our spiritual and physical survival. Our politics oscillate between the consolidation of bureaucratic controls and outbursts of impotent, if symbolic, fury. The rule of law, as Stanley Diamond says, represents "the chronic symptom of the disorder of institutions." Science, which was to liberate us, imprisons us in abstractions; passion and compassion atrophy in the hands of professionals who turn their concepts into fetishes. So-called students of man, who study man because he has become the problem, are driven by a search for abstract models within which to capture and hold fast the flow of human reality. What began as a fraternal endeavor to understand men in their concrete similarities and differences, in order to comprehend human possibilities, is rapidly becoming one of the "policy sciences," a discipline of human control, the very denial of humanity. Prometheus yields to Procrustes both in our culture at large and in our study of it.

It is this growing denial of human freedom, the diffusion of the false consciousness created by the increasingly technetronic order (to use Zbigniev Brzezinski's appalling and approving term) that Stanley Diamond raises his voice against in these essays.

In his opening essay "The Politics of Field Work," Diamond reaffirms that field work is the ground for human encounter, ultimately encounter with ourselves, not the fixing of signs on a piece of paper or upon magnetic tape by an investigator who turns himself into a recording machine. The anthropologist's hut provides no neutral ground, constitutes no privileged sanctuary. He and his tribal interpreter meet in a real world, tense with exploitation and the exercise of power. They cannot hide from each other; there is no hiding place. Determining one another, each asserts for the other his humanity and human possibilities. The field experience is, then, a political experience; it demands that the anthropologist expose the forces that imprison him and that he seek to expose the forces that imprison the native.

But what must an anthropology look like if it is to be a study of human freedom and liberation, of human possibility and necessity? It must have a sense of shared humanity: "It is our consciousness, as a species, that enables us to empathize with what we do not directly share," says Diamond. Anthropology requires "speciational consciousness" so that the anthropologist can approach other societies with the confidence "that his humanity is equal to the task of registering differences." It must address itself to real human beings, not empty concepts, for it is "human decisions which create the alternatives that are open to choice." Human beings not only "reflect cultural events but synthesize experience and have the capacity to react in creative and unexpected ways." (See "What History Is.") Such a new anthropology would have to affirm man's capacity for re-creation in confrontation with the high priests of determinism—politicians and professionals—who preach resignation before the tyranny of their official definitions of reality. Such an anthropology must also turn its back on British social anthropology, ever obsessed with the problem of (colonial) order, the concerns of the traffic cop and the prison matron. It will have to distance itself also, as Diamond does in his discussion of Lévi-Strauss, from a Cartesian anthropology that strips cognition of meaning and affect, denies the integral relation of theory and praxis, and thus represents men as the eternal victims of their brains, ceaselessly driven to assemble and disassemble mental elements, forced forever to enact these *ad hoc* schemes in an imitation of life. These are, Diamond tells us, images of our own alienation through which we ceaselessly redefine and refine the problems of our own time.

But—and this is the central question of these essays—where shall we find human beings not alienated from their passions and their work? In primitive cultures, answers Diamond. It is through communication with the primitives of past and present, and with our own primitive possibilities, that we can create an image, a vision, a sense of a life once led by all men and still led by some, a life richer and more intricately human than our own. To do this we must learn to see that life from within, as these fellow human beings still see and feel it; we must learn the "uses of the primitive." Thus Diamond sets for us and for himself a triple task; to comprehend the primitive world as primitives do, to see our world from the vantage point of the primitive, and to link this understanding to the unexpressed aspects of our nature. For Diamond, then, the primitive is both a historical phase in man's career, and an existential aspect of his being. If primitive peoples created societies that exhausted a whole range of human possibilities, civilized men have failed in the equivalent task. It is from this multi-dimensional vantage point that Diamond defines and contrasts primitive and civilized behavior in "The Search for the Primitive," and "The Rule of Law Versus the Order of Custom." It is in this perspective that he discusses, in a brilliant and representative essay, Plato's *Republic* as the classic model of the Western state, exhibiting in an early but perfect form all the quintessential characteristics and stigmata of civilization. This new anthropology to which Diamond has given a voice is, then, communication, and the creation of new possibilities for communcation between the primitive and the civilized. As we construct a vision of the primitive in ourselves and our time, we can also posit new possibilities for ourselves. And that demands of us, finally, political action consistent with our insights. In a century that legislates official definitions of human nature and then sanctifies them through the operations of the state, we must return to the root. "The root," as Marx said, "is man." In demystifying civilization and concretely explicating being in primitive society, Stanley Diamond writes the prolegomena for a Marxist ethnology, and an existential anthropology.

Eric R. Wolf
New York City
Spring 1972

PREFACE

My original intention was to write a book, in one concentrated burst of energy, on the theme explored here, and to that end, I carefully kept notes and references for a dozen years. As that file grew, remaining more or less unused, I wrote these twelve related essays and then realized that I had, in fact, written the book. Each essay represents a chapter in an integrated argument. Three—"Civilization and Progress," "Schizophrenia and Civilization," and "The Myth of Structuralism"—have not previously been published. I have significantly revised and extended the remaining eight, in order to elaborate their meaning and sharpen my purpose. But I have not forced the chapters into an absolutely logical and unilinear sequence. Rather, each chapter explores an aspect of the basic theme: the immediate human significance of the breach between civilized and primitive culture, between state and stateless societies. Chapter 8, for example, deals with civilized law as the antithesis of primitive custom, Chapter 7 with the civilized problem of 'mental illness' in primitive perspective, Chapter 5 with Plato's *Republic* as the antithesis of primitive society, and Chapter 9 with an analogous critique of the Book of Job. The argument of the book is probably expressed most fully in Chapter 4, an inductive model of primitive society in contrast with civilization.

These cultural-historical antitheses, and the consequent split in consciousness evident everywhere in modern society cannot be transcended until a revolutionary transformation occurs, equal in scope and depth to that which initiated civilization about 5,000 years ago. The point of this work is that nothing less will suffice. If we are ever to outlive the trauma of history, I believe it can only be through the resolution of the primitive-civilized conflict in our society and in ourselves. It is the task of anthropology to help trace the contours, and confront the imperatives of that conflict, while giving us a glimpse of another human possibility. Otherwise, the discipline is pointless.

These essays are offered, then, as a modest antidote to the alienation, guilt, anxiety and fear to which human beings are condemned in modern imperial civilization. If they are of any use, I shall be grateful, particularly at a time when the American people have a chance to see nakedly for themselves the social reality they have been educated to celebrate and lulled into accepting.

I thank my students of the past 20 years—at UCLA, Brandeis, Syracuse, Columbia, and the New School for Social Research—for listening and creatively responding to the ideas set forth here. They have helped me more than I have been able to help them.

Stanley Diamond
Halesowen,
Worcestershire, England
August 1973

1

INTRODUCTION: CIVILIZATION AND PROGRESS

Civilization originates in conquest abroad and repression at home. Each is an aspect of the other. Anthropologists who use, or misuse, words such as "acculturation" beg this basic question. For the major mode of acculturation, the direct shaping of one culture by another through which civilization develops, has been conquest. Observe, for example, the Euro-American "influence" on the South Vietnamese, or the fact that white Protestant Anglo-Saxons who settled in New England learned a few things from the aboriginal Indian peoples (of which the writers of history for civilized children make so much), and that black slaves "contributed" African rhythms to southern American music. In all these instances, one group was dominant and the other subordinate. Such examples of the diffusion of cultural traits suggest the struggles that have taken place within various societies. When—as generally happens—this diffusion is traced as an abstract exchange, somehow justified by the universal balance sheet of the imperial civilization, the assault by civilized upon primitive or traditional societies is masked, or its implications evaded. The propagation of basic elements of ancient Egyptian culture along the eastern Mediterranean strip was, for example, a precipitant of political and economic conquest. The politically "weaker" peoples were confronted with a single set of alternatives, rooted in the Egyptian experience. This historical fact is then reflected as a law of development; as civilization accelerates, its proponents project their historical present as the progressive destiny of the entire human race. The political component is obscured by deterministic arguments from natural law, natural

1

history and natural science. Anthropology as a civilized discipline has, despite the pretentious relativism of many of its practitioners, "reluctantly" shared these ethnocentric notions of historical inevitability. Political decisions, however, are rather more existential in their nature. They can be literally decisive; they are implicated with problems of will and authority. For popular—as opposed to imposed—politics is people in groups deciding to act in order to reject, create or maintain a given form of social life. Civilized peoples and civilized disciplines have, therefore, been particularly sensitive to political action on the part of "backward" peoples which created the possibility of autonomous societies and alternative cultures. In the mind of the imperialist, the world is small, and loss of control in one area threatens the whole. The fabric of world culture, our oral or inscribed literary, esthetic and religious inheritance, may be, as anthropologists are prone to put it, a "multicolored fabric"; but since the rise of civilization that fabric has been woven on a political loom.

No matter how far we range in time and space, from Teotihuacan to Angkor Vat the tale is always the same. No matter what distinctions we encounter in language, art, religion, cultural style or social structure, the history of civilization repeats itself, not as farce, which Marx supposed to be the fate of all historical repetitions, but as tragedy. In the shadow of this tragedy, the achievements of civilization are reduced to their proper proportions. They were intended for the use and pleasure of the very few at the expense of the skill and labor of the many.

The original crimes of civilizations, conquest and political repression, were committed in silence and that is still their intention, if not always their result. For most of the victims, through most of human history, could not and cannot read or write. It is sometimes said that they had no history. That is a complex opinion—false, yet profoundly true in a way not intended. It is false because it assumes that history is a matter of documents. Conventional historians, who live by documents and, therefore, consider them sacrosanct, would deny authentic history to most of the human race for the greater period of time on this planet. The opinion of H. Trevor-Roper, Regius Professor of History at Cambridge University, is typical: "Perhaps in the future there will be some African history to teach. But at present there is none. There is only the history of Europeans in Africa. The rest is darkness. . . . "

Africa, along with all other areas inhabited by human beings has both a "pre-history" and a "history" recorded in the migrations of people, the artifacts found in the earth, the connections traceable among myriad languages, and the oral traditions of indigenous societies. Africa is the locus of predominantly unwritten, deeply self-conscious human experiences, the ensemble of which constitute the only authentic definition of history. Even so, documents exist; in the Western Sudan, for example, the Kano chronicle provides information about events ten centuries old. Of course, that kind of "history" is necessarily skewed by the official attitudes of invading groups; the distortions are probably of the same magnitude as the information that has come to us, filtered through the scribes, priests and courtiers of eleventh-century England, or, for that matter, the journalists and closet academicians of the twentieth century. But Trevor-Roper is, in a sense that he would not admit, perfectly correct; most men, whether Africans, medieval Europeans, or working-class Englishmen, have lived in the "darkness" to which they have been confined by those who record and rationalize the career of civilization. For their histories, in Africa, for example, were of no use to the European historian—not being reified, they could not be endlessly mined for the sake of either the academic specialist or the establishment he represented. When Trevor-Roper claims, therefore, that Africa has no history, he means that Africa has no history that *he can use*.

Those people who *could* write, the scribes and priests of Egypt, Babylonia or China, were rarely disposed to record the attitudes of those they taxed, subordinated and mystified. Writing itself was initially used to keep tax, census and other administrative records; it was, in short, an instrument for the recording of official histories, invented by bureaucrats. The oral tradition, the ceremony, the round of daily life, the use and manufacture of tools by the people at large did not depend on writing, nor did they need to be reflected in writing. The compulsive rite of civilization is writing, and the compulsions of the official concept of reality are both experienced and expressed in the exclusive mode of cognition signified by writing. This fixation on one-dimensional realities is particularly evident in the attitude of the ethnologist whose civilized insistence on recording the exact and proper form of a ritual, the exclusive mode of marriage or descent, the precise code of behavior, may reveal his own motivation and certain shortcomings of scientism, but fails to resonate with the variety and flexibility of primitive social usages. The connection between Malinowski's insistence on word-perfect magic among the Trobriand Islanders and his clinically compulsive personality, as reflected in his diary—"a diary in the strict sense of the term"—is a case in point.

Writing was one of the original mysteries of civilization, and it reduced the complexities of experience to the written word. Moreover, writing provides the ruling classes with an ideological instrument of incalculable power. The word of God becomes an invincible law, mediated by priests; therefore, respond the Iroquois, confronting the European: "Scripture was written by the Devil." With the advent of writing, symbols became explicit; they lost a certain richness. Man's word was no longer an endless exploration of reality, but a sign that could be used against him. Sartre, the Marxist existentialist, understands this; it is the hidden theme of his autobiography, *Words*. For writing splits consciousness in two ways—it becomes more authoritative than talking, thus degrading the meaning of speech and eroding oral tradition; and it makes it possible to use words for the political manipulation and control of others. Written signs supplant memory; an official, fixed and permanent version of events can be made. If it is written, in early civilizations, it is bound to be true.

History, then, has always been written by the conqueror; the majority of people have traditionally remained silent, and this is still largely the case. It is the civilized upper classes who, conceiving their positions as determined by God, talent or technology, create the facts of history and the deterministic theories which justify both the facts and their own pre-eminence. Thus we have no conventional way of knowing what the "ordinary" peasant in Bronze Age China or early dynastic Egypt felt, thought or suffered. Even Shakespeare found it necessary to deal with kings and nobles when exploring the human soul. The Greek novelist Kazantzakis tells us that he was not impressed by the ideologues when he visited Russia shortly after the Revolution. Rather, standing in Kremlin Square, he shuddered at the snarl of rage that rose from the endless parade of peasants, soldiers, workers and urban riffraff. This is the sound that is rarely recorded. It is, rather, the chain of conventional historical chronicles that defines the "mainstream of civilization," and makes us certain that history as we know it is somehow inevitable, and must be the record of the fittest survivors.

In the beginning, conquest and domestic oppression were indistinguishable. As the earliest societies that began to consolidate as states expanded territorially, local peoples were conquered and incorporated as lower-class subjects or slaves into the evolving polity. We find this pattern everywhere—in the Nile Valley some 5,000 years ago; in England following the Norman invasion; among the Incas of the Peruvian highlands; in the valley of Mexico prior to the Spanish conquest; in the coastal forests of West Africa in the sixteenth century. Imperialism and colonialism are as old as the state; they define the political process. In Dahomey, for example, any person born within the territory claimed by the emerging "king" was, by right of conquest, a Dahomean subject. His ultimate obligations to the nascent state, the political definition of his humanity, took precedence at least abstractly over his local, kin-mediated, social existence.

After the initial consolidation of the state, as V. Gordon Childe relates, the ancient Egyptians colonized the eastern Mediterranean littoral and that, along with their economic imperialism and punitive expeditions, stimulated state-building among local peoples. This archetypal imperial process is worth examining. The importation of raw materials, needed for the development of Egyptian industries as well as for funerary ceremonies, was financed from the royal revenues. Copper and turquoise were mined in the Sinai. Expeditions equipped by the state, escorted by royal soldiers, were periodically dispatched across the desert for this purpose. Similarly, cedarwood and resins were imported from North Syria. Ships bound for Byblos* were equipped and provided with trade goods by the state; government officials led expeditions to the upper Nile and brought back gold and spices.

The major purpose of this traffic was to secure luxuries and magic substances or raw materials; while peasants and laborers still used stone tools in the fields and quarries, soldiers were armed with metal weapons. This trade also helped sustain new

---

* An ancient Egyptian colony, from whose name the term "Bible" is derived.

classes—merchants, sailors, porters, soldiers, artisans and clerks were supported from the surplus revenues collected by the pharaoh. More specifically, the effects of the imperial trade on Byblos were as follows: the Egyptians needed cedarwood for tombs, boats and furniture; they obtained it from Lebanon, and shipped it from the port of Byblos, close to Beirut. Before the rise of civilization in Egypt, Byblos had been the site of a neolithic town. As early as 3200 B.C., the Giblites had been self-sufficient fishermen and farmers. But the consolidation by conquest of the Egyptian state from a series of neolithic villages strung out along the banks of the Nile turned Byblos into a primary supplier of raw materials for the use of the Egyptian upper classes. In satisfying the Egyptian demands, Byblos abandoned the economic self-sufficiency of its neolithic structure, and came to depend upon a foreign market. One is reminded of Rousseau's observation: "Alexander, desiring to keep the Ichthyophay dependent on him, forced them to give up fishing and to eat foodstuffs common to other peoples." Moreover, Egyptian traders and officials settled there in order to secure their interests, and the Egyptians "instructed" the Giblites in the administration of the city and the management of their money, establishing what was in effect a protectorate. A stone temple was built in the city, decorated by immigrant Egyptian craftsmen; and the Giblites learned the Egyptian script, the language of commerce.

As time went on, Byblos became a pre-industrial city, a market for raw materials, and a further center for the diffusion of the new social economy. But it should be noted that the imposed elements of Egyptian civilization tended to remain static in Byblos. The Imperium changed the nature of the indigenous society, which retained certain of its cultural traits by adapting them to the new structure, but Byblos, in the classic colonial mode, did not and could not keep pace with further developments in Egypt. While the Egyptians improved their script, for example, the Giblites maintained for a millenium the archaic characters which they had originally adopted. The imperial process, then, increased the affluence of the Egyptian upper classes, and converted Byblos into a little Egypt through the direct effect of the division of labor needed to supply raw materials for the related tasks of administration and defense. This, in turn, led to the impoverishment and dependence of the majority of people engaged in fishing and farming.'

A similar chain of events was set in motion by the imperial thrust of Mesopotamia, which resulted, after 2500 B.C., in the breakup of the neolithic communities and their replacement by urban civilization. Here again the "secondary centers" remained provincial, compared to the "dynamic" metropolitan powers. But self-replication, which is both the need and the desire of the imperialist center, was not always accomplished so directly. The nomads of Sinai, for example, those "wretched Bedouins," refused to mine copper for the Egyptians in return for manufactured trinkets. Workers from Egypt, under the eye of the royal army, had to do the job. And in other areas, such as Nineveh, the primitive farming settlements were forcibly converted into imperial towns. Eventually these archaic civilizations (Egypt, Sumer, India), through direct or indirect conquest, reproduced themselves throughout the ancient world. "Initially, on the borders of Egypt, Babylonia, and the Indus Valley—in Crete and the Greek Islands, Syria, Assyria, Iran and Baluchistan, and further afield on the Greek mainland, the Anatolian Plateau, South Russia, villages were converted to cities and self-sufficient food producers became commercially specialized." Only those who lived in the most remote areas could escape this process; only the nomads of the desert denied its reality. Like the primitives who flee civilization, they refuse to cooperate or to alter their image of themselves, as imperialism invests each secondary and tertiary center.

More than 2,000 years after the inception of archaic imperialism, the same imperatives are constantly at work. In 416 B.C., the Athens of Plato and Socrates, then at war with Sparta, refused to recognize the right of the inhabitants of Melos to remain neutral. Thucydides reports, truthfully in spirit if not in fact, a dialogue between the Melians and the Athenean envoys in which the latter reject all reasonable and humane argument. Power, they say, is what counts in this world; and it would be better for Athens to be defeated by Sparta than to reveal so damaging a weakness to other subject peoples by accepting the friendship of defenseless Melos. The Melians insist on their independence and reject the honor of becoming an Athenean colony. The Atheneans then attack Melos, killing the mature men and selling the women and children into slavery. Thereafter they colonized Melos themselves. This was the same Athens that condemned Socrates as a traitor a few years later. The two events taken together, the one externally imperialistic, the other internally repressive—remind us of the still more ancient association between this twin dynamic of the state, which converges to a single process at the origins of civilization itself. And it is always useful to remember that in Athens, at the height of its cultural achievement, there were at least three slaves to every free man. This fact is reflected in the classic utopian projections of civilization, as instanced in the work of Thomas More, where it is assumed that a special class of the disenfranchised will engage in "black labor." And in Plato's *Republic*, that prototypical apology for the state, the workers and farmers constitute lower orders of being.

Civilization has always had to be imposed, not as a psychodynamic necessity or a repressive condition of evolved social life, as Freud supposed, and not only in terms of the state's power securing itself against its own subjects, but also with reference to the barbarian or primitive peoples who moved on the frontiers. Native communities were the ground out of which the earliest, class-structured, territorially defined civilizations arose. Internally, these native peoples were transformed into the peasant and proletarian "masses" who supported the apparatus of the state. No matter how "necessary" the political structure of civilization may have been initially, the progressive degradation of the independent native communities remains a truth of history. No rationalization for the existence of the early state can alter the fact that the majority of the people were always taxed in goods and labor far more than they received from the state in the form of protection and services.

Even if we acknowledge the necessity—due to population pressure, scarcity of land, water and other resources—for political constraints in the earliest stages of state formation, there is no inherent reason for it to have taken the oppressive form that it did—except for the burgeoning anxiety of those removed from direct production about their economic and political security. That security seems to have been all the more problematic when we assume along with Marx, Morgan, Engels, Radin, Childe and Redfield that primitive societies are proto-democratic and communalistic, and further, that the character of the neolithic communities that immediately preceded the rise of the earliest civilizations could be similarly defined. For primitive customs and habits so long in their formulation could hardly have been transformed without very great resistance. The consequent struggle between the state—the civil authority—and the constituent kin or quasi-kin units of society is the basic social struggle in human history. It is still reflected in local attitudes and institutional buffers against the center, even where distorted.

Their anxiety about not being self-supporting, along with the anticipation of such resistance, seems to constitute the motive for the upper classes' elaborate extortion of wealth from the direct producers. But even if we accept the necessity of the political transformation of society and agree that no state could survive unless "surplus" wealth created by the emerging peasants and workers was appropriated for the support of the classes not directly engaged in production, this does not account for the accelerating inequities in the distribution of wealth. The widening gap between the rich and poor as ancient civilizations developed could not have been due simply to scarcity, or to the need for supporting specialists removed from subsistence activity. Rather, it was due to increasing expropriation. For as Marshall Sahlins has pointed out, the richer a society, the greater the distance between its classes, and the greater the concentration of wealth at the summit. Nor was the archaic concentration of wealth a function of its presumably rational reinvestment. Not only were the uses of wealth irrational, inflating the tautology of power, but redistribution in the form of public works or services eventually increased, rather than lessened, the gap between classes. The dynamics of archaic civilization reveal the pathology of wealth—wealth as power, or luxury as "well-being"—and the inadequacy of the distribution of wealth. By 3000 B.C. in the Middle East, such rationalizations for the state, which also apply to monopoly capitalism, are apparent. As Marx understood, the processes of state formation and function are generalizable beyond the specific form of the state.

The critical question, then, is that of the socioeconomic exploitation and the concomitant loss of the cultural creativity and autonomy of the vast majority of human beings. Conspicuous extortion from worker and peasant was a confirmation of power;

but power, so reified, not only confirmed social status, it also displaced anxiety about the actual powerlessness of the privileged, which was a result of the loss of their direct command of the environment. The sheer accumulation of wealth, the antithesis of primitive customary usage, was thus compensatory, a sign of the fear of impotence. It is a response of the alienated in pursuit of security; the manipulation of people is substituted for the command of things. As civilization spreads and deepens, it is ultimately man's self, his species being, which is imperialized.

But according to the evolutionary determinists, the support of emerging artisans, soldiers, bureaucrats, priests by workers and peasants, a division of labor and class which presumably insured greater productivity in a given area subject to an accelerating population-resource ratio was rational, if not spontaneous. Specialization of function is supposed to maximize economic results (but the political question is always "for whom"); it breaks down the multi-dimensional functioning of the person in the primitive neolithic community, and leads to the institutionalizing of the division of labor, as not only determined, but socially desirable. The division of labor provides, in turn, the internal logic and coherence of class-structured society. Markets, middlemen, administrators became necessary because property had to be guarded and regulated, and exchange values established; thus the mutually dependent relations of the basic producers to the middlemen and the rulers are "completed" (mystified) in the structure of the state. The state appears as the inevitable sum of its social parts; its ideology is the projection of a unity by the "naturally" differentiated. If the process of civilization had unfolded in this way, as simply an adaptive machine, then all social ills can be ascribed to inadequate technology or "geometric" increases in population; correlatively, scarcity, and hence competition for scarce goods and services, could be put forward as the major factor in the growth of the state. Scarcity may even be conceived as a meta-principle, an existential condition of the human race which, satiated in one area, will find reason to compete in another. Thus, scarcity is conceived as a natural, not a social phenomenon.

The point is that the capitalist social dynamic and consequent logic of scarcity and the abstract rage to consume (the other side of the coin of affluence), combined with the positivism of

Protestant culture, has rationalized the dynamics of civilization as rooted in human nature. Human nature is conceived as a system of reflexes tuned to detect and overcome scarcity. Society, not to speak of civilization, is conceived of as *ab initio* the visible structure of the struggle for what is scarce—food, women, land, material resources, power. It is only when the positivist mind abreacts under the influence of drugs or alcohol that a more spacious view of the human past and potential appears, and then its images tend to be mechanical, dissociated, admittedly unreal. But ordinarily, the positivist spirit abandons the contingencies of history for the constricted certainties of evolution. Law is its touchstone, or as Tylor put it, "if there is law anywhere, it is everywhere"—and civilization is accepted as a rational contract negotiated by sane men aware of their limitations. So goes the capitalist view of the nature of civilization, which reflects the accumulating 7,000-year-old myth of the state. But even at its best, in the form of a liberal ameliorative rationalism, its proponents will call on the power of the state when tried by the prospect of radical change. The capitalist view is only a minor deviation from the aristocratic conception which accepts the received class and occupational structure qua structure as rational, but wants to put the right people in the right places. Some, it seems, are leaders, and others followers by virtue of their birth, talent, training, capacity. Where the emphasis is on talent, the aristocratic rationale for the state, as in the *Republic* dissolves into a meritocratic view. And the latter, in turn, is always in danger of dissolving into racism, which feeds back into the argument of birth, sometimes refined to a genetic point.

None of these conceptions is correct. Yet they remain the only possible explanations for the existence of civilization, if we do not ground ourselves in the converse existence of primitive society, and in a theory of exploitation which can only be based on the latter. In primitive cultures, wrote Malinowski, "there are no rich people and paupers, no people of great power; nor yet people who are oppressed; no unemployed, and no unmarried." And further, "before the advent of military pursuits and political power, which appear late in human evolution, there occurred no taxation, no confiscation of private property by chiefs or other tribal potentates."

Exploitation, then, is the hidden process which contradicts all totalitarian or amelioristic rationalizations for state power. All revolutionary theory is based on this civilizational process. Marx, in particular, identified exploitation as the appropriation of a surplus—initially, in the earliest civil societies, in the direct form of tribute and labor service. Its modern, monetized and ultimate form is surplus value—that is, the appropriation of a certain portion of the labor power of the worker by the capitalist, expressed as an inadequate wage. In Marxism, all "private" profits flow from surplus value, although the organs of the state maintain the ancient, more direct forms of expropriation—taxation, conscription, the right of eminent domain, etc. The point is that the theory of surplus appropriation, including that of surplus value, is the critical issue for revolutionaries; any doctrine of social change which omits this is reduced to the effort to modify the distribution of wealth within a bureaucratic state, conceived as essentially rational and necessary, and when cruel, inescapably so.

The opportunity for exploitation is obscured by the emphasis on the obligation to serve; the bureaucrat is said to be a civil servant, the monarch is said to serve his people, and so on. The case for the unity of the state is no more than a mystification of exploitation.

From the beginning, that sine qua non, the continuous production of a "surplus" in support of the State apparatus, was not spontaneous; it required the mediation of political authority. As Robert McC. Adams has maintained, there was no imminent logic in surplus production. The fact that primitive cultivators can produce a surplus does not mean that they will; or put another way, the occasional use of a surplus for ceremonial, symbolic and reciprocal exchange purposes is of a different order than the routine production of a surplus in support of other classes and occupational groups. But this classic statement of the problem is inadequate. The terms must be refined if we are to begin to understand the process. The imposition of tribute in kind on local communities in, say, the Nile Valley, cannot be understood as drawing on a productive base which is somehow divided into a "subsistence" segment (supporting and reproducing customary functions of the group), and a "surplus" segment (set aside for the tax collector, or otherwise directed to the support of nonproducers). Surplus production is not an abstract economic category. It is, rather, the portion of goods and services expropriated from the direct producer in support of other classes or occupations. But that expropriation cuts directly into so-called subsistence production; it reduces the share of the direct producer in his own product; it represents the alienation of his labor power. Subsistence production among primitive peoples should be understood, then, as the economic effort required to reproduce society as a whole, a society in which the individual participates fully.

But with the advent of the state, production is more or less rapidly depressed, to the point where the merely biological functions of the cultivator are replicated, within a constricted range of social functions. This is true *subsistence* production, whereas the conventional use of the term with reference to stateless societies implies, or should imply, no more than the absence of specialized cash cropping for commercial marketing. The production of a surplus conceived as merely an increase in production over that needed to reproduce the traditional society of a local group is a politically-inspired economic myth.

The occupational and class division, which depends on the basic producers, does not, of course, happen all at once. In the earliest stages of state formation, the peasant was also an artisan, echoing primitive usage. Analogously, in the aboriginal state of Dahomey, every man was supposed to be able to roof a house, build a wall and cut a field. And most people in the major Yoruba "towns" in West Africa work as farmers, as did many of the inhabitants of the largest communities in ancient Sumer and prehispanic Mexico. An "appreciable proportion" of the inhabitants of Islamic Middle Eastern cities have also been farmers, cultivating adjacent fields. The point is that the expropriation of labor power was initially a process of *relative* impoverishment; it was limited by the immaturity and relative weakness of the early state, and by the consequent recognition of the emerging peasant-artisan as the source of all wealth.

The separation of functions between peasant and artisan was accelerated by the direct confiscation of the artisan's labor time, indeed of the artisan himself, by the civil power; the carpenter or potter was, literally, "in his majesty's service." Artisans may become further specialized in the manufacture of military equipment and that, in turn, reinforces emerging class distinctions. But it was the ostentation of royal courts, with their thousands of retainers, which most effectively subordinated the artisan to the civil power. At Susa, the palace staff in the Early Dynastic Three Period numbered about 950 people; but after Mesopotamia was unified by Sargon I, over 5,000 men are reported to have eaten daily in the royal palace.

As the peasant evolved from the primitive cultivator, the artisan became differentiated from the peasant so that, even as separate persons, they were not necessarily confined to the same household. At the same time, the traditional barter market allowed for the confiscation of goods by the civil power, thus fixing the artisan more firmly in his identity as an artisan. As the part-time specialist wandered from market to market, from group to group, offering his services in order to pay his taxes and find food, he also diminished his connection with the land. The point is that the division of labor, like the production of a "surplus," required the mediation of political power; the humanity of both the producers and the consuming classes is gradually sacrificed. Poverty, political imposition and social degradation reduced the life of the toiler to an economic imperative, to a question of sheer subsistence; the symbolic content and the social meaning of labor progressively declined. Even the everyday tools and implements of the lower classes, which are usually manufactured by craftsmen in order to produce a wide range of goods, can be distinguished from the elite artifacts produced by specialists who concentrate on a narrow range of work. A Berber housewife may tan her own skins, but the production of Morocco leather in Fez demands 20 consecutive operations, each performed by a different, highly trained work group. The result is that the poor were increasingly deprived of superior tools, while their esthetic and inventive impulses declined. The implications of this process, which begins with civilization, will be understood if one recalls that the primary inventions on which civilization itself depended were the work of primitive neolithic cultivators. At the same time, the specialized artisans, divided into their guilds and under the command of the royal court, create their objects in a craft rather than a human environment, and in response to an external, specialized and conspicuous demand. This may and can lead to the efflorescence of certain styles—"a master carver may design and add the finishing touches to a piece of work" —but it also leads to boredom; as the reputation of the master is inflated, so the specialized apprentice is relegated to chiseling out the design.

This degradation of the artisan's life for the sake of the object, is also basically economic; like all assembly-line procedures, it cuts costs. But cost-cutting, which is one of the rationalizations for the division of labor, is a political, not an intrinsically "economic" process. For the efficiency and high technical skills supposedly involved to not reward the majority of artisans, nor do their goods reach the majority of consumers. The mobilization of the artisans simply made their products available to the upper classes at the prices and in the quantity that they found socially desirable.

But if the lower classes were degraded, and the artisans in effect imprisoned, the nonlaboring classes were only free in fantasy— their dissociated dependence on the work of others was, as we have seen, a pathological condition; at the same time their symbolic lives were deformed by their partial and fanciful functioning in the world. This growing division between classes and occupations, and their consequent reification, is the social basis for the split in human consciousness which civilization institutionalizes. The potential integrity of the person remains unrealized; only society as a whole seems to have this integrity, and the conception of the person as a social reflex becomes credible because it reflects social reality. The related breach between mental and manual labor to which Marx alludes is both a symptom of and a cause for the alienation of persons from themselves, reflected in the mind-body dualisms with which civilization conjures; and that in turn is epitomized in the rise of academic philosophy.

These dualities, which reflect the class structure and the division of labor in archaic civilizations, were classically evident in northwestern Cambodia. For an indeterminant period, up to about 800 A.D., a number of societies that were just then becoming centralized existed along the Mekong River. They have been described as "kingdoms, loosely held together ... with chieftains ... villages ... [or] village communities." The peasantry remained relatively free, labor relatively undifferentiated, authority relatively traditional, within the autonomous local groups. But with the development of "irrigation agriculture," a new state, religion and ruling class became possible and were, in fact, created.

As irrigation led to the multiplication of crops and increased population, the peasant became specialized as a mere laborer on the land. On this productive base there developed a strongly centralized state, signified by an emperor cult, "the divine king on the mountain." The consolidation of royal authority here, as elsewhere, was inherently contradictory—the more the king was objectified as a political fetish, the more circumscribed were his actions, and the more powerless he became in actuality. Compared to the old chiefs of the late neolithic villages that preceded the rise of the state, he was impotent, bound by the existing order, otiose and remote, after the pattern of civilized gods. The Cambodian state was actually run by aristocrats and theocrats. As they grew richer and more alienated, the villagers sank to the level of a working force, and when mentioned by name in the priestly inscriptions they are called "dog," "cat," "loathsome," "stinking brute," etc. As the population continued to increase, the surplus—that is, the confiscation of the fruits of local labor—also grew while the people, incapable of reproducing their traditional social lives, "fell into ever greater misery." And all the while, the "immense dams glittered in the sunlight," and "rice paddy upon rice paddy" stretched "away to the horizon." As their localities were denuded of art and artisanship, "the temples," suborning the skill of the artisans, "rose ever more vast and beautiful." Angkor Vat was, and remains, the material evidence for the monumental alienation of a whole people. Those who built it and those whose labor paid for its construction, neither planned nor commanded the finished product; the Temples of Angkor Vat towered over an oppressed peasantry; they had no place in what remained of the local community. And the ruling oligarchy manipulated the meaning of these monuments as symbols of power. As for the artisans, such structures were no longer their work, the expression of their human being, but merely edifices to which they were compelled to contribute their labor.

These ceremonial centers of power and tribute were, of course, common in the ancient world. The administrators, soldiers, landlords and artisans who populated the *Ch'eng*, the traditional Chinese administrative center, were supported by tribute, in rent or taxes, imposed on the peasantry of the hinterland. In the valley of Mexico, Tenochtitlán was the annual tributary center for luxuries of all kinds, clothing, and over 50,000 tons of food—borne on the shoulders of porters. The inflated wealth of imperial Rome, and the Mongol capital of Karakorum were similarly based. In each case, the monarch was able to redistribute periodically a certain portion of the tribute to the inhabitants of the capital city. And this had the classic imperial effect of binding the ruled to the ruler (a tenuous bond) within the metropole, in a common enterprise. But, we must remember along with Marx, that to the degree men are socially determined, they are irresponsible agents of history; the revolutionary perspective, not to speak of the imperatives of revolutionary conflict, does not include moral condemnation.

It is likely, for example, that the ancient peasants and workers collaborated in their own exploitation. Once the structure of the original community had been weakened or transformed, the sheer need to keep body and soul together, meet domestic obligations, confront police and military coercion, along with the hope of individual reward, priestly mystification and other familiar factors, would have served well enough to inhibit men from acting on or even recognizing their own, more fully human interests. But that, of course, does not inhibit them from rebelling. On the other hand, sufficient autonomy was preserved by the local groups which produced the resources for the support of the state to make the system viable; the priestly-military-bureaucratic oligarchies could not destroy the basis of their own sustenance without destroying themselves. The state, then, permitted what it could not command. As civilization evolves, the central authority permits less, commands more; and states grow more, not less, totalitarian.

We must conclude that the development of the early civilizations as instruments of oppression was the result, not of some environmental or technical imperative, but of the new possibilities of power which men in certain positions found it necessary to cultivate and legitimate. As Starobinski has pointed out, the idea of liberty as a human possibility, was not to be invented until the French Revolution. "Reinvented" is a more accurate term, for as Boas and Marx understood, freedom as a concept does not exist among primitive peoples because society is not perceived as oppressive. Exploitation, like the idea of liberty, is a complex social-economic-psychological invention diffusing with civilization itself. In this sense, the grossly inegalitarian aspects of civilization are contingent, not predetermined. This view, of course, implies a good deal about human nature—mainly that, given the opportunity and driven by certain needs, some men will compound their profit and seek an illusory freedom, based on the exercise of power, at the expense of others. In reality, of course, they are bound to those whom they exploit.

On the other hand, there is ample historical evidence that the great majority of people have always been suspicious and resentful of political power as such. The only fully participant societies have been primitive; they lack explicit political structures and, subsequently, exploitation, in the basic, civilized definition of the term. Whatever else we may say about men as political beings, it is clear that the great majority of them have viewed the exercise of political power as either irrelevant to, or destructive of their daily concerns.

Yet we have no way of knowing how many abortive rebellions may have been launched by slaves or peasants exasperated by taxes and labor service, or by artisans commanded to work for the ruling class in ancient civilizations. We do know, for example, that in Polynesia, during the earliest intimations of state formation, when the big chiefs failed to redistribute the goods of the community according to custom, local uprisings resulted. In traditional China, many landlords lived in the walled towns because their garrisons were a defense against peasant rebellions. And there is a rare Egyptian document dated about 2000 B.C.—"the story of the eloquent peasant"—which attacks the extortionate behavior of the bureaucrats. Another document, dated some centuries later, in the form of a letter to the correspondent's son, advises him in the most dramatic terms, to become a scribe so that he may escape a manual laborer's or a peasant's life of degradation.

For 5,000 years peasants have rebelled, by evading the imposition of the central power, or by directly attacking its representatives. But only in this century has the peasantry become a revolutionary force. In the West, peasants have been liquidated as a social class since the rise of commercialism and industrialism. The proportion of people on the land constantly diminished—in both the United States and the United Kingdom, for example, currently about 4 percent of the people live on the land—and those remaining are, of course, not peasants but itinerant laborers, full-fledged farmers or corporate agricultural workers. Therefore, the problem of the peasant qua peasant has solved itself, albeit within a capitalistic framework. But this is not true elsewhere. The processes of urbanization and industrialization linked to the revolutionary ascendancy of the bourgeosie in most of Europe quickly reduced the ranks of the peasantry, and cash-cropping businessmen-farmers emerged while the new technology converted the countryside into an extension of the city. This has not happened among the ancient peasantries of Africa, Asia, Latin America, or the Near and Middle East. There, the peasants, in some areas declining to rural proletariats, either have the potential to become restive or are already revolutionary. Their emergence in new rural forms, their relationship to the national institutions and to the urban populations, their actual and potential political weight are central to any projection of the future conceived on a global scale. Unlike the Western "self-liquidating" peasantry, the existent peasantries of most of the world will not wither away through social and economic attrition. Their intolerable living conditions, steadily worsening since the upper neolithic period, and their self-consciousness, will not wait upon the blind processes of urbanization and industrialization which changed the social contours and demography of Europe. The peasants are there; they constitute most of the world's population, the link between archaic and modern civilizations. They are the poor who are getting poorer, both intranationally and internationally, as the Western world gets richer.[1]

The problem of the peasant is manifold. He is suspended between primitive subsistence cultivation and a market economy. Even in so-called "closed" peasant communities within larger national frameworks—as in parts of Bolivia—the relative absence of marketing connections does not inhibit direct or indirect political or religious ties to any given establishment. But by and large, it is the association with the national market that provides the paradigm for the peasants' linkage to the larger, politically organized national center. That is, as a number of theorists have maintained—a peasantry represents a "part culture"—a society which, historically viewed, has lost the power to replicate itself. As we have noted, peasants have characteristically functioned and emerged in "archaic" civilizations of one type or another. Their voluntary associations with the center of power have never been significant. As in the pre-revolutionary Russian *mir*, there were no tight state controls, but rather tribute was paid in kind or in labor service granted through the mediation of an indirect internal ruler. Peasants in the emerging world, and in Africa particularly, are not closely wedded to the state in any positive sense. Such peasantries have materialized as a result of the collapse of archaic political societies under the onslaught of colonialism, or else they have developed from the entrapment of primitive peoples in modern markets and new political contexts. The point is that peasants are limited in their revolutionary consistency and movement by their traditional suspicion of external political and economic obligations. At the same time, if the peasant is able to reach a reasonable accommodation with an external authority, the trajectory of that accommodation tends to be self-reinforcing—as, for example, in northern Nigeria—and revolutionary activity may be regarded as more of a threat than a hope. Basically, peasants are more exploited than they exploit. This is a psycho-social and political fact which tends to contradict, or at least make difficult, revolutionary initiative among them. Peasantries work directly on the land, cultivate for their own subsistence, and are typically at the mercy of the urban markets in their effort to get a decent return on their cash crops. Family members may be "exploited" in terms of labor time and access to prized goods, but intra and interfamilial cooperative arrangements tend to absorb much immediate tension.

Given these general characteristics of the peasantry, it is understandable that their image of revolutionary change is not congruent with that of the urban worker, the middle-class liberal, or the traditional revolutionary theorist. What the peasant wants is an adequate amount of land, low taxes, minimal national political interference in his network of local associations and a good return on his produce. The peasant who has been motivated to emerge from a condition of intolerable exploitation tends to stop his revolutionary activities once he has attained the goals just mentioned. On the other hand, where either socially determined scarcity of resources or new abundance leads to the possibility of socioeconomic stratification in an already depressed, civilized peasantry, the peasant has proven himself to be fully capable, in the former case, of exploiting landless countrymen and, in the latter case, of multiplying his holdings so that he assumes the position of a minor landlord. In any case, the generalization that "ordinarily" the peasant works directly on the land and does not permanently exploit anybody, still holds.

One concludes, therefore, that the peasant must be stimulated to fully coherent and purposeful revolutionary activity by cadres (including peasants) who claim a total view of the emerging social condition for three reasons: tenuous identification of the peasantry with a national center; paradoxically, the conservatism of the peasantry when it has made some accommodation to the center; and the incomplete character of the peasant's revolutionary aims. In any case, the Western peasant as a self-liquidating social type liquidated in the West must become, through the dialectics of revolutionary growth, willing to transform himself in terms of the emerging world. Rural life, in one form or another, must survive; agricultural production, of course, remains essential, but the peasant as traditionally defined will eventually become a casualty. Communes, state farms and collectives develop in his place; many peasants, transiently or otherwise, migrate to cities; and consistent revolutionary pressure ultimately transforms the fabric of peasant life, no matter what its traditional form. All of these paradoxes and historical accumulations serve as obstacles to furthering national and/or socialist revolutions where the majority of the people remain peasants and where they cling to a meliorative view of their own best interests as peasants, traditionally alert to the fact and possibility of further exploitation.

But it should also be noted that large-scale displacement in the countryside as a result of wars and an alien military presence can trigger contemporary peasant resistance—first in a national, and then in a socialist form, as in China and Vietnam. But that requirement is itself a measure of the peasant's ambiguity; he provides the revolutionary potential, yet remains the revolutionary problem.

The transformation of primitive people into an archaic peasantry is, then, a process as old as the state itself, but it is not confined to the great seminal civilizations. It is evident in the English state, for example, as it began to crystallize during the late Anglo-Saxon period. But with the world hegemony of modern European civilization, the business of state-building, including the incorporation of indigenous peoples, is so monopolized by alien imperialists and so accelerated by modern technology and the demands of the market, that the internal dynamic changes its character. In the earliest civilizations, the development of the peasantry from a primitive base must have been a long and complicated business, since it was an aspect of the unprecedented evolution of new political and economic institutions—class structures, commercial markets, centralized government, a more "elaborate and efficient" division of labor. In contrast, modern imperialism rapidly converts self-supporting African or East Asian primitives or depressed peasants into cash-cropping farmers who produce for export. The metropolitan power compels people to work on plantations, in mines, and build roads to link the latter with ports that develop into cities; and at the same time, the pre-industrial cities of the archaic civilizations—Ibadan in Western Nigeria, for example—are penetrated by modern structures.

Forced labor, in a variety of forms, is a common colonial phenomenon. But it is basically in levying taxes that the imperium compels the native to find new ways of earning cash, driving him into export cash-cropping, or converting him to wage labor in European installations and attaching him to a commercial market. The native's roles as trader and consumer, responding to manufactured needs, become mutually reinforcing. Correlatively, modern imperialism, including colonialism, stimulates a reaction which mirrors the structure of the imperial power itself. The peoples of the exploited area are transformed into an external mass, or proletariat, connected ultimately with the metropole. When the modern imperium "bestows independence" upon polities which it has arbitrarily formed in colonial areas, it follows logically that the inheritors of power are more or less friendly antagonists of the abdicating rulers (who have defined the very territories which the former inherit); and they maintain their associations in a variety of ways. It is only in the course of a war of national liberation, which is at the same time an ethno-genetic struggle, the struggle to form a nation, engaging the energies of the people from top to bottom, that the implications of independence can be understood. For if it is a truism that independence cannot be granted, but must be earned, it is equally clear that the aggressors in wars of national liberation are inevitably the colonial powers and their indigenous representatives. Therefore, it should be obvious why the two major revolutions of the twentieth century have not occurred in conventionally defined colonial areas, but were generated in an ancient civilization, China, and an archaic European polity, Russia. It seems that the more direct and profound the experience of colonialism, the less revolutionary is the reaction. Russia, subject to immediate Western influence, modernized on, and therefore converges to, a general European model.[2] China, a civilization of greater autonomy, continuity and depth, is generating new forms of social life—dialectically related to the spirit but not duplicating the letter of the past.

The Chinese, who have a deep and continuous experience with culture, are attempting to eliminate bureaucratic growth, demystify education, and relate town to country, mental to manual labor—while inhibiting the emergence of new classes. As they slowly and arduously improve their general standard of living, they also avoid the artificial consumerism, the pejorative display and use of wealth, which is an inherited goal and impulse of Western society. In China, a superficially modern, but basically archaic civilization of peasants is transforming itself into a socialist polity; the implications of this process for dialectical evolution as opposed to unilinear modernization—are obvious. For the Chinese know that no central power, archaic or modern, has ever ruled the whole body and territory of the Chinese peasantry. The nucleus of Chinese civilization was in the great bend of the Hwang Ho—and the reach of the traditional Chinese state had always exceeded its grasp. This holds true for all archaic civilizations—for example, that of India did not extend much beyond the Indus Valley. But the Chinese seem to be approaching this issue both as a revolutionary problem and an anti-bureaucratic opportunity.

Civilization, then, has evolved in two major phases, ancient and modern. The ancient states of China, Egypt, Babylonia, India were—in their restricted primary range—and along with their satellites and descendants, peasant-based and slow to develop. But the older civilizations are primary, in the sense that they were the original locus for the primitive transformation. The imperial thrust of these nuclear civilizations stimulated state-building almost everywhere, despite variations in style and differences in scale—except, perhaps, in the aboriginal new world. The classical civilizations of Greece and Rome that are ancestral to the Western experience are the heirs of the ancient Near Eastern cultures mediated through Crete and the Aegean. Thus actual history—not merely logical, abstract and determined evolutionary sequences—

becomes the locus of our concern. History was the will of men before it became man's fate, and it is always in the name of man that the most abstract and abysmal crimes are committed. In civilization the members of the antagonistic classes share a deepening false consciousness which persists up to the moment that they reject the inevitability of their respective positions, no matter how rationalized or sanctioned.

In its imperial phase, politically dynamic modern civilization invests the static ancient civilizations. The immobile political conflicts between the traditional local group and the archaic centers are gradually replaced by the new comprehensive movements to modernize. This "modernization" is confined, for the most part, to the growth of a new middle class made up of administrators, intellectuals, managers and businessmen who share a local variant of the imperial culture; meanwhile, the condition of the peasants and the urban poor worsens. Thus civilization comes full circle in the modern imperial period, as the British occupy India, and "protect" Egypt; the French annex Lebanon, and so on. Finally, the Europeans who "discover" and migrate to America reduce the aboriginal population at will. The transformation of primitives into peasants is no longer possible, since particularly in North America it is a question of primitives confronting a farming and manufacturing society. In Middle and South America, the primitive peoples are also decimated; only the peasants who worked the land in the Mexican valley and under the Incas survive, but even they are converted into plantation workers, serfs, peons. As civilization propagates itself, the remaining primitive peoples become increasingly marginal, not only geographically, but also culturally. They are no longer the raw material for the state-building process. They are superfluous, and so if they cannot be transformed, they are destroyed. The terms of their transformation are dictated by the imperial powers and their brokers, in the name of civilization.

Primitive peoples have been fascinated, repelled, conquered, administered and decimated by civilization, but they have hardly ever chosen to civilize themselves. In the middle of the eighteenth century, Rousseau understood this very well:

> It is an extremely remarkable thing for all the years that Europeans have been tormenting themselves to bring the savages of the various countries in the world to their way of

life that they have not yet been able to win over a single one, not even with the aid of Christianity; our missionaries sometimes make Christians of them, but never civilized men. Nothing can overcome the invincible repugnance they have of adopting our morals and living in our way. If these savages are as unhappy as it is claimed, they are, by what inconceivable depravity of judgment do they constantly refuse to civilize themselves by imitating us or to learn to live happily among us—whereas one finds in a thousand places that . . . Europeans have voluntarily taken refuge among these natives, spent their entire lives there, no longer able to leave such a strange way of life . . . .

Yet, in the last analysis, despite everything we insist on defining civilization as progressive. And if that is the case, it follows that the major means of propagating civilization—imperialism—must also be ultimately progressive. This opinion has been shared by reactionaries and radicals alike. A British governor of Nigeria, exemplifying the reactionary argument, is quite capable of admitting that England had no right to be in Africa in the first place, but once there, the affirmation goes, the government did have certain responsibilities and it discharged them supremely well. "Admittedly by force," good government has been substituted for tyranny, human sacrifices and slavery had been abolished and material prosperity had been secured for the country. "Under the Pax Brittanica the country grew rich." This was accomplished, we are told, without "any attempt to force upon Nigeria all of the doubtful advantages of modern civilization . . . each tribe had been permitted and encouraged to preserve such of its customs and ideas as are not repugnant to natural justice and humanity." However, "the more terrible fear of the supernatural still remains and will remain until Christianity and education drive out superstition." The arguments for imperialism are always false, contradictory or irrelevant and, as the instance of the Nigerian-Biafra war reveals, they have no predictive value whatsoever. It is easier to believe the candid rationalizations for imperialism than to question them, for questioning them means questioning Western cultural assumptions; the meaning of civilization is at stake.

With specific reference to Nigeria (the classic colonial case), the country was, in the first instance, the invention of a colonial power in search of trade, markets and geopolitical advantage. In evaluating Nigeria, the colonialist is confronting his own handiwork. One would hardly anticipate a negative judgment. As we shall see, radicals are not free of this compulsion. The image in the mirror also accounts for the agony of decolonialization; the colony is not only a profiteering exercise, it is also a test and revelation of the imperial culture. The investment is not only in oil, nickel, tin and an advantageous market, but also in a language, a cultural style, an interpretation of history and a civilizing mission which links ideology and economic purpose. Imperialism is, among other things, a complicated exercise in cultural narcissism. The upper classes in the metropole are drawn to it in order to retain their power and their image of themselves; that is one reason why colonies have been retained even when they seemed to be losing money for the metropolitan governments. Colonial failure is perceived as symbolizing failure at home, and that could increase the restiveness of the domestic lower classes.

But I do not wish to underestimate the political-economic argument. The colony is a piece of property, and property does not have to show a consistent return; it can always be held against a future need or possibility of profit. Deficit colonial social accounting is more than balanced by the profits made by trading or mining combines, or multinational corporations such as the United Africa Company—not to mention the personal chances for profit and prestige the colony affords metropolitan subjects. Moreoever, imperialism and colonialism cultivate dependence; they inhibit the evolution of social alternatives in the subordinate areas. And that shields both the economic interests and the way of life of the imperium against competition.

Equating "civilization-imperialism and progress-prosperity" does not work on other grounds. There is no way to measure, in our terms, the well-being of native societies that are not organized as capitalist or pre-capitalist states; how does one measure "scarcity"? Even so, the "prosperity" of the conquered is an illusion. It is said, if not understood, for example, that Nigeria, having been invented, prospered in the perspective, and for the benefit of England. But, within Nigeria itself, only an elite actually "bettered themselves," and they were cut off from their own people. This elite was two-layered: one part consisted of indirect rulers, indigenous native authorities paid by the British in order to execute British intentions, thereby losing their traditional position, and evolving as a naked ruling class, as did the Emirs in northern Nigeria. It also included local businessmen, politicians and intellectuals; their social prestige and economic prosperity set them apart from the vast majority of peasants, workers and petty traders. Moreover, the growth of Nigeria as a market for British goods, export cropping for cash, taxation, the drawing of native peoples into trading networks, the growth of cities as import-export centers and related factors, eroded the substance of that native life which indirect rule was supposed to preserve. The division between the native authorities and the rising young politicians-businessmen-intellectuals (these new vocations were frequently practiced by the same person) was perhaps the least of the splits encouraged by colonialism. New classes—urban and rural proletariats, market-oriented peasantries, a middle class largely dependent on the metropolitan power—developed and struggled over the resources left to them in the colonial economy. Such internal divisions were the inevitable result of colonial rule and colonial rule then justifies itself in terms of such divisions. The colonial power seeks to become the arbiter of colonial conflicts which it stimulated in tne first instance. In so doing it assumes precisely the role to which all civilized political authority pretends both at home and abroad—the state as arbiter. But in actuality the colonial power will always support the group, class or persons' most congenial to its own interests, just as a domestic state will, in the long run, support those interests which invented it. In the Nigeria-Biafra conflict, for example, England, presumably above the battle, supported its own federal creation. The role of the colonial power as arbiter is further rationalized by the ethnic conflicts which result from arbitrarily imposing colonial boundaries and forcing "national" identities into existence that are purely political, and have little or no cultural-historical significance.

The movement toward a traditionally-based national identity is then considered irredentist, as in the cases of Biafra or the southern Sudan, but it can only be judged as such with reference to colonial gerrymandering in the first place. Therefore, the "responsibility" of the imperial power grows overwhelming, since it cannot resolve the contradictions generated by its own rule. At that point the pressure to withdraw formal sovereignty becomes intense, even in the absence of a powerful and unified independence movement. But should such a movement exist, its intention—the achievement of independence—is likely to be in accord with that of the metropolitan power. The only question that remains is whether the ex-colony and the metropole will continue to profit the ruling classes in both countries. If the answer tends to be negative, neo-colonialism, a colonialism without "responsibility," is established in the name of independence. The Ivory Coast, for example, flourishes superficially on metropolitan loans, tourism, hotels and primary export cropping. But if the answer tends to be positive, if the ruling group in the ex-colony understands the antagonism between itself and the metropole, and seeks a united anticolonial movement, then revealing decisions are sometimes made. In 1958, when Guinea, alone among the former French colonies in Africa, voted against joining the Association of French States, de Gaulle withdrew every resident French technician and halted all further aid within hours. The Guinean rebuff was conceived as a profound cultural rejection and a vote of no confidence in the French government. Accordingly, French investments there could not be considered secure. Analogously, when China began to contest the ideological hegemony of the Soviet Union, and to question Soviet socialism, the Russians refused to renew their formal aid agreement after 1956. In 1959, they abruptly cancelled the Nuclear Assistance Treaty they had entered into with the Chinese; and in 1960 they withdrew all remaining Soviet technicians in a matter of days. The point is that the imperialist imagination can neither permit nor conceive alternatives in subordinate areas and will use all means to abort them if they should develop. Thus, imperialism fulfills its own prophecy; and the metropolitan power seeks to impose its concrete form of society as a theory of growth.

The British claims in Nigeria, England's pivotal colony, deserve further attention because they are so typical—with reference, for example, to the argument about metropolitan abolition of slavery. Large-scale commercial and chattel slavery initiated by the Europeans in the fifteenth century on the coast of West Africa overshadowed ancient Arab efforts further inland. Indigenous "slavery" in Africa, which included pawning and related practices, had been relatively mild; slaves could inherit property, become the heads of families, and their children typically assumed the status of free men; thus they were incorporated into the kinship and village structure. In the native state of Dahomey, for example, any man born in the territory, no matter what his paternity, was by definition a free man, or "commoner." Arab slavery could be as cruel as the European kind but in those African areas which were influenced by Islam, the domestic aspects of slavery were emphasized more strongly than in the European institution.

Although the imperialists claim credit as Christians for halting the slave trade (Britain finally abolished slavery in 1807), they rarely acknowledged starting it, or pursuing it to a degree and with a rationalized ferocity unprecedented in human history. Slavery was as immoral and un-Christian in the sixteenth century as it was in the nineteenth; it was not abandoned because of deepening moral perceptions; Christianity had not changed. Rather, slavery was abandoned by the more commercial European nations in conflict with the more feudal and agrarian ones, because: it began to interfere with the more lucrative sources of trade, such as palm oil; and the slave market had been glutted and the growth of manufacturing was rendering the institution obsolete. It was perhaps cheaper to support an industrial worker receiving a minimal wage than a slave, for whose total welfare the master was supposedly responsible, although slaves, not to mention "free" laborers, died by the thousands for lack of care. Besides, it would have been absurd to import slaves to work in mines or factories, since they would have to compete with domestic labor, of which there was a more than adequate supply. Nor had England any means of absorbing slaves on the land; there were no plantations in the country, and by the sixteenth century the English farmer had long since been defined as a "free" man. Slavery was only pursued for profit on the extensive plantations of the new world, particularly in the American South, where domestic field labor was in short supply and slaves could be cheaply housed, fed and cared for. Moreover, slaves of an alien race could easily be treated as objects in a polity wherein they had no history, and, therefore, no rights.

The loss of the American colonies helped account for England's declining interest in the slave trade, but imperialism holds no principle constant except that of self-interest. The English government under Palmerston aided the South during the Civil War and came very close to declaring war on the North, at the same time that it was policing the slave trade off the coast of West Africa. The British government, which was then in the hands of the aristocracy, was naturally sympathetic to the agrarian Cavaliers of the American South. But they also looked forward to cheap American cotton for the mills of Lancashire, along with a widening American market for goods manufactured in Britain, a market that would be assured should the South win. The Puritan North, on the other hand, was a potential competitor, and was, in fact, waging the war to extend its commerce and industry throughout the nation and on the expanding frontier. So far as slavery was concerned, England struggled to supplant it by another form of trade in West Africa and would have been compromised only in principle, not in fact, by a southern victory. The natural rate of increase in the United States would have substantially kept up the supply of blacks without further trading in Africa. Moreover, the cotton gin had increased the output of black plantation labor exponentially, relative to the number of workers, thus making slavery more economical than ever, so that further importation of slaves was hardly necessary. But even if England had not calculated in this way, support of the South, encouraging chaos in her former colony, gives the lie to imperialist apologetics. Since they shared an affinity for the industrial North, it was the workers and the rising bourgeosie—not the men in political power—who restrained the British government from declaring war.

Thus the rise of modern slavery was responsive to social and economic conditions; the question of morality was abstract, irrelevant. The course of modern slavery epitomizes false consciousness in history, except for those slaves who refused to accept their servitude, or those actual or potential slaveowners who rejected the use of slaves, taking whatever social risks were involved in such an action. Slavery was the most direct and brutal form, the incarnation of imperialism. When it was no longer necessary, it was supplanted by mercantile colonialism, and finally by neo-colonialism—economic manipulation at a distance. Imperialism evolves, but it is never self-liquidating.

Along with the abolition of slavery, the Christian mission has also been represented as an impulse for modern imperialism. Colonialists assumed that "universalistic" religions, of which established Christianity was representative, were inherently superior to the "paganism" of local cults. But it hardly needs to be pointed out that the competition between the missions of the various Christian sects, along with the almost continuous warfare between various Christian polities reflected in the colonial arena, failed to impress pagans who were being instructed in the subtleties of scripture. Moreover, primitive religions were fully capable of absorbing or duplicating the essentially Christian symbols and meanings divorced from metropolitan power. The "particularism" of primitive religions cannot be equated with a lack of depth; it is rather a symptom of the territorially delimited societies with which they were associated. In theological perspective, the Christian churches have been clearly associated with established social and economic interests. This is less true of primitive religions, whose symbolic formulations rise from and are in touch with the whole of human existence, and which therefore express a more authentic religious consciousness than has been evident in churchly dogma. The point is that primitive religions are culturally particularistic, but within the given culture, universal in their synthesis of man-society-nature. Christianity, it should be remembered, did not become ecumenical until after it was transformed into the Roman church; until recently, non-Catholic Christians had a hard time escaping damnation in the view of the church, a perspective reciprocated by its Fundamentalist opponents. But Hell is unknown in less exclusivist primitive religions.

The universalism of Christianity is no more than a symptom of the imperial control by Western civilization of the cultural space of other peoples. Correlatively, Christianity, in time, links classic to feudal and feudal to modern civilization. Institutionalized Christianity is therefore an aspect of modern imperialism; the church has rarely questioned the inevitability of progress—that is, of the inevitable triumph of the West—nor has it ever launched a significant critique of imperialism at home. Rather, it has served as a link between classes, while sanctioning the continuity of political authority; the "conflict" between church and state is always a division within the same domestic establishment, no matter how it may appear to the contestants. Individual Christians, whether Protestant or Catholic, may, of course, interpret and seek to use their faith in emancipatory ways, at home and abroad, but to accomplish this they are almost always compelled to subvert the churchly establishment, as is the case today in Brazil, Chile and Columbia; the radicalization of the church there means no more than the radicalization of a few prelates. But these factors aside, the British claim that imperialism directly propagated Christianity, or that its purpose was deeply Christian, is without substance. In northern Nigeria, Christian missions were prohibited until shortly before independence in accordance with the mystique of indirect rule, which was supposed to preserve the indigenous, more or less Moslem, authority.

Apologists for imperialism, whether reactionary or radical, frequently take education as a further example of imperialism's progressive effect—if not, so far as the radicals are concerned, of its intention. Continuing with Nigeria as an example, the subject matter of education there has been rather selective. The university-trained indigenous elite was cast in the British mold; they studied British history, English literature, the humanities, the classics. They were certified according to the standards of and in affiliation with the British educational establishment. They learned English habits, manners, attitudes and expectations. If black Africa was their point of origin, then African England became their conscious or unwitting projection of the future. Translated into metropolitan terms, they were by cultural—if not economic—definition, upper-middle class, and that consciousness was constantly reinforced within the university milieu. However, members of the black university elite did not achieve equality with their tutors, only recognition from them. At the same time, they became further isolated from their own people and tradition. The predictable result of all this was academic snobbery. The African elite assimilated the attitudes of their English models toward "uneducated Englishmen," a species of white man to whom it was legitimate to feel superior. The educated black was encouraged to look down on uneducated blacks and whites alike, and thus displaced the hostility he might ordinarily have felt toward his metropolitan mentors. His snobbery was an acute defense against his own sense of not being fully accepted; it was the snobbery of the English *arriviste*. The training of the university elite, and to a certain degree the secondary school candidate, thus paralleled the class character of higher education in the metropole. The difference was that the indigenous elite, isolated from lower-class blacks and whites alike and disassociated from a native establishment, could only secure its own interests. In contrast, the public schools and universities of England represented the tradition of British rule, both at home and abroad.

In the colonial university curriculum, technical and scientific subjects were avoided, since they were not considered prerequisite to the creation of gentlemen-administrators. More importantly, technical and scientific training was expensive; adequate teachers and equipment could hardly be spared for colonial service. Technical training, shorn of its academic and scientific mystique, but representative of the country's needs, was also neglected. White expatriots could fill those jobs that represented the metropolitan conception of colonial needs. But above all, scientific and technical training meant handing over the keys to the kingdom—science symbolized, technology actualized power, the threat of real autonomy. Even at home, the metropole prized these resources. Science was a bureaucratic mystery, whereas technology was merely pragmatic and, consequently the domestic engineer was the captive of either the government or the corporate economy and that became the colonial definition of science and technology.

But training in the Western conception of the humanities constituted a kind of deracination; it was a form of cultural conditioning. Native languages, literature and history were paid scant attention. So far as the social sciences were concerned, reification cooled revolutionary ardor, turned lived problems into clinical cases, meticulously distinguished theory from practice, and encouraged the professional aspirant to be value-free, yet sensitive to the demands of his career. If the social sciences, along with the academic humanities, supported the status quo at home, this was even more evident abroad.

Lawyers, of course, functioned in the British tradition. The very language of the law persuaded the indigneous lawyer to take on the metropolitan view of justice and politics. Like the social scientist, the lawyer also learned to pride himself on being value-free—as dedicated to procedure as the former is wedded to technique. He was in effect the opportunistic member of an estate which pursued its own "legitimate" material and professional interests. The lawyer inclines towards disengagement; his natural arena is the court, the ultimate symbol of the civilized and colonial establishment. There, he earns his living by engaging in an abstract legal contest; cases concern him in the context of legal principles, but political principles, which include the rationale for the existence of the courts in the first place, remain unchallenged. Both the law and its practitioners are conservative. It follows that legal training, which meant training in British law, was prized by both colonialists and students. For the former, it helped strengthen the bonds between the colony and the metropole, and for the latter, it was a safe route to the top.

Thus university education, and to a lesser extent secondary education were obvious agencies of imperialism. Examinations, standards and requirements reflected or were directly linked to the metropolitan academy. But primary education in southern Nigeria was initiated and supported by the *missions*, not the colonial government. Partly as a result of this circumstance (as the missions were largely Catholic, and the metropolitan church, Anglican), among the Igbo-speaking peoples of the Southeast, the primary schools were incorporated into the multitudinous village communities, remaining more or less under local control. Among the Yoruba of the Southwest, on the other hand, the educational system was more fully centralized and rationalized in accordance with the aboriginal distinction between Igbo and Yoruba organization. The Igbo were perhaps unique in their ability to adapt Western primary education to local usages; for example, the students in a given village might be transformed into a cooperative work group, discharging nonacademic tasks when called upon. Older children also assisted, and saw to it that the younger ones understood their obligations, thus greatly diminishing the isolation and mechanical peer affiliations generic to the foreign educational structure. The competitive elements in that structure were converted into a kind of title-taking, which reflected the competition for titles in the traditional society without losing the sense that a superior title implied superior responsibility. Finally, Western education among the Igbo was conceived of by the Igbo as a purely pragmatic undertaking, mediated by the individual, but undertaken for the good of the group.

However, in almost every other case throughout the colonial world, the very structure of schooling was an analogue on the factory system, an imposed form of industrial culture. The new hierarchies of formal education, the school as a locus of socialization, disengaged the student from his local setting, while ostensibly providing him with individual means of mobility in colonial society. Schooling did not draw upon local usage; traditional learning had occurred in the absence of such formal institutions and through the normal variety of social groups and activities. These qualifications, however, do not apply to northern Nigeria where, in the virtual absence of mission schools, formal education for the mass of depressed peasants was nonexistent. In fact, northern Nigeria, with the largest population in black Africa, was the seat of archaic civilizations for perhaps a thousand years before colonial conquest, and thus lent itself most readily to indirect British rule. It was not the recipient of what a former governor of Nigeria, with the contrived ambivalence of the sophisticated civil servant, has called "the doubtful advantages of Western civilization." Christianity had not been introduced on any scale worth considering, nor had education, to which Christianity had been linked in southern Nigeria. Even slavery was tolerated in the north, although slave-raiding was prohibited. That is, those who had been slaves at the time of colonial superimposition were not directly emancipated by British rule. Given the prohibition on raiding, along with the stipulation that all children born after April 1, 1901 were to be considered free, it was assumed that the institution would die of attrition. However, the subtle class and rank gradations that persist in northern Nigeria reflect the pre-colonial structure. One scholar has assessed the situation as follows: "The prohibition on slave recruitment under British rule has left these relations intact. Wherever ex-slave and master remain in contact, the ex-slave or his descendent is still the master's *dimajo* while the master is *ubangiji* (father of the inheritance). Thus slavery has turned into serfdom, and the *dimajai* of today are described by the masters as *talakawa* (commoners), *bayi* (slaves) or *yanuwa* (kinsmen) according to the context. In one sense, the *dimajai* are just as much slaves as ever they were in the last century. In another, they are free commoners, like other *talakawa*, and at law they are now formally responsible for their own offenses. Few are really distinguishable from other Moslem Habe, whose culture is now their own."

The economic changes that took place in northern Nigeria were the result of the colonial engagement of the peasants in a world market, and the political changes that occurred were in reaction to dynamic events in southern Nigeria, a reaction largely confined to the colonially subserviant northern elite. The situation in northern Nigeria, the most strategic area in British Africa, makes it clear that even the manifest pretensions of imperialism must be dismissed. Therefore, when radical scholars such as Thomas

Hodgkin and conservative administrators such as Sir Alan Burns agree that the nineteenth-century European penetration of West Africa was intended to spread Christian civilization, develop education and halt the slave trade, they are both equally wrong. But their agreement reveals the depth of the imperialist mentality, which is obliged to define itself as progressive.

This question of progress is critical. The idea itself is rather odd; civilizations other than that of the contemporary West have been ethnocentric, imagining themselves to represent the height of human achievement. The Egyptians, Chinese, Greeks, medieval Islam, the Romans, the feudal European church, all defined themselves as peerless, a notion that was concentrated in but by no means confined to the upper strata of their respective societies. But the purpose of imperialism, as engaged in by pre-industrial societies, was political and economic control. Other cultures may have been judged strange or inferior, but it was not explicitly assumed that the imperial mission was to transform society in the image of the dominant power, even when that occurred to some degree. However, with the rise of industrialism and the related ideology of science, the total conscious transformation of society and nature was, for the first time in human history, considered both possible and desirable. Imperialism thus takes on the appearance of a joint enterprise; as a metropolitan power evolves towards greater efficiency, technological sophistication and a command of the environment, it cultivates the same motives within the subordinate and dependent cultures. In the modern era, the mission of civilization is simply civilization itself. And the idea of progress becomes an ideal which both the imperium and the "emerging" societies strain to achieve. Their futures have been plotted, because it is assumed that their pasts are either shattered or irrelevant.

Europe does not doubt the superiority of its techniques or its vision; imperialism is a mission that can be "objectively" evaluated. But their fulfillment implies a universal polity. Imperialism is conceived as a leveling—and, at the same time, a progressive—force. The cultures of societies everywhere are reduced to the common denominators of their respective metropolitan powers, and imperialism as world hegemony becomes the paradigm for world government. Accordingly, the imperialists, at one with spokesmen for world government, suspect indigenous nationalism. But as Malinowski pointed out, in unwitting agreement with Marx, the nation, as opposed to the state, is the basis of culture. The nation is the generator of custom, the creative aspect of a whole people, the community of language and tradition linked through a society situated in a continuous territory. The assault on the nation, or the statist distortion of nationality which results in chauvinism, are equivalent political assaults on the creativity of a people. The sinister and disingenuous Fascist appeal to the *Volk* represents the extreme of chauvinism; in fascism, the totalitarian state—the bureaucratic fulfillment of monopoly capitalism—uses the longing of people for authentic community as leverage for political manipulation. Language becomes the opposite of what it symbolizes, and therefore contradicts that which is actually experienced—the pseudo-*Gemeinschaft* is called a *Gemeinschaft*, the collective masquerades as a community.

As nations are subordinated by and incorporated into states, nationalism becomes a political weapon. But it is always a sign of its opposite, of cultural insecurity, of the lack of cultural definition within the bureaucratic reach of the state. But nations precede states in history, and show signs of outlasting them. Historically viewed, they are the cultural forms that succeed primitive society. For example, in pre-colonial Eastern Nigeria, the Igbo-speaking peoples, numbering about four million, constituted a primitive nationality; they had no centralized bureaucracy, no socioeconomic classes. The autonomous villages traded and intermarried, but the extent of such relationships never comprised the whole of Igbo-land. People in any given area may have been unaware of the existence of Igbo-speakers beyond their immediate territorial horizon. Nevertheless, the Igbo shared a mutually recognizable culture and certain limited, if effective social mechanisms; they also spoke dialects of the same language. But the self-conscious, microcosmic marital and linguistic boundaries of the tribe did not define the total Igbo situation. Nor did the Igbo constitute a territorially definable, politically articulated protostate. As an objectively definable and unself-conscious primitive nationality—a nation of concretely but incompletely linked villages—they and similar peoples clarify, by contrast, the bourgeois *nation*-state which emerges in modern Western civilization. But the latter determines the conventional political and academic awareness of the modern problem of nationality; Westerners conceive of nations as bourgeois nation-states.

In the post-bourgeois world, the persistent efforts of the Basques, Bretons, Serbo-Croatians, Australian aborigines, New World blacks and Indians, Biafrans, Italo-Americans, Scotch and Welsh, among others, to identify themselves within contemporary bureaucratic states may be a significant symptom of economic disadvantage; but it also represents the dialectical return to ethnicity. These movements reflect the statist distortions of national consciousness, but at their most vital they are demands for the perpetuation of cultural diversity in politically viable form on an economically viable basis. Imperialism, or any other thrust toward world government, seeks to inhibit the reformulation of old, and the formation of new nations; it generates ecumenical concepts; it is the negative side of world consciousness, society, culture. Imperialism is incarnated today in the multinational corporation, but this technocratic model on a global scale, commanding all significant facets of culture, is currently confined to the Western imagination. It is the projection of the socioeconomic needs and cultural realities of Euro-America. The historical contradiction is obvious: a "world government," which would represent an evolved speciational consciousness, would not have to be established by force, and would not be imperialistic; therefore it would not have to be established at all. Its constituent communities would have reached a degree of sophistication and free communication that would render an international political bureaucracy obsolete. At the same time, if what has actually happened in history is any guide, these constituent communities, relieved of bureaucratic superimposition, would create a variety of cultural forms and languages, duplicating, on a higher level, the symbolic processes—the variety of forms so evident in primitive societies. Thus ethnogenesis, the creation of cultural groups, would become a continuous process.

Imperialism seeks to absorb and nullify all contradictions; but the basic apology for imperialism remains the idea of progress. The brutality of the means of conquest, the erosion of other cultural possibilities, the necessity of political tutelage, even economic exploitation for the benefit of the metropole are all rationalized in that context. Their unintended consequences are conceived as positive; enlightened self-interest, it is fancied, ultimately resolves itself in the universal good. Therefore, imperialism strives to appear as a joint enterprise, a collaboration of cultures, on the analogy of class collaboration for the health of the state. The manifest and "scientifically demonstrable" superiority of the West seems to be the logical denouement of the history of the species. And it is just here that the actuality, with all of its obvious and admitted imperfections, is mystified by the ideal of Western civilization, projected as no less than the goal of humanity—a goal which all rational men are obliged to share. If Europe is faithful to its own heritage, the rationalization runs, and fully realizes its potential, then it is bound to become the civilization of the world—everyman's fate. It follows that every contact of any consequence between the European and the "natives of other lands" has been in bad faith. The missionaries, the businessmen, the soldiers, the colonial administrators, the anthropologists, all of these approach other cultures as raw material to be used in their own interests.

Social progress, it was assumed, inhered in the working through of these political, commercial and scientific interests; and that in turn reflects the illusory cultural logic of mercantilism—namely, that the sum of the behavior of individuals motivated by profit will secure the prosperity and progress of society at large. But no matter how the issue is put, at home or abroad, faith in progress as the outcome of their techniques and ideas justifies Western civilized men to themselves. One must acknowledge further, that that faith is the dominant idea of Western civilization. In its name, Western man rationalizes not only his self-interest, but also his failures. He does not perceive his failures as the result of his goals, nor of his motives, but rather of the means at his disposal, or of his human limitations. For he cannot surrender the notion of progress without destroying the rationale for his entire civilization. No matter how critical he may be of the realities of his society, he clings to his progressivism as he would to his sanity. It is the notion of progress that mediates his alienation, and makes it possible for him to construct a reality which he does not actually experience.

But his commitment to progress is really less a faith than a compulsion. No matter what aspects of Western culture he assumes to be potentially or actually superior to the cultures of other times and places, the case for superiority is always weaker than the intensity of his argument. This argument is, therefore, grotesque, a deformation of consciousness. For the idea of progress is not based on a rational analysis of our civilization. It springs from the disequilibrium of the system in which Western man finds himself. The social structure of the United States, for example, limits the uses of technology. Corporate capitalism is misrepresented as "free enterprise," or as the realization of the revolutionary spirit of the eighteenth century; Thomas Jefferson is linked to General Motors. Modern technology, society and ideology are always out of joint with each other; and this sensed disjunction generates the idea of progress. Caught in the contradictions of society, Westerners see themselves as ciphers of history; incomplete and always waiting to be completed. Disintegrated by the extreme division of labor, by competition for goods and services and status rivalries, they obsessively anticipate integration. The idea of progress is, above all, the precipitant of unresolved social and personal conflicts in modern civilization, conflicts that feed on themselves. It is the awareness of this conflict, along with the effort at resolving that creates the sense of unresolved movement towards specific goals which are defined as progressive.

A comparison with primitive societies permits us to understand this point more fully, for the structure of primitive societies is perceived as permanent. Progress is a reality of personal growth, a progress *through* society, not *of* society, as the individual moves from experience to experience on what the Winnebago call the "road of life and death." The infant may be conceived as the reborn spirit of a deceased ancestor. The child and the adult typically succeed the infant through a ritual cycle that sanctions learning and experience in a sacred order, and may culminate in the person becoming an elder, who, dying to the world, then reemerges as an ancestral spirit, sometimes in the womb of a grandson's wife. The primitive custom of calling a parent by the name of the child, technically termed "teknonymy," reflects this cycle.

"Progress," in primitive societies, if this Western conception can be applied to them at all, would be a metaphor for spiritual transformation. The contradictions of growth through the various phases of the life cycle are socially recognized, ritually expressed and dialectically resolved.

The *couvade*, as practiced, in the tropical forest of South America, is a case in point. Customarily the husband repairs to his hammock for several days during his wife's labor and immediately after she has given birth to a child. He acts with unusual circumspection, since he is assumed to be a custodian of the infant's spirit. He behaves as if he had undergone the birth experience, and the geneology of the child is underscored by his actions. But, more significantly, the couvade is a visible symbol of a complex shift in the relationships involved in childbirth, centering on the male as a point of reckoning. Childbirth transforms the respective roles of, and the relationships between, the sexes. Husband and wife are now being mediated by another person, and their behavior towards each other changes. For the male, the transition is from lover to husband, son to father, generally from a position of lesser to greater social responsibility. Complementary transformations involve the wife; but in her case, childbirth symbolizes its own reality. The focus on the male not only compensates for the absence of a sharply defined critical event in his life, but also engages the woman in the meaning of the male experience—which includes the continuity of his connection with the child—just as he had been directed to the meaning of her experience during pregnancy and its immediate aftermath. Like other rituals which center on one sex, it also epitomizes shifts in the behavior of the other, even when the latter transformation is less public. The couvade, then, can be understood as a crisis rite socially expressing an existential transition experienced as risky and formidable within the cultural context of a given people. The contrast with the conventionally disengaged and disoriented male in similar situations in our society hardly needs to be remarked.

Just as the systemic conflicts in modern civilization generate our idea of social progress, so the inevitable conflicts of growth generate the idea of personal progress in primitive society—but such primitive conflicts are resolved; they are shared, understood and socially structured. The person, does, in fact, evolve through hierarchies of being. But in our civilization, the person is reduced to a status, a reflex of society, and it is society which is supposed to progress. In primitive societies, the "becoming" of personal growth is balanced by the "being" of personal realization on all significant levels of existence and, therefore, our perception of history is simply irrelevant. On the other hand, compelled by their conflicts, Westerners are always trying to find concrete evidence for their superiority; they feel that they represent the West, the logical inheritance of the past, civilization itself.

Our culturally compulsive need to believe in progress is one thing, but the rational evidence is quite another; in fact, the evidence is weak. It is, however, worth examining. Anthropologists seem to have reflected more on this question than historians, and perhaps more explicitly than philosophers, since they are concerned with the variety, evolution, development and attrition of culture from its prehistoric origins to the present. One would suppose, therefore, that anthropologists would be more skeptical about civilized claims to superiority, and that they would be less ethnocentric and more responsible in their judgments than other members of the academy. But before considering the case for progress, the idea needs a somewhat sharper definition. "Progress" means advancement to a better condition, not simply evolution or development. Evolution implies a systematic outgrowth of one form from another; one may refer, for example, to the evolution of the automobile from the wheeled cart, or of a steamship from a wind-driven vessel. Similarly, one may refer to the evolution of institutions, such as marriage or the family, evolving from polygyny to monogamy, from extended groups to nuclear units. Or, one may have in mind the evolution of whole societies, such as capitalism evolving out of feudalism. But evolution is not quite the same thing as development—institutions, tools and events, all these may develop without changing. They may simply replicate themselves or expand, as in the case of the automobile industry. However, modern industrial civilization does not base its case on evolution or development, but rather it bases it on superiority and, therefore, on the concept of progress, the notion of progressive change.

Academicians are almost unanimous in their support of the idea of progress, which is readily enough understood in the light of the priestly and scriptural origins of the academic profession. Exceptionally, Franz Boas, the founder of academic anthropology in the United States, stated that he would always give more credence to the opinions of ordinary people on important issues, except technical ones, if the former were sufficiently clear, because intellectuals were bound by convention and identified, for the most part, with the received authority. Yet even Boas had a qualified faith in the progress of civilization, a faith which he shared with A.L. Kroeber, his best known student. Boas and Kroeber defined the progress that has actually occurred in civilization, and the areas in which it can continue to occur, as follows:

BOAS	KROEBER
1. In science and technology.	1. In science and technology.
2. In the extention of in-group, ethical commandments against murder, rape, theft, etc. to larger and larger out-groups.	2. In the decline of magical thinking (he exempts religion here).
3. In the increase in the health, safety and comfort of the individual.	3. In the lack of social obsession with psychophysiological processes— such as puberty and menstruation.
But progress cannot be defined in terms of the form of society. Anarchy may be one man's ideal, and centralized authority that of another man.	4. In the decline of bodily mutilations for religious or cosmetic purposes.
	5. In the growing humanity of civilization, manifested in the opposition to slavery, torture, slaughter of prisoners of war, etc.
	6. In the quantitative accumulation of culture traits.
	But, after all this he draws back and states that wiser living and happiness constitute progress and wonders, in the teeth of his own apparent judgment, whether that has, in fact, occurred.

The superficiality of these judgments reflects the sociocultural situation of the anthropologist; his conclusions, therefore, bear no relation to his competence, or to the inherent implications of his work. First of all, science and technology are not necessarily related. Man was a technician long before he was a scientist; more pertinently, science and technology, reified and divorced from the human context and from social application, are no more than mechanical fetishes. The belief in the progress of an abstract science or technology is a peculiarly Western fallacy. Western man fantasizes, understandably enough, that he will one day be replaced by the robot or the computer. But that is a projection of his own immediate feelings about his contemporary self; this replacement has already begun. Therefore, it is only from the *standpoint of the machine*, representing the disengaged category of "science and technology," that progress remains possible; in order to maintain the fiction of progress, Westerners entertain the notion of negating humanity itself. And this, in turn, is related to the irrational production of commodities, over which ordinary people have no control, but which they are conditioned to consume. In the joint perspective of the worker and the consumer, the machines take on a life of their own—after all, they have not invented them, and have no voice in their use or replication. The imperious ring of the telephone, for example, interrupts all other activities. Its trivial, dissociated and obsessive use reflects both the alienating character of the society that prizes it so highly, and the transnational corporations that profit from it. Thus the telephone as ordinarily used becomes a sign, not of communication, but of the lack of communication, and of the consequent compelling desire to relate to others, but to relate at a distance—and in the mode of a frustrated orality. The telephone is not an abstractly or inherently "rational" instrument, but an integrated aspect of the repressive culture of monopoly capitalism.* In our society, the machine becomes the mediator, and finally the locus of dissociated personal impulses.†

Kroeber's emphasis on the quantitative accumulation of culture traits is similarly unacceptable; it implies that progress can be measured from the standpoint of a culture, a superorganism. But the real issue is qualitative; it concerns participation in a culture, the personal command of cultural possibilities. For example, the mere existence of a civilized dictionary containing 100,000 words bears no relation to the working vocabulary of a bank clerk, which is probably poorer than that of an Eskimo, or an illiterate Swedish or Greek peasant. Like the category "science and technology," the toting up of culture traits in society at large is abstract arithmetic, irrelevant to the competence and capabilities of persons. It is no wonder that Kroeber, along with other anthropologists, typically tends to reify culture, to view it as growing and developing with a life of its own—like the coral skeletons of sea polyps.

---

* Monopoly capitalism seeks to overcome its contradictions by producing goods and services that absorb and displace attention from the isolation and frustration that its form of society generates; these objects and services then become necessary, a sign of progress, a proof of prestige for those who "own" them, a symptom of class collaboration, and a way of holding the people at large, who have no other alternatives, to ransom. They are, in other words, addictions.

† This psychosocial fact led Norbert Weiner, the architect of cybernetics, into a crusade against his own creation.

Boas refers to the extension of in-group ethical commandments, but that, of course, has not occurred. For example, the interesting fact that the great majority of murders in the United States occur within families or among close friends and acquaintances, denies the logic of this progression. Moreover, the intensity and duration of modern war, on the basis of modern science and technology, is not only unknown among primitives, but murder, rape or theft among the primitive in-group is also a rare occurrence. Still another criterion, the increase in the health, safety and comfort of the individual, is not only impossible to measure "objectively," but if measurable in the terms stated, would require a bourgeois yardstick. The anthropologist does not mention transcendance, spiritual growth or maturation. And he overlooks the increase in the subtler diseases—cancer, schizophrenia, arteriosclerosis. The recently rediscovered pollution of the environment (Rousseau documented that in the eighteenth century, Marx and Engels in the nineteenth), the rise in the rate of industrial accidents, and the unhealthy character of daily life, all militate against the notion that the species has been improving itself in these areas. Moreover, Boas unaccountably overlooks the increasing immiseration of most of the people of the world during the past 5,000 years. He concludes with a concession that is precisely wrong: there can be no progress in the forms of society; for they are a matter of preference, which the anthropologist conceives relativistically, in terms of temperament. But it is, for example, the social organization and culture of capitalism, in historical contrast with, say, an Eskimo band, that must be correlated with the possibility of human fulfillment and the understanding of the human condition. Boas's negative point is conceived in the impossible perspective of a mind standing completely outside of society; rather than being the foundation of human possibility, society becomes a matter of choice, a mere fashion.

Kroeber emphasizes somewhat different, but related, conditions. The decline of magical thinking is hard to reconcile with the obsessive-compulsive neuroses that Freud identified as a central process in the personality of modern Western man. Correlatively, magical thinking is replacing religion in the Western consciousness, rather than the other way around. The mechanical manipulation of persons and of nature, the identification of the ego with externals, the triumph of secularism, and the flourishing of a thousand and one cults which promise reward without any realistic means, the efflorescence of drugs, which means treating the mind as a machine—all these related processes signify the increase, not the decline, of magical thinking.

The lack of obsession with what Kroeber calls "physiological processes" (an astonishing formulation for an anthropologist) is actually the lack of ritual focus on the crises of life, which physiological processes symbolize. In the primitive consciousness, the body is both reality and symbol; it is lived with, experienced, understood; thus Kroeber's "obsession" is, in reality, a celebration, not a degradation. By the same token, the decline of bodily mutilation for religious purposes signifies a decline in religion, and an avoidance of pain as a symbol of growth. What has actually declined, is the perception and understanding of sacrifice, the gift of the body as a token of the spirit. Meanwhile, bodily mutilation for cosmetic reasons has increased. Surgical operations on faces and breasts, the use of all sorts of devices to improve the clothed appearance of the body, and the general large-scale investment in cosmetics grows with the reduction of self to status, of reality to appearance, in modern Western civilization.

Kroeber's opinion, expressed after the second World War, about the presumed civilized opposition to slavery, torture and slaughter of prisoners of war, is hardly worth considering. It does not distinguish between the various forms of "slavery,"—primitive, archaic and modern. Nor is torture ethnologically interpreted—for the torture of prisoners of war among the Iroquois, for example, was a cruel test and a challenge, but it was not ideologically based; they had no intention of "brainwashing" the enemy. In fact, Iroquois prisoners of war were frequently adopted into the tribe, supplying labor, but eventually they could regain their dignity and achieve Iroquois status, either directly or through their children. Kroeber's final concession is safer than Boas's; he is, after all, uncertain—he feels that "wiser living and happiness" are the real issues involved. But, in contrast with his positive indices of progress, Kroeber makes no effort to define either wiser living or happiness. The curiously shallow observations of both Boas and Kroeber in this matter, observations which are at variance with their understanding of the primitive world, illuminate the academic character of the ethnologist, his fundamental incapacity to seriously criticize his own society and his willingness to adopt a language that denies his experience.

Yet, we are told by another anthropologist—V. Gordon Childe*—that "It is futile to deplore the superstitions of the past as it is to complain of the unsightly scaffolding essential to the erection of a lovely building. It is childish to ask why man did not progress straight from the squalor of a 'pre-class' society to the glories of a classless paradise, nowhere fully realized as yet." (But in denying the question, he nevertheless asks it.) "Perhaps the conflicts and contradictions, above revealed, themselves constitute the dialectics of progress." The basic contradiction that Childe refers to here is between the growth of population—in his opinion, a sign of progress—correlated with late neolithic technology—and the consequent rise of class-structured states which, leading to war, destroys men. At the same time, the archaic state represses the technological initiative which led to its conception; slaves are readily available; religion and magic invest temporal power. "In any case," Childe continues, "[these] are facts of history. If we dislike them, that does not mean that progress is a delusion, but merely that we have understood neither the facts nor progress nor man. Man made the superstitions and the institutions of oppression as much as he made the sciences and the instruments of production. In both alike, he was expressing himself, finding himself, making himself."

The insistence on progress here, although somewhat more sophisticated than the expressions of Kroeber and Boas, is no less mechanical; for a dialectical argument would not fall back upon the notion of man finding himself, but would rather look forward to the necessity of a revolutionary reconstruction of Western civilization, on the prototype of the "squalid" neolithic pattern which the author elsewhere memorializes. It is not at all "childish" to ask why man did not progress straight from the squalor of a "pre-class" society to the glories of a classless paradise. That is precisely where the question of exploitation intrudes, and it must be asked directly, not merely rationalized as a process. For, theoretically speaking, there is no reason at all why grossly differentiated distribution and consumption of wealth must exist in a politically organized society. In fact, the contrary assumption is the argument for modern socialism. And China, as noted, is

---

* more precisely, an archeologist

attempting to transform itself from a largely archaic civilization into a communist society—while suppressing the growth of pejorative vocational, class or bureaucratic interests. That was the manifest meaning of the cultural revolution. The term "squalor" is, of course, gratuitous, as is "glories"—the use of each term should be seen relative to the other. By referring to past squalor and future glory, the archaeologist reveals the kind of bitter detachment which leads one to accept man in modern civilization as "expressing himself, finding himself, making himself," thereby justifying the whole course of civilization as inevitable. In the guise of man determining himself, he accepts man as determined— whatever happens in the future must, therefore, be similarly conceived—leading to the conclusion that modern civilization is the most progressive of all civilizations, despite its drawbacks.

But more importantly, these anthropologists evade the problems of conflict and alienation. As I have tried to point out, the peasantry has always felt itself estranged from the center, and impoverishment notwithstanding, has built up a network of defenses against the assault of the state. It is only in modern civilization that the state dynamic compounded by secondary imperialism—is totalitarian, and dissociation from our human possibilities, our species being, increasingly acute. Modern civilization cannot be simply weighed in the abstract balance of promise and denial, of oppression and freedom, of science and superstition —particularly at a time when pure science itself has become a superstition, and where the superstitions of the primitive past are being understood as systems of belief that reflect a multidimensional reality. The question, rather, is one of learning the reasons for our alienation, denying the inevitability of history and understanding that for 40,000 years man survived and formulated his own existence in the absence of the state. Western man cannot afford to mystify his situation as being "progressive," except in the sense implied by Marx. Perhaps the most alienated can, by confronting and acting on their own condition, free themselves. Only then can we speak of progress, which is always, in part, a primitive return; a reformulation of old impulses in new situations and social structures. The task is Herculean; to confine the state as a form of society to the anthropological "museum of antiquities." The following chapters are dedicated to the exploration of that proposition, and its necessity.

2

THE POLITICS
OF FIELD WORK

From the beginning it was a star-crossed field trip. In August of 1959, accompanied by my wife and daughters, I flew down from Rome to Kano, across the Mediterranean and Saharan Seas, from the most permanent and vulgar of European cities to the most typical and enduring of Hausa cities. For centuries the town had been the port of entry for the caravans that converged upon it from the trans-Saharan routes. Kano had been one of the original seven Hausa states, founded, according to the chronicle that bears the city's name, in A.D. 999. Today it is the largest and most important city of the western Sudan, the very essence of Moslem Africa. It is the economic hub of northern Nigeria, a rail and road depot, and the center of an export trade in groundnuts, the most important cash crop of the Northern Region (directly supporting at least five million people) and, along with cocoa and palm products, the mainstay of the country's economy.* Since I had decided to undertake a field study of a pagan people on the Jos Plateau, it seemed appropriate to enter the country through this ancient gate. We floundered down through the savage squalls that are characteristic during the height of the rainy season in northern Nigeria and landed at the International Airport at five o'clock on a bleak morning. The trouble, which seemed minor at the time, began at customs. The immigration officers wished to know my purpose in entering the country. I produced my credentials, gave them a letter of introduction, and was asked my place of proposed

---

* Oil has now become prominent.

residence and the name of the organization with which I would be associated.

It should be realized at once that Nigeria was not a settler's colony. Unlike Kenya and the Rhodesias, Nigeria, along with the other British-occupied territories in West Africa, had adopted a policy of strictly controlling the number and kinds of Europeans permitted to enter the country. The usual explanation for the origin of this policy had been that climate, disease and terrain made the place uncongenial for European settlement. These may be factors, but they do not constitute an explanation, for if they were sufficient then no formal policy would have been necessary. A political issue seems more pertinent.† Settlers eventually will cause trouble for the mother country, which then has to choose between the interests of the native people, who will look to the Metropole as certain Iroquois tribes did to the British, and its own subjects. The latter may antagonize the local people by land grabbing and social prejudice and the related forms of exploitation; or they may develop so vested an interest in the colony that the ties with the Metropole are severed. The history of the New World where England learned this lesson too late is ample evidence. In any case a settler's colony cannot be accommodated to the classic pattern of indirect rule, in the modern British experience, pragmatically initiated in India and pursued by design by Goldie and Lugard in northern Nigeria. Thus the strict control of immigration and the rules of residence and work have the effect of maintaining metropolitan sovereignty (and securing overseas economic opportunities) while apparently reinforcing the well-being of the natives.

The Nigerian officials had become understandably jealous of their prerogatives in this matter, particularly during the period following self-government and preceding independence. When I sought to enter Nigeria, there were no more than 16,000 Europeans resident in a country with a population of 40 million (now controversially counted at 55 million). The great majority were clustered in the cities of the south, particularly in Lagos.

---

† Of course, the nature and extent of economic resources peculiar to a colony, its geopolitical position and the politicomilitary power of its inhabitants are factors determining whether an area developed into a settlers' colony. But other things being equal, a nonsettlers' colony is a happier one for a Metropole.

Controls were stricter in the Northern Region where the political structure was more rigid than in the East or West, since the British had utilized the hierarchical Fulani apparatus, itself superimposed upon the previous Hausa structure, in order to rule the region. Northern Nigeria, constituting three-fourths of the land area of the country and containing more than half the total population, had always been considered a most successful experiment in indirect rule, enabling the British to maintain the colony with a minimum of investment, a maximum of trade, and the least possible political ferment. These efforts had failed in the Eastern Region because of the democratic and decentralized character of Igbo society. Indeed, the women's riots at Aba in 1929 symbolized the inception of the mass movement toward freedom in West Africa: they swept the colonially appointed chiefs out of office and, in that year of Western economic depression, these women traders, incensed by rumors of taxation, wrecked the trading companies that were buying cheap and selling dear, and doing so under the protection of an alien political apparatus. The riots summed up the colonial business, which the Igbo had grasped from the beginning, in a nutshell. In the Western Region, indirect rule had gained leverage with the Yoruba-speaking peoples because of their system of paramount chiefs, but this was complicated by the existence of traditional counselors and other customary checks on the power of the Obas. Moreover, in both the east and west as opposed to the Fulani-Hausa north, a university-trained elite had begun to develop between the world wars. The elite did not fit into the administrative structure. They constituted a force toward new party and parliamentary institutions—the first wave of the colonial revolution but by no means the last. Of course, it was only in the Fulani-conquered areas of the north, the anchor of British sovereignty in West Africa, that indirect rule worked smoothly. In those sections not penetrated in depth by the Fulani, particularly in the pagan areas of the Jos Plateau to which I was headed, indirect rule had foundered because of the difficulty of finding appropriate native authorities. Chiefs, who were often only messengers, were supplied for the uses of the conqueror under the threat of force.

But I was only to understand these political processes later when I became inadvertently involved with them and learned, the way anthropologists are said to learn, by participant observation.

At the time that I was asked my address and purpose at the immigration desk at the International Airport in Kano, I did not realize the full background and import of the question. As it happened I did have a prospective address, but it was imprecise. I had arranged to rent a house several miles from the city of Jos from a tin company that had recently been bought out by a large American corporation. Jos had developed into a bustling city of about 70,000 on the basis of the tin fields which had first attracted the Niger Company, the fine point of British penetration in Nigeria, to the High Plateau. Tin was the leading mineral export of the country, and its high-quality oxide ore was found in an area that had been ethnographically little explored. The pagans of the High Plateau were among the most primitive peoples still functioning in Africa. The conjunction of a remote and inaccessible area, a primitive population, a modern industry and a relatively new urban center made the plateau a particularly inviting place for anthropological inquiry. Moreover, the native peoples of the plateau, indeed of the province generally, were known for their independence and disinterest in the civilization that was growing in their midst, and I found that prospect attractive, also. As it turned out, there was a further problem of which I was unaware. The fierce desire for independence which had kept the Fulani at bay and had later frustrated the classic British design for indirect rule, was now finding political expression, feebly at first, and haltingly, as Nigeria approached independence.

The plateau had become the vanguard of a movement challenging the dominant political party of the Northern Region, the Northern Peoples Congress (NPC). The Congress was the party of the emirs, dominated by Fulani-Hausa elements, and had been encouraged by most British colonial officials. But dissident groups, connected with the major political parties in the Eastern and Western Regions, had begun to crystallize—notably the United Middle Belt Congress (allied with the Western Region's Action Group) and the Northern Element's Progressive Union (allied with the Eastern Region's National Convention of Nigerian Citizens). Much of the activity of these parties was concentrated on the plateau where, of course, the local cultures had no historical connection of any kind with the archaic Fulani-Hausa political apparatus. Indeed the societies of the plateau pagans had been fundamentally uncivilized, that is, they were not politically structured. The UMBC and NEPU had hoped to attract pagan support, not only on the plateau, but throughout the Middle Belt. Indeed, in the new and independent Federation of Nigeria, which was about to be discussed in London, the platform of the UMBC called for a separate Middle Belt state (NEPU, which drew its strength from dissident Hausa elements, was proportionately less positive on this matter). Obviously, the establishment of regional autonomy for the Middle Belt would weaken the north critically; the population would be reduced by one-third and the land area by one-half. Instead of politically, geographically and demographically dominating the Nigeria that was approaching independence, the north would shrink to more historically justifiable boundaries, thus permitting a more dynamic and progressive national government. The Middle Belt issue was critical, and the Jos Plateau was considered by the Northern Region's government as one of the most prominent threats of their continued sovereignty.

I was, then, journeying to an area that was ethnographically important, which I knew, and politically explosive, which I did not know. Yet there was no better vantage point from which to view and assess the local roots and national turmoil of Nigerian politics than the Jos Plateau. There, in the cockpits of the Middle Belt, parties and peoples of the three regions* of Nigeria met, mingled and fought. The predominantly pagan population of the province, numbering more than half a million, created an enclave beyond the immediate reach of northern officialdom, in which riotous political discussions and criticisms had to be tolerated. Southerners, notably Igbo and Yoruba, were at home in the city of Jos, and even the colonial officers were less committed to the monolithic north that was emerging out of indirect rule than were their counterparts in other provinces of the region. Moreover, the typical Hausa peasant, habituated to centuries of oppression and thus, on the surface at least, resigned and fatalistic, was rarely encountered on the plateau or in the province at large. In retrospect, it is clear that by 1959, in the view of the NPC, the plateau was a bone in the throat of the north, and all the more so since the indirect income from the tin mines was the biggest single

---

* Since this writing, a fourth region, the Midwest, has been established in southern central Nigeria, to be succeeded by the present 12-state system.

item in the budget of the Northern Region. Yet, in order to understand this, it was not enough merely to visit the plateau; one had to get a taste of its politics. Fortunately, that is what in small measure happened to me. I was transformed inadvertently from a theoretical bystander to an observant participant.

ENTERING THE FIELD

The business began when the customs officer at the International Airport at Kano, after checking my credentials and keeping a copy of my letter of introduction, filled in my entry permit. Since I had made arrangements to rent the house from the tin company, he simply assumed that I was employed by them, although I had explained my mission in detail and indicated this on the back of the permit. It was a logical error on his part. There were no unconnected residents in Nigeria. A man was either a civil servant or a company employee, that is, if he planned to stay in the country for any length of time. There was hardly any category into which an anthropologist unaffiliated with Nigerian institutions could readily be put; moreover, Europeans or Americans planning to settle in Plateau Province for at least a year more likely than not would be associated with the mining of tin. But I failed to notice on that weary morning that my purpose in coming to Nigeria had been misinterpreted on my entry permit. Some months later this was to be pointed out to me by an Anglo-Irish assistant superintendent of police, a man with a confidential manner and cold eyes.

We stayed in Kano for a few days—just long enough to get the feel of that bright harsh city, casting stark Islamic shadows. I plowed through the filthy markets (Islam has a private, not a civic conscience), appreciated the big clean-lined mosque, and marveled at the gaiety of five blind beggars, walking, arms linked, through the square. But, as elsewhere, I was struck by the children with the fly-encircled eyes, that unremarked symbol of social decay throughout the Sudan and the Middle East. I wandered, also, through the introverted alleys of the old town, where Islam turns a blind eye to the world yet lives so intensely and indecipherably within, each devout or unspeakable in his measure. But even here, in northern Nigeria, one could sense the body of Africa throbbing under the cloak of Islam like a great bird under a hood. I was familiar enough with the Middle East; it was Africa I was after, in order to quicken an academic specialty, and we were not sorry to leave Kano. But first I was able to arrange, by lucky circumstance it seemed then, for a Hausa- and English-speaking Igbo cook, steward, interpreter and general factotum to join us at a later date at Jos.

The trip to the plateau, a distance of perhaps three hundred miles by road, was trivially eventful. We drove southwest of Kano through the zone of most intensive groundnut cultivation that forms an ellipse around the city, onto the broad empty Sudan savanna in the direction of Funtua, a small divisional emirate in Southern Katsina Province. We had to abandon the taxi after all four tires had blown out, but finally managed a lift into Funtua in the glossy American car of a prosperous, inquisitive and unusually talkative Lebanese trader, a groundnut middleman who was returning to Zaria from a business trip to Kano and would soon go home to Beirut rich on small steady profits and parsimonious living. The three focal points of activity in Funtua town were the petrol station, the Emir's palace and the local office of the United Africa Company. The palace was surrounded by retainers of one kind or another who were curious but not helpful. The Emir was inaccessible, asleep, and no one would dare predict the time of his awakening. From time to time the petrol station sprang to life as a produce truck or Mammy wagon, lopsided with passengers, pulled in for service, rest or refreshment from the trays of white-robed, itinerant Hausa peddlers. It took courage of a high order along with faith in God (a message inscribed in a variety of metaphors above several windshields) and the capacity to live dangerously in the moment to drive or trust oneself as a passenger in these vintage vehicles. They seemed to have been picked off the junk heaps of Europe; actually most were assembled in Nigeria from imported frames to meet local needs, and to make as much money as possible. Their wrecked and burnt out carcasses were a familiar sight on the native landscape. But what I remember best about Funtua is the soft-eyed, African woman, who seemed a single being with the swooning child on her hip, watching us pensively from the center of the jabbering crowd that surrounded us as we walked.

After a delay of several hours, I was able to find a truck bound for Zaria that was willing to take me and our baggage; my family had driven on with the Lebanese. We turned southeast into Zaria Province, through typical Guinea savanna country, broken by occasional plots of Guinea corn and millet and empty of human habitation, as all African landscapes appear to the unsubtle, urbanized eye of the stranger. We spent that night in a government rest house on the outskirts of Zaria town (most northern provinces are named after their principal towns); there, while being served a Hausa interpretation of a depressing English meal by a Kanuri waiter with slashed cheeks, we had our first contact with British colonial officials on tour. Each seemed an island unto himself, remote, ostentatiously self-engaged in trivial ways to avoid intercourse with another. They were a pale and miserable company. The administrative adventurers of the nineteenth century—Lugard, MacLean, Burton—had dwindled to clerks charged with foreclosing the empire in its last frontier. Yet despite the social distance between them, they seemed not uncomfortable together.

The following morning we rented a taxi in the old town, less Middle Eastern, more open, frank and African than Kano, and headed southeast, climbing up through park land and wooded hills to the Jos Plateau. Later this brief trip from Kano through Funtua and Zaria to Jos was to be inflated as a survey of the northern provinces, including Borgu division, a Yoruba center, and that is why I mention it here.

The tin mining company from whom I had rented the house was about five miles northwest of the city in a village area called Gwong. The main office and staff dwellings were strung out along a road that disappeared into the hills surrounding the city. The land itself was rented by the company from the local pagans—the Anaguta, I was to discover—for a nominal yearly fee, since no expatriate organization was permitted to own land outright in any of the major regions of Nigeria. The company had moved its mining operations off the plateau and out of the province to Tiv country in the Benue area, and columbite had surpassed tin as its major commodity. The tin fields of the plateau were approaching exhaustion, having been worked out by European companies that displaced vast areas of top soil in the process; and by 1958 the international quota on tin production had driven most prospectors out of the business and drastically cut back the profits of even the largest operators. But the director of the company with whom I had negotiated, a Greek by birth, who had been in the country for 35 years, first as a trader, then as a prospector, and finally as an executive, had sensed the trend in the early years of the war. He had been able to switch to columbite, which is found in association with tin ore, and had become an important producer of that strategic heat-resistant mineral. But although three-fourths of the world's columbite supply was in Plateau Province and adjoining provinces, its industrial future was uncertain; its use quite specialized, extraction difficult and expensive, and it required a high price per ton to keep operations profitable. American stockpiling until 1955 had led to a columbite boom, but the market was now declining rapidly, and the director of the company was pleased to sell his majority holdings to a large American corporation. Like many expatriates, he felt the old colonial Nigeria dissolving under his feet; independence was looming, his friends were leaving, his money had been made, and he was looking for a country that would not tax his bank reserves too drastically. But I had come to study, and to associate with, Africans and had no direct concern with the problems of expatriate businessmen.

The house was well situated. A tiny compound of beehive huts lay about 75 yards from its rear entrance, in a Guinea corn field that stretched to our back yard. This, as it happened, was one of the compounds of the nominal chief of the Anaguta. There was a constant, casual traffic of women naked to the waist, bearing head loads, to and from the hamlets that lay a short distance on all sides of the company dwellings. By late afternoon we could hear the sound of drums echoing against grim and rocky hills, where the pagans lived in compounds that we knew were there but could not see. Moreover, we were less than a quarter of a mile from the strangers' settlement, the Sabon Gari or new town, a kind of suburban slum in which Nigerians from other parts of the country clustered on the edge of northern cities. Sounds of joy floated up from the strangers' settlement and, mingled with the pagan drums, lit up the darkest of nights. This was an excellent field headquarters.

None of the tin company personnel knew the names of the pagan villages in the surrounding hills, nor had they ever visited them; they were vague about the tribal name. Without exception they were afraid of Africans like these pagans, whom they could not dominate, and contemptuous of Africans they could dominate. The colonial officers in Jos, who were turning over at an alarming rate as independence approached, were equally uncertain about the Anaguta, and this increased my curiosity. The Anaguta had never been studied, although there was an occasional reference in the literature; they were, it seemed, a most elusive people, yet they were the aboriginal owners of the territory on which the city of Jos and its environs were located. Here was a sort of suburban primitive culture, buried in its rocky habitat, difficult of access, yet only a few miles as the crow flies from the most Europeanized city in northern Nigeria. I had not decided on a people with which to work before leaving the States—the Jarawa and the Birom were likely prospects, but both were somewhat better known than the Anaguta and, it was said, easier to reach. I decided to take things as they came, and set out in pursuit of the Anaguta.

A few weeks after settling down at Gwong, the Igbo factotum whom I had hired in Kano* joined us with his pregnant wife. Pius was an intelligent, adaptable, quick-witted young man, a baker by trade, with a varied and sobering experience of colonial housewives. He came from a hamlet in Owerri Province in eastern Nigeria, the most populated area in West Africa, almost as dense as the Nile delta. Like many of his countrymen, he found it necessary to leave home at an early age because there were too many children, too many legitimate claims, and not enough good land left in his family. Being an Igbo, he was also of a litigious turn of mind; and, of course, he was eager to learn and explore. Pius knew the north, having lived in Kano for many years, and had a mild contempt for the genuflections of the Hausawa before their social superiors. No Igbo, he would say, ever bows to any other; "We are all equals, we are all brothers." He was even capable of patronizing the political leader Zik. "Zik tries," he would repeat, with sly disapproval, "Zik tries." But of course, as with every other unsophisticated Igbo I have ever met, Zik was the apple of

---

* After we left Nigeria, I heard that Pius had returned to Kano—and there he probably died, in the massacre of 1966.

his eye, the symbol of his pride.* I had hired Pius, or rather, he had hired me, for his excellent English and Hausa, and because, being an Igbo, he would serve as a knowledgeable guide on a trip that I planned to the Eastern Region. I had hired him also to avoid any possible complication that might arise from employing a local man in my household.

But Pius created local associations. His full name, Pius Owerri, whether conferred or adopted I did not know, was a conjunction of statuses that placed him at once. He was, first of all, a utilitarian Catholic and a conventionally religious man. On our trip to southeastern Nigeria we were to discover a relatively relaxed and apolitical Catholicism that melted self-protectively into the cultural and physical landscape. Framework churches, open to the sky, flourished in Pius's native province, thrusting themselves up through the bush every few miles, looking like so many unfinished Gothic sketches. Owerri, Pius's patronymic, announced his birthplace to any Igbo anywhere in Nigeria, and put him in immediate touch with his countrymen. In no time at all, Pius, a stranger on the plateau, had established contact with an obscure Catholic mission where his wife was to be delivered some months later. And he had joined the Owerri branch of the Igbo Progressive Union in Jos, a combined fraternal, insurance, uplift, recreational, and marching and chowder society, undeniably but elusively political, that exists wherever Igbos congregate. Other West African peoples may be as itinerant, out of choice or necessity, as the Igbos, but none has developed to such a remarkable degree this method of maintaining social ties, cultural activities and political solidarity. Igbo particularism was strong, yet it did not contradict their nationalism, for Igbos claimed that the creation of a united Nigeria was precisely their *special* mission. This conviction did not endear them to colonial or Hausa-Fulani authorities, nor did the old colonial residents ever forget that it was the Igbo who first exposed the inadequacy of indirect rule. Moreover, Igbos made stiff-necked servants: their inclination to talk man-to-man was considered presumptuous. And their mutual aid groups, set up in foreign provinces by a people who were notorious for their

---

* Azekiwe's political mistakes after independence in 1960 and his defection to Nigeria from Biafra during the Civil War have finally discredited him among Igbos.

political irritability, although legitimate and within the law, helped fix the image of the Igbo as a natural subversive.

Pius was politically aware, but he was not, at this time in his life, politically engaged. He had his hands full trying to keep house, placate a homesick, scolding wife and keep his intricate finances in order. He had spun out his connections in and around Jos as innocently as a bird builds a nest, and he joined the Union as a matter of course. While Pius went about his business, I began to make preliminary contact with the Anaguta, whom I had first mistaken for Jarawa, climbing through the hills in the company of a Jarawa farmer in Hausa dress who had visited us one day out of curiosity. It was necessary to hike ten to twelve miles daily in order to visit several of the widely dispersed compounds, jot down a few words and make my presence known to astonished and amused natives. The adults, of course, had seen white men before in the Jos area but, with few exceptions, from a distance. No white man had ever visited these compounds. Many of the younger children, who had not yet strayed beyond their hamlets, fled, unbelieving, at my approach; many a babe in arms screamed in outrage. European contacts hardly existed, yet the European presence hung over these hills.

It probably was easier for me to get used to them. I quickly came to appreciate the mature, deeply experienced, deeply incised faces of the older people. These were the most expressive, most fully human faces I have ever seen. They made me feel pity and shame for the cosmetic, contrived, acquisitive, vain, uniform, despairing and empty faces that are familiar even among the elderly in the cities of the West. Every conceivable emotion was etched into the faces of the Anaguta as deeply and as harmoniously as the herringbone scarifications that ran symmetrically down each side, from temple to chin. No single emotion or idea dominated; there were no caricatures, no masks.

I had worked briefly among mountain Arabs in Israel, and they had impressed me immensely by their independence and dignity. But for centuries they had fluctuated between being peasants and predators; they understood the market, the elementary tricks of statecraft, and had an instinct for the city. Most of my field training had been among Europeans, or European-derived peoples in Israel, and although my theoretical and monographic reading had led me to think otherwise, I had about reached the conclusion shared by most contemporary, academic anthropologists—primitive peoples are really just like us. Or, if characterological differences can be noted, they are variations on a common human theme, molded within cultural, but not cultural-*historical*, dimensions. I no longer believe this. There are profound qualitative distinctions between primitive and civilized peoples, glossed over by anthropologists anxious to remove the stigma of inferiority from the term *primitive* and still embarrassed by Voltaire's impertinent attack on Rousseau. Whatever their cultural styles, civilized peoples resemble each other much more closely than they do primitives, and of course the converse is true. The human constitution is everywhere the same, and both the subtlest and most profound human needs are universal, but they are more completely realized, if in inimitable ways, by primitives than among ourselves. That is, primitive peoples understand the preconditions of a human existence. That is what struck me when I first looked into the faces of the Anaguta.

The only face that seemed ordinary—in that gallery I remember so distinctly—belonged to one of my interpreters. He was a young man, the first and only Anaguta to have attended secondary school, the only Anaguta who spoke any English and one of the dozen or so nominal Christians among them. His features were mobile but blank. They moved from feigned innocence to a frank low cunning and back again. He was the only Anaguta I encountered who was capable of social cringing. He was hell-bent on improving his wordly status, which meant becoming a nominal Nigerian, a consumer of European goods and an employee of the Zaria Tobacco Company. But he believed in nothing except appearances, and he was unskilled at them, for he was an absolutely new bourgeoisie. Yet Audu was a poignant figure, groping his way into the outer world, away from a people that scorned it, condemned by their indifference to be a weak, slippery, unhonored, faithless pioneer. He was the only African I have ever met who smiled thinly and seemed incapable of laughter.

Just as their faces were tempered and refined by a direct and disciplined experience of life, so were the Anaguta bodies. The women usually went naked on their home grounds except for a pubic covering of leaves, although they had adopted a kind of sarong for trips to more modest and licentious places. The native working garments of the men were breech clouts or loin cloths;

they wore blankets or cotton togas on more formal occasions. Most of the time, most of the Anaguta exposed most of their bodies. Wherever the Christian and Islamic establishments have penetrated or the body-mind schism has developed, the body has been conceived as an instrument of sin, so Europeans and Hausa alike regarded the Anaguta as *naked* pagans, that is, natural sinners. Their uncovered bodies were not pretty, either cosmetically or in the sense of having achieved the Greco-Roman ideal of physical perfection. But they were tough, graceful and used. There were no gross, distorted or repellent bodies among them; each displayed a natural proportion of working parts and no withered functions. After a while I found these active, unself-conscious bodies beautiful, precisely because they were used and, among the old, weathered by use; even the breasts of the women, lank and leathery from suckling children year after year, dropped in a natural contour from straight backs and appropriate shoulders. These features seemed, of course, ugly—hideous is the word I often heard—to fastidiously concupiscent Europeans and Moslems. Living among the Anaguta was a lesson in anatomy. I learned the proper shape of calf and thigh, trunk and buttock, neck and shoulder, even when somewhat diminished by hunger. And I discovered how epicurean and dissociated was our urban image of the body, how *fetishistic*, in the technical psychoanalytic sense, how shamefully aware are we of what we hide, in contrast to the Anaguta, who scarified and circumcised for symbolic reasons, to mark an event, to inscribe identity, to test courage, but neither feared nor worshiped the body in itself. What the Anaguta thought of European faces and figures, I do not know. But I do remember the words of a Jarawa prostitute, drunk in a palm-wine market, who confronted a European, "There is *one Baturi* with a good face." *One* white man. It stuck in my mind.

Pius, of course, was no more primitive than I, although we were civilized in different ways. As an Igbo, a Nigerian, a successfully acculturated man and a blooming citizen of the world, he was puzzled by the Anaguta and suspicious of them. His people had been exposed for 400 years and more to the soldier, the trader, the slaver and the missionary—generally to the underside of civilization—and had developed remarkable means of coping with it and assimilating what they had learned to their own ends. Igbo solidarity, equalitarianism, love of the land and highly developed social reflexes have primitive roots, but the transformations in Igbo society had long since shifted their forms and functions. All that these Africans fully had in common was the color of their skins. They still shared rhythm and laughter and a certain ease of movement. I suppose that the psychological precondition of these traits, though not the cultural cause, is a generous and disciplined gratification of the senses in infancy. The more civilized the person the less pronounced these traits. Pius could be melodramatically superstitious, as he proved to us one night when we were collecting secret society masks in Ibibio country near Calabar just before a mass burning by missionaries, but his random and shallow superstitions were a civilized rather than a primitive phenomenon. He had a few strategic, self-protective beliefs, but no longer any faith. The Anaguta made Pius uneasy. He considered himself their superior and could never comprehend why I spent so much time in their company. As for the Anaguta, they were totally indifferent to Pius.

THE FIRST WEEKS: SETTING UP THE HOUSEHOLD

After the first few weeks at Gwong, our compound took on an even greater assortment of incommunicants, although from the outside it might have seemed that a conspiracy was being hatched. Our arrival created a flurry of interest, which we did not encourage, among the tin company staff occupying the half-dozen houses in the vicinity of the office. I asked a few tactical questions of the director, the Chief Inspector of mines in Jos, and several assorted colonial officers, who either knew little of the Anaguta and cared less or had confused them with some other people. There was to be one exception to this uniform unconcern, but I did not discover it until much later. I listened while these officers and company men, to my surprise, bewailed the character of British rule in northern Nigeria. I even nodded sympathetically when one important administrator remarked, rather too simply: "We have supported the Emirs right down the line, and when the people rise against them, as they certainly shall—if we have not by that day cleared out of the country, they will murder us in our beds."* But I did not solicit his remarks and did not improve upon them. The fear of being murdered in bed seemed endemic among the old Jos colonials, whose ranks, I should add, were being armored by colonial dinosaurs from the most remote outposts of a shrinking empire, seeking one last assignment in northern Nigeria before returning home to the new reality.

We made no courtesy calls, failed to sign the Resident's book, invited no Europeans to our house save a Canadian doctor, a domesticated adventurer who became my enduring friend. We neither socialized nor joined any of the several clubs at which the higher-class English residents of Jos tried to amuse themselves. The fact is that I was not concerned with colonial Nigeria, but with what remained of aboriginal Nigeria, and I could not take seriously the claims or prerogatives of the White Man's Nigeria nor the rigamarole of colonial society. I was to understand later that the only real vulnerability of the British colonial aristocracy is in not being taken seriously. They can survive anything but being ignored. Look past them, fail to be impressed, imply even unwittingly that their day is done, and these finely trained, routinely brave men are defeated.

As a leave center for Europeans throughout Nigeria and headquarters of the tin and columbite business, Jos had a relatively large "permanent" European population; and it had developed the character of a tiny settler's colony. The Europeans exchanged their imported amenities within the small area of the city and its immediate environs, holding themselves aloof from the pagans who occupied the further suburbs to the edge of the high plateau and beyond. Even when Europeans and pagans inhabited a common physical space, they moved in different dimensions, without seeing each other. This helped fold the European aggregate back on itself, creating a hierarchy of trivial statuses and an electric circuit of tension and rumor. Unlike Lagos, Kano, Onitsha, Ibadan or Kaduna, Jos had no great chiefs, no high African politicos, no educated African elite with whom the European could communicate without betraying his sensibilities. One must remember also that every colonial is basically a material or spiritual profiteer. He comes to extract, earn, administer, win to a cause or faith, and he brings his superior manner and technique

---

* Of course, in the end it was the Igbo who were murdered in their beds.

with him; he could not be a colonial, I thought, if he came to learn or to look for a lost humanity. That would make him disloyal to his government, his company or his church or, if he were a social scientist of a certain type, to his profession.

It was into this concentrated settler's enclave that we entered, quite unwittingly, and in which we did not participate. Then Pius—Igbo, impudent and independent—joined us, apparently a servant but behaving like a friend. His native background automatically elicited my anthropologist's respect, and I was ashamed that he was my servant. After Pius came Taru—Anaguta, a son of the British-recognized secular chief of the tribe. It took me several weeks to arrange an interview with the chief, who, I finally discovered, lived in the compound just behind our house. And it took several months before I found out that he was not the real authority among the Anaguta, insofar as they could be said to have one. But Abamu was friendly and, after first passing himself off as a Jarawa, he agreed to send me his oldest son as an assistant. Taru turned out to be a cheerful outcast, an authentic deviant. He was in his late thirties, unmarried, with no compound of his own, and it was said that no woman would stay with him, although they found him attractive. The trouble with Taru was that he was an intellectual who had become inordinately curious about Europeans and other non-Anaguta and had decided to spend his life observing, although he never showed any desire to join them. His mother was a Birom woman, purchased in marriage by his father and still the old man's chief wife, dominating his second compound up in the hills. This divided parentage may have stimulated Taru's curiosity while making him a willing outcast. For Birom women were formally deprecated by Anaguta, who had not traditionally practiced the bride price among themselves and, rather ethnocentrically, interpreted it as an insult to the woman's family.

Taru was a natural student of man; he learned by osmosis, and his relaxed and joking manner belied the strength of his insights. He wore a garment so tattered and nondescript that I cannot recall its color or shape, and he frankly disliked working with his hands. He spoke the languages of the Birom, the Jarawa, the Nyango-Irigwe, the Jere, the Buji and the Rukuba. Unlike other Anaguta who spoke a slow pidgin version of Hausa, he was beautifully fluent in that lingua franca of the Northern Region. He knew

Fulfulde, the original language of the Fulani, still spoken by the pastoralists but largely replaced by Hausa among the Fulani of the town. Taru was an indescribably gentle man, with yellow eyes and a ferociously charming yellow smile that could unsettle Pius and make those who did not know him back away; he looked like a black lion. He was my constant guide and companion, escorting me everywhere through Anaguta territory, everyone's friend without trying, a man of natural and impersonal courtesy, but he was not much use as an informant on the routine customs of his people. He was interested only in the unusual—in leading me to old burial urns, sacrilegious to touch, in exploring caves in which the Anaguta may once have lived or at least sought shelter, in guiding me through the sacred groves, in pointing out stone axes that his people may have made and certainly used for cutting sacred wood. He did all this with the utmost detachment and good humor; there was no delinquency in his makeup, no spite. He knew that his culture and perhaps his people were dying out; he understood my interest, but he did not seem to share my concern. This lack of concern was, at first, difficult for me to accept. But finally I came to understand that Taru and the Anaguta generally regard the future in a way hard for us to imagine. For them, the future is not a cumulative, progressive and novel experience through which tomorrow is conceived to be better or at least "different" from today. It is, rather, an endless repetition of an established human pattern within which individual variety flourishes without disturbing the whole; the execution of ritual and the observance of custom fix the master pattern and make life viable. Past, present and future are conceived of as cyclic phenomena, and the pursuit of the cycle, even when leading objectively to the Anaguta's decline, remains subjectively sustaining. The Anaguta were bent upon preserving their historical existence, not denying it, by withdrawing from civilized contact. The ritual bracketing of birth and death, man and nature, the present, the past and the future, good and evil, the thing and the person, remolds the finality of any experience with which they are objectively faced. Thus the Anaguta are able to confront situations which would panic a Western group, made brittle by the certainty of its secular commitments.

As it is, the Anaguta seem to have made a series of critical choices, adding up to a single conscious decision not to try to adapt to the new world growing up around them. With insignificant exception, they refuse to migrate from their dwindling lands; do not convert to Christianity or Islam, do not encourage their children to go to school; do not send vanguard groups to settle in the town and search out new possibilities of livelihood. They are disinterested in agricultural resettlement schemes; do not work for Europeans; and like most Plateau pagans, they shun the tin mines. They are not even interested in Nigeria; some do not understand what the term denotes, most cannot conceptualize it. The majority have been no further than ten or twelve miles from their native hamlets; they have heard of Kuru, but not of Ibadan. Planes fly over their hills, dotted with tiny beehive huts; once they were frightened, now they are unconcerned. Electricity, the cinema, trucks, automobiles, the artifacts of white civilization, do not arouse their curiosity. They retreat and retreat, physically and culturally, pursuing the fragments of ancient usages. Yet no nativistic idea or messianic tremor compensates for their flight. But we must understand this response from the perspective of the Anaguta. They believe their native territory is at the center of the world, where space and time intersect, and that, for them, is equivalent to living as close as possible to the Gods.

The Anaguta are faintly inquisitive but not fascinated by white men, whom they formally regard as spirits, *andoogubishee*, in one aspect ancestral, in another local, the inhabitants of their sacred groves, to be used, placated and prayed to by their priest chiefs. Having categorized white men, they have named the nameless, and somehow having conquered that problem, can relate to them. But this does not exhaust their perceptions of white men—it merely conceptualizes them in a useful way. White men are, in a certain sense, *andoogubishee*, but *andoogubishee* are not merely white men. This kind of logic is not at all Western. The assumption is not classically syllogistic: the individual Anaguta is not saying that some, but not all, *andoogubishee* would, therefore, be white men. Rather, he is claiming that white men are a form which *andoogubishee* may take, without fully projecting the essence of either white men or *andoogubishee*.

The Anaguta accept things as they are, immerse themselves in surfaces, grasp them with all the senses, and are not embarrassed by changes of shape, form or emphasis. They even have a tale that places white men in natural history. Whites, they say, came from the bottom of lakes and rivers, where they were like fish. Then they climbed onto the land, and from the land up into the trees; only recently have they descended, just having lost their tails, which is why they look so much like monkeys. They do not dislike these occult monkeys, but they need not be awed by them—they have found a place for them in Anaguta lore, perhaps by adapting a Hausa folk version of a well-known European theory. As they can be pragmatic about the supernatural, so they accept the presence of whites; or rather, to the Anaguta, everything that exists is natural and there is no need to be alarmed. It is even possible for them unconcernedly to accept the white man as a fully human being, despite the partial classification as an *undoogubishee*, or as a recently evolved animal.

Taru neither respected, feared nor hated white men, although he considered them less enduring than Africans. "You are not the first *Baturi* we have seen," he would remind me from time to time (meaning, in other words, "we will outlive you yet"). I noticed that he was always very careful not to be exploited by me, even in the name of friendship, and made a quiet fuss about receiving the modest wage for which he had asked exactly at the appointed time, or else he would not stir from our compound.

Taru was indefatigable. He could sleep under any conditions, anywhere, any time. He bathed like a cat, had a body like a whip, and thought nothing of walking 20 miles to a millet-beer market, or scrambling for hours through rugged country with an awkward and heavy load on his shoulders. Sometimes at night we would sit on the ground while he played plaintively on a small reed harp, singing of some obscure event in his peoples' past, in complicated and beautiful harmonies that exhausted the meaning of intimacy.

This internal exile had no close friends among his own people and seemed merely tolerant of his relatives. But he did argue, rather wistfully it seemed, for my support of a younger half-brother who was trying to enter elementary school against the wishes of his father, the Chief. If Taru had gracefully detached himself from his own people, they reciprocated by not taking him seriously, although they neither humiliated nor rejected him. With great amusement he used to call me *Pozo*, ("Elder") because I had grown a beard and therefore presumed above my status, for only elders wore beards among the Anaguta; he did not believe that any white man could really be an elder.

Taru was uninterested in Anaguta women. But he had a quick eye for the erectly tall, beautiful, spectacularly gowned and turbaned Fulani women who walked the trails to Jos with calabashes of sour milk on their heads. He could talk to them in their native tongue, and proud and reserved as they were, they always had time for Taru. After he moved in with us, these birds of paradise made our back yard a regular stop on their way to town. There they sat, applied exotic pigments to their faces and looked for Taru in his quarters.

Obviously it was seductive to find in Taru an idealized image of myself as an anthropologist threading my way between two cultures. I tried not to see that I, thinking of myself as an outcast, was *invulnerable* and, therefore no matter what my intentions, uncommitted. For how can commitment have any meaning when there is no real moral or spiritual risk? I still held to the illusion of the "innocent" anthropologist. Although intellectually, of course, I knew better. I was just fully beginning to realize that anthropology had become a privileged way of maintaining distance in the name of science, not only from the people one "studied," but from one's own cultural predicament, from oneself. This had not been tested by my experience in an Israeli kibbutz, where my identity as a Jew, my total participation in the community and the need to define my antagonism to Zionism and relation to Israel broke through the abstraction of my role as an anthropologist.

Our next permanent guest was Audu, my Anaguta interpreter, who was finishing his penultimate term in a secondary school about 30 miles from Jos. Then came Umaru (Audu's older brother) and wife; they, along with Sako, the eldest brother, who merely visited, became my chief informants on the day-to-day life of the Anaguta. Audu's family was unusual. They had been recommended to me by Taru's father and the Rukuba teacher at the local native administration elementary school in Gwong. They were the only upwardly mobile family among the Anaguta. Audu had become their trembling vanguard. Both parents were long deceased, and Sako had assumed the father's place and was responsible for the family's upward and outward thrust. Atypically Anaguta, from childhood Sako had been awed by and drawn to the white man's technology. Many years before he had walked 30 miles to a mining station out of curiosity and there had heard a radio, but he was ridiculed as a liar when he tried to describe it at home. When the Europeans began to come in greater numbers (in the 1930s) and Jos took shape as a city, with roads on which four-wheeled animals appeared, he realized that the Anaguta would have to adapt themselves to the new ways if they were to survive. Despite his dissenting view of their situation, Sako never lost caste among his own people, probably because they sensed that his interest was not self-serving. He was highly respected and was said to have the capacity to become invisible in moments of crisis. This blessing was bestowed; it could not be learned or even summoned up at will by the few who were endowed with it. Sako never boasted of this gift or even claimed to possess it; he left that to other people. When he was still a young man, he had been seen pulling a leopard off a child; as he grabbed its tail, Sako is said to have disappeared, and the animal fled. There were a few false claimants to the gift of invisibility, the most respected of occult powers among the Anaguta; but people paid no attention to them. A man who sat by a trail trying to foster the illusion that he was invisible would be seen and heard, and humored by being ignored. *The power to become invisible*—what greater gift could a people fleeing before civilization desire?

It is possible to climb to the peak of a hill in the heart of Anaguta territory and look down on the white roofs of Jos, a few miles to the south; if it is late afternoon in the rainy season and a mist diffuses the air, the city, insubstantial, shimmers in and out of view. Or on blazing afternoons, from the sudden perspective of a mountain trail, the bulk of the city of Jos contracts, and it appears as just another bright patch on an endless, ancient landscape. The Anaguta play with these perspectives; from the heights they command they know every visage of the city in each season and hour. But the city is not an optical illusion, however illusory may be the purposes that established it or the ends it pursues.

How ironic it was that Sako, one of the few possessors of the gift of invisibility, should have been aware of the need to come to terms with the superior power that was encircling his people. His people had clubbed him and left him for dead when he enrolled Audu as the first and for years the only Anaguta student at the district elementary school; but he neither struck back nor changed his course. There were other incidents over the years, but Sako survived them with self-respect. After he had become a regular visitor to our house, he was charged by a younger man of his lineage with betraying tribal secrets and was publicly slapped. I was being given rituals, part of the living body of the people, it was said, and it was true as everyone knew, for I had explained my mission to all who would listen. Even the subtler aspects of the charge were true, for what sacred thing was I giving the Anaguta in return for what they were giving me? What could I give them? But the man who slapped Sako—and there was no greater insult—was considered a malcontent, jealous of his position and secretly interested in getting closer to the Europeans. So Sako was praised for ignoring the insult conceived in hypocrisy. On another occasion, Sako invited me to a most solemn ceremony—the symbolic reenactment of the Anaguta's victory over the Fulani, which helped keep the Islamic horsemen off the plateau. We were both under attack that afternoon—he verbally by members of the family that had accused him of disloyalty, and I by a frantic warrior who made several passes at my head with an ax. The majority of people present stood by observing us but not looking at us. When we held our ground, the tension broke; I at least was never to be troubled again. Sako, the conciliator, continued to be considered the honorable enemy of his peoples' intentions. Unlike Taru, who was a voluntary outcast and regarded as a harmless deviant, Sako was quite conservative, even exemplary, as a husband, a father, a worker and a believer. Thus his unique desire to accommodate the Anaguta to the outer society was conceived as profoundly threatening.

Sako was not successful. His efforts had been narrowed to the scope of his own family. Audu might escape his Anaguta identity, but he was not influencing his tribesmen. And Umaru, the middle brother who came to live with us, was also preparing to abandon his people, as they were bent on abandoning the world. Both Umaru and Audu were in a pitiful, not a tragic situation, because they were unaware of what was happening to them and were incapable of choice. They had learned from a strong brother that change was the only salvation. But they had no support from their own people and were faced with indifference on the outside. Inevitably, with little moral or material capital, finding themselves and their people inadequate, ignorant of the society into which they were emerging, lacking modern, specialized skills with little chance of developing any and pitifully ashamed of themselves, they could only hope to survive by bluff, self-deception and other modes of cheating. Audu had not worked on the land for years; as he had been his brother's pioneer in elementary school, he was the only Anaguta to have attended secondary school. With luck, this deracinated yet uncultivated man might become a clerk or a minor civil servant in a country full of peasants. The British are ambiguously grateful for the contribution of these West African clerks to whom they gave the busy work of empire; these underpaid, undereducated, bewildered boys earned the conqueror's contempt as they bent awkwardly to his needs. And those more glorified clerks—the barristers—earnest, literate, precisely educated men, who were scrupulously intentioned yet, with few exceptions, served as domestic agents of foreign administration and partners in the enterprise, helped seal the metropolitan intentions. But technical education or the cultivation of knowledge about Africa, its history, geography, cultural variety and unity were neglected. It did not fit the half-unwitting strategy of colonialism.

What happened to Umaru I, an unwilling agent of change, saw myself. Umaru had learned a distaste for manual labor from Audu, who had in turn absorbed it from the colonial environment of his school. By the time he moved into my compound he, a Christian like Audu, already considered himself superior to his tribe. He was bursting with abstract piety, but he spent all of his money on European clothing, utterly ignoring his wife, who roamed our back yard naked and finally left him to return to her brother's compound with their two small sons, thus, after the custom of sister exchange in marriage pursued by the Anaguta, jolting Umaru's sister out of *her* marriage, since such arrangements are reciprocal. The fate of one marriage determines the other, the initial agreement having been entered into by two unrelated male friends. This did not disturb Umaru too much, because he was wooing a young Anaguta woman who had married a Birom, had lived briefly in Kaduna and was the only Anaguta who had up to that point left the Jos area and then returned home in disillusionment. She had a sophisticated Hausa air, wore pretty robes and appeared to her former peers as an empty-headed, preoccupied snob. Umaru's behavior, which had been satisfactory as an informant, became impossible as an Anaguta. His money wages made him feel superior to his wife, who ordinarily would have earned the few shillings a year needed to pay his head tax by selling firewood or a few garden vegetables. Living in my compound reversed this process; now his wife was immobilized and he had the negotiable coin. This also enabled him to neglect his land. He was unable to hire outsiders, and no Anaguta cultivated for wages. Nor, to my surprise, would his relatives or friends maintain his compound in his willful absence. If he had been ill they would have been glad to help, or if he had needed extra hands they would have organized a work group; but this was sheer neglect, and even if he intended to return one day they felt no obligation to encourage what they considered delinquency. The choice had to be Umaru's, not mine or his family's. The breach was made formal when Sako, on a routine visit to our compound, brought Umaru's hoe with him and handed it over wordlessly. Personal relations remained friendly enough between Umaru and his lineage, but he was now on his own.

On the other hand, Umaru never shared a shilling with his friends or relatives. At first this struck me as pure greed. But I came to realize that the logic was as impeccably traditional as that of his kinsmen when they returned the hoe. Only the context was misapprehended. Umaru was now a wage worker; he was earning his keep by his own efforts, he was not living on traditional land. No fellow tribesman was contributing in any way toward Umaru's livelihood; thus none had the right to a share in his wages. The unspoken principle of Anaguta economics—to the laborer shall go the fruit—was now being applied in a quite different milieu. Umaru accepted this but he did so naively. He was no longer functioning in a cooperative society; he had no guarantee of productive work, and he had no sense of the intricacy of the new economy that would not, in fact, reward him in direct proportion to his efforts. That is, Umaru had no conception of a market economy, certainly not of the capitalist system or of his terribly insignificant bargaining power. The Anaguta had never developed internal markets, had no system of currency, and were subsistence cultivators. Umaru had not even the chance to acquire the elementary shrewdness of the peasant in selling to the city. Indeed Anaguta, who habitually counted by the duodecimal system, often paid twelve shillings for the Hausa ten. Umaru was incapable of a depersonalized business exchange; that was not the way goods and services circulated among his people. Even though he gloried in being a paid employee, he regarded himself as a protector, a father, a brother, a kinsman. Umaru imagined that he had exchanged a little compound for a big one that required less work, afforded more prestige and had many more amenities. I tried to play the part of compound head, although I liked Umaru less than the unsentimental Taru. But objectively, Umaru had moved from one world to another. My compound was the flimsiest of shelters, and I knew that his grand and simple expectations like those of innumerable others resembling him, would be shattered. I could not explain this to Umaru. He had no place to which to return, and who was I to tell him that he had little chance of succeeding in the way he had anticipated. So I watched him as he luxuriated in his new European vest and trousers or in his white Hausa cap and gown—jaunty, confident, apparently free as a feather is free but actually at the mercy of every current of air, and rootless—neither Anaguta nor Nigerian, nor pagan, nor Christian, a man losing his identity in the pursuit of an illusion. Later, when I could no longer stand what I had come to understand, I tried to discuss these matters with his people, but they had already thought beyond me.

Lucas completed our household. He was a debonair young man, a recent secondary school graduate and an acquaintance of Audu's, who spoke superior English and Hausa. Lucas was an Ankwe, from the Shendam division, the southernmost sector of Plateau Province. Like many converted plateau pagans, who had an antipathy to Islam because of Fulani attempts at conquest and who were influenced by the relatively large number of missions in the province, Lucas was a Christian. He was also an eagle scout, and the conventional excellence of his character had won him a guided tour to England. But there was more to Lucas than that. He had a penetrating, detached intelligence, which emancipated him from interpreting human behavior in racial terms. Yet I had seen him shudder with the repressed mortification that a naturally superior man of low social status is likely to experience when ever so subtly slighted by his merely social, merely European superiors. Lucas had shrewdly sized up the structure of the new Nigerian society, at least in the North, and had calculated his chances. But he was torn between his desire to become a doctor and swifter roads to success. Unlike Audu, he came from people who were rapidly responding to European and Hausa stimuli and from a family that had been acculturated in depth; his father had been an Episcopalian minister. Lucas's aspirations were understood and supported at home; indeed, he seemed the prototype of the young man anywhere who has left home in order to make good in the big city, except that the colonial experience had made him more adaptable and experienced than his Western counterparts. Moreover, he felt that the fate of his kinsmen depended on his success; he was obliged to reciprocate their support, and this made him rather more socially ruthless and fraternally responsible, more nepotic, than he otherwise might have been. At the time Lucas joined us as my chief interpreter and research assistant, he had not yet decided about continuing his education and was looking for an interim job other than clerking, which bored him. He was also curious about America and had toyed with the idea of applying to an American university for a scholarship, so we met each other's needs. I was glad to have him. After we left Nigeria, he wrote me wistfully about the "charming Anaguta" but he turned down the offer of an American scholarship and decided not to become a doctor. He accepted an appointment at an Officers' Training School in England, no work for a young man of his timber and especially absurd in Nigeria, but a quicker, perhaps explosive route to the top.*

This then, was our more or less permanent African household—Pius, steward and cook, and his wife; Taru, Chinese hobo of a primitive, guide and companion; Umaru, informant, and his wife; Audu, informant and Anaguta interpreter; and Lucas. Two Igbo, four Anaguta, one Ankwe. Five Christians, three of plateau pagan background, and two pagans. Three literates, two semiliterates, two illiterates. No Moslems, no Hausawa, which, it turned out, was contrary to colonial habit.

GETTING MORE DEEPLY INVOLVED

Strangely enough, this nuclear group never jelled socially. Each

* I have since learned that just before the Civil War he finally achieved his ambition, as a commanding officer in the Nigerian Federal Army.

went about his business quite independently of the other except, of course, when the necessity of working with me threw them together. Otherwise, they came and went at random, giving the compound the appearance of a place in which something unusual was going on as, indeed, I hoped it was. This atypicality was heightened by the fact that Africans entered through the front door, and I spent a good deal of time in the yard, which, after the custom of the country, separated the main dwelling in which we lived from the quarters of the Africans. The living room was a working office; those African associates with whom I was not engaged drifted in and out as they pleased. When I was not tracking down a compound in the hills, usually accompanied by Taru and often by my wife with her cameras, I could be seen sitting in my front office with Lucas, Sako, Umaru or Audu, and later there were others, inquiring into Anaguta society along an English-Iguta, English-Hausa or English-Hausa-Iguta circuit. At the same time I was bending to the task of learning Iguta, a hitherto unwritten language, by writing down texts, collecting vocabularies and showing off the little I knew on every possible occasion, which was the best way to learn a little more. Since I had come to the plateau to study a pagan people in the vicinity of Jos, I had counted myself lucky in landing a house on the territory of a practically unknown group and had gone right to work on the principle that one can do field work anywhere. It did not strike me that expatriates and official Africans alike would be willing to suspect the bearded man who went everywhere with a miniature tape recorder, whose wife was always taking pictures, who was moreover constantly in the company of natives and capable, or so it seemed, of speaking to the pagans in their own language. Yes, I was said to be an anthropologist, they thought; but was I or, if so, was that all I was. I had not reckoned with the settlers' colony character of the expatriate community, which could amplify a stranger's footfall to the sound of a marching army. Nor had I realized the critical political importance of the pagan areas of the Middle Belt to the dominant parties of the (then) three regions of Nigeria, but especially to the NPC, as frustrated in winning the allegiance of the plateau people as the Fulani had been in their efforts to conquer them and the British, indirectly, to rule them.

I had considered the possiblity of moving into an Anaguta compound and settling my family in Jos; should the Anaguta have accepted me on such short acquaintance, the idea would have been impractical even for a Mary Slessor. The euphorbia-enclosed compound was a maze of tiny interconnected huts through which a family's social and sexual life pulsed. In a year's time, I could not learn to live and work as an Anaguta and anything short of that would have been a waste of my energy and an outrage on their privacy.

More pertinently, as I learned among the Arabs, the Anaguta would have seen through any effort of mine to pretend to Anaguta identity. I had to be what I was in order to maintain their interest and respect and cultivate a reciprocal understanding. To understand them, I was compelled to understand myself. And one participated in their lives when one was invited; one had no clinical, no objective right to participate. Nor was my field experience in an Israeli border kibbutz comparable. There I had lived for 19 months in a one-room wooden hut, on the edge of the settlement, without water or other amenities; the children had been committed to the children's house, my wife and I had worked in the various branches of the *meshek* or economy, and I had been accepted as a *de facto* member of the society. But the relationship had been reciprocal; I, a Jew, had earned my role as an observer, even to the point of taking my turn at patrolling the Jordan border which the kibbutz, at that time, impinged upon, a job agreed to because the defense of my family and necessarily that of the community *in which I chose to study* by living there, seemed to me a moral necessity—although my actions in no way implied ideological agreement with either Zionism or kibbutz collectivism. Moreover, I had been invited, early on, to become a permanent member of the community—a community which had a strong sense of its continuity with the state of Israel.

My relationship to the Anaguta was defined in a wholly different way. It was not reciprocal; my induction into a clan (as among the Iroquois), or into blood brotherhood (among the Arabs) could only be a traditional gesture. These societies were under colonial assault; objectively, the future had ceased to exist for them. Whatever my intention, I remained an outsider. I could not have survived on their staples—millet beer or acha gruel—nor have withstood the cold nights of the long dry season or the violence of the rainy season on that steep ground without access to civilized shelter. There were, of course, no utilities available;

supplies would have had to be carried in at great inconvenience. Moreover, I would certainly have been an early victim of one or more of the water-borne parasitic diseases for which the region was notorious. I would have had to spend an unreasonable amount of time boiling water, cleaning food and so on. This was imperative in European quarters; in a native compound it would have been impossible, unless so stocked and transformed by modern equipment that it would have ceased being a native compound, and that would have defeated my purpose. I was fortunate that our house was well within the borders of Anaguta settlement.

At night, if I did not hear the sound of ceremony in the Anaguta hills, I would often drive in to Jos and roam the native streets, listening and observing, usually ignored, occasionally insulted as someone whom I could not see spat "*Baturi* bastard," mistaking me, I told myself, for the other kind of European. My mode of life, my opportunities, the very clothes I wore were an insult to these disinherited. From a little social distance, anthropologist, colonial administrator, business man seemed alike. From a greater distance, only the color of the skin was visible, and beyond that any man on the social horizon might be an enemy. Colonizing civilization had created these distances; good intentions were merely precious and sentiments cheap. The Africans who jeered at me in town were no better men than I. But once human hatred finds an affective occasion and a plausible excuse in the repressions and inequities of civilization, it is implacable. What could I reply? It is not so easy to hate the crime but love the criminal. It is not even simple for most of us to purify ourselves of our small, private enmities.

Certainly, if the church understood anything, it understood that. Had the missionaries come in fear and trembling before the judgment of their own history, to be forgiven, or had they come, insensibly, merely to forgive? Sometimes at night I could hear thinned-out African voices rising in the childish, rote refrains of Protestant Sunday School songs, from an enclosure run by a missionary sect, rigid with abstinence. Once later, in Ekot, in the steaming bush near the Cross River in southeastern Nigeria, we were put up for the night at a mission hospital by a young Irish priest. I was richly wined and dined in his quarters, he having changed from habit to civvies, and the evening closed with his singing "When Irish Eyes Are Smiling" accompanied by an ancient record, long after I had retired to his absent colleague's bed. He had become a priest, he said, because it was a good job for a likely Irish lad (like Pius, he had too many brothers and too little land), and he believed in spreading the Gospel. He kept in touch with the outer world by reading *Life* magazine religiously; the Africans whom he confessed through a slit in the concrete wall of the rectory, hardly existed for him. He stated, in so many words, that his task, like his colleagues, was to save as many souls as he could by applying the essential formulae. Apart from his interest in eating and drinking, he seemed an abstemious man, although his colleague had, according to my host, fathered several children—which did not affect the rather dissociated way in which that colleague conceived *his* mission. When I left he said, with the air of a man conferring a small impersonal favor, that he would pray for me; I said, "Thank you, Father," in appreciation of the uproarious evening we had spent trying to communicate from his planet to mine.

But afterwards in Jos I encountered a missionary of another kind, a member of another Irish order who had been in Nigeria for 40 years. He was so keenly indifferent to this world, so experienced in suffering that he was able to identify fully with the Africans who had been hurt by it and he looked upon the rich and neurotic West with casual contempt. But Africa was leaving itself and him behind, and he was preparing to die without returning home. As I walked the streets of Jos, it seemed to me that the earth was stiffening in abstract, stereotyped hate. How were we to recover our primary capacity to let hate flow so that we might love? How were we to turn hateful energies to creation before we perished; how were we to ride the back of Blake's burning tiger? That was what I was looking for among the primitive Anaguta, or what was left of them in the aftermath of colonialism. How were we, the civilized, to recover our *senses*?

Later I was to discover that that was the question asked by the Sengelese novelist C.H. Kane when, in *L'Aventura Ambigué* he invents a dialogue between a traditional and a Europeanized African:

> His world [the poorest peasant's, begins the traditional African] does not admit of accident. It is more reassuring than yours, despite appearances.

Maybe [replies the Europeanized African]. Unhappily for us, it is my universe which is the true one. The earth is not flat. Its banks do not overlook the abyss. The sun is not a lamp hung in a bowl of blue porcelain. The universe which science has revealed to the West is less immediately human than ours, but admit that it's more solid . . . .

Your science has revealed a world round and perfect, of infinite movement. It has reconquered that world from chaos. But I think it has also left you open to despair.

Not at all. It has freed us from fears . . . puerile and absurd.

Absurd? The absurd is your world. . . .

The dilemma then, is to sustain the world, the *traditional* world which we perceive with all our senses and grasp in metaphors, against the conceptions of modern science, of contemporary industrial society. The sun *is* a lamp hung in a bowl of blue porcelain. It is also an explosive thermonuclear field wherein hydrogen continuously transforms into helium. Each "reality" is of a different order; but the scientific abstraction has overcome the consciousness of Western man and distorts the very definition of humanity. The anthropologist, confronting the native, must constantly struggle against reducing both himself and the other to ciphers in a scientific experiment. This has nothing to do with making friends or influencing people (anthropologists are pretty good at that), but recognizing that what they are and what they know is necessary to our survival, while the converse is more than false. For our existence is systematically obliterating theirs.

In the towns, African humanity is arranged in fluid masses around market stalls, mosques, dance halls, stores; any flickering point of interest attracts a geometric crowd. The world's goods are distributed very thinly through these masses. It is possible to buy things—even parts of things—in miscroscopic quantities. Once I bought a single match from the head tray of the ultimate retailer. The original shipment, no doubt, had descended in diminishing lots from importer and wholesaler to stores, stalls and trays, swelling the profits and the number of profiteers while bringing the overprized ware to the most impoverished consumer. In one sense these new cities of Africa were no more than elaborate depots for the trading companies—everyone buying or selling something in the redolent, swarming markets; under the wings of vultures, a wilderness of petty entrepreneurs. Big traders gave birth to little traders but never cut the cord. They held the peasants in their credit by subsidizing the production of peanuts, palm oil or cocoa. Cultures have been ruined for the sake of modern mercantilism, and societies conquered so as to secure unimpeded trade. Millions of people, stimulated to produce for the Europeans in little lots that became enormous shipments, in towns like Jos bought back some small expensive thing that seemed cheap because of its size or inferior quality—tiny individual measures of production and consumption, but they commanded all the surplus sinew and strength of British West Africa. No wonder Europeans were uneasy around Jos. The "white man bastard" was the unseen presence, the invisible master. He rarely materialized; his goods stood up for him. Conquest by trade was indirect conquest; indirect conquest was best served by indirect rule.

The city laughed and chattered at night in a hundred tongues, but it seemed to me to be groaning. It was always a relief to leave Jos and take up my pursuit of the Anaguta, who were matching invisibility against invisibility, indirect response to indirect rule.

As the weeks rolled by, our presence became more conspicuous by our absence from European circles and the flowering of our compound into a web of African activity. Pagan women wearing headboards and with babies wrapped on their backs used our back yard as a short cut home from market. Taru's Fulani friends primped every morning beneath a particular tree. Drummers, flutists and other musicians were always welcome for a recording session. And there were many occasions when the cement walls reverberated under the powerful, intricate rhythms of the big Anaguta drums. People danced frequently in our back yard, and once several dozen warbling Jarawa women, trailed by a large crowd, suddenly arrived in front of the house adjoining the tin company office. Then there was the time that we invited the Miango* troupe, the most explosive dancers in northern Nigeria, to perform in an open field across from the local court not far from our compound. Armed with a police permit, they moved across the city from their settlement to ours, leaping, their bodies curved like brown fish in the sun, drumming, piping and singing, followed by most of the Miango community. They put on a show that rocked the countryside for us, themselves and hundreds of

---

* The local name for Jos Nyango-Irigwe.

Anaguta who filed down from their compounds, and sobered a passing British doctor who had spent 12 years in Lagos and could not believe what he was seeing. At that time I had no way of knowing that the Miango, the most consciously and intelligently acculturated of plateau pagans, and the Anaguta, the most elusively defiant, were making common cause against Birom control of the Jos Division native authority. The Miango and most of the Jarawa in the neighborhood of Jos were ready to use traditional Anaguta claims to the city and its environs to depose the British-supported, Hausa-oriented Birom Chief and to lift the pagan areas around the city out of Birom control. The Miango and Jarawa were already under the Anaguta Chief of Gwong District. But Abamu, the Chief and Taru's father, had no political sense and moreover was of little consequence among his own people. At any rate the Anaguta were unconcerned. But it was now possible for anyone who was compiling a dossier or making mental notes to have me involved not only with national but local politics.

THE AUTHORITIES ARE THREATENED AND BECOME SUSPICIOUS

My alien presence in Gwong already had given rise to unfriendly speculation by the authorities. I tried, for example, to interest the Divisional Educational Officer in the case of an Anaguta elementary school student who, oddly enough, wished to continue his education. We had a quiet, unfruitful conversation. The officer was perhaps a bit too frigidly polite, and I a trifle too enthusiastic. We were also paying the tuition of some 20 Anaguta children at the local elementary school. It was only about 12 shillings per term per child, but their parents could not afford the fee. And we enrolled a Jarawa waif who had attached himself to our household with the consent of his sister. The sister, a speechless prostitute in the New Town, had vermilion eyelids and rose cheeks and a face clenched in the agony of such pleasures. Some years earlier she had left a disintegrating compound in a half-abandoned Jarawa hamlet, taking her brother with her, to take her chances in the city.

In one form or another these modest and unofficial efforts echoed around the colonial circuit, and word came back to me from an acquaintance in the next province that some presumptuous American was raising a hell of a row insisting that hill pagans be sent to school, which was not the case at all. But it took several more concrete events to precipitate official action.

The first of these events occurred a couple of months after our arrival in Gwong. Pius's wife had returned from the hospital, and he, having by that time knit himself snugly into the Igbo community, arranged for the infant to be unveiled at a naming ceremony in our compound. On the appointed day a group of his fellow townsmen from Owerri Province, whom he had met at the Igbo Progressive Union in Jos, arrived bearing gifts and prepared to bestow a name on their compatriot's daughter. It was an impressive display of Igbo egalitarianism. Pius was a servant, but the dozen men ranged around the table he had set up in the back yard and drinking the beer he had provided included professionals and businessmen, merchants and mechanics and a single policeman. The latter was so obviously Igbo that, even if I had then been aware of the possibility, I would never have taken him for a police spy, although the species, official and otherwise, was common in northern Nigeria. Moreover, the man was in uniform.

The women in their Sunday robes clustered around mother and daughter. The men drank their beer, ribbed Pius on his fatherhood and spoke of home. The yard hummed with gaiety. Pius had asked me to share a glass with his guests, which I did, responding to a toast to Zik, later President of Nigeria, but then the Premier of the East and head of the NCNC, not then in compromising coalition with the NPC at the Center.

Immediately thereafter, I left to take my family on a drive through Birom country, south of Jos. When we returned, about an hour later, the compound was deserted, and Pius was standing bowed and withdrawn, drying glasses in the kitchen. It seems that the chief assistant to the director of the tin company, who lived in a nearby house, had suddenly appeared, inquired whether I was home and then suggested that the party be broken up. Although he was not a pious man, he had given Sunday, along with my absence, as the reason. This chief assistant was a hearty, strongly built, busy fellow, with a tea strainer of a moustache and a face like that on the label of Beefeaters' Gin. But he was also a devious bully, haughty before the submissive Hausa clerks who worked in the office and humble before the boss. It comforted him to think that the boss was just a Greek, some kind of a Wog, despite his carefully trimmed British accent, which almost but never quite betrayed him, and his languorous, pale white, unoccupied, upper-class British wife. Beneath the bluff, Sergeant Major exterior, the chief assistant was a terrified small bourgeois who had found his way to the colonies, horizontal mobility being a good substitute for the upward mobility that he could not have achieved in England because of his limited chance for education and inconsequential connections. He had lived well in northern Nigeria, playing an upper-class charade, buying service and respect in a passable accent, and he dreaded above all the prospect of returning home to descend to what would be considered his rightful place in society. So he courted the boss like a lover, for his dismissal would have voided his entry permit, and neglected his wife; his marriage was misbegotten anyway, and from time to time he drank himself helpless. His wife, an angular, intelligent English woman, was once a schoolteacher but was now growing incompetent in the colonial atmosphere which rusted her skills while inflating her prestige. For that reason she feared the return home as deeply as her husband. Later she made an effort to reach us when the going got rough but fell back exhausted on the other side.

The chief assistant was hardly the man to stand up to assembled Igbos in someone else's back yard. He had to be selective about the Africans he insulted—so as not to endanger his stay in Nigeria—just as he clung to the Levantine boss who enjoyed insulting this Englishman he owned. He had been polite, I am sure, to Pius and his friends—out of fear. But this was a job for the director, who was less discriminating in his approach to Africans; and the chief assistant called the director out to officially enforce the reprimand. The director habitually referred to the Africans as bastards and was always trying to make his Hausa employees and servants jump by shouting at them at the top of his voice from the shortest possible distance. The idea seemed to be to catch them unaware, a sport that he felt was appreciated all around.

The Igbo were not impressed by the director's argument—in my back yard and on Anaguta land—that African celebrations were not permitted on his property. He was obstructing a naming ceremony, and they argued with him man to man. In a shorter time than it takes to tell it, the director threatened to call the

Senior Superintendent of Police, with whom he was on friendly terms, and shouted that Pius and his baby were bastards, and who could properly name a bastard. He went on to charge them with creating a disturbance, which was not true, and at this they reluctantly left. Pius was ready on the instant to take the case to court, but the others would not have it. Southerners were, just then, suspected and disadvantaged in the North. The political battle against southern associated parties was gaining force and "northernization" of business and government was gaining momentum. Charges could easily be trumped up against these southerners, and they were uncertain about the extent of the tin executives' influence.

The next day I went to see the director. Pius had been humiliated in front of his friends. He looked uncertainly to me, "the other kind of European," for moral support, and I would not have people interfered with in my house. At the outset the director and I were patient with each other. I explained to him, as one expatriate to another, that Nigeria was not a settlers' colony, that it was impractical and immoral to push Africans around; and I gave him a short, cordial course on the deficiencies of the colonial mentality. He responded by assuring me of his respect for me and my work and then read to me from the unwritten manual on old colonial behavior. Africans, he said, were children. It took decades to understand them, and no amount of book learning could equal his experience. They had to be treated with a firm hand since they had no direction of their own, and if you gave them an inch they would take a mile. If they were not biologically inferior to whites, they were at least a thousand years behind them. He said he had really been guarding the propriety of my house in my absence and also the little frontier community in which we all lived. And he told me how Africans were prone to committing atrocities. This, I recalled, was a favorite topic of conversation of his new English secretary, a preternaturally competent, good-natured, earthy woman, neat as a pin, who had spent too many years in the Rhodesias where she had been briefly married and widowed, and who clothed her unusual sexual fantasies in African dress. I informed the director that attitudes such as his were making it difficult for the white race. I told him that he was never to interfere with my affairs again. He said that my affairs were public affairs; he had recognized two prominent members of the Jos branch of the NCNC among the party in my compound, and if I thought that that was a baby-naming ceremony I was laughably wrong—it had been a political meeting, and he was within his rights in breaking it up because all political meetings in northern Nigeria required a police permit. Moreover, they had been toasting Zik when he interrupted them, and what further proof did I want. Igbos, he said, his eyes turning red, were arrogant and tricky. He was beginning to shake, afraid to insult me directly and afraid not to, so I walked out, telling him to stay away from my legally rented premises, knowing that only a religious conversion could breach that wall of prejudice and frustration.

But I did not know that he had already informed the Senior Superintendent of Police that I had subsidized a large and noisy rally of the NCNC in my compound. At that time Hausa-Igbo tensions in northern Nigeria were high; the conception of the coalition government composed of the NPC and NCNC had not yet taken shape. The Igbo were politically active and outspoken, and the memory of bloody assaults by the Hausa on the Igbo in Kano was still strong. This added another complication to the complex and (to the NPC) dangerous balance of forces in the province. In a matter of weeks the colonial circuit of rumor had amplified Pius's private naming ceremony to a lavish reception arranged by me for a hundred prominent members of the NCNC, honoring that southern "radical" and suspected enemy of the north, Zik,* on his birthday. Word even spread to adjoining provinces and frightened a fellow anthropologist who was professionally addicted to looking at social processes objectively and had a strategically healthy respect for the status quo.

By that time I had attracted the attention of the British police, who were determined to keep northern Nigeria a model of colonial stability; but I do not think that I was under direct scrutiny. I was known, however, in African and European circles for rather different reasons, so it should not have surprised me, as it did, when a newspaper reporter knocked on the door one day and asked for an interview. He was a representative of the *Daily Times*, the leading national newspaper, published in Lagos in English as were most Nigerian papers. He told me that he had heard that an

---

* Dr. Azikiwe ("Zik") took office as Governor-General of Nigeria following independence in 1960; after Nigeria became a Republic he was installed as President by the coalition NPC-NCNC government.

anthropologist was studying hill pagans in Gwong and would be grateful if I explained this newsworthy mission to him. I did not object in principle and, feeling that I could learn as much from him as he from me, I invited him in. I followed the Nigerian press carefully and was well aware of its shrewd but figurative interpretation of the news. In the American press proper facts are typically made trivial in shallow and uninformed contexts. The Nigerian press was the converse; it had an instinct for the sense of events, with or against the facts, although it was capable on occasion of reaching heights of fantasy. I was forearmed, but Patrick, the reporter, was disarming. He was of Igbo parentage, born in the North, personable, poised and eager. I explained at some length my efforts among the Anaguta and the auspices under which the study was being conducted; he seemed interested but took no notes. He had come with a colleague, who was so quiet and inconspicuous that I was completely unaware of him; indeed, I never saw him again or found out who he was. Presumably he was a witness to my remarks, but whether innocently, that is, journalistically, or in some other capacity, I do not know. But one way or the other, in what were to be fairly frequent trips to the office of Patrick's newspaper, he was never in evidence.

Patrick finally asked me my opinion and impressions of the current Nigerian scene. I said that I only had some general ideas about the North, not having visited the other regions, and would discuss these with him but strictly off the record, not for publication. He agreed at once and we began a lively discussion.

The gist of it was as follows. The North was a terribly poor and economically underdeveloped area. This was due in part to indirect rule, which had paved the way for and encouraged smallholder cash-cropping. Indirect rule had been successful where Fulani sovereignty had been strongest and unsuccessful in the pagan areas where political chiefs had had to be appointed by the British in order to collect taxes where none had been collected before and to keep the King's peace in the vicinity of trade routes. The NPC, the party of the Emirs, grew out of and merged with, the administrative structure of indirect rule and therefore could not and would not encourage democratic participation in government at the grass roots. As was well known, Lugard's system was fundamentally undemocratic in application; it rewarded and strengthened those already in power, made them dependent on the Colonial Authority and disengaged them further from any connections they may have had with the people at large. In theory, I indicated, indirect rule was supposed to use native institutions, not merely established or appointed political chiefs, but it had failed to do so. Had any real effort been made for example, to transform traditional, cooperative economic systems or native authorities into modern agricultural, marketing or labor cooperatives? Actually, the British had done very little *directly* to develop the North; there was hardly any evidence of capital investment beyond the necessary transportation grid in the service of trade. The colonial process had been one of pacification and extraction. The British colonial apparatus had been superimposed upon the cruder, tributary and slave-ridden Fulani system, itself a type of archaic colonialism. It was also interesting to discover that where the Fulani had not conquered, indirect rule had failed and the NPC had not taken root, as among plateau pagans; and opposition political parties making a direct appeal to an untutored electorate had emerged but these had been stimulated by southern elements. It seemed incongruous, I concluded, that the Colonial Office should consider northern Nigeria the prime example of a successfully managed colony, particularly when so many English officers in the field, in administrative generations gone by, had written so many reports and books criticizing the nature and assumptions of the undertaking.

Patrick, a member of the NCNC, grew very serious, agreed emphatically, and contributed interesting material of his own. When he left, he promised, at my request, that he would submit to me any item intended for publication and would prepare a brief notice on my study of the Anaguta but would not, of course, use any remarks that might incite the regime. Being a certain type of journalist, this promise he failed to keep. Several weeks later a prominent story appeared in the *Daily Times*, misidentifying me and quoting me selectively and luridly. There was only a single passing reference to my work among the Anaguta, the supposedly original intent of the interview. No mention was made of regional politics, but the North was characterized as the most backward area in Nigeria. Patrick had obviously used me for his own purposes. Breach of confidence aside, the story was inaccurate enough to justify a letter to the editor. But I decided that it would be unwise to attract further attention and let it go. After all, the

Nigerian press was full of statements by natives and visitors evaluating and criticizing every aspect of the local scene. Patrick's story, in contrast, had been relatively modest. But later it was easy enough to visualize official thought processes: an American anthropologist lives in Gwong, apparently studying pagans whose claim to Jos is being used in an effort to shift the balance of power in the area; he considers indirect rule undemocratic and the North an impoverished and oppressed region. Exploiting academic license, he plants a story in the press which can be used by enemies of the established regime. Obviously, the man is an agent of some kind, probably an agent provocateur. If not, he is having that effect and it is all the same. Could it be that the Americans want a democratic North as soon as possible? After all, Azikiwe and Nkrumah were educated in the United States; both are notorious enemies of political chieftancy, colonialism and indirect rule. But the man may not be acting in the interest of the American government. Perhaps he takes his orders from the Soviet Union. Perhaps that was his role in Israel.

Logically enough, anthropologists are frequently taken as spies because of the inquisitive nature of their work; their concern with local affairs in the remote places to which they go, their tendency to fade into the background of local custom in living up to the canons of participant observation. They have, also, a certain limited academic immunity; they travel freely, and what better cover could a secret agent desire. A logical case can be constructed, and often has been, against any anthropologist in the field almost anywhere in this era of inescapable crises. Of course anthropologists are *spiritual* double agents. That is, they are marginal to the commercial-industrial society that created them, but they eagerly explore the areas opened up to them by colonialism. Anthropology is an academic discipline, but it also implies revolt, a search for human possibilities. Police agents instinctively suspect that sort of thing.

Perhaps a few anthropologists have actually been government agents, or, less officially, have reported unpublished findings to appropriate government agencies for aggressive purposes; they are beneath contempt. But most such suspicions originate in the psychologically totalitarian concept of "objective guilt." That is, the effect of a man's behavior, measured against the intentions of a dominant political power, becomes sufficient cause for him to be identified as a spy, a traitor, and so on. His own intentions or actual connections are irrelevant. Ultimately, on that basis, a case could be constructed against any citizen anywhere; it would be unnecessary for him to be an anthropologist. But the theory of objective guilt has the curious effect of creating opposition to any system or agency that makes use of it. To fear being mistaken for an enemy of a regime is the beginning of political wisdom, that is, it is the first step toward becoming an opponent of any oppressive regime. This then is not merely an anthropological matter, although anthropologists are perhaps in a good position to make inquiry. Nor is it even a national or colonial affair but a familiar and universal threat in an age of systematic terror. Still, I had no intention of becoming involved "objectively" or otherwise in local Nigerian politics. Therefore, my private talk with Patrick had been an error in judgment.

By December I felt that the initial phase of my work in Gwong had been completed. After involved negotiations I had finally met the real, traditional authority among the Anaguta, a Priest Chief, a holy *primus inter pares*, whom I was permitted to provide with millet beer at 40 paces (to approach him more closely would have contaminated him). Three months later I was permitted the right to talk to him providing I did not look at him. Thus we decided to undertake our planned tour of southeastern Nigeria, including a visit to Pius's hometown, and the southern Cameroons. The purpose of the trip was to see Igbo land, to visit a few plantations north and east of Calabar, which are rare in British West Africa, and to buy, if possible, artifacts for a university museum. The southern Cameroons was then a separate region within the Federation of Nigeria. The beginnings of a plantation economy had been developed there under German administration prior to the First World War. The highlands were also celebrated for wood carving and bead work. There had been some agitation for an independent Cameroons, reported in the Nigerian press, and a plebescite was to be held in 1959. But it was generally felt that the electorate would choose to remain connected with Nigeria. At any rate that was not then a problem of concern to me.

Our trip lasted about a month, including a strange tropical Christmas Day in the Oban Hills, where Christian ceremony was expressed in variations of native mortification of the flesh. One young man showed us a dagger through his wrist, another, his palm pierced completely by a sharpened reed. In both cases, no blood, no pain—only the slow beat of drums and a circle of grave witnesses.

We toured the bush trails and brisk towns of Igbo land, crossed rivers in every conceivable way, including a poled raft that was exactly the length of the wagon. Later I had to drive the empty vehicle across a wooden suspension bridge 100 feet above the river, swinging 20 degrees to either side. The roadbed was an inch or two narrower than the wagon, but inching crabwise, and encouraged by a silent, smiling crowd on the far bank that materialized from a compound in the forest, I managed to make it. It was the denoument of a 60-mile short cut through the bush, and we were too exhausted to turn back. The bridge was to collapse shortly thereafter.

From there, we climbed the new trails north of Calabar to the precipitous one-way strip that wound through jungle up to Bamenda, the highland center of the southern Cameroons. The plantations were open-air factories that had stilled and routinized the bustle of African life and created a restless labor force. Featureless rows of concrete dwellings had replaced the lovely, lofty thatched triangular huts of the region. I was content that these plantations had no real future in southern Nigeria. But the arts of the carver and the potter were still alive in the villages.

In Bamenda I was directed to speak to a Mr. Foncha, who was connected with the Antiquities Commission, to determine whether certain objects for which I was negotiating could be taken out of the country. It turned out that I had a good, long, hair-raising talk with him about many things, both sacred and profane, while he was immobilized in his compound with a fractured collarbone, and a rainstorm of unimaginable violence kept me at his bedside for several hours. Foncha, it developed, was the head of the Opposition Party, which was working toward Cameroonian independence and which to everyone's surprise won the election some months later, catapulting him into the Premiership. This was taken as a blow to Nigerian prestige in general and a threat to northern territorial integrity in particular, since the precedent set by the southern area could have been followed by the northern Cameroons. I had traveled, in short, from one sensitive Nigerian area through Igbo land, itself a region suspect in the North, to another politically uncertain place. From Plateau Province through southeastern Nigeria, the southern Cameroons, and the return. I could not have followed a more sensitive itinerary if I had planned it that way.

By the time I returned, British colonial and northern Nigerian agents had identified me as an active enemy of the regime, and I was to be instructed further in the subtleties of colonial control. As it happened, they only anticipated my politics in this particular matter. My experience finally caught up with my abstract understanding. I found myself in a position to learn that Nigeria, the model colony, soberly "tutored" for independence, was actually the epitome of colonial failure, a consequence of imperialism at its worst. And, when the time came, that led to my commitment to the struggle for Biafran independence.

3

ANTHROPOLOGY
IN QUESTION

*In a sense, by dint of studying man, we ... have made ourselves
incapable of knowing him.*

—Rousseau

Anthropology, abstractly conceived as the study of man, is
actually the study of men in crisis by men in crisis. Anthropologists and their objects, the studied, despite opposing positions
in the "scientific" equation have this much in common: if not
equally, still they are each objects of contemporary imperial
civilization. The anthropologist who treats the indigene as an
object may define himself as relatively free, but that is an illusion.
For in order to objectify the other, one is, at the same time,
compelled to objectify the self. On this score, the anthropologist
betrays himself as inevitably as he does the native whom he
examines. Therefore, when Lévi-Strauss, whom I take to be both
the most representative and the most elusive of contemporary
anthropologists, argues that, as the offspring of colonialism,
"anthropology ... reflects, on the epistimological level, a state of
affairs in which one part of mankind treats the other as an
object," he tells us only half the truth.[1] The other half is critical.
For the anthropologist is himself a victim, and his power of
decision is a fiction, embedded as it is in the exploitative
foundations of civilization. Edmund Carpenter relates a case in
point: the presumed results of an official experiment in
communication to which he lent himself in Australian New
Guinea. Although questioning the ethic of the undertaking, he
argues that the disorganization, indeed the destruction of the
village culture under systematic electronic assault (tape recordings,
film and so forth) which his team initiated, could be justified only

by the knowledge gained of analogous processes in our, the colonizing, society.[2]

Unless the anthropologist confronts his own alienation, which is only a special instance of a general condition, seeks to understand its roots and subsequently matures as a relentless critic of his own civilization, the very civilization which converts man into an object, he cannot understand or even recognize himself in the man of another culture or that other man in himself. Thus when Lévi-Strauss finally insists, with an admirable consistency men who share his views fail to achieve, that as an anthropologist he cannot invidiously compare societies, that to assume the legitimacy of one is to legitimate all, he does so as a pure relativist, a natural scientist of man.[3] This implies a suspension of what our society isolates as values, and all serious reflection or action that comes from them. Values become aspects of a cultural code and are no more meaningful than parts of speech. This "privileged" situation of the anthropologist is, in fact, the quintessence of alienation. For he must behave *as if* he had no judgment, *as if* his experience were inconsequential, *as if* he denied history, *as if* the contradictions between his origins and his vocation did not exist. Moreover, he will imagine that he has no politics, and he will consider that a virtue. One is reminded of Ruth Benedict's argument that if our society created unemployment, it was only logical to assume that the unemployed should be treated with dignity; or analogously, that under colonial conditions, the British did better with proud people and the Dutch with those who were more accustomed to humiliation. Therefore, a reshuffling of sovereignties was theoretically in order.[4] In this admittedly banal example, which has not yet developed into scientific relativism, symmetry of values, the logical structure of the cultural code, is the paramount consideration, the meta-value of the relativistic professional. He may know better, but he may not admit to knowing better as an anthropologist.

The split between the person and the professional reaches the limits of irony in the study of man. It is, of course, prefigured in military and civilian bureaucracies; in the organization of the state itself, wherein the person adapts to a single status and a "professional" ethic, the ethic of domination. The "professional" anthropologist is an alien, although—perhaps because—he claims the whole of the Western tradition for his ancestry. Claiming everything, he is in danger of being nothing. Indeed, he is estranged three times over: first, in his own society, along with the generality of his fellow citizens; second, in the choice of his profession; and finally, in relation to those whom he studies.

Such an anthropologist must sooner or later define himself as an "entropologist" (Lévi-Strauss' term)[5] and rest on the prediction of the ultimate thermodynamic leveling of all culture. If the possibility of self-knowledge is denied by the anthropologist as the goal of his inquiry, then the structures or forms, of which history is merely an aspect, become ends in themselves, and they are entropic. This denial of self-knowledge by Lévi-Strauss, most evident in his confrontation with Ricoeur and others at a symposium organized by L'Esprit in 1963,[6] is worth examining because it exemplifies scientism in its ethnological form and almost succeeds as an objective, relativistic statement.

THE *L'ESPRIT* SYMPOSIUM

On two occasions during the roundtable discussion Ricouer asks: "But if I do not understand myself better by understanding [primitive peoples], can I still talk of meaning? If meaning is not a sector of self-understanding, I do not know what it is."

The first time Lévi-Strauss replies: "In my perspective, meaning is never the primary phenomenon: meaning is always reducible. In other words, behind all meaning there is a non-meaning, while the reverse is not the case. As far as I am concerned, significance is always phenomenal."*

The second time Lévi-Strauss replies: "I find it quite legitimate that a philosopher who poses the problem in terms of the person should raise this objection, but I am not obliged to follow suit. What do I understand by meaning? A particular flavor perceived

---

* Lévi-Strauss the ethnologist is actually saying that he is not interested in meaning (significance), which he regards as *merely* (and always) phenomenal. For him, the primary phenomenon is not meaning but non-meaning, which lies behind meaning and to which, he believes, meaning is reducible. But the reverse is not true; that is, non-meaning is never "reducible" to meaning. In short, Lévi-Strauss is concerned with the primary or underlying structures of non-meaning, which nonetheless govern meaning. Lévi-Strauss, so to speak, reverses the focus of the phenomenologist; he had substantially dismissed phenomenology in *Tristes Tropiques*.

by a consciousness when it tastes a combination of elements of which any one taken alone would not produce a comparable flavor.... The ethnologist tries to recover the meaning... to reconstitute the meaning... by mechanical means he constructs it, unwraps it, and then after all he is a man, so he tastes it."

Later on, Lévi-Strauss, in response to Jean Lautman elaborates on the question of meaning: "I am trying to make an analysis of man.... This undertaking is to find out how the human mind functions.... I have a feeling that the ethnologist does the same thing for collective ensembles that the psychoanalyst does for individuals [with reference to the theory of the mind, not therapeutic praxis].... *I do not believe that the self-analysis undertaken by the mind will improve it; I am completely indifferent as to whether it improves it or no. What interests me is to find out how it works and that is all* [emphasis added]."

But questions remain. Jean Conilh asks: "I wonder if this problem you have raised is not the following: Each time we attempt an interpretation of savages is this not always ultimately a way of finding a meaning for them so as to understand ourselves? ... Is our problem to classify or to find a meaning? "

Lévi-Strauss answers: "To be sure, I think that one of the reasons for the attraction ethnology exercises even on non-professionals, is that its inquiries have powerful motivations within the heart of our society, interpreting as they do a number of our society's dramas.... We ought to recognize that whether we are ethnologists or merely interested in ethnology it is for *scientifically impure reasons* ... nevertheless if ethnology is to deserve recognition some day for its role in the constitution of the human sciences, it will be for other reasons."

The anthropologist implies, in other words, that structuralism, or whatever the name of the contribution ethnology is destined to make to the understanding of mind, is a higher truth, on the analogy of Freudian theory, in contrast to the psychoanalytic praxis. It is just here that the relativism of Lévi-Strauss breaks down in the espousal of an objective, objectifying and scientific conceptualism—a conceptualism, moreover, which is and must be literally useless. "Its importance ... depends on results whose interest lies on another plane"—thus Lévi-Strauss admits his belief in the unique theoretical superiority of an immaculately abstract and analytic logico-deductive science of the ultimate forms of reality, which has reached its zenith in Western civilization.* Although he refuses to locate himself in any particular philosophic tradition, Lévi-Strauss has in fact become a mediator of final concepts. And this is a view which, according to Alexadre Koyre, has its origins in Plato at a certain juncture in the history of our civilization coincident with the rise of the academy. Thus, Lévi-Strauss's higher mission is academic and ethnocentric.

Despite his intricate concern with the meaning and operation of symbols, which he actually degrades to the function of signs, Lévi-Strauss stops at the "reality" of structuralist and psychodynamic theory. He fails to consider, for example, that Freud's theory of the mind is one of many possible complementary "explanations" for phenomenal experience; or that it may, perhaps, be taken as a root metaphor. It is therefore clear that to the limited degree that Lévi-Strauss appreciates phenomenology ("significance" is always phenomenal), it would have to be in the conceptual vein of Husserl not in the existential perspective of Merleau-Ponty. Moreover, the only conceivable but by no means inevitable proof of psychodynamic theory is in its instrumentation, that is, in psychoanalysis, the latter being the origin of, while remaining dialectically in touch with, the "higher" conceptual effort. More to the point, no scientific concept outlives consistent counterindicative application. And one should add that the concept divorced from application, as in the instance of Einstein's Unified Field Theory, is an esthetic curiosity, a deficient category of myth. The history of Western civilization is, after all, littered with dead scientific concepts. It is ironic that Lévi-Strauss understands so well the presence of technology in the absence of formal scientific systems in primitive societies on the one hand, while he insists on the ultimate superiority of such systems on the other, despite the historicity of the concepts they generate. In any event, it is clear that his concern is to discover no less than the "true" nature of "minding," which, in his idiom, implies an

---

* During the *L'Esprit* confrontation Lévi-Strauss seems to disavow the conclusion of *La Pensée Sauvage*, in which he had made a plea for a synthesis of primitive and civilized modalities of thought. He viewed them as complementary to the modern scientific enterprise; their equivalence, therefore, becomes a live, historical issue not merely an abstract, timeless matter. But even then he seems to imply that only the modern mind can understand the significance of the synthesis.

ambition to understand the final character of the human universe. It is equally clear that he believes an inevitable requirement for such understanding is objectification and that the resultant knowledge is superior to that which all other types of cognition provide us with.

But objectification is least of all a mental operation. Objectification on the scale which concerns us evolves with civilization itself; it is an ensemble of processes—a political process involving the legal subordination and definition of the person within the state, a social process coincident with the elaborate division of labor and the rise and conflict of classes, a psychological process through which the civilized consciousness becomes alienated from labor, nature and society as a whole. Correlatively, objectification finds its intellectual analogue in the analytic-abstract modality of thought which, reflecting further on itself, emerges in one form as "structuralism." We should also bear in mind that Lévi-Strauss is not interested in technology as such, with which modern science is to some extent associated; he is concerned, rather, with a pure principle of understanding, a principle he has succeeded in detaching from both its origins and its social or technical functions. He wishes, it seems, to be a mathematician, whose integers are necessarily devoid of content and meaning. Jean Conilh intimates this when, during the course of the *L'Esprit* confrontation he says: "Have you not constituted a philosophy and a philosophy of our time? ... In that case, I can reject this philosophy and go back to primitive mentality, reading it on another level, the level of symbols, for example, and find a new meaning for it."

But Lévi-Strauss does not interpret objectification as alienation, even though he tells us that "anthropology is the daughter of this era of [colonial] violence." On the contrary, he contends that the "state of affairs in which one part of mankind treats the other as an object" makes it possible *"to assess more objectively the facts pertaining to the human condition"* [emphasis added]. Therefore, one must conclude that, *as an anthropologist*, Lévi-Strauss has no important argument to launch against the imperialism that he describes nor against the condition of his own society. As a matter of fact, as a highly trained member of that society he would seem obliged to confess that his understanding of "reality" has been furthered; for him objectification is above all a purely mental operation. Ricoeur, who one imagines could hardly agree with this implicit assessment, in fact terminates his response to Lévi-Strauss at the *L'Esprit* roundtable as follows: "as far as you are concerned there is no 'message': not in the cybernetic, but in the kerygmatic sense; you despair of meaning; but you console yourself with the thought that if men have nothing to say, at least they say it so well that their discourse is amenable to structuralism. You retain meaning, but it is the meaning of non-meaning. The admirable, syntactic arrangement of a discourse which has nothing to say. . . . "

THE PROBLEM OF SELF-KNOWLEDGE

The key to Lévi-Strauss' "meaninglessness" is, I believe, his rejection of self-knowledge, which is in turn the root paradox of modern anthropology. If self-knowledge is irrelevant, so is self-criticism, which is impossible without self-knowledge. Moreover, both self-knowledge and self-criticism are meaningless in the absence of a normative sense of human nature, which Lévi-Strauss' radical relativism and formalism inevitably contradict. His relativism breaks down, as we have seen, with reference to his own professional task; perhaps we are obliged to say more specifically that his relativism is that of the scientific observer and is not a naive cultural relativism. His formalism constricts the human enterprise within an ethnologically defined cultural unconscious, limited in its functions though generating a variety of formal analogues. But there is no real possibility of novelty, volition, substance, synthesis. Lévi-Strauss' complementary oppositions, around which he chooses to organize his ethnographic data, do not permit synthesis (not to speak of transcendence) and, therefore, they do not permit growth. That is, they are *structural*, not *human* ambivalences. It is hard to decide whether so high-pitched a determinism is rooted in a theory of human nature or culture. What is more likely is that we have been presented with a closed hypothesis concerning the nature of culture that is reducible to a dogma concerning the nature of mind. It is equally hard to decide whether Lévi-Strauss is a pure natural scientist or the cold poet of a formalist esthetics, until one realizes that in his work, more clearly than in that of any thinker of our time, the two visions are revealed to be identical. But above all, it is important to recognize Lévi-Strauss' determinism, his negation of history as a human possibility.*

Criticism of self or other, of our society or theirs, depends on the definition of human needs, limits and possibilities arrived at through the constant effort to grasp the meaning of the historical experiences of men. In this anthropological "experiment" which we initiate, it is not they who are the ultimate objects but ourselves. We study men, that is, we reflect on ourselves studying others, because we must, because man in civilization is the problem. Primitive peoples do not study man. It is unnecessary; the subject is given. They say this or that about behavior (who has not been impressed by the wisdom of his informants?); they engage in ritual, they celebrate, but they are not compelled to objectify. We, on the contrary, are engaged in a complex search for the subject in history, as the precondition for a minimal definition of humanity and, therefore, of self-knowledge as the ground for self-criticism. The questions we bring to history come out of our own need. The task of anthropology is to clarify these questions.

THE EIGHTEENTH-CENTURY: ROUSSEAU

Jean Conilh touches upon the problem as follows: "In the eighteenth century we find writers discussing the Good Savage in relation to the questions they were asking about themselves. In the bourgois colonialist epoch we find a conception of the primitive which presents them as inferior. . . . "[9]

Manifestly, the two views Conilh contrasts would seem to be merely rationalizations of the interests of the respective pre- and post-revolutionary societies. Certainly, nothing could be clearer

---

* Contrast this with Rousseau: "Nature commands every animal, and the beast obeys. Man feels the same impetus, but he realizes that he is free to acquiesce or resist; and it is above all in the consciousness of this freedom that the spirituality of his soul is shown. For physics explains in some way the mechanism of the senses and the formation of ideas; but in the power of willing, or rather of choosing, and in the sentiment of this power are found only purely spiritual acts about which the laws of mechanics explain nothing."[8]

than that imperialism was the source of the idea of the inferior savage. But further reflection leads us to a deeper assumption, namely, that in the nineteenth century, the period of bourgeois political and class consolidation within the Euro-American sphere, the very image of man was progressively degraded and *that* was reflected in the shift in conceptions of the primitive. Put another way, the distrust and repression of human nature, the mark of the nineteenth century bourgoisie, were expressed as anthropological assumptions. And these assumptions about man in general, were projected onto primitive men, those particular others.

There is a further nuance in the distinction between the eighteenth-century Good Savage and the nineteenth-century inferior savage. In the nineteenth century, just as the social organization and techniques of modern industrial capitalism emerge as a world force, so the idea of inevitable progress in the name of science becomes a fixed ideology. The revolutions having succeeded and then, quite obviously, having failed in their social promise, it appears as if all the frustrated passion were mobilized behind the idea of the dominance of science. This, in turn, had been foreshadowed in the high expectations, the excitement concerning the future of science so evident in the eighteenth century. But there are very important distinctions. For the eighteenth century, science, celebrated even by the poets, the spirit of reason incarnate, and the vision of the scientific society was utopian, a vision that Fourier and others later tried to realize. Moreover, the celebration of reason was balanced by a bitter and sophisticated critique of actual social conditions on the one hand and the sense of the indivisibility of existence, in its esthetic, sensuous and rational dimensions, on the other.

In the eighteenth century, men could still be rediscovered; mankind was an open system. The great questions concerning the nature of man and culture were being reformulated; it was the axial episode in the modern consciousness. The term "Good Savage," synonymous with natural man, was both an historical definition and the ground for the perfectability of man. Rousseau asks: "What experiments would be necessary to achieve knowledge of natural man? What are the means of making these experiments in the midst of society?" He charges: "For the 300 or 400 years since the inhabitants of Europe have inundated the other parts of the world, and continuously published new collections of voyages and reports, I am convinced that we know no other men except the Europeans, . . . under *the pompous name of the study of man,* everyone does hardly anything except study the men of his country."[10] Rousseau calls for a proper anthropology, the purpose of which is self-knowledge and the means the authentic understanding of others. As a representative of his time, he is interested in a critical and revolutionary discipline.

THE NINETEENTH-CENTURY: MARX

In the nineteenth century, on the other hand, the concept of the primitive no longer implied the search for natural man. In the hardening scientific perspective, primitive characteristics were regarded as remote in time and space; they were at the base of the evolution towards civilization; and civilization had been identified as a unilinear, inevitably progressive movement. Although doubts were evident, for example, in the work of Morgan and Tylor, the secular trend was conceived to be from the inferior to the superior. This investment in the notion of progress in the nineteenth century was the beneficent aspect of a morbid process, which can be epitomized as the conquest of nature—including human nature. Imperialism was a political manifestation of the struggle against nature and man, associated with the notion of the inevitable superiority of Western civilization. The means at hand for conquering primitive and archaic peoples helped rationalize the scientific perspective in which they were viewed as inferior. Coincidentally, reason (the scientific utopianism of the eighteenth century) was transformed into functional (or, better, reductive) rationality which was ideally evident in the mechanisms of the market and embedded in the apparatus of industrial capitalism. The arena for rationalization becomes the whole of human existence. As reason is reduced to rationality, the esthetic and sensuous aspects of the person are repressed; that is, they are brutalized or sentimentalized. The ethos of "achievement"—what in other contexts is called the "performance principle"—develops in antagonism to human nature or, rather, constricts the definition of human possibilities.

Even revolutionaries do not escape; they are, after all, shaped by the forces they seek to transcend. Marx, for example, abandoned the scientific utopianism of the eighteenth century, though he acknowledges his indebtedness. He was obliged to take into account, while accounting for, nineteenth-century capitalism —both in its domestic and foreign manifestations. Accordingly, the early Marx justifies imperialism as being "objectively" progressive; only thus could the frozen structures of archaic civilizations be broken down and progress become possible. He was to give up this view, which remains the classic rationalization for colonialism, although he never developed any coherent alternative. Similarly, Marx shifted his opinion on the question of Irish liberation. Originally, he was opposed to that movement because he assumed that the potential solidarity of the British working class and the impoverished Irish could be more important strategically and more significant historically than the national question. He changed his mind in later years on the ground that Irish independence would deprive the English establishment of a diversionary tactic and force the English proletariat to express their frustrations against their own ruling class. In each instance, that of imperialism and that of the Irish question, Marx dealt with the problem in the language of an abstract, world-historical process.

But he displayed no such ambivalence about his own society. Marx anticipated and worked toward a revolution which he assumed could occur under the social and material conditions of nineteenth-century capitalism. He did not counsel patience or call upon the workers to await the inception of a more advanced technology. Indeed, as Venable asserts, he defined patience as utopian.[11] That is, he did not subordinate what he conceived to be the interests of the European proletariat to any other class or population anywhere in the world. The European proletariat, who had reached the extremity of alienation, were the cutting edge of the world-historical process; their actions were the precondition for the freedom of all. Marx, of course, was the seminal theorist of alienation. He understood the human predicament in modern society, and he undoubtedly believed that the social situation which gave rise to it had to be fought through on its own terms and that any other course would be evasive. His enthusiasm and strangely unreal hopes for the momentary fraternity of the Paris commune, seem to indicate his frustration about the ordinarily alienated character of revolutionary imperatives. Still, in centering on "progressive" Europe, Marx was certainly a man of his time.

Indeed, the most fruitful of the Marxist terms of reference derive from the time. More generally, they relate to "history"—in the Marxist lexicon, to civilization. Prehistory (the period of primitive, classless, communal society) and the post-historical societies (presumably, free of alienation) are hardly subject to conventional Marxist analysis. The historical materialist terms of reference, grow more cogent as class societies mature and harden, as states emerge, as civilization develops. This is what Rudi Supek, the Yugoslavian sociologist, seems to imply when he writes: "Marx's well-known statement . . . namely that 'the methods of production of material life condition the process of social, political and intellectual life in general' is valid only for a firmly structured society with highly developed material production."[1][2] It follows, therefore, that only in primitive societies can we begin to understand the full potential of the generic-symbolic capacities of men.

The extreme division of labor, which dissociates man from himself, the reduction of persons to limited functions situated in classes, and the splitting of the cultural universe into antagonistic economic, social and ideological sectors, are, first of all, real events, and only then do they become analytic categories. Marx emphasized that he was describing, not fantasizing history. He was not an *a priori* builder. Nor can Marxism be turned into a theory of material limitations; if it can be epitomized at all, it is a theory of social, hence political, constraints on material possibilities. It is therefore dialectic in method and must be distinguished from all types of reductive materialism or technological determinism.

Put another way, Marx recognized the disjunction between available technology and the maximum social use of technology in civilization, as well as the competing economic interests generated by that state of affairs. That is, Marxism is based on the social process of exploitation in terms of class conflict, and the question of class consciousness becomes the critical political question. Therefore, Marxists view conventional politics as a screen for economic interests, and the economic factor as relatively invariant over the long term. But as Supek points out, "Marx, in fact, does not mean that the method of material production conditions the contents but 'the process' of social, political and intellectual life."[1][3]

Marxists do not, for example, "reduce" art when they seek to relate the esthetic process to social and economic constraints; nor do they deny that the artist may "rise above his time." As dialecticians, it would indeed be awkward for them to deny that. The Marxist point is that art is not merely an epiphenomenon on an economic base, but a creation which reflects its social limitations, although it can be, like religion or revolutionary theory, symbolically transcendent. Nonetheless, only when men *act* politically, not only through esthetic and religious symbols, to change the economic basis of their lives in accord with their "truly human" interests, can they begin to make history. It is at this juncture that the analytic categories of Marxism, derived from the actual history of civilization, are avowedly negated by its goal, a classless communitarian society. For it is anticipated that in such a society labor will become socially reintegrated, and economic exploitation will disappear, along with the primacy of economic interests. Hence, class conflicts will no longer serve as the motivating force in history. In projected communist societies, with the reintegration of labor, the person can be redefined as a unified esthetic, rational, sensuous being. Analogously, where economic, social and ideological sectors of culture have been reintegrated, causal analyses, which arise as a result of intolerable disjunctions, such as that between mental and manual labor, become irrelevant. Thus, analytic objectifying social science will lose its foundation and its function. Even historical materialism was not conceived as a contribution to academic social science. It was supposed to sharpen its wits in praxis and lose itself in revolutionary success.

In this emphasis on praxis, Marx is very close to Rousseau, who had stated, "Man is not made to meditate, but to act." Of course, Rousseau's meditations were, in their relentless, pertinent self-examination, *acts*. For Rousseau, as has been said, "Theory and practice, thought and life, the abstract and the concrete [can not be divorced]." Moreover, in propounding a theory of society most in accord with the possibilities of human nature, the *natural society*, to which he imagined all history was tending, Marx extends and completes the tradition of Rousseau. If Rousseau is the paradigmatic thinker of the eighteenth century ("With Rousseau," asserts Goethe, "a new world begins"), Marx plays that role in the nineteenth. He is the Rousseau of the post-revolutionary period of bourgeois class consolidation, but he also conceived himself as living in a revolutionary interim. He had absorbed most of what was useful in the evolutionary theories of his time. He lived at a time in which Rousseau's (or for that matter Herder's) worst intimations of the future had been realized.

It is hard to conceive a Marx without a Rousseau; between them, they constructed an astonishing critique of the origins and fate of the modern consciousness. They were both familiar with the paradoxes of history, and they represent a critical tradition which binds their centuries together. Yet, their differences reveal the discontinuities between the two periods. Marx was basically committed to Europe; he faced the juggernaut squarely, and he imagined it transformed through its structural contradictions, understood and acted on politically. Europe was the key to the future, and for most of his life he seemed convinced that progress, despite the proliferation of new problems, was a historical reality. Progress was no longer just an eighteenth-century projection; it was for Marx and Engels also a realization. Rousseau on the other hand was from the beginning alive to the human possibilities that he sensed in the primitive cultures Europeans had been systematically destroying for the sake of progress and profit. Rousseau believed in the perfectability of man, but he was profoundly skeptical of the European argument for progress.

The categories of Marxism, then, delineate the realm of alienated history. They are not intended to reveal the details of a liberated, classless society but only to outline its general character and, of course, pronounce on its necessity and desirability. It follows that Marxism provides us with the impulse but not the means for understanding the primitive, classless (gentile) cultures of the past. Marx and Engels both borrowed from and converged to Morgan on that score, but their purpose was to chart the prehistoric evolution of society toward the state. Primitive cultures were for them the ground of all future historical movement. Moreover, Marx indicated that they served as the paradigm for the idea of socialism; socialism would achieve "that which men had always dreamed about," Marx believed.[16] But primitive cultures were not to be approached on their own terms, although Engels could be euphoric on the subject.*

---

* What splendid men and women were produced by such a society! All white people who have come into contact with unspoiled Indians [admire] the

Nonetheless, it would seem that nineteenth-century progressivism inhibited Marx and Engels from a further inquiry into the actual conditions of primitive culture. Marxism did not generate an ethnology but a critical and revolutionary analysis of civilization, particularly of modern capitalism, based on the fundamental questions asked of their own time and place. An ethnology in the tradition of Marx and Rousseau *is* possible, but it would have to be based on the converse of the Marxist analytic and critical categories, since it deals with societies that are the converse of civilization (and so, of course would owe much to Marx). Only in this way could one generate interpretive, comparative, historically self-critical descriptions of primitive cultures. Anthropology is impoverished to the degree that it does not explicitly center on such questions as the following (which were, of course, anticipated in the eighteenth century):

---

personal dignity, uprightness, strength of character and courage of these barbarians.

We have seen examples of this courage quite recently in Africa. The Zulus a few years ago and the Nubians a few months ago—both of them tribes in which gentile institutions have not yet died out—did what no European army can do. Armed only with lances and spears, without firearms, under a hail of bullets from the breech-loaders of the English infantry—acknowledged the best in the world at fighting in close order—they advanced right up to the bayonets and more than once threw the lines into disorder and even broke them, in spite of the enormous inequality of weapons and in spite of the fact that they have no military service and know nothing of the drill. Their powers of endurance and performance are shown by the complaint of the English that a Kaffir travels farther and faster in twenty-four hours than a horse. His smallest muscle stands out hard and firm like whipcord, says an English painter. That is what men and society were before the division into classes. And when we compare their position with that of the overwhelming majority of civilized men today, an enormous gulf separates the present-day proletarian and small peasant from the free member of the old gentile society. ... However impressive the people of this epoch appear to us, they are still attached to the navel string of the primitive community. The power of this primitive community [had to be] broken. But it was broken by influences which from the very start appear as a degradation, a fall from the simple moral greatness of the old gentile society. The lowest interests—base greed, brutal appetites, sordid avarice, selfish robbery of the common wealth—inaugurate the new, civilized class society. It is by the vilest means—theft, violence, fraud, treason—that the old classless gentile society is undermined and over-thrown. And the new society itself, during all the two and a half thousand years of its existence, has never been anything else but the development of the small minority at the expense of the great, exploited and oppressed majority; today it is so more than ever before."[17]

What is the quality of social life and individual consciousness in a primitive culture in which:

—there is a predominantly natural division of labor, the person engages in a variety of tasks, and no significant disparity between mental and manual labor exists;

—neither classes, class conflicts, nor exploitative political structures exist;

—social contradictions are minimized or resolved and existential contradictions are celebrated and socially experienced;

—the available technology is maximally utilized for human needs, that is, man commands the means of production;

—technology has developed in an empirical but nonscientific context and is embedded in ritual relations;

—kinship, rather than object relations, define and link society and nature; and

—the idea of *social* progress does not exist?

What is the range of definitions of human nature?

What is the character of violence and what are the social occasions for violence?

What are the goals and means of education (learning) in the absence of formal schooling?

In short, what is concretely meant by the claim that our sense of primitive communal societies is the archetype for socialism?

An anthropology rooted in the manifold implications of such questions shares the eighteenth-century vision of the human potential. It is important to realize, following Hobsbawm, that there is a precedent in Marx.

It is certain that Marx's own historical interests after the publication of *Capital* (around 1867) were overwhelmingly concerned with [primitive communalism; and, further, a reason for] Marx's increasing preoccupation with primitive communalism [was] his growing hatred and contempt for capitalist society.... It seems probable that he, who had earlier welcomed the impact of Western capitalism as an inhuman but historically progressive force on stagnant precapitalist economies, found himself increasingly appalled by this inhumanity. We know that he had always admired the positive social values embodied, in however backward a form, in the primitive community, and it is certain that after

1857-8 . . . he increasingly stressed the viability of the primitive commune, its powers of resistance to historical disintegration and even—though perhaps only in the context of the Narodniki—discussed its capacity to develop into a higher form of economy without prior destruction.[18]

But this is not to say that the result was a systematic ethnology. It does, however, imply that the primitive-civilized paradigm central to the eighteenth century increasingly commanded the attention of Marx, who, in this sense also, extends and completes the tradition of Rousseau.

TWENTIETH-CENTURY PROFESSIONALISM

The ethnocentric and abstract progressivism of the nineteenth century preadapts anthropology for the uses to which it is put in the twentieth century, the period in which the study of man becomes rationalized as an academic discipline and *as a way of life for anthropologists*. Amateurism evaporates; the tradition of Rousseau and Marx is not furthered but is either misunderstood or abandoned; and the study of man lends itself to the manipulation of peoples in the very course of observing them. This is the case not only politically but intellectually. Significant questions are trivialized and trivial questions made to appear significant in the struggle for professional position and academic reward.

At the same time, relativism emerges as the dominant theme in twentieth-century anthropology and seeks to redress nineteenth-century ethnocentrism with specific reference to the allied notions of progress and the presumed inferiority of primitive people. One finds that evolutionists can be relativists; social anthropologists associated with the British colonial office can be relativists; empiricists can be relativists; and so on. Relativism is at its best a liberal response to, and a "humane" mediation of, whatever society seems viable in the eye or imagination of the anthropologist. But at its worst relativism proves popular not only because of its corrective role in the profession of anthropology; it is in accord with the spirit of the time, a perspective congenial in an imperial civilization convinced of its power. Every primitive or archaic culture is conceived as a human possibility that can be "tested"; it is, after all, harmless. We at our leisure convert the experience of other cultures into a kind of sport, just as Veblen's modern hunter mimics and trivializes what was once a way of life. Relativism is the bad faith of the conquerer, who has become secure enough to become a tourist.

Academic relativism knits together anthropologists of diverse schools. Boas and those whom he trained, for example, established (and it is a brilliant achievement) that there are no inferior cultures, races or languages; and correlatively, that races, languages and cultures are historically not functionally related. They strived to appreciate and understand cultural diversity.

But this twentieth-century abreaction is caught in contradictions from which it cannot escape. Cultural relativism is a purely intellectual attitude; it does not inhibit the anthropologist from participating as a professional in his own milieu; on the contrary, it rationalizes that milieu. Relativism is self-critical only in the abstract. Nor does it lead to engagement. It only converts the anthropologist into a shadowy figure, prone to newsworthy and shallow pronouncements about the cosmic condition of the human race. It has the effect of mystifying the profession, so that the very term *anthropologist* ("student of man") commands the attention of an increasingly "popular" audience in search of novelty. But the search for self-knowledge, which Montaigne was the first to link to the annihilation of prejudice, is reduced to the experience of culture shock, a phrase used by both anthropologists and the State Department to account for the disorientation that usually follows an encounter with an alien way of life. But culture shock is a condition that one recovers from; it is not experienced as an authentic redefinition of the personality but as a testing of its tolerance. These experiences have also been compared to psychotherapeutic encounters, in that the career of the anthropologist and the integrity of his professional function are clinically examined. The tendency of relativism, which it never quite achieves, is to detach the anthropologist from all particular cultures. Nor does it provide him with a moral center, only a job.

One is tempted to say that relativism puts the soul of the anthropologist in jeopardy. But the relativistic stance is usually demystified in practice, and the anthropologist discovers that he is a middle-class Episcopalian Anglo-American or a second generation urban American Jew, whose cultural identity reasserts itself along with his prejudices. It is at this recurring point that relativism is reduced to a professional posture, the bedside manner of the anthropologist, and is divorced from his actual life.

As cultural relativism becomes thoroughly objectified and professionally self-conscious, it passes into scientific relativism and seeks to rid itself of all purposes extraneous to the detached scientific examination of cultural mechanisms. Self-knowledge, engagement, the involvement of the anthropologist in any activity other than his profession, are potential contaminations. The cycle is completed: participation in all cultures finally appears and is scientifically justified as equivalent to participation in none. This is assumed to be the key to an understanding of the human situation. And it is here that Lévi-Strauss emerges as the anthropologist of his time.*

But the avoidance of the implications of the Rousseauean and Marxist tradition does not work. Reductive materialism, the formal appreciation of primitive cultures, the collapse of the historical sense, the refusal to put one's society in a critical perspective, lead only to academism—and, in reality, convert the anthropologist into an instrument of that imperial civilization which his calling originally set in question.

THE CRITICAL METHOD

How, then, can anthropology be reconstituted? Intellectually, this is not as formidable a task as it sounds. The problem is one of reformulation rather than discovery or invention. Nor is it primarily a question of devising new methods or fancy ideas. We begin with the primitive-civilized dichotomy. If one examines the methods and conclusions of Rousseau, it is possible to understand the ground of this fruitful ethnological habit.

Rousseau was concerned with two complementary tasks. On the

---

* One can understand why Paul Radin alone, among the anthropologists of his generation, insisted that the only acceptable ethnology is the life history, self told, by members of indigenous society. Radin defined this as both the method and the theory of ethnology which had, eventually, to be assimilated to history, and in that perspective he severely criticized the Boas school, especially Mead and Benedict. Radin's view is necessarily incomplete (he himself asked critical questions of the data throughout his career); but what is more pertinent is that his view was exactly the reverse of the objectifying trend. He spotted it and tried to combat it early on.[19]

one hand, he was engaged in a journey to the center of the species in order to understand the "natural" precivilized man as a human possibility. He situated that possibility in prehistory and viewed certain realities in modern civilization, with which we have become all too familiar, as a threat to its further realization. On the other hand, he was engaged in a journey to the center of his own civilized being. The first task was historical, the second personal; and they are, of course, related. With the former, he projected a model of primitive society, incorporating limited data, in quite the way contemporary anthropologists do. He called, as did the later Marx, for a much wider exploration of the lives of primitive people than had hitherto been possible in order to discover "the real foundations of human society." He was fully aware of the difficulties involved: "it is no light undertaking to separate what is original from what is artificial in the nature of man. And to know correctly a state which no longer exists, which perhaps never existed, which probably never will exist, and about which it is nevertheless necessary to have precise notions in order to judge our present state correctly."[20] What are we to make of this typical Rousseauan paradox?

Rousseau is here laying down the foundation for a normative and comparative mode. At the same time, he views all the information available to him in the perspective of the civilized predicament, about which he has incontestable data and in which he himself is a datum but not a passive vehicle. He has no illusions about the possibility of a perfectly objective portrait of primitive man, because he clearly recognizes that that portrait must be both the result of his own questions and his own introspection. Although Cassirer, among others, is disturbed by the apparent disparity between Rousseau's recourse to data, and the projection of a qualitative model, this turns out to be no less than the inevitable method of anthropology.

Rousseau, then, utilizes data and at the same time constructs a model based on the logical and historical opposition between himself as a prototype of modern man and the primitive peoples with whom he is concerned. Need it be repeated that he never uses the expression "noble savage"? Along with Morgan and Marx he sees the deep past as prologue; nor did he ever suggest or imagine the possibility of turning back history. The latter was a deduction, as he put it, in the manner of his adversaries—which he anticipated (rather than let them have the "shame of drawing it")—and demolished. His impulse to understand primitive people is the other side of the impulse to understand the largely inexperienced but imagined possibilities of himself as a civilized person. This attempted synthesis, which embraces data, a model and introspection that clarifies further what one is observing, is the first and among the last lucid expressions of what anthropologists do or should do.

Although Rousseau established the primitive-civilized paradigm in modern anthropology, he did not invent it. Its history is rooted in the history of civilization, but tracing it would be an exercise in an almost infinite regression. One would eventually arrive at that hypothetical point where man in civilization asks the question—in whatever symbolic form—who am I? And since contrast is the only mode of seeing, man must conceive of himself in relation to what he assumes himself to have been and to what he one day hopes to become.

The second aspect of Rousseau's understanding is evident in his *Confessions*. They are among the most enduring revelations of a fully conscious modern man. Perhaps the first modern man, Rousseau strips himself to the bone. And once again he is less interested in the precise sequence of events than in their meaning. He is not a diarist. When his critics accuse him of misrepresentation, they misunderstand the convoluted problems of memory and construction of self, the question of truth that transcends the presentation of facts. Any confession, like any attempts at ethnology, has to be a fiction, a constitution of reality.

Interestingly enough among social scientists, "confessions" that describe the confrontation with the people being studied seem peculiar to anthropologists. Anthropologists, despite their professional protestations, seem concerned with ultimate questions about the nature of men.

Thus, they have always generalized about primitive peoples. The problem is to ask questions of these people and of ourselves of the type that I have tried to outline. Such questions are not new; but by making them central, we change the ethnological focus. It is not even a question of further field work but of reflection and synthesis. The data is voluminous, the ground for working toward conclusions exists. How many anthropologists have generalized about primitive peoples—Boas, Kroeber, Lowie, Radin—and how consistently, on the basis of restricted information?

Lowie is typical: "The Eskimo (and most other primitive peoples) generously share what food and shelter are available .... "[21] How may one take that statement apart? What is meant by *generously*? What are the penalties for not acting that way? How does Lowie know that most other primitive peoples behave in the same way? What does the ethnographer mean by *primitive*? And so on. Such questions are valid and more or less answerable. But the answers do not explode the paradigm, they help define it further. Lowie's statement remains accurate, if imprecise—but not trivial—for in contrast to ourselves most primitive peoples share the necessities of life. And that becomes one of the definitions of the primitive experience. One must note that Lowie's orthodox field work was limited to North American Indians, notably the Crow of the Plains, who had long since been confined, as he himself states, to reservations when the anthropologist appeared among them. Obviously, no anthropologist has worked in more than two or three primitive societies. In short, anthropologists are in the habit of referring to the primitive modalities of existence in terms of their own immediate experiences; and their familiar references to "my people," are symptomatic. But "my people" is also a proprietory expression, implying an invention, in which the anthropologist unwittingly includes himself.

This historical construction is not, nor can it be, based upon so-called rigorous examination of the full range of empirical data. The notion that data can somehow independently exist without a paradigm, even if unconscious, is obviously an illusion; such data would be no more than a catalogue of random observations. Goethe put the matter succinctly: "The highest wisdom would be to understand that every fact is already theory." The historical intuition (for the theoretical construction must also be an intuition) comes out of an inherited paradigm that is constantly renewed in the reflections of civilized men.

THE CRITICAL ALTERNATIVE

The political reconstitution, as against the intellectual reformulation of anthropology, is more complex, because it requires not only reflection and synthesis but a different kind of work in the world. We are living in a period of unprecedented destruction of languages, cultures and nations under the assault of highly centralized bureaucratic states. Culture, the creation of shared meanings, symbolic interaction, is dissolving into a social mechanism, directed by signals. This, of course, accounts for the rebellion of the young against functional rationality and their search for some kind of meaning, a rebellion which need not be overt; and often looks like cynicism, conformity, apathy.

Clearly, the study of man can reconstitute itself only in the struggle against the conversion of men into objects, in our own society and elsewhere. Anthropologists who recognize this may now decide to turn to the arena in which most men, notably peasants and primitives, the conventional objects of study, are recreating themselves as subjects in the revolutionary dramas of our time. In accordance with their competence, these anthropologists are likely to declare themselves partisans in the movements for national liberation (the nation being the basis for culture) and social reconstruction (which begins with socialism, the name for the ancient and persistent paradigm for the rights and possibilities of man). If field work remains possible for them, it will not be in the pursuit of their careers but independently, as amateurs, in order to learn, not to "examine," in dynamic and possibly revolutionary circumstances.

But since when has anthropology been comfortable in the academy? And since when have academic concentrations of intellectuals accomplished what they pretend? As the recent Yale University Study Commission on Governance put it: "Considering how overwhelming a proportion of intellectuals are gathered in universities, it has always been puzzling why so few great intellectual achievements spring from them." Moreover, "there [is] 'a great deal of truth' in the allegations of radical critics that universities are class institutions with complacent and self-indulgent faculties that forget to ask fundamental questions."[2 2]

Those anthropologists who choose to reformulate the questions of Rousseau and Marx can at least be sure that the study of man is not an end in itself; it will be negated in the knowledge of men.

4

THE SEARCH
FOR THE PRIMITIVE

As soon as a man appears who brings something of the primitive along with him, so that he doesn't say, "you must take the world as you find it," but rather "let the world be what it likes, I take my stand on a primitiveness which I have no intention of changing to meet with the approval of the world," at that moment, as these words are heard, a metamorphosis takes place in the whole of nature. Just as in a fairy story, when the right word is pronounced, the castle that has been lying under a spell for a hundred years opens and everything comes to life, in the same way existence becomes all attention. The angels have something to do, and watch curiously to see what will come of it, because that is their business. On the other side, dark, uncanny demons, who have been sitting around doing nothing and chewing at their nails for a long time, jump up and stretch their limbs, because, they say, here is something for us, and so on.

—Kierkegaard

This thing we call "civilization"—all these physical and moral comforts, all these conveniences, all these shelters, . . . constitute a repertory or system of securities which man made for himself like a raft in the initial shipwreck which living always is—all these securities are insecure securities which in the twinkling of an eye, at the least carelessness, escape from man's hands and vanish like phantoms. History tells us of innumerable retrogressions. . . . But nothing tell us that there is no possibility of much more basic retrogressions than any so far known, including the most basic of them all: the total disappearance of man as man and his silent return to the animal scale, to complete and definitive absorption in the other.

No small part of the anguish which is today tormenting the soul of the West derives from the fact that during the past century—and perhaps for the first time in history—man reached the point of believing himself secure. Because the truth is that the one and only thing he succeeded in doing was to feel and create the pharmaceutical Monsieur Homais, the net result of progressivism! The progressivist idea consists in affirming not only that humanity—an abstract, irresponsible, non-existent entity invented for the occasion—that humanity progresses, which is certain, but furthermore that it progresses necessarily. This idea anaesthetized the European and the American to that basic feeling of risk which is the substance of man. . . . Human history thus loses all the sinew of drama and is reduced to a peaceful tourist trip, organized by some transcendent "Cook's". . . . This security is what we are now paying for.

—Ortega y Gasset

The Pandora's Box which I propose to reopen is vast, complex and many-chambered. The problems it contains range from the historiographical to the theological and technological, but I am going to state the case as simply and strongly, indeed as naïvely, as I can.

It may seem surprising that anthropologists cannot agree on a definition of *primitive*. After all, we have more or less systematically studied peoples characterized in that way for at least a century. A few anthropologists even deny the existence of special emphases in native cultures which might, in turn, justify the concept *primitive*. This should not put us off; it is a common fashion in our hyperanalytic age. Physicists, for example, are not at all certain about the attributes of atoms, not to mention the lesser particles, which no human eye has ever observed directly; they seem infinitely divisible and complex, they appear in a variety of states, and it is hard to determine where they begin or end. Yet the atom continues to exist as a conceptual model, as a shorthand way of organizing confusing and inaccessible data. The concept is operative, even if a few hyperpositivistic physicists would deny its descriptive validity. With appropriate modifications, we might similarly describe the relationship of biologist to cells, the geneticist to genes.

The point is that this ambiguity is not the result of too little information or not enough quantifiable science. It arises, rather, from a fashionable mode of looking at the world, a way we have of disorganizing, or disintegrating, our data. One is reminded of the tale told of the aging physicist, who could not walk across a room for fear of falling through the enormous distances that he knew existed between the microcosmic particles that composed his environment—if, I should add, particles they were. This hyperanalytic attitude would seem to be, more than anything else, a reflection of the minute division of labor demanded by our contemporary industrial society, of certain cultural assumptions and of the equation of science to the machine. It is the very opposite of the primitive view, which is synthetic or holistic—but I shall deal with this more fully below.

Here it is enough to suggest that our hesitation in defining "primitive" is paralleled in most other disciplines with reference to their major subject matters. It is not a function of ignorance but of a scientific style, which has grown unreasonably opposed to the idea of fundamental assumptions, of synthesis and of conceptual models, important as such skepticism may be. Still, any human discipline or any science that shrinks from epistemology and "metaphysics" (in Collingwood's sense, the science of first assumptions) reduces itself finally to mere mindless technique.

THE CRITICAL TERM

Primitive is, I believe, the critical term in anthropology, the word around which the field revolves, yet it remains elusive, connoting but never quite denoting a series of related social, political, economic, spiritual and psychiatric meanings. That is, *primitive* implies a certain level of history, and a certain mode of cultural being which in this essay I shall make a further attempt to formulate.

This mode of cultural being is continuously obliterated or attenuated by the processes of civilization and more radically so than we are usually able or willing to acknowledge; as a result, the image of an identifiable, cross-cultural, pre-civilized and, yes, a priori human possibility has practically disappeared from our conceptual lexicon. Unyielding cultural relativism, cultural determinism and social scientism are, in part and each in its own way, rationalizations of a civilization that has forgotten what questions to ask of itself. These attitudes have helped blunt the sense of universal human need, conflict and fulfillment which has been most adequately expressed, in the past, through art and religion. It is, I believe, a singular task of anthropology, no matter what its practitioners call themselves, to assist in the reformulation of pertinent life-preserving questions.

The search for the primitive is the attempt to define a primary human potential. Without such a model (or, since we are dealing with men and not things, without such a vision), it becomes increasingly difficult to evaluate or understand our contemporary pathology and possibilities. For instance, without an anthropology bent on rediscovering the nature of human nature, the science of medicine may survive, but the art of healing will wither away. For healing flows from insight into primary, "pre-civilized" human processes; it presumes a knowledge of the primitive, a sense of the minimally human, a sense of what is essential to being human.

In order to understand ourselves and heal ourselves in this age of abstract horror, we must regain the sense of the totality and the immediacy of human experience. In order to determine where we are, we must learn, syllable by syllable, where we have been. The sense of history is for a society in crisis what relentless self-searching, psychoanalytic or otherwise, is for the individual in crisis—it is releasing and enriching, cathartic and creative, and it may be the only thing that saves our lives. History implies exhortation, because it is confession, failure and triumph. It is the measure of our capacity, the link between man and man, the key to ourselves. The lack of a sense of history, or the mechanistic view of it as immutable and inevitable, is the death of man. The only inevitable, literally unavoidable, events are, accidents and certain categories of natural phenomena which, in the human perspective, have the fatality of accidents.

Yet, the "post-historic" creature, necessarily congealed in a bureau and reduced to a function, is a common enough plotting of the future.[1] This image of the human termites of tomorrow, each exuding its specialized bit of culture to what is conceived as an infinitely rich and almost palpable social whole, used to be one of Kroeber's favorite predictions, which he based on Wheeler's work with insects and his own attitudes toward men.[2] All those who assimilate human history to natural history, or mechanize it, help dull the sense of history and prevent men from confronting themselves. The penalty we pay for blunting the historical sense is dissociation, both social and individual; the tripping of the fuse on the bomb will under such conditions become only the ultimate incident in the course of a chronic cultural illness—something abstract that we nevertheless do.

"When we contemplate the past, that is history," Hegel said, "the first thing we see is nothing but—ruins." Out of these ruins of civilization, we must win through to a whole but concrete vision of man. Every thinker of consequence from the beginning of the industrial revolution to the present has, in one way or another, warned us of this necessity. Darwin, Freud, Marx, Einstein, L.H. Morgan, Tylor, Henry Adams, Paul Tillich, Boas, Kierkegaard, Sartre have urged us to a vision of the responsibility and autonomy of man. Modern anthropology itself germinated in a search for the historical contrast to our own intolerable condition, in a search, that is, for the primitive. It was, no doubt, an expression of remorse for the ideological and technical conquest of the planet by western Europeans, themselves restive in a culture they had learned to wield as a weapon. It follows that the anthropologist has been the disengaged man *par excellence*, dissatisfied at home and questing abroad. He is a scout sent out by a civilization in turmoil to find a resting place and learn the lay of the land. He is a type of domesticated Ulysses, Joycean, not Homeric.

Modern anthropology is the search for man in history, undertaken by a society threatened with automatism. In broader perspective, anthropology may be said to begin with civilization, certainly with the Greeks, and perhaps with the Babylonians, the Egyptians, the ancient East Indians or the Chinese. It would be instructive to study the records of the latter four civilizations in order to determine how far anthropology had advanced among them and what forms it took. Wherever civilization arises, the primitive in man is subordinated; it withers away, grows attenuated or is replaced. Thus the puzzled search for what is diminished, the search for different ways of being human, for the primitive (which is anthropology) begins. Even Plato, who was probably the most beneficently civilized man in history, pays tribute, in the beginning of *The Republic* to the satisfactions of his bucolic version of primitive life, which he feels plausibly constrained to replace by his towering and totally civilized Utopia. Plato understood that civilized man cannot know what has been gained until he learns what has been lost.

Plato spent his life trying to define and create a model of civilized man in civilized society. All of his work is a kind of anthropology of civilization, a vast exploration of political society. It should interest us that it ends on a note of despair. For in *The Laws* Plato is no longer struggling to grasp, *to create*, civilization as part of an expanding human consciousness; his final social statement is frankly repressive and pragmatic, and prophecy becomes mere prediction. In *The Laws*, human nature has become the enemy, and we recognize civilization. Freud, had he permitted himself the luxury of philosophizing, would have analyzed the Plato of *The Laws* perfectly, just as Plato, had he acknowledged the primal necessity of *poiesis*, of ritual, would have been able to penetrate more deeply into the nature of that primitive, actually rustic, life which he nostalgically abandons in favor of the ideal state. Yet in *The Republic*, in contrast to *The Laws*, whether we like it or not, we are caught by a vision of man finding himself in civilization, although in ways that are hardly viable since they exclude, rather than incorporate, the primitive.

If Plato concerned himself with the problems of civilization, ranging from the esthetic to the technical and legal, at a time when civilization in Greece had become an insoluble problem, other philosophers, writers, travelers and historians have been more deeply concerned with uncivilized people. Their descriptions vary immensely, and many are clearly projective or otherwise distorted, but what runs through them all, whether drawn by Herodotus or Tacitus, Ovid, Seneca, or Horace, Columbus or Camöens, Montaigne or Gide, Rousseau or Monboddo, de Bougainville, or Melville or Conrad, is the sense of contrast.* Civilized men are

---

* It is hardly necessary to note that this problem of contrast is an explicit, major theme in the work of many modern students of society, e.g., Redfield, Radin, Sapir, Tylor, Boas, Maine, Maitland, Morgan, Marx, Engels, Tönnies, Freud, Fromm, Weber, Durkheim, Mauss—and a minor theme in Kroeber, Linton, Benedict, Fortes and a host of others.

here confronting what they presume to be primordial; they are saying, "this is the way we were before we became what we are, this is the other side of our humanity." That is the anthropological statement, and it will always remain the anthropological question.

Paradoxically, as civilization increases in depth and scope, anthropology proliferates, but it becomes increasingly professionalized. The urgency of the central question is lost sight of; it is even denied and the question is repressed *because* of its urgency and the risks we must undergo in attempting to answer it. The very circumstance, then, that leads to the deepening need for the anthropological search, that is, the expansion of civilization, also converts anthropology into a narrow discipline with mechanical techniques and trivial goals. It may even come to pass that the central question—what part of our humanity we have lost and how and why we have lost it and how and in what form we may regain it—will cease to be of concern to anthropology. Perhaps significant statements about man will no longer be made by anthropologists, just as most sociologists no longer say anything very compelling about society, or political scientists about politics, economists about economics, and so on, precisely because these fields, reflecting the larger division of labor in our culture and its increasingly analytic attitudes, have grown further and further apart. But man cannot be subdivided endlessly; the most critical tissues escape the scalpel; it is the entire organism which must be studied. Correlatively, history cannot be quantified.

In the beginning, bureaucracies counted—people, goods, land— in order to muster, levy and control, *to record those facts* which became the basis for civil imposition.[3] It follows that in the logic of history, a bureaucratized discipline is first and foremost a quantifying one. Later, quantification becomes an end in itself, not just, a problematic and limited means, as it always is in the human sciences. The principle of evaluation is absorbed into, or subordinated by, this numbers game—an abstract ploy of counters that avoids policy, principle and meaning by presuming to rise above them. The new pedantry is the pedantry of the machine.

Anthropology is becoming too civilized, too abstract, too bureaucratized. It is being transformed into just another specialized exercise, a symptom of our civilization, congruent with it rather than antithetical to it. The latter is its true patrimony, and it should be a vocation of anthropologists to make this truth known.

My contention, then, is that the term *primitive* has content in anthropology and that the attempt to explore its implications remains our central task, precisely because we are so civilized and so in need of a deeper vision of man. It is in this way that anthropology can become a revolutionary discipline, though it may often seem the most remote and eccentric of inquiries.

THE WORD ITSELF

It is generally agreed that the English word *primitive* is a direct adaptation of the medieval-modern French form *primitive*, which is the feminine of *primitif*. The only change, apart from the shift in accent from the last to the first syllable, is the shortening of the final *i* in English. The first documented appearance of the word in English is in a Middle English tract on surgery, *circa* 1400, where it is spelled *prymytiff* and has the meaning "primary" or "original" (*causes prymytiff*), a denotation which it has retained through its history. Another very early usage appears in a statement of Henry VII at York, *circa* 1486, containing the phrase "primative patrone." Here *primative* implies "earliest," "original" and "primary," not only in time but in rank. The *a* in *primative* may reflect a dialectic variation or, what is more likely, it may be derived from the old French *primat*, which meant a leading dignitary in the Church. It is of some interest to note that the dual meaning of contemporary word *primate* ("a ruling ecclesiastical figure" and a "biological order comprising lemurs, tarsiers, monkeys, apes, and men") has its origin in the feedback between two lines of descent from the original Latin term, *primus*, one denoting rank, the other temporal order.

The first modern spelling of the word (the adoption of the French feminine form), seems to have appeared in the title of a book published in 1581—*Positions wherein those Primitive Circumstances be Examined which are Necessarie for the Training up of Children*. As an anthropologist, I find this a particularly congenial text. Here primitive has the sense of "primary," with the added nuance of "basic."

The French *primitif* is derived from the medieval Latin *primitivus* (*primus* = first + *ivus*, a later adjectival ending), meaning earliest or oldest. *Primitivus* was originally used in postclassical Latin as a grammatical term to indicate archaic words (*verba primitiva*). It was not until the medieval period that *primitivus* gradually came to mean "primary," "earliest" or "oldest." Actually, it does not appear in English and Irish Church texts until the twelfth century, when it began to supplant *pristinus* and *priscus*.

Primitivus can be ultimately traced back to classical Latin *primus*, through the derivative adverb *primitus* ("in the first place"), and the cognate adjective *primituus*. *Primus*, of course, means "first" or "earliest" and is the superlative corresponding to the Latin comparative *prior* ("earlier"). *Primus* is, moreover, related to *pristinus*, ("existing in, or as if in, its first state") and to which *priscus*, synonymous with *pristinus* except that the thing represented no longer exists; both words were eventually replaced by *primitive*, as indicated. Their denotations were purely temporal, reflecting Cicero's use of *cascus* ("old" or "ancient"), a cognate of *priscus* when referring to time past. Lucretius, it may be noted, is even more diffident; in *De Rerum Natura*, he simply adopts such constructions as *tunc* ("then"), and *nunc* ("now").

The classical Latin forms are probably based on the Homeric adverb and Attic preposition and conjunction *prin*, which means "before." This, in turn, derives from the presumptive proto-Indo-European root *pri*, which also has the sense of "before." In Latin, therefore, the prefixes *prim, prin,* and *pris* are extensions of the proto-Indo-European *pri*. A cognate prefix *pra* exists in Sanskrit (in Doric Greek also); in the former language the words *prakkalina* and *prathamakalina* mean "belonging to an earlier time," which is very close to the etymological "primitive."

All major European languages except Greek seem to have adopted the word *primitive* from a medieval (Church) Latin source; whether the word was mediated through the medieval-modern French, where it first appeared in the 14th century, is, except in the instance of English, difficult to determine. In Spanish, Italian and Portuguese *primitivo* is the current form; in Romanian (which may have borrowed it directly from postclassical Latin), German, Dutch, Flemish, Danish, Norwegian, Swedish and Hungarian *primitiv* is used; in Latvian—*primitius*; and so on. There is a parallel word in Greek—*protogonos*, meaning "first born," that is, "earliest" or "oldest."

In none of these languages does the term *primitive* have an etymologically pejorative significance. Although all languages associated with civilized polities do seem to have words that etymologically imply the inferiority of other groups, such as the Sanskrit *mlechha*, the Greek *barbaros* and the English *uncivilized*, the word *primitive* lacks this structural implication. Even *savage* does not suggest anything more in its derivation than "living in the woods," that is, "close to nature" (from Latin *siluaticus*, an adjective Latin *silva*). And the word *pagan* is ultimately derived from Latin *pagus*, meaning "village," but originally signifying "a boundary post stuck into the ground." More precisely, the Latin *paganus* descends from *pagus* and means, successively in time, "villager," "peasant," "civilian" and finally "heathen." Thus the evolution of Rome from "a boundary post stuck into the ground," that is, a compact between villages, to the emergence of the Church is symbolized in the history of the word *pagan*. But for most of Roman history before Constantine a pagan was a villager, a peasant and, perhaps, by literal implication, a man of peace (*pax*) in contrast to the civil-military representatives of the state.

Primitive, *pagan* and *savage* are, then, three perfectly respectable words. But *primitive* is the most widely disseminated, in the most recognizable forms, in major languages and has, even today, the least pejorative associations, signifying merely a prior state of affairs, a relative sense of origins. Therefore, I see no reason for abandoning the word, as is periodically suggested, hedging it with quotes, prefacing it with the inexplicit irony of "so-called" or replacing it with limited and misleading expressions such as "pre-literate."* The task is rather to define it further and so help to reach agreement on what *primitive* means.

PRIMITIVE IN TIME AND SPACE

How are we to locate primitive peoples in time and space? In attempting to answer this question, I shall tentatively adopt the

---

* The presence or absence of writing as a criterion of primitiveness is inadequate. The complex, advanced horticultural societies of the Guinea Coast and South America lacked writing, yet they were, as we shall see,

following scheme, based on four very broad phases of development. The first phase extends from the initial appearance of culture in the Lower Paleolithic, some half-million years ago, to approximately 10,000 B.C., roughly the Paleolithic-Neolithic period of transition. This tremendous span comprises, from the standpoint of succeeding phases, the phase of *cultural origins*. Whatever information is available rests on rather slender archeological evidence. We know next to nothing concerning the origins or then extant forms of language, social organization, religion and so forth; most of the formative, nonmaterial aspects of culture remain inaccessible to us. The study of contemporary primitive peoples sheds no clear light on these matters; such inquiries give us no insight into the dawn of human consciousness for we make suppositions based on material—including esthetic—artifacts, assuming always that our knowledge of contemporary pre-civilized groups is applicable, and then, of course, the argument becomes a tautology. What I mean to say is that the anthropological term *primitive* applies, or should apply, to the condition of man prior to the emergence of civilization and following those earliest periods of cultural growth culminating in the Upper Paleolithic. However, the typical institutions of primitive peoples, which I shall discuss below, have long established histories; so far as I am aware, we have never witnessed, nor have we a record of, the ultimate origins of these institutions.

The second phase begins about 9,000 B.C. and lasts until the inception of an archaic form of state organization, or civilization, emerging *circa* 5,000 B.C. in the Middle East, but varying in time

---

archaic *civilizations*. Another difficulty involved in the use of the literate-pre-literate criterion (apart from the prediction inherent in *pre*) is the differential distribution of the trait of literacy within societies that have been classified as literate and therefore nonprimitive. The overwhelming majority of Chinese, for example, have been unable to read and write throughout Chinese history. This is also true of extensive peasant areas in Europe. In contrast, Japan with a peasant society base still largely operative prior to World Warr II is said to have attained the highest literacy rate in the world.

There is no doubt that beyond a certain socio-economic level, literacy is a necessary development in any society; it is essential to the acceleration, accumulation, and increasingly complex fiscal-military controls associated with civilization. The mere existence of writing among a tiny fraction of the populace, as in China before World War II, makes literacy an ambiguous measure. It is, then, the use to which literacy is put and its correlation with society in depth, that converts it into a proper historical diagnostic. The point that literacy is a secondary, not a primary, tool and symptom of civilization.

widely around the world. For example, marginal peoples of the High Nigerian Plateau or interior New Guinea are only now becoming involved in political society. This phase, from the Paleolithic-Neolithic transition to one or another early form of the state, is the germinating period of cultural forms that can be called primitive and is reasonably accessible to anthropological scrutiny and reconstruction. This is the location in time which Levi-Strauss considers primitive, and, as Lovejoy indicates, it is the settled condition which Rousseau sensibly attempted to outline in his *Discourse on the Origins of Inequality*.[4] It is at this juncture, reached at different times at different places, that the historical and contemporary dimensions of the concept *primitive* heuristically coincide in a scientifically acceptable way.

The search for origins cannot effectively be pushed back beyond the Paleolithic-Neolithic transition; even the most peripheral peoples—the Bushmen, Eskimos and probably the Australians—share basic features with so many other native groups that they can hardly be considered representative of an earlier phase of development, and if somehow they are, the differences are not pertinent for the present purpose. *Primitive*, then, refers to widely distributed, well-organized institutions that had already existed just prior to the rise of ancient civilization; it does not imply historically an inchoate time of cultural origins nor psychiatrically the period when supposed primary processes were directly expressed.

But these well-established primitive institutional patterns do not disappear with the emergence of archaic civilizations, the third phase in this provisional scheme, encompassing political societies in the Mediterranean Basin, the Middle East, the Near East and the New World.

These archaic societies embrace people who are primitive, who are in transition from primitive to peasant status or who have been converted into full-fledged peasants, culturally influenced by and economically dependent upon market centers; they are marked by pre-industrial towns whose citizens and slaves discharge commercial, ceremonial, administrative and military functions.*

---

* I should note that I am here avoiding the vexing category *feudal*. In Europe and probably in Japan feudalism, which is primarily a type of political society, followed the dissolution of archaic state systems. In parts of East Africa, for example, Ankole feudal conditions were apparently generated by

Probably most of the world's population still lives in this archaic, apparently exhausted social environment. Certainly the majority of people studied by anthropologists are found within one or another variety of archaic political structure, whether or not that structure has maintained its integrity. In certain cases, the centralizing mechanisms may even have disappeared, but local groups survive and continue to resonate their previous associations, as among Meso-American and Hausa peasants and, in a historic instance, as in medieval Normandy after the disintegration of the Carolingian Empire.[6]

I should re-emphasize that this third cultural phase can develop either prior to, or in the total absence of, agriculture and writing. Advanced horticulturists in West Africa, for example, produced a considerable surplus, which supported a type of organization that included: (1) a complicated system of taxation and conscription; (2) a developing class system; (3) a rudimentary bureaucracy whose primary function was fiscal-military administration of fairly well-defined territories; (4) pragmatically conceived civil laws, which arose, at first, to expedite taxation and conscription; and (5) chiefs or kings who began to wield secular power within an infant political structure which maintained many of the forms, while changing the substance, of the previous primitive institutions. At the same time, these advanced horticultural societies rest on, and indeed can only survive by, drawing their strength from a base which remains genuinely primitive, according to criteria that I shall attempt to indicate below.

The fourth cultural phase is the modern state, that is, contemporary civilization, coincident with the maximal politicization of society. This process began with the mercantile and scientific revolutions and continued through the industrial revolutions in Western Europe; it is now, of course, diffusing rapidly in a variety of forms throughout the world. As maximal political societies advance, primitive and archaic traits crumble within their borders and on their frontiers. Put another way, the primitive characteristics which managed to survive under the surface or in the formal ideological patterns of archaic civilizations and among the most isolated peoples, became casualties to the

---

the subordination of primitive cultivators to warrior herdsmen; this pre-state fuedalism is evident in the varying forms of clientage and land tenure that developed.[5]

total revolution stimulated by the extension of modern civilization.* Authentically primitive and maximally civilized traits are as antithetical as it is possible for cultural attributes to become within the limits of the human condition. This is, however, the present fact of history and it constitutes the problem of this society, for the sickness of civilization consists, I believe, in its failure to incorporate (and only then to move beyond the limits of) the primitive.

PRIMITIVE—A POSITIVE DEFINITION

It follows from the foregoing that there are two direct field opportunities for studying primitive groups. One can either pursue the few remaining peripheral peoples, those uninvolved in any archaic superstructure and reached by only the most superficial of modern civilizing influences; or alternatively, one can study the more remote local groups associated with still existent archaic civilizations, always attempting to distinguish, of course, between primitive and peasant traits.† It is this correlation of the two

---

* As in the instance of reincarnation, which can reasonably be considered a formal, archaic elaboration on ritual death and rebirth among primitives.

† I have been fortunate in having been able to undertake field work among a quite marginal group of horticulturalists, the Anaguta of the Nigerian Middle Belt, and in an archaic society, mountain Arabs on the Israeli-Jordan border. I have also studied a modern and, in a certain sense, a hyper-civilized community: the Israeli-kibbutz. The point is that the average anthropologist probably investigates no more than two or three different societies in the course of his career; reflection and reading fill out his training. Thus, the basis of his generationalizations is always empirically limited. Moreover, our most important generalizations are interpretive, as they must be in any historical discipline concerned with the problem of meaning and not merely with the surface of social facts.

There is no ultimate, contemporary authority in these matters, and it is even doubtful whether further information is necessary. The problem is one of integration and synthesis; yet, as Kierkegaard was perhaps the first to indicate, no total or totally objective system is scientifically possible, because man in history is never complete.[7] When all is said and done, we can only express considered opinions on the most significant matters in anthropology or related fields; their relative wisdom will depend upon the depth and imagination of the observer and on the reality of his commitment; confirmation depends upon what men decide to do in history and even then may be objectively ambiguous, or, what is worse, merely academic. At any rate, it is at least clear that the profounder facts *do not* speak for themselves.

directly available categories of primitive with archeological, including documentary, evidence that results in a generalized conception of primitive life, fusing historical and contemporary information.

This is not to deny the uniqueness or societal individuality of one primitive group vis-á-vis another; indeed, the possibility of differential cultural emphasis seems to be greater, even if subtler, among relatively discrete and self-sustaining primitive societies than among civilized groups. One society may emphasize property displays, another the manufacture of baskets of all shapes and sizes, and so on; each emphasis being the hyper-accentuation of diffused or generic, social, economic, or psychological tendencies, which often have the idiosyncratic character of sport or play. But in contrast with civilization, these distinctions fade as the basic similarities are illuminated, for the variations that do occur are elaborations of those fundamental themes that are the very definition of the primitive; they happen within certain limits, and do not threaten the integrity of the society. Moreover, historical contrasts between primitive societies and maximal civilizations are far more fundamental than: (1) "horizontal" variation among primitive societies employing similar subsistence techniques; and (2) primitive societies employing different subsistence techniques, for example, hunters and gatherers as opposed to simple horticulturalists. The distinctions between the most marginal hunters and a local group in an advanced horticultural society are, of course, significant in many respects, but I am interested here in the substantial similarities that exist, even in such cases.

I will not linger on negative definitions of *primitive*, on what is not primitive in language, religion, magic, art, psychological function and so on. The historical model I hope to induce is just that, a model, a construct, which limits and helps define the range of variations on a level of organization termed *primitive*. Although specific instances and usages are cited, this does not imply their universality insofar as form is concerned. But the functional equivalents of the formal modes specified certainly seem to exist everywhere in the primitive world and certain fundamental attributions of meaning also seem universal among primitives.

But first I wish to repeat that all primitive peoples are marginal to the mainstream of modern history, primarily because of such "accidents" of habitat as removal from the developing centers of civilization. In the sense already noted, contemporary primitives can be roughly conceived as our contemporary, pre-civilized ancestors. Their ten interrelated characteristics, aspects of a prism, are outlined in the following sections.

Communal Economies

Primitive societies rest on a communalistic economic base. This is not to say that everything in such societies is owned in common, which is clearly not the case, but rather that those material means essential to the survival of the individual or the group are either actively held in common or, what is equivalent, constitute readily accessible economic goods. The group can be defined as the customary, cooperative work unit, ranging in size from one or more nuclear families, as among the Eskimo, through the various extensions to the clan or group of clans; or the group can be defined as can be a locality, a village, part-village, or village cluster. In any event, the work unit may shift according to season, purpose and need.

Exceptions to this communal condition dissolve under close scrutiny. For example, it is claimed that members of Hottentot joint families "own" particular cows in the family herd, but we find that they cannot privately dispose of them. It is similarly assumed that individuals "own" particular watering places, but we discover that access is never denied to other people in need of it.[8]

On the other hand, true private property does exist among primitives, in the form of tools made by the individual, breechclouts, back scratchers and similar "extensions of the personality." However, private property of this type does not constitute primitive capitalism; this does not exist, at least among primitives. The private property that can be identified is either not essential for group survival, is readily duplicated by any individual in the society and therefore need not be owned communally, or is of so personal a nature that it cannot be owned communally.

If primitive capitalism is an illusion, the critical question of primitive property has, unfortunately, been obscured by both the partisans and the antagonists of the concept of primitive communism. The partisans too often seemed to be stating that everything in primitive societies is owned in common, including wives and children at one stage, thus conjuring up a false image of an absolute, monolithic, social, economic and psychological collectivism.[9] But their antagonists just as often misconstrued the nature and function of the private or personal property that does exist among primitives. Individuals were said, for example, to "own" incorporeal property—songs, magic spells, curing rituals and so on. This may be true, but it is irrelevant to the economic base of primitive communal society. Moreover, such prerogatives tend to be widely distributed; even where certain of them are concentrated in the hands of shamans or medicine men, they remain readily available to other people, in exchange for goods or services that are by no means scarce. Knowledge of esoteric lore is also widely distributed; any elder is likely to know the details of a particular medicine rite, although its exclusive administration may be the profession and prerogative of certain individuals. But even this preference can be waived in the absence, illness, or death of sanctioned persons. In authentically primitive communities, esoteric lore seems to be more publicly known than we have usually supposed.

There are other ways in which attitudes and social behavior have been confused with basic economic functioning, thus further obscuring the issue of primitive property. For example, primitive societies frequently emphasize competitive games, ceremonies, property displays, property giveaways and so on, but such competition, whether assuming an economic form (as in the Kwakiutl potlatch) or an esthetic form (as in the wonderfully spontaneous and satirical Eskimo songs) does not endanger and is irrelevant to the communal functioning of the economic base. Indeed, this type of competition, even when subserving other functions, can be understood also, in a ritual context. The Eskimo songs, for example, are creative and socially bounded ways of discharging hostilities built up in the ordinary course of daily life; they do not lead us to characterize Eskimo society as competitive in the mercantile and capitalist sense.

Even in the proto-states of East and West Africa, the underlying social units, the joint families or clans, work cooperatively and hold land in common, although a certain portion of the surplus they produce is siphoned off for the support of the rudimentary civil power.

The general point, then, is that primitive societies uniformly possess a communal economic base; economic exploitation of man by man, as we know it in archaic and modern civilizations, is absent. Even where a degree of exploitation develops, as in the proto-states—usually through the payment of tribute or labor service—it rarely results in the economic ruination of one group or individual by another. Thus, we find that in primitive society in the ordinary course of events, no man need go hungry while another eats; production is for use or pleasure rather than for individual profit. Just as primitive society is not competitive in a basic structural sense, it lacks a genuinely acquisitive socio-economic character. In the words of Evans-Pritchard "In general it may be said that no one in a Nuer Village starves unless all are starving."[10] Laurens van der Post spoke to this point as follows: "An old hunter in Africa, the simplest and wisest man I ever knew, once said to me, 'The difference between the white man and the black man in Africa is that the white man 'has' and the black man 'is'."[11]

Correlatively, there are no economic classes in the sense that any paramount group may be said to own the means of production, although a chief may symbolize in his person the property rights of a particular unit. It follows that primitive economies are natural economies; they lack true money. I mean by this that the three related and defining attributes of civilized money—that is, money as an abstract, intrinsically valueless medium for appropriating surplus, storing value and deferring payment or delaying exchange do not adhere to primitive money. The latter serves as a counter or symbol of value, as in native Dahomey, where cowries were used to represent tribute that was actually collected, in kind, by the king's agents.[12]

Even this role of primitive money is marginal. Exchange among primitives is usually effected by barter or gift. These converge toward being donations, akin to sacrifices,[13] that is, not merely a giving of goods but a giving of oneself. In such transactions the object is progressively enriched, its symbolic character heightens; conversely, in the rationalized modern market each partial, impersonal exchange reduces the symbolic constitution to a calculation, a sign. While civilized money tends to alienate man from his labor by transforming his labor into an abstract commodity, by detaching it from him and by transferring considerations of "worth" and "value" from a human to a marketing context, primitive exchange has the contrary effect: social value and social effort are always directly expressed and understood; they strengthen the sense of community. Indeed, the major emphasis in most forms of primitive exchange seems to be on *giving*, and this may be accompanied by attitudes ranging from hostile to the generous. As Barnett states of the Indians of the Northwest coast: "Accumulation in any quantity by borrowing or otherwise, is, in fact, unthinkable, unless it be for the purpose of immediate distribution."[14]

The Winnebago, for example, tell us that *they* give as follows:

1. Have someone make a dummy out of grass and dress it with whatever objects he wishes to receive as gifts. If he wants a horse have him put a bridle crosswise around the body of the dummy; if he wants clothes, have him dress the dummy up in Indian clothes.

2. The maker of the dummy then places it near a gathering of people or where he expects such a gathering to take place. He sits down near his dummy.

3. When a second participant sees the dummy he goes over and either kicks or strikes the man who made it, at the same time giving him one of the objects he desires. Others may join in upon the same conditions.

4. The participants only stop kicking the dummymaker when someone, preferably a warrior who at some time or other had cut up an enemy in war, cuts up the dummy.

5. As soon as his bruises permit him, the man who made the dummy gets up, gathers all his gifts together, and goes home.[15]

The primitive gift may serve an "economic" purpose, within a reciprocal system, but like all significant activities in primitive society, it is multi-functional, a focus for the expression of a wide range of emotions and purposes.

We can conclude, then, that in primitive society, there is no morbid individual anxiety about the fundamental right or opportunity to work as a peer among peers; this is simply not at issue. The expectations of food, clothing, shelter and work are not juridical because they are unexceptionable. The rights and duties involved are completely customary. The basic economic structure functions rationally.

Leadership Roles

In primitive societies, the major functions and roles of leadership are communal and traditional, not political or secular. The chief of a clan, or the patriarch of a family, are respected as the embodiments of clan, family or tribal heritage. In many societies, a clan chief is simply the oldest member of the group. Obeisance toward these figures is symbolic, a sign of respect for one's tradition and thus of self-respect. It is not the result of coercion or an institutionally manipulative social act.

Leadership may also be situational, and based on skill. Primitive societies abound in "chiefs." In any one tribe, there may be a hunting chief, work chief, dance chief, women's chief, age grade chief, and fishing chief. These leaders function only in specific contexts and for limited periods of time; usually, their primacy is based on capacity in the particular activity. It does not carry over into the round of daily life; and, almost everyone in the society is, at one time or another, in a "chiefly" position. W.H. Rivers makes this point as follows:

> When studying the warfare of the people of the Western Solomon Islands, I was unable to discover any evidence of definite leadership. When a boat reached the scene of a headhunting foray, there was no regulation as to who should lead the way. It seemed as if the first man who got out of the boat or chose to lead the way was followed without question. Again, in the councils of such people, there is no voting or other means of taking the opinion of the body. Those who have lived among savage or barbarous peoples in several parts of the world have related how they have attended native councils where matters in which they were interested were being discussed. When, after a time, the English observer found that the people were discussing some wholly different topic, and inquired when they were going to decide the question in which he was interested, he was told that it had already been decided and that they had passed on to other business. . . . The members of the council had become aware, at a certain point, that they were in agreement, and it was not necessary to bring the agreement explicitly to notice.[16]

Leadership may also be a function of generalized rank and

status, which automatically accrues to every normal member of the group through the mere fact of his having attained a certain age or undergone certain experiences. In the latter case, a qualification is necessary. Every normal man will have the opportunity to achieve status via certain experiences, but not all men will be equally successful. Statuses may be hierarchically organized in primitive society; but they are not scarce, and their formal distribution and function is part of a historically selective, if "unplanned," rational paradigm.

Moreover, the association of major, traditional leadership with shifting, situational and "automatic" types of status leadership, reduces the occasions for what can be termed "broad spectrum" social hostility, while diminishing the alienation that develops in response to arbitrary, remotely exercised, and impersonal authority. In these respects and others, primitive systems do not squander their substance by inequities woven into the social fabric. In a profound psychological sense, primitive societies are democratic, though they are not reductively "equalitarian." Equality is not construed as identity in primitive life. Leadership is reasonably distributed and exercised.

The Legality of Custom

It is a logical corollary and a historical truth, that in primitive societies, laws as we know them do not exist. Society operates through custom and by well-understood informal sanctions, not by means of a legal apparatus administered from above in the interest of this or that group, that is, not by codified laws. There are no special legal functionaries; there is no specific and exclusively legal apparatus. The multitudinous occasions for law that we are familiar with in civilization, for example, commercial rights, governmental levy and bureaucratic function, simply do not occur in primitive society. As Tylor put it, "one of the most essential things that we can learn from the life of rude tribes is how society can function without the policemen to keep order."[1][7] There are certain obvious exceptions to this generalization, for example, the Plains Indian buffalo police, but they are the exceptions that prove the rule, explicable as the result of particular circumstances; they are neither permanent formal groups, nor manifestations of an over-arching legal order.[18]

In the proto-states, of course, specialized laws, courts and judges had begun to develop, but at the primitive base of these archaic societies, the traditional, customary machinery continued to operate.[19]

Among primitives, then, there is no body of law and no permanent supportive militia standing apart from, and above, the people at large. Thus, that curious aspect of alienation that arises in all political societies, the division between "we" and "they," the citizen versus constituted public authority does not develop.[20] The people and the militia, the people and the tradition are for all practical purposes indistinguishable. Among primitives, the public authority is representative in fact; there is no constitutional theory. In civilization, the theory of public authority adhering to one or another form of government is paramount, but representation, in fact, becomes problematical.

Conservatism and Conflict Resolution

Primitive societies tend to be conservative; they change slowly compared with technologically dominated cultures; consequently, they do not manifest the internal turbulence endemic in archaic or contemporary civilizations.* The fact that sanctions are customary is not the only reason for the relative conservatism of primitive life. A more significant factor is that primitive societies tend to be systems in equilibrium. They are not disrupted by institutional conflicts, although they contain well-structured, often cyclical conflicts among institutions; and of course, personal conflicts do exist. The former is exemplified in the limited struggles among sodalities and in certain types of institutionalized deviancy; the

---

* Technical development alone may seem, at first glance, a perfectly objective measure of progress, as many social scientists still contend. But in the perspective of a primitive society, whose culturally defined needs are being adequately met by the available techniques, it might seem otherwise. A prologue to a theory of progress is perhaps implicit in the argument I am presenting but does not seem worth pursuing, since it is already part and parcel of twentieth century disenchantment with "perfectly objective" measures of human affairs.

latter in the ordinary play of personalities, which may intensify to witchcraft. Indeed, the built-in social mechanisms for the expression of hostility which these structured conflicts partly are, help strengthen the social fabric; the society, so to speak, recognizes and provides for a wide range of human expression.

Despite, or rather, because of this, society to the primitive is apprehended as a part of the natural order, as the backdrop against which the drama of the individual life unfolds. It is sanctified by myth, revealed in ritual, and buttressed by tradition. The social network is perceived as a more or less permanent arrangement of human beings vis-à-vis each other. Since the basic needs for food, clothing, shelter and, as we shall see, personal participation are satisfied in all primitive cultures in a socially non-exploitative manner, revolutionary activity is, insofar as I am aware, unknown. It is probably safe to say that there has never been a revolution in a primitive society; revolutions are peculiar to political societies. Indeed, the Messianic and nativistic movements that have periodically swept primitive cultures under the threat of external destruction, indicate the relative state of institutional grace in which they ordinarily function.

The primitive, then, is a conservative; his society changes its essential form only under the impact of external circumstances or in response to drastic changes in the natural environment. Institutional disharmonies never reach the point of social destruction or, correlatively, of chronic, widespread individual disorganization.

Cultural Integration

It follows that, in primitive societies, there is a very high degree of integration among the various major modalities of culture. Between religion and social structure, social structure and economic organization, economic organization and technology, the magical and the pragmatic, there are intricate and harmonious correlations. These correlations have two major effects: (1) they tend toward the optimal practical efficiency of the system; and (2) they integrate a whole series of emotions and attitudes around a given activity, rather than isolating or abstracting the activity from its human context. An obvious example of the first effect is the maximal use of technology by primitive economic systems. So far as I know, no primitive economic system is dysfunctional with the available technology. Neither does it utilize technology in a wasteful or inefficient way, no matter what bizarre means are brought into play to dispose of surplus beyond the point where the subsistence needs of the group are met or to stimulate exchange. The second effect is exemplified in the validation of practical activities by magico-religious means, as in the classic case of the expert Trobriand canoe maker, who confirms the step-by-step construction of his craft with spell and incantation.

This typical primitive usage needs to be differentiated from magic in civilized society. The latter is usually detached from pragmatic activity, is indeed a surrogate for action in the world. Primitive magic, despite its mechanical character, integrates the activity into a traditional universe, whereas civilized magic acts out the possibility of achievement without effort—the genie conjured from the lamp—as a result of despair, of the *impossibility* of acting in the world. This "abracadabra" effect, whether expressed in neurotic obsessive-compulsive maneuvers, the flourishing cults of southern California, the procedures and promises of astrologists and palmistry, or the reification of, let us say, "money" as the key to "happiness," all represent the practice of pure magic-growing, as Redfield indicated in his studies of Yucatan, with civilization, and growing, it should be added, at the expense of the religious consciousness. For modern magic develops logically out of our conception of nature as a machine.

A rough and simplified model of functional integration in primitive society is provided by a type of joint family structure widely distributed throughout Africa, although parallels are found in other major ethnographic areas. The nucleus of such a (predominantly) unilateral, unilocal family may (if it is patrilineal and patrilocal) consist of the patriarch, one or more younger brothers and his and their sons and unmarried daughters; around the nucleus circulate the wives of the male members. The culture in which this residential unit is the critical social group can be analyzed as functioning on three primary, interrelated levels:

Dominant ideological activity	= ancestor worship.
Dominant social unit	= joint family.
Dominant economic activity	= shifting horticulture.

These three particular forms or usages, representing the major, reciprocating levels of the society, constitute the core of the culture. They are, so to speak, the culture in essential cross-section. Obviously, they do not comprise the entire culture, but each is critical on its level and is functionally correlated with the critical forms and usages on the other levels. When we say that such a culture changes, we mean, in effect, that the core processes have changed, and they always change in a demonstrable relation to each other.

In this system extensive areas must be regularly cleared, cultivated with hoes and periodically abandoned; this requires a cooperative labor unit, which happens to be efficiently achieved by a group of nuclear families residing together and related generationally as, in this example, through the male line—a joint family—in a structure sanctified by ancestor worship.

I am not implying here that shifting horticulture, joint family structure and ancestor worship are inevitably linked traits. Ancestor worship functions in systems that are not predicated on shifting horticulture. Joint families exist in the absence of any kind of horticulture. And shifting horticulture is associated with ideological and social complexes which cannot be precisely defined as ancestor worship or joint family organization. The linkage of forms in the model outlined above is historically and functionally but not inevitably, determined. Moreover, I am not suggesting that religion is merely epiphenomenal to a socio-economic base—even though ancestor worship, for example, persists as long as the joint family-horticultural system maintains its integrity. The native religion, will absorb Christian elements when under missionary assault, if the social economy remains relatively unshaken, but it disintegrates rapidly when the society to which it is immediately relevant crumbles. In this sense, the socio-economic base may be considered an independent variable, the religion a dependent variable. But this applies only to a particular *form* of religion, not to religion as such. Even the specific forms of religion must be viewed as social inventions and not as automatic projections of a particular social economy, just as a social form viable to a particular technology is also an invention and not a logically inevitable development. Another way of putting this is as follows: in primitive societies, the superstructure is not reducible to the economic base; that reductive process begins with the exploitative economic relations of civilization. "All our inventions," said Marx, "have endowed material forces with intellectual life, and degraded human life into a material force."

That is, religion *qua* religion is a fundamental mode of cultural behavior, correlated with other modes but not caused by them. It is, I believe, as absurd to assume that religion germinates in economic and social factors as it would be to claim the opposite—that the roots of economic (or social) activity lie in religion. They are equal and equally ancient needs—capacities and propensities of human nature, related in their generality in ways that are incredibly complex and far from evident. Moreover, when the form of a major ideology such as ancestor worship collapses, its insights and postulates do not vanish from the consciousness of men; they become part of a universal inheritance.

Returning now to the specific joint family structure under consideration, the land cannot be alienated or sold because the primitive living within the system views the earth as the dwelling place of his ancestors; it is *terra sancta*. Thus, we can trace a functional connection between religion and land tenure, an economic factor.

The patriarch is the family priest, the living link to the ancestors and thus the embodiment of family tradition. Yet he serves also as coordinator—though not necessarily field chief—of the cooperative labor unit and as the channel for the distribution of the social goods produced. The family itself is not only a labor force but a ceremonial group; it is, so to speak, its own congregation. Thus, connections between socio-economic and ideological factors are readily identified.

The patriarch functions also as the arbiter of disputes within the family and in many instances, among families. He, therefore, discharges a social task having political and juridical aspects.

When the family grows beyond the size at which it can efficiently operate, given its ecological circumstances, a new joint family buds off from it into free clan or village lands. The new patriarch, who may be a younger brother or an older son in his compound of origin, sets up a new establishment; this is considered a culturally heroic act. He may be regarded as a culture hero—and ecological necessity thus becomes permeated with a moral purpose, which to the primitive moving within the system, is not segregated from other purposes and may indeed be said to be primary.

In short, within the typical joint family structure, there develop complex correlations among economic, social (including political and legal) and ideological factors; particular persons function in a multiplicity of ways, and specific activities bind a wide range of responses. These correlations do not unite *all* economic, social and ideological activities; only the major ones on each level are involved, the sum of which are essential to the survival of the group. The others, whether economic, social or ideological, are subsidiary as, for example, fishing is among cultivators.

To the primitive acting within the society, the major elements interpenetrate in a circular, self-reinforcing manner: all aspects of behavior converge in a system that strives toward maximum equilibrium. We, of course, can and do analyze out the component parts of the system; we, as outsiders, can demonstrate that changes in technology, in the mode of making a living or in land tenure introduced by Europeans, shatter the joint family structure, and with it, eventually, ancestor worship; civilization is compelled to dissect the corpses it creates. But the primitive moves within this system as an integrated person. His society is neither compartmentalized nor fragmented, and none of its parts is in fatal conflict with the others. Thus he does not perceive himself as divided into *homo economicus, homo religiosus, homo politicus* and so forth. For example, the Yir-Yiront, an Australian people, make no linguistic distinction between work and play. The primitive stands at the center of a synthetic, holistic universe of concrete activities, disinterested in the causal nexus between them, for only consistent crises stimulate interest in the causal analysis of society. It is the pathological disharmony of social parts that compels us minutely to isolate one from another, and inquire into their reciprocal effects.

As Sapir implied, this primitive holism is in startling and significant contrast to our own conflict-filled, isolating and abstract—our increasingly civilized—experience of society.[21]

Participation in Society

The ordinary member of primitive society participates in a much greater segment of his social economy than do individuals in archaic civilizations and technically sophisticated, modern civilizations. For example, the average Nama male is an expert hunter, a keen observer of nature, a craftsman who can make a kit bag of tools and weapons, a herder who knows the habits and needs of cattle, a direct participant in a variety of tribal rituals and ceremonies, and he is likely to be well-versed in the legends, tales and proverbs of his people (a similar list could be drawn up for the Nama female). The average primitive, relative to his social environment and the level of science and technology achieved, is more accomplished, in the literal sense of that term, than are most civilized individuals. He participates more fully and directly in the cultural possibilities open to him, not as a consumer and not vicariously but as an actively engaged, complete person.

However we may conceive the future of civilization, primitive society was certainly the source of this aspect of Marx's definition of communism: it will become possible for men "to do one thing today and another tomorrow, to hunt in the morning, fish in the afternoon, rear cattle in the evening, criticize after dinner... without ever becoming hunter, fisherman, shepherd or critic."

A major reason for this functional integrity is in his mastery of the processes of production; that is, the primitive, in creating a tool, creates it from beginning to end, uses it with skill and controls it. He has no schizoid sense of it controlling him, and he has direct access to the fruits of his labor, subject to the reciprocal claims of his kinsmen. This subtly inflected reciprocity cannot, in depth and detail, be explored here,* but it is sufficiently reflected in Kenyatta's words:

> Before the advent of the white man the institution of serfdom and wage-workers was unknown to the Gikuyu people. The tribal customary law recognised the freedom and independence of every member of the tribe. At the same time all were bound up together socially, politically, economically, and religiously by a system of... mutual help, extending from the family group to the tribe.[22]

In contrast, glance again at the frequently drawn portrait of the fractionated worker emerging in modern civilization (not to

---

* Marshall Sahlins has elaborated the point brilliantly in *Stone Age Economics*.

mention the serf or slave who occupied the stage before him), compelled to sell his labor power as a marketable commodity. Indeed the worker who appeared after the industrial revolution began to regard himself as a commodity, as a tool or an extension of a tool—the very opposite of the primitive view of the tool as an extension of the personality. The modern worker and to varying degrees his predecessor in archaic civilization became alienated, specialized and morally estranged in the process of production. This is evident in the history of the industrial process; when the worker is reduced to a motion, he can be replaced by a machine. But the persistent civilized appreciation of hand, as opposed to machine-made objects reflects, historically and existentially, the resistance to the process. Correlatively, the power of the "owners" or chief executives, became an inhuman power.* But their freedom is a pseudo-freedom, for it is based on the coercion of subordinate groups; they are bound to those whom they exploit. Their social ties grow manipulative; their privileges—irresponsible. Nor do the managers, technicians, bureaucrats and clerks escape this fate. It is the present agony and peril of all classes and grades in civilized society. If civilized production has helped disorganize modern man and deprive him of his moral center, primitive production helped to integrate primitive man.

Moral Order and Tribal Organization

A fundamental reason for the holistic and moral, but not moralistic, character of primitive society is that it is organized on a kin or tribal basis, not on a political basis. All significant

---

* Goldenwieser gives an interesting linguistic illustration of this: "When the executive speaks, words emerge from his lips not unlike mechanical tools which, having established contact with those spoken to, make them go through their paces. Such words are brief, as precise as possible, and thoroughly impersonal."

He continues by drawing a contrast with the example of a more primitive function of speech: "But we also speak to reveal content, inviting the one spoken to to participate in our ego. . . . Here personality comes to the fore, time flows easily, what counts is the enhancement of the moment through psychic interplay. . . . Such was the conversation of primitive folk . . . here folk-lore thrived and mythology took form. Such also is the conversation of peasants, with its proverbs, allusions, metaphors, its pithy descriptions and composed narratives."[23]

economic, social and ideological functions are discharged within and among kin or quasi-kin groupings, whether these are nuclear families, joint families, clans, clusters of clans, or the various types of sodalities. Society thus functions on a personal, corporate and traditional basis, rather than on an impersonal, civil and individualized basis. The words of a Pomo Indian are pertinent:

> In the white way of doing things, the family is not so important. The police and soldiers take care of protecting you, the courts give you justice, the Post Office carries messages for you, the school teaches you. Everything is taken care of, even your children, if you should die, but with us the family must do all that. Without the family, we are nothing, and in the old days before white people came, the family was given first consideration by anyone who was about to do anything at all. That is why we got along. With us the family was everything. Now it is nothing. We are getting like the white people, and it is bad for the old people. We had no old people's home like you. The old people were important. They were wise. Your old people must be fools.[24]

Kin units, then, together with the technically nonkin institutions patterned after their image (age grades, specialized friendships, cooperative work groups, male or female clubs, etc.) comprise primitive society. Although the immediate biological family is everywhere evident, it is usually found merged within a larger unit.[25] The important point is that all meaningful social, economic and ideological relations have a kin or transfigured kin character. Even within the most extensive clan organizations, where hundreds of people may be said to descend from a common ancestor and the actual blood relationships may either be entirely attenuated or completely fictitious, people still behave toward each other as if they were kin.

This personalism, splendidly illustrated by Hallowell, is the most historically significant feature of primitive life and extends from the family outward to the society at large and ultimately to nature itself.[26] It seems to underlie all other distinctive qualities of primitive thought and behavior. Primitive people live in a personal, corporate world, a world that tends to be a "thou" to the subjective "I" rather than an "it" impinging upon an objectively separate and divided self. Consciousness for the primitive is the most common condition in the universe, a perception that is also found, in more civilized and abstract forms, in the work of Whitehead, Haldane and Teilhard de Chardin.

Negative traits of primitive society, such as witchcraft, represent the dark side of this personalism. Yet primitive witchcraft seems significantly distinct from the civilized species of witchcraft, which is apparently the result of rigidly repressed urges and projected feelings of guilt. Among primitives, witchcraft seems to arise rather from the intensity of personal life, which produces unusual sophistication and subtlety about people and in certain areas, a dangerous sensitivity. Yet, the belief that people can make other people sick contains its obvious truth; it need not be based on chronic insecurity in human relations and is not only the result of scientific ignorance. Indeed, further studies of the types of people who are considered witches, within a given primitive society and cross-culturally, should be illuminating, for example, in terms of the conception of the witch as an inordinately narcissistic person, a bad mother or unfulfilled woman.* As the Gikuyu say, "To live with others is to share and to have mercy for one another," and, "It is witch-doctors who live and eat alone."[2 7]

At its most positive, however, primitive personalism is the "one touch of nature that makes the whole world kin"; it suggests the quality of "co-naissance," of universal relatedness, of being born together, which, interestingly enough, the French Catholic Existentialist Paul Claudel, reaching deeply into his own consciousness, has illuminated in his art.

The Non-Platonic Mode of Thought

This brings me to the observation that primitive modes of thinking are substantially concrete, existential and nominalistic, within a

---

* Among the Anaguta, a witch (*ukiri*—the most obscene word in the language) was identified after a social consensus was reached through dreams experienced by many people, in which one particular person appeared constantly as a threatening or destructive agent. Anybody could, in theory, become a witch, but the actual incidence was quite rare and usually resulted in the suicide of the person concerned. Even in such cases, being a witch was considered an unfortunate attribute for which the person was not, in his very "essence," condemned. The individual who was acting as a witch (this is more accurate than simply calling the person a witch) was never accused directly, but ultimately in subtle yet well-structured ways the message struck home.

personalistic context.* This does not suggest a lack of abstract capacity (*all* language, *all* culture and convention flow from this phylogenetic human endowment), but it does indicate an emphasis functional with the kinship structure of primitive society and a lack of concern with the specific type of abstraction that may be called, in the Western civilized world, Platonic.

Boas wrote:

Primitive man, when conversing with his fellow man, is not in the habit of discussing abstract ideas.... Discourses on qualities without connection with the object to which the qualities belong, or of activities or states disconnected from the idea of the actor or the subject being in a certain state, will hardly occur in primitive speech. Thus the Indian will not speak of goodness as such, although he may very well speak of the goodness of a person. He will not speak of a state of bliss apart from the person who is in such a state. He will not refer to the power of seeing without designating an individual who has such power. Thus it happens that in languages in which the idea of possession is expressed by elements subordinated to nouns, all abstract terms appear always with possessive elements. It is, however, perfectly conceivable that an Indian trained in philosophic thought would proceed to free the underlying nominal forms from the possessive elements, and thus reach abstract forms strictly corresponding to the abstract forms of our modern languages.... [And further] If we want to form a correct judgment we ought to bear in mind that our European languages, as found at the present time, have been moulded to a great extent by the abstract thought of philosophers. Terms like "essence, substance, existence, idea, reality," many of which are now commonly used, are by origin artificial devices for expressing the results of abstract thought. In this way they would

---

† Here, I am adopting terms that have grown within a civilized philosophic tradition. But this is not to imply that primitive are technically or self-consciously existentialist, nominalist and so on. We can, however, approximately, so classify their modes of thinking. Perhaps it would be more suitable to refer to *existentializing* and *nominalizing* tendencies, but this is a quibble, since the nominal forms of such labels cannot be used precisely to identify even the appropriate civilized systems of thought.

resemble the artificial, unidiomatic abstract terms that may be formed in primitive languages.[28]

I can only add that my own experience with primitive modes of thinking bears this out completely. For example, the Anaguta, of the High Nigerian Plateau, never count in the abstract but count only with reference to concrete things or people; the numerals change form according to the classes of objects being counted, but are not grammatically concordant with them. Yet the Anaguta are fully capable of grasping number unrelated to particular objects. But they do not deify or reify number; there is no occasion for doing so in their society, and the idea seems meaningless to them.

Similarly, in explaining the meaning of a proverb, a concrete context is always presented, for the abstract idea is regarded as inconclusive. Context and existence rather than essence constitute the established aspects of thought. So, for example, the Anaguta say: "Demean the man's character, but never the man himself." This means that a man must be judged on what he *does*, for what he *is* is not only inaccessible but can lead to many contradictory actions. That is, one can never reach a final judgment on his manhood, only on this or that aspect of his behavior.

Here it is worth noting that Dorothy Lee, in classifying Trobriand thought as essentialist, uses *essence* in an ambiguous manner.[29] She does not adopt the Platonic definition (of essence as an ideal or universal form, imperfectly and variously reflected in earthy particulars) but claims, in effect, that each concrete particular (for example, tubers, in varying conditions or stages of growth) is distinctly named and conceived to have its own being, or essence. But this is actually a nominalist as opposed to a conceptual realist position. The particulars do not refer back to an abstract universal; the individual thing is the ultimate reality. Lee's pure Trobriand essences are, I believe, better described as singular existents: the category "essential" confuses the issue.

The existentialist, rather than the technically essentialist, mode of Trobriand thought is further indicated, even if inadvertently, by Lee when she states: "The magician does not *cause* certain things to be, he does them. . . . It follows that the Trobriander performs acts because of the activity itself. . . . "

I would also restate Lee's insistence on the irrelevance of causality to Trobrianders as a reflection of the typical primitive holistic and synthetic view outlined above. The lack of concern with causality can thus be understood as the absence of an analytic, specialized, "scientific" approach to nature and society. But this lack of concern, it must be emphasized, is with the elaboration of objective theories of causality; it does not obstruct the sequence of empirical efforts involved in any given task.

Finally, it seems that Lee contradicts herself in claiming that, although the position of a thing or event in a pattern is of paramount importance to Trobrianders, this does not reflect a concern with relationships. Obviously, I take the contrary view, that is, the intricate arrangements of people vis-à-vis each other, the kin nature of primitive culture, is mirrored in the concern with pattern and order, and disorder, in things and events.

However, what F.S.C. Northrop has called a "naive" form of realism is commonly expressed among primitives, emanating, it is evident, from their personalism.[30] But this realism is not of a conceptual character and may be assimilated to the existentializing tendency. Spirits, for example, are individuated; they concretely exist. As Paul Radin definitively put it:

> It is, I believe, a fact that future investigations will thoroughly confirm, that the Indian does not make the separation into personal as contrasted with impersonal, corporeal with impersonal, in our sense at all. What he seems to be interested in is the question of existence, of reality; and everything that is perceived by the sense, thought of, felt and dreamt of, exists.[31]

And an Eskimo poem makes this quite clear:

There is a tribe of invisible men
who move around us like shadows—have you felt them?
They have bodies like ours and live just like us,
using the same kind of weapons and tools
You can see their tracks in the snow sometimes
and even their igloos
but never the invisible men themselves.
They cannot be seen except when they die
for then they become visible.

It once happened that a human woman
married one of the invisible men.
He was a good husband in every way:
He went out hunting and brought her food,

and they could talk together like any other couple.
But the wife could not bear the thought
that she did not know what the man she married looked like.
One day when they were both at home
she was so overcome with curiosity to see him
that she stabbed with a knife where she knew he was sitting,
And her desire was fulfilled:
Before her eyes a handsome young man fell to the floor.
But he was cold and dead, and too late
she realized what she had done,
and sobbed her heart out.

When the invisible men heard about this murder
they came out of their igloos to take revenge.
Their bows were seen moving through the air
and the bow strings stretching as they aimed their arrows.
The humans stood there helplessly
for they had no idea what to do or how to fight
because they could not see their assailants.
But the invisible men had a code of honor
that forbade them to attack opponents
who could not defend themselves,
so they did not let their arrows fly,
and nothing happened; there was no battle after all
and everyone went back to their ordinary lives.[32]

The Uses of Ritual Drama

In primitive society, the ritual drama is a culturally comprehensive
vehicle for group and individual expression at critical junctures in
the social round or personal life cycle, as these crises are enjoined
by the natural environment or defined by culture. In such
ceremonies, art, religion and daily life fuse, and cultural meanings
are renewed and re-created on a stage as wide as society itself.

In a sequence from archaic to modern civilization, we can trace
the process through which religion, drama and daily life split
apart. The drama, the primary form of art, retreats to the theater,
and religion escapes into the church. The sacraments, those
formalized remnants of the primitive crisis rites, and the "theater,

the play," develop into carefully cultivated and narrowly bounded conventions. Civilized participation in culture becomes increasingly passive, as culture becomes increasingly secularized.

Among primitives, rituals are cathartic and creative. They are cathartic in that they serve as occasions for open, if culturally molded, expressions of ambivalent feelings about sacred tradition, constituted authority, animal and human nature, and nature at large.

A good example of the cathartic expression of ambivalence toward the sacred occurs in a Wintun's Hesi ceremony which Barrett calls "the acme of Wintun ceremonialism." The clown directs his comic assaults at the leader:

> When the captain of the host village was singing as he marched slowly about the inside of the dance house, one of the clowns staged himself before the captain and marched slowly backwards in step with him, while delivering joking remarks concerning the leader's ability to sing and the particular song he was voicing. This did not seem in the least to disconcert the singer, who continued to sing in his gravest manner: but his song was not received with the usual seriousness.[33]

Ritual expression of ambivalence toward constituted authority is illustrated among the Anaguta. Men who are being initiated into the status of elders had the right publicly to challenge elders of long standing, who were still physically vigorous, to a combat with clubs. This took place within a circle of young, newly initiated men dancing slowly to the beat of drums and the sound of horns. No man could be struck above the trunk, and the challenge need not be given or accepted. But for those who desired to do so, this final phase of the men's initiation ceremony afforded the opportunity to work off hostility against particular elders who might have abused their authority. Painful injuries occasionally resulted. Physical cowardice or bluster were exposed, but did not brand a man beyond the situation, and, as noted, there was no obligation to participate, although it was honorable to do so. Nor did the ceremony threaten the general respect in which the elders were held; on the contrary, the institutionalized expression of ambivalence helped buttress the social structure generally.

These rituals are also creative in the dramatic revelation of symbols and the anticipation and elaboration of new roles for individuals; they make meanings explicit and renew the vitality of the group.

The Nama role-transition rites are indicative. At puberty, childbirth, the death of a spouse, the contraction of certain diseases, the slaying of an enemy in war, the killing of a large game animal and similar occasions, the individual is said to be in a condition called *! nau* (in an unclean, labile or dangerous state). During these periods, he is suspended between two statuses and is considered to be dangerous to himself and to others; he is *of* the tribe but not *in* it. Therefore, he is isolated, and placed in the care of an immune guardian, who has passed through the *! nau* period for the identical event. In order to be restored to normality, a person must undergo a ritual cleansing, participate in a common meal with people who have emerged from the same situation and then be re-introduced into the life of the tribe by his guardian, at a ceremonial dance. The person is, in short, reborn.[34]

These experiences lead to a hierarchical development of the social self, which, in turn, assimilates contradictory forms of behavior without traumatic consequences. Among the Indians of the American plains, for example, the status of warrior could be succeeded by a status of a higher order—that of "Peace Chief," honored for his wisdom and experience. He was the guardian of the well being of the people; his balanced judgment prevailed over the special interests of the warriors.

Put another way, the primitive rituals are creative in the reduction and cultural use of anxiety arising out of a variety of existential situations. Birth, death, puberty,* marriage, divorce, illness—generally speaking, the assumption of new roles, responsibilities, and psychological states, as these are socially defined and naturally induced—serve as the occasions for the ritual drama.

These experiences can be perceived as a progressive spiritualization of the person throughout the life cycle; among certain peoples a woman is said to become pregnant through the incorporation of a grand parental spirit who is then reborn, but not precisely duplicated, at the actual birth of the infant. This is not to say that primitive peoples are unaware of the connection

---

* Puberty may be, as Radin believed, the primary, pivotal rite of mankind—fusing as it does economic and sexual maturation while polarizing male and female and projecting polarity onto nature at large.

between intercourse and conception, but rather that they are capable of sustaining both realities, the metaphorical on the one hand and the reductively biological on the other, without contradiction. Analogously, when Australian aboriginal elders whirl their bull-roarers or churingas, said to represent the voices of the ancestors until the moment when the "truth" is exposed to the young men at initiation, the duality of this truth can be transcended. For it is understood that the elders have the power of summoning, of creating the voices of the ancestors. Unfortunately, the positivism of Western-trained anthropologists have time and again led them to make irrelevant distinctions between the two aspects of reality represented in these instances. In any event, the life cycles of primitive peoples are not merely a series of moments bounded by discrete ritual structures; rather, the ritual structures symbolize the continuous, dynamic process of social maturation. Naturally, the formal ritual structure varies from culture to culture, but the functions are mutually assimilable.

Such rituals are, I believe, primarily expressive, as opposed to the predominantly binding, compulsive, "ritualistic" behavior encountered as neurotic phenomena among civilized individuals.*

The primitive ritual also differs from ritualized group occasions in civilized society; the latter strive toward repression of ambivalence rather than recognition and cultural use. One can hardly imagine a "burlesque of the sacred"[36] taking place at, let

---

*An Eskimo game bordering on ritual, reported by Peter Freuchen, is illustrative: "There was also the rather popular game of 'doused lights'. The rules were simple. Many people gathered in a house, all of them completely nude. Then the lights were extinguished, and darkness reigned. Nobody was allowed to say anything, and all changed places continually. At a certain signal each man grabbed the nearest woman. After a while, the lights were put on again, and now innumerable jokes could be made over the theme: 'I knew all the time who you were because—: several old stories deal with this popular amusement. It should be said that—crude as it may seem to use—it often served a very practical purpose. Let us, for instance, say that bad weather conditions are keeping a flock of Eskimos confined to a house or an igloo. The bleakness and utter loneliness of the Arctic when it shows its bad side can get on the nerves of even those people who know it and love it the most. Eskimos could go out of their minds, because bad weather always means uncertain fates. Then suddenly someone douses the light, and everybody runs around in the dark and ends up with a partner. Later the lamp is lit again, the whole party is joking and in high spirits. *A psychological explosion—with possible bloodshed—has been averted*" (italics added)[35]

us say, a patriotic ceremony; in this sense all state structures tend toward the totalitarian. But, among primitives, sacred events are, frequently and publicly caricatured, even as they occur. In primitive rituals, what we would call the fundamental paradoxes of human life—love and hate, the comic and the tragic, dedication and denial and their derivatives—are specified, given free, sometimes uninhibited, even murderous "play" in quite the sense that Huizinga uses that word.* But let us remember, to adopt an extreme example, that even ritualized cannibalism or the torture of the self or others, recognize and directly confront the concrete humanity of the subject. The purpose of ritual cannibalism is not only the humiliation of the enemy, but also the absorption of his heroic human qualities. In a way that is repugnant to civilized sensibilities, cannibalism was a bloody sacrament, perhaps the first sacrament. Torture, whether inflicted on the self or others, is, of course, sadistic and masochistic, but it was frequently a test of endurance, of manhood and of the capacity for spirituality. Here, for example, is what the Eskimos say: "Let the person who wants a vision hang himself by his neck. When his face turns purple, take him down and have him describe what he's seen."[37] But it should be noted that in no instance is the purpose of primitive torture the conversion of the victim to the torturer's point of view; ideological imperatives are not the issue.

Yet the sanguine and terrifying aspects of primitive life, which civilized individuals could hardly sustain, precisely because of the immediate personal contexts in which they occur, do not begin to compete with the mass, impersonal, rationalized slaughter that increases in scope as civilization spreads and deepens.

This impersonal process should not be confused with the primitive attitude towards strangers. It has been frequently assumed that the stranger is not perceived as a human being by the members of any given primitive society and, consequently, can be treated in a subhuman way. But this notion, in any event not to be

---

* "The concept of play," writes Huizinga, "merges quite naturally with that of holiness . . . any line of tragedy proves it. By considering the whole sphere of so-called primitive culture as a play-sphere we pave the way to a more direct and more general understanding . . . than any meticulous psychological or sociological analysis would allow. . . . Primitive. . . . ritual is thus sacred play, indispensable for the well-being of the community, fecund of cosmic insight and social development. . . . "[40]

confused with civilized estrangement, is contradicted by both psychological deduction and ethnological evidence. Psychologically, the intensely personal, including totemic, associations which link man to society and society to nature, argue against the validity of assuming that the stranger is an exclusive exception. As Marshall Sahlins put it: "Ordinarily, savages pride themselves on being hospitable to strangers."[38] Nor does the fact that many primitive peoples call themselves by the name which represents "human being" imply anything more than recognition of their uniqueness in a state of nature. Indeed, the dialectic between the uniqueness of the human being and the understanding of his commonality in nature, defines a dynamic perception in primitive culture. The primitive attitude towards the stranger, then, is not a reflection of the latter's nonexistence as a human being, but of his *lack of status as a social person*. It follows that some way must be found to incorporate the stranger into a recognized system of statuses before one is able to relate to him specifically. Among the Australian aborigines, the complex system of marriage classes and descent groups permits an individual to orient himself almost immediately on the territory of a strange band hundreds of miles from his native area. Adoption of prisoners of war, or the incorporation of a white man into an aboriginal galaxy of living spirits serve an analogous purpose. The point is that in primitive society a person must be socially located and named before his human potential is converted into a cultural identity. Among the Igbo-speaking peoples of south-eastern Nigeria, and this is typical, an infant is a human but not a social being until he is given a name at an elaborate ceremony some months after his birth. In fact, throughout the life cycle among many primitive peoples, naming expresses the need to reintegrate all aspects of the developing personality into the social group. Persons may have multiple names at any given time in their lives, and names may also be given when they assume new roles and statuses. Tylor understood this aspect of the ethnology of naming very well although his progressivistic perspective, is, of course, unjustified: "Lower down in the history of culture, the word and the idea are found sticking together with a tenacity very different from their weak adhesion in our minds, and there is to be seen a tendency to grasp at the word as though it were the object it stands for, and to hold that to be able to speak of a thing gives a sort of possession of it, in a way that we can scarcely realize." Perhaps this state of mind was hardly ever so clearly brought into view as in a story told by Dr. Lieber. "I was looking lately at a negro who was occupied in feeding young mockingbirds by the hand. "Would they eat worms?" I asked. The negro replied, *"Surely not, they are too young, they would not know what to call them."*[39]

To the degree that the person, or aspects of the person, are not named, to that degree the person remains a "stranger," even within the group. Thus we can distinguish between internal and external social strangers among primitives, and the structure of estrangement in civilization.

In this connection, how can I ever forget the shock and horror expressed by an Anaguta informant of mine, whom I had persuaded to attend an American (war) movie in a nearby town. This man spent several hours acting out, in my presence, the indiscriminate, casual, unceremonious killing which he had witnessed on the screen. It was almost impossible for him to believe that human beings could behave in this way toward each other, and he decided that it must be a special attribute of white men—superhuman, and at the same time, subhuman. He finally sublimated the experience to the character of a legend. It was his first movie.

The point is that the wars and rituals of primitive society (and the former usually had the style of the latter), are quantitatively and qualitatively distinct from the mechanized wars of civilization. The contrast is not merely in the exponential factor of technology multiplying a constant, homicidal human impulse; in primitive society, taking a life was an *occasion*; in our phase of civilization it has become an abstract, ideological compulsion. The character of this contrast is implicit in the words of George Bird Grinnell:

> Among the plains tribes with which I am well acquainted—and the same is true of all the others of which I know anything at all—coming in actual personal contact with the enemy by touching him with something held in the hand or with a part of the person was the bravest act that could be performed . . . the bravest act that could be performed was to count coup on—to touch or strike—a living unhurt man and to leave him alive, and this was frequently done. . . . *It was regarded as an evidence of bravery for a man to go into battle carrying no weapon that would do any harm at a distance*. It

was more creditable to carry a lance than a bow and arrows; more creditable to carry a hatchet or war club than a lance; and the bravest thing of all was to go into a fight with nothing more than a whip, or a long twig—sometimes called a coup stick. I have never heard a stone-headed war club called coup stick [italics added].[41]

Such a war is a kind of play. No matter what the occasion for hostility, it is particularized, personalized, ritualized. Conversely, civilization represses hostility in the particular, fails to use or structure it, even denies it.

In that uncanny movie *Dr. Strangelove*, for example, the commanding general of the Air Force and the Soviet Ambassador, who have clumsily managed to attack each other, are admonished by the President: "Gentlemen, no fighting in the (computerized) war-room." The point is that in civilization "hostility" explodes with a redoubled, formless bestiality, while we, so to speak, look the other way, refined and not responsible. One is reminded of the character of Dr. Strangelove, whose repressed, crippled, gloved hand, struggled constantly to choke him to death; this schizoid tension is not exorcized until the bombs fall, until the indescribable energies are released, and the paralyzed professor rises with joy from his wheelchair, finding his personal apotheosis at the moment of the extinction of the species.

We wage increasingly impersonal wars, and unlike the Crow, kill at increasing psychic distance from our victims. Or note the contrast with the notorious Jivaro, whose women, fearing his spirit, sing to the shrunken head of an enemy during the last in a series of head hunting rituals:

Now, now, go back to your house where you lived
Your wife is there calling you from your house.
You have come here to make us happy
Finally we have finished
So return.[42]

Civilization blames its crimes on its leaders, more sophisticatedly on abstract, historical forces and finally, abandoning these culprits, despairs utterly of man. Dissociation culminates in depression.

But such unbalanced despair is not reflected, so far as I am aware, in the oral traditions of primitive peoples.

That dissociation and depression were evident in our response to the episode at Mylai, which further reveals the nature of modern civilized war generally, and hence the nature of our society. That is to say, it is part of the culturally and psychically dissociative process which threatens the existence of all of us. By dissociation, I mean, elaborating on my previous reference, the process through which we lose touch with the meaning, the predicate of our own behavior—with our own humanity, and the humanity of the other. That militaristic conception of the person, acted out at Mylai, is generic to state organizations. The first political societies, as Tylor tell us, were patterned after armies— and the conception is alienated, irresponsible, ultimately absurd in the political sense. Political absurdity is the converse of what can be termed existential absurdity; existential absurdity is confronted in primitive society and typically celebrated, not only as an aspect of ritual, but in the omnipresent, ambivalent, tragicomic, mythological figure of the trickster.

Modern mass society creates the modern mass soldier, as a reflection of itself. The effort is made to train him as a deadly bureaucratic machine; in fact he may even shortly become obsolete to be replaced by machines, as the General of the American Army anticipates. And this would certainly follow the history and logic of automation. On the other hand, this reduced person, this bureaucratic soldier, has a repressed affect which can explode, given the weapons at his disposal, into the most obliterating behavior. He kills, whether by bombing at a distance or face to face—but he kills, it should be re-emphasized, at great psychic distance. "We might as well be bombing New York," said an Air Force Officer in Vietnam. This distance is compounded, of course, by the ethnocentrism which the United States as an imperial power instills into its citizens. But the modern mass soldier does not have to hate the specific enemy, which is an inverted way of saying that he does not necessarily recognize the humanity of the specific enemy. When the massacre at Mylai is compared to the routine bombing from the air of similar villages in the so-called "free fire zone," populated by other "Pinksvilles" (how more dissociated can a reference to a human habitation be), the comparison is, it seems to me, psychodynamically valid; the distinction is real but insignificant. For example, in the face to face encounter at Mylai, the American soldier typically dehumanized the South Vietnamese civilians as "gooks."

But this was a false concretization, expressing in a stereotype, the needs of the soldiers involved, and irrelevant to the actual existence of the object. Killing a "gook," or a Jew, remains killing at a distance, although physical proximity demands more of the psyche than bombing from the air; the total dissociation of the former is converted into the direct subjective distortion of the latter. The point remains that the people killed were insufficiently alive in the consciousness of the killers—and this mirrors the actors' inadequate sense of their own humanity. What we were facing at Mylai, then, is not an incident, not even a policy, but the tragic course of a civilization.

Certain ritual dramas or aspects of them acknowledge, express and symbolize the most destructive, ambivalent and demoniacal aspects of human nature. In so doing, they are left limited and finite, that is, they become self-limiting. For this, as yet, we have no civilized parallel, no functional equivalent.* Even the primitivistic drama of Christianity, with its civilized insistence on the vicarious experience of pain and joy, has become refined and collectivised to the vanishing point.

Transcendance and Individuation

If the fulfillment and delineation of the human person within a social, natural and supernatural (transcendent) setting is a universally valid measure for the evaluation of culture, primitive

---

* Meyer Fortes expresses a parallel idea: "I do not mean to imply that everybody is always happy, contented, and free of care in a primitive society. On the contrary, there is plenty of evidence that among them, as with us, affability may conceal hatred and jealousy, friendliness and devotion enjoined by law and morals may mask enmity, exemplary citizenship may be a way of compensating for frustration and fears. The important thing is that in primitive societies there are customary methods of dealing with these common human problems of emotional adjustment by which they are externalized, publicly accepted, and given treatment in terms of ritual beliefs; society takes over the burden which, with us, falls entirely on the individual. Restored to the esteem of his fellows he is able to take up with ease the routine of existence which was thrown temporarily off its course by an emotional upheaval. Behavior that would be the maddest of fantasies in the individual, or even the worst of vices, becomes tolerable and sane, in his society, if it is transformed into custom and woven into the outward and visible fabric of a community's social life. This is easy in primitive societies where the boundary between the inner world of the self and the outer world of the community marks their line of fusion rather than of separation."[43]

societies are our primitive superiors. This is not meant as a play on words. What I mean is that in the basic and essential respects which are the concern of this paper, primitive societies illuminate, by contrast, the dark side of a world civilization which is in chronic crisis.

The primitive realization of the person can be termed *individuation*, and it is the antithesis of ideological individualism. Ideological individualism is a reflection of what Redfield calls *individualization*; the latter is a symptom of civilization and denotes the increasingly mechanical separation of persons from each other, as a result of the shrinkage and replacement of primitive, organic ties by civil, collective connections. The pathological loneliness, the schizoid character that Sullivan identified as a prevailing pattern in American life and as the substratum of psychoses is the corollary of civilized individualism. This obsessive ideological individualism is, like values, a reification; indeed it is one of our most reified "values." The more assiduously we pursue, discuss and examine "individualism"* the more its "essence" eludes us.

We hardly need to be reminded that the recognition and confrontation of this sense of personal isolation has been a major, if not the major, theme in the work of the most important contemporary artists and philosophers, as Jung, for example, has noted with reference to Picasso and Joyce.

What we call romantic love, for example, the underlying theme in contemporary American popular culture, is grounded in the sense of personal isolation. As the family is reduced to a discrete biological group consisting of parents and children, as kin ties attenuate, the affective burden of the family increases. But the very social process which intensifies the emotional pressures on the family make it less and less possible for the family to realize

---

* Goldenweiser expressed it this way: "The factories flooded society with machine-made commodities, all cut to pattern, disindividualized and standardized. From pins to houses, ... from I.Q.'s to Ph.D.'s, mechanical unformity settled upon industrial lands.... The material base thus transformed tends to affect other aspects of life and thought. Power, speed, efficiency [results], organization, centralization, size, quantity—tend to become universal standards. Society, material and spiritual, begins to move in the direction of a socialized Super-Robot, built after the pattern of a machine."[44]

these expectations. Not only has the family ceased to be the center for economic, political and cultural activity, but each member is typically involved with one or another collective for the greater part of his waking life—the school, the factory, the business. Moreover, the confusion of sexual roles, among other factors, diffuses the identities of the respective mates and generations vis-à-vis each other and leads to a mechanical dependence on peer groups. More specifically, the fragmented family cannot satisfy the dependency needs of its members because the social reality of the nuclear unit has been thrown into question by its loss of function. The family does, however, stimulate dependency needs and then, because of inadequate resolution, intensifies frustration while maintaining a high level of infantile expectation. Since the resolution of dependency needs is basic to the reciprocating experience of love, the romantic lover falls "in love" or, as one popular song complained, "Falling in love with love is falling for make-believe." It is love as an abstraction, rather than the actual loving of a person as a being in the world, that dominates the romantic consciousness and transforms the whole notion of the romantic, which implies empathy with the inwardness of the other into its opposite—a sentimental longing, a desire to incorporate the other.

The projections of romantic love, then, are the result of the deprivation of affect within the nuclear family immobilized within a bureaucratic society. To the person "falling in love," the other is the epitome of all stimulated but unresolved, imagined but unexperienced relations with the family—father, mother, sister, brother, aunt, uncle, *baby*.

These projected needs are so intense that they overshadow the reality of the loved one; the lover feels that all expectations can be satisfied in the beloved's magical presence, just as an adequately cared-for infant responds, more realistically, to the existence of the mother. As the popular songs have it, "You Are My Everything," "Oh Baby, What I Couldn't Do with Plenty of Money and You" and so on, ad infinitum. The anticipated romantic union wears thin at the moment when one party surrenders the impossible demands in frustration and seeks another surrogate for all the differentiated affective relations of which he has been deprived or, more rarely, suddenly sees the other as a person with comparable needs and resources. Divorce or estrangement is the usual result of the unrealized and unrealizable promise; and it is no more than an acting out of the bitterness of estrangement in the most intimate phases of socialization in the family of origin. Romantic love, culturally defined, is not an expression of feeling, but of frustration at feeling's absence. One might add that the disaffection of the young seems, to a significant degree, to be the result of the failure of the notion of romantic love. The society of the young, in its cultural aspect, may be seen as the result of an effort to invent widely ramifying kinship connections, to make them economic and socially effective and to live through them in diametric opposition to the exclusivity of romantic prerogatives. The problem is whether this impulse can find a political form—rather than dissipate itself as a psychodynamic overreaction. Nonetheless, impressive numbers of young, middle class people have come to understand that romantic lovers rid themselves only rarely of their multiple expectations, which are reinforced in the sentimental projections of the official popular culture. Rarely do such lovers accept each other realistically rather than merely legally or fatalistically. This is not to exhaust the definition of romantic love, a religious heresy in Western civilization since the Middle Ages, wherein the other was worshipped as God, the converse of recognizing God in the other, which is the essence of Christian love. The medieval heresy has a different social root and a transcendent, as opposed to a sentimental, character. Romantic love was never the basis for marriage in the Middle Ages. But this is not to deny the occasional achievement of a relationship of what may be called "passionate comprehension," perhaps unique to our society, when the demands on the other are moderated because the symmetrical needs of the self are understood.

Among primitive peoples, of course, the experience which we define as romantic love is largely unknown; affective relations are differentiated and discharged throughout the life cycle and kin groups or kin surrogate groups are the center of cultural activity.

Among the Winnebago, for example, no mere mouthing of an ideal of love can gain an individual either admiration or respect in the absence of the appropriate behavior. Consonant with this attitude is the degree of love insisted upon; one cannot love everybody equally. Above all, say the Winnebago: "Do not love your neighbor as you love those of your own house. Only if you are wicked will you love other people's children more than you do your own." Obviously, we confront here a non-platonic, technically existential and nominalist view of life, or better, of living. To love everyone alike is impossible, and a statement to that effect would be not only insincere, but unjust, because it would lead to the neglect of those whom one ought to love most, if one is to learn to love at all. In this mode of cognition, one deserves neither credit not discredit for giving expression to normal human emotions. It is the context, the concrete effects that count. It is wicked to love other people's children as much as your own, it is wicked to love your wife to the detriment of yourself and family, and it is wicked to love your enemy while he is your enemy." One's relationship to one's enemy is not a distortion of love, it is, therefore, not obsessive: one experiences "enmity"—concrete, particular and limited. In these Winnebago formulations, there is no significant disassociation between subject and object, subject and predicate. That breach has gradually widened throughout the history of civilization and can only be understood as a result of complexly interacting economic, cultural, cognitive and semantic changes.

The contrast with the Winnebago is worth exploring further. Among them, for example, one has no right to the glory of a war party if one enters upon it in the wrong spirit. But just what does that mean? In the autobiography of a Winnebago Indian,[4][5] a man is represented as being about to join a war party because his wife has run away from him. "Such a man," the author insists, "is simply throwing away his life. If you want to go on the war path, do not go because your wife has been taken away from you, but because you feel courageous enough to go." This is explained as follows: "When you get married, do not make an idol of the woman you marry, if you worship her, she will insist upon greater worship as time goes on and it may be that when you get married, you will listen to the voice of your wife, and refuse to go on the war path. Why should you thus run the risk of being ridiculed. After a while you will not be allowed to go to a feast. In time, even your sisters will not think anything of you. You will become jealous, and after your jealousy has reached the highest pitch, your wife will run away. You have let her know by your actions that you *worship* a woman, and one alone [note the warning against reifying or fetishizing the object]. As a result, she will run away

163

from you. If you think that a woman, your wife, is the only person you ought to love, you have humbled yourself. You have made the woman suffer and made her feel unhappy. You will be known as a bad man, and no one will want to marry you again. Perhaps afterwards, when people go on to the war path you will join them because you feel unhappy at your wife's desertion. You will then, however, simply be throwing your life away." What this would imply in the woman's perspective is as follows: She must not permit herself to become a slave of love in response to being fetishized. She must run away, rather than permit herself to indulge her own narcissism and the other's dependence. In her case, the weakness would consist of reducing the man to a pseudo-child, and herself to a pseudo-mother, which hopelessly contradicts her existence as a working partner and autonomous person.

The complexly evolved moral discrimination evident in the quoted passage is clear; compensatory, indiscriminate, projected and reified violence is, like reified love, and essentialized values, held in contempt. For the results are obvious—"loss of life, suicide and the dragging of innocent people into your calamity," those, for example, who are going on the war path properly prepared spiritually. In other words, the discreet expressions of what we generalize as violence are spiritually intricate ritual acts among the Winnebago.

Conversely, impulses towards integration, even toward love are time and again converted into their opposites in our civilization, as the Marquis de Sade was capable of understanding. Violence is the name we give to our thwarted creative energies and ordinary human expectations, to our failures, to our fear of ourselves, of what we are capable of doing.

Violence, love and values are, then, related reifications in our society. We talk about values or morality, in the deep sense of the term at the moment that the sacred character of human experience becomes problematic, and, when compelled by our social structure, we segregate values from the general flow of our experience. As soon as we become capable of analyzing values they have become—in that other sense of the term—commodities, detached from ourselves, objects for the social scientist.

Similarly, with *violence*. Violence is a concept that we name and create, as a thing in itself, when we confront the inexpressible energies of people trapped in the structure of civilization. Violence, like love and values, needs to be demystified as a transcendent linguistic idea somehow reflecting either an ultimate creation of the demiurge—a final category, or an immanent genetic entity. *What we do not know about violence*, is a function of our unwitting insistence on turning it into an essence, and therefore the knowledge of essences must become a classic philosophical problem in our civilization.

What we violate, do violence to, we hypostatize: our moral syntax has no predicate. Hence we speak of doing *good*, good for its own sake, or *evil*. We convert each into a pure substantive, beyond experience, abstract. That is what Paul Radin meant when he observed that the subject (or object) to which love, remorse, sorrow, may be directed is regarded as secondary in our civilization. All have the rank of virtues as such: they are manifestations of God's if not of Man's way. But among primitives, in this instance the Winnebago, whom Radin knew intimately, the converse holds. Morality *is* behavior, values are not detached, not substantives; the good, the true, the beautiful or rather, the ideas of these things, do not exist. Therefore, one does not fall *in* love, one loves another; and that is an intricately learned experience, as hate, in a certain sense, also is.

Here is the paradox: rationalized, machanized and secularized civilization tends to produce standard, modal persons rather than natural variety. The individual is always in danger of dissolving into the function or the status. This if Goffman's thesis in *The Presentation of Self in Everyday Life*[46] and in his studies of total institutions, which it must be added can only base themselves on *incompletely developed persons*. But ultimate role playing or infinite masking of the self is not universal. It may be dramaturgical or theatrical, as Goffman describes the process, but it is not dramatic. The dramatic has its roots in the catastrophies and paradoxes, the meanings of ordinary existence, first celebrated and given form in the primitive ritual drama. Mere dramaturgy has as much relation to the living, historical heart of drama as religion has to religiosity. Indeed, such conventional play acting is the antithesis of the drama. Yet is is instructive that a civilized sociologist should, while accurately describing the intricacies of collective role playing, mistake the construction of a *persona* for the development of the self.

In the name of individualism, civilization manufactures stereotypes: Dumb Doras, organization men, or Joe Magaracs, whose prototype, in the popular tale, is transformed into the very steel that he helps produces. Such stereotyping usually leads to a culturally formed stupidity, a stupidity of the job itself, which grows to encompass the person, feeding on itself as both a defense against experience and the result of being deprived of it. But the psychologically isolated individual, cognitively, instrumentally, and affectively dulled by the division of labor and threatened by leisure yet somehow treasuring the idea that, in his name, society functions and battles are fought, is unknown in primitive society. To be "detached," "unattached," or "objective" (that is, object-oriented) becomes, as civilization advances, both the symptom of a social condition and the expression of an intellectual attitude. Yet it is precisely this kind of "individualism" that inhibits the growth of the indivisible person, that inner union of contraries.

Conversely, in primitive society, authentic individuation is more likely to occur, because the pre-conditions for personal growth, which I shall shortly attempt to summarize below, are present. Paul Radin, one of the most deeply experienced field anthropologists wrote:

> Free scope is allowed for every conceivable kind of personality outlet or expression in primitive society. No moral judgment is passed on any aspect of human personality as such. Human nature is what it is, and each act, emotion, belief, unexpressed or expressed, must be allowed to make or mar a man.... Limitations to this expression naturally exist—but these flow directly from an intense and clear-cut appreciation of the realities of life and from an acute sensitivity to group reaction.[47]

Radin sums up his viewpoint as follows: "Express yourself completely but know yourself completely and accept the consequences of your own personality and actions." Jomo Kenyatta attempts a similar assessment: "The African is conditioned, by the cultural and social institutions of centuries, to a freedom of which Europe has little conception...."[48] And Christopher Dawson, referring to the tribal background of the Celts, agrees:

> Nevertheless, though the tribe is a relatively primitive form of

social organisation, it possesses virtues which many more advanced types of society may envy. It is consistent with a high ideal of personal freedom and self-respect and evokes an intense spirit of loyalty and devotion on the part of the individual tribesman towards the community and its chief.[49]

I believe these statements to be substantially true, which is to say that they accord with my experience. The point is that primitive man is not a mere reflex of the group. On the contrary, the group is "embedded, indeed embodied, in the very individuality of the individual."[50] Anyone who has ever witnessed a ceremonial African dance will certainly agree that the individual's sense of personal power and worth is immeasurably heightened by the communal nature of the event. It is as if the person is expressing an energy beyond his own. Yet the bodily movements, the facial expressions, often the steps, vary from person to person—the individual style comes through. Such an organic group is the converse of the mob, that is, a collectivity of detached individuals losing themselves in some furious activity, seeking an anonymous union. The mob is a civilized phenomenon not a primitive one; it is the collective in frenzy, the repressed emotions exploding outward without restraint or form, balance or responsibility. The image of the mob is part of our image of the city, and the city is the carrier of the best and the worst of civilization.

But the primitive society is a *community*, springing from common origins, composed of reciprocating persons, and growing from within. It is not a collective.[51] Collectives emerge in civilization; they are functional to specialized ends, and they generate a sense of being imposed from without. They are objectively perceived, objectifying and estranging structures. Leopold Senghor spoke to this point as follows: "Above all, we have developed cooperation, not collectivist, but communal. For cooperation—of family, village, tribe—has always been honored in Black Africa; once again, not in collectivist form, not as an aggregate of individuals, but in communal form, as mutual agreement."[52]

A collective has the form of a community but lacks the substance; it is involved with the concept "public," which is not at all the same as the idea of the social. The fully functioning, highly individuated member of society is the antithesis of the public man. "A public," wrote Kierkegaard, "is neither a nation, nor a generation, nor a community, nor a society, nor these particular men, for all these are only what they are through the concrete. . . . The public will be less than a single real man, however unimportant,"[53] That is a dreadful statement. Let me put it this way. The public is a reification, a projection of our partial lives and its mode of existence, its expression of energy, its *revenge* is what we have come to call violence, and the problem of violence.

I wish to review, extend and present for further exploration some of the most critical aspects of the primitive features already outlined. Among primitives, we customarily encounter within the web of kinship:

1. Good nurturance. The infant's psychophysiological contact with a "mothering one" is both extensive and intensive. Whatever childhood disciplines are imposed (and they vary widely from society to society, in time of imposition, mode and content) they function within a dynamic affective field.*

2. Many-sided, engaging personal relationships through all phases of the individual's life cycle, further developing and strengthening the sense of self, and others, for these are reciprocal processes. This dynamic, multi-layered sense, and actuality, of self, cannot be understood in the one dimensional terms of "ego" psychology; the primitive self cannot be reduced to an ego but is the result of a hierarchy of experiences, incorporated into an increasingly spiritualized being as maturation proceeds from birth through the multiple rebirths symbolized in the crisis rites, to ancestry of others.

   I would further hypothesize, that the socialization process

---

* Throughout the High Nigerian Plateau, for example, children are customarily force-fed water by hand during infancy. The infant may scream, become furious, and even momentarily lose consciousness. But this amuses, rather than disturbs the mother, for she knows well enough that she is not committing a hostile act. She remains firm, but persistent during the brief conflict. Afterwards, the infant quiets down very quickly and is rewrapped into his secure position on the mother's hip or back. It is this unfailing association with the mother and mother surrogates, that makes the infant receptive to the customary disciplines, and renders them nontraumatic. The "instinctual" life is neither feared by adults, nor harshly repressed in children.

among primitives results in a high modal capacity to relate things and events, that is, to think. This most striking (indeed, defining) component in human intelligence would seem to be a function of the "quality and nature of concrete affective relationships" at critical points in the life cycle. The conceptual or abstract capacity is, of course, the ability and desire to make connections and not, necessarily, to deal with abstractions in the Western philosophic sense. Just as the primitive people I have known give an over-all impression of alertness and intelligence, so people who have become specialized in civilized political economies frequently impress one with the automatism of their responses, and their boredom. Boredom is a highly civilized characteristic, not a primitive one; but these probable relationships between social-historical character and intelligence have hardly begun to be explored.[54]

3. Various forms of institutionalized deviancy. These have the effect of accommodating idiosyncratic individuals to the group while permitting unconventional behavior. In such cases the deviant may be both privileged and penalized, but he does not become a social derelict.

Among certain American Indians warrior societies—the Cheyenne Contrary Ones, or the Crow Crazy Dogs—the most inappropriate behavior was tolerated. But the young men who were granted this license to invert customary behavior had to reciprocate by exposing themselves in battle, which usually meant engaging the enemy in the most unexpected and direct ways. Here, for example, is what the Crow say about the matter:

—Act like a crazy dog. Wear sashes and other fine clothes, carry a rattle, and dance along the roads singing crazy dog songs after everybody else has gone to bed.

—Talk crosswise: say the opposite of what you mean and make others say the opposite of what they mean in return.

—Fight like a fool by rushing up to an enemy and offering to be killed. Dig a hole near an enemy, and when the enemy surrounds it, leap out at them and drive them back.

—Paint yourself white, mount a white horse, cover its

eyes and make it jump down a steep and rocky bank, until both of you are crushed.[55]

4. The celebration, and fusion, of the sacred and the natural, the individual and society, in ritual. Through ritual, life culminates in the form of drama; social and existential anxieties are creatively used.

5. Direct engagement with nature and natural physiological functions. Thus the sense of reality is heightened to the point where it sometimes seems to "blaze." It is at this point that the experiences of primitive and mystic converge, for mysticism is no more than reality, perceived at its ultimate subjective pitch. And this, in turn, brackets the pragmatism of the primitive with his mysticism, while linking the "ordinary" man to the shaman. The focus in each case is the same, the difference is the degree of intensity. Merely filthy or nasty attitudes about natural functions are rare—although broad, even wild (trickster) humor—is commonplace. This Paiute song is typical:

In the old time women's cunts
　　had teeth in them.
It was hard to be a man then
Watching your squaw squat down to dinner
Hearing the little rabbit bones crackle.
Whenever fucking was invented
　　it died with the inventor.
If your woman said she felt like
　　biting you didn't take it lightly.
Maybe you just ran away
　　to fight Numuzoho the Cannibal.

Coyote was the one who fixed things,
He fixed those toothy women!
One night he took Numuzoho's lava pestle
To bed with a mean woman
And hammer hammer crunch crunch ayi ayi
All night long:
"Husband, I am glad," she said
And all the rest is history.
To honor him we wear
　　our necklaces of fangs.[56]

6. Active and manifold participation in culture. This, together with the preceding, contributes to feelings of individual worth, dignity and competence.

7. As Leach, Boas, Weltfish and others have emphasized, the natural environment is perceived more esthetically than is commonly the case in civilization. Artisanship is highly prized and widespread among primitives; the continuous contact with finely and individually made everyday objects helps to make personal, and charge with meaning primitive surroundings. "Among primitive people," concludes Boas, "goodness and beauty are the same."[57]

8. Socio-economic support as a natural inheritance. Conversely stated, socio-economic risk is equitably distributed throughout society. Therefore, no crippling anxieties or doubts about personal worth derive from that fundamental source. This, in addition to all preceding points, explains the minimal occurrence, or absence, of civilized types of "crime" in primitive society.

These prominent features of primitive society should lead us to anticipate an exceedingly low incidence of the chronic characterological or psychoneurotic phenomena that seem to be growing with civilization, as Meyer Fortes, among others, has indicated.[58] This reflects my own experience; I would add only that the disciplined expressiveness of primitive societies, together with traditional social and economic supports also results in a greater tolerance of psychotic manifestations, or better, converts the latter into a normal, bounded human experience.

THE PROSPECTS

The individuation, personalism, nominalism and existentialism so markedly apparent in primitive society continuously reinforce each other, and as we have seen, they are fully consonant with the social structure. Similarly, it is interesting to note that Heidegger believes that the break in the Western tradition between the pre-Socratics and Plato, that is, between what I would roughly identify as pre-civilized and civilized conceptions, is symptomatic.[59] Each interrelated mode may be summarized as follows:

Primitive (pre-civilized, pre-alienation) existentialism is evident in: (1) the ritual expression of the primary needs of the person in nature and society. Meanings are questioned and resolved and a literal "being born with others" or co-naissance[60] or "the free abandon of communion"[61] occurs. As Boas puts it: "The readiness to abandon one's self to the exultation induced by art is probably greater [than among ourselves] because the conventional restraint of our times does not exist in the same form in their lives;"[62] (2) the emphasis on existence rather than essence; (3) the responsibility of the individual to self and society; and (4) the lack of concern with analytic modes of thought.

Primitive personalism is revealed in: (1) the web of kinship; (2) the organic community; and (3) the apprehension of consciousness throughout society and nature.

Primitive nominalism is focused in: (1) The emphasis on concrete particulars and contexts; (2) the naming of *existents* in nature and society, in dream and reality; and (3) in the fact that ideas, as such, are not, typically, hypostatized or reified.

Primitive individuation is nurtured by: (1) The full and manifold participation of individuals in nature and society; (2) the intensely personal socialization process through which individual qualities are delineated; and (3) the expression of society in the person and the person in society.

The four dominant qualities, or modes of thinking, or psychological perspectives, or ways of behaving—they are all of these simultaneously—find their antithesis in the prevailing modes of conduct and thought that arose and steadily intensified with the growth of civilization.

In each of these critical areas—critical because it is within their parameters that the crisis of civilization is expressed—civilized behavior may be characterized as increasingly: (1) essentialist; quantification becomes etherealized, which is, as we have seen, a political, philosophic and, finally, a scientific process. Western science is conceived in Galileo, but Plato is the Godfather;[63] (2) abstract and analytic; (3) impersonal and mechanical, in short, (4) collectivized, that is, involved with aggregates of individuals, in pursuit of specialized activities that tend to transform their human associations into technical, or even merely spatial, arrangements. Personae are substituted for persons.

Despite Western civilization's pride in science, and perhaps because of it, its mode of behavior is increasingly magical, publically, with reference to commodity fetishism, and behavioristic and mechanical manipulation of all sorts, including advertising; and privately, the equivalent of these public expressions, with reference to obsessive-compulsive neuroses. These identifications of the "ego" with externals, these security operations absorb far more energy in our society than they do among primitive people; that is, what can be technically defined as magical behavior has grown, not diminished with civilization. And this is pure magic, substitutive of effective activities in the world, rather than correlated with them, just the contrary of the case among primitive people. Moreover, explicit behavior toward the supernatural, is, in our society weighted on the magical, that is, the mechanical end of the magico-religious continuum . . . the method of religion being a projection of the personal, in the typical mode of the primitive world.

Our pathology, then, consists in our dedication to abstractions, in our collectivism, pseudo-individualism, and lack of institutional means for the expression and transcendence of human ambivalence. Conversely, the negative aspects of primitive personalism find their own subjective balance, but cannot be objectively checked.

Our illness springs from the very center of civilization, not from too much knowledge, but from too little wisdom. What primitives possess—the immediate and ramifying sense of the person, and all that I have tried to show that that entails—an existential humanity—we have largely lost. That is what civilization must selectively incorporate; we cannot abandon the primitive; we can only outgrow it by letting it grow within us. For thousands of years of a cultural development antithetical to ours, man deeply defined his nature; let us make that, which the poets have always known, very clear.* All notions of progress, and rationalizations

---

* Gary Snyder exemplifies this consciousness:
> As a poet I hold the most archaic values on earth. They go back to the Paleolithic: the fertility of the soil, the magic of animals. The power-vision in solitude, the terrifying initiation and rebirth, the love and ecstasy of the damned, the common work of the tribe.
> There is a level of mind which must be distinguished from the purely ecstatic, where the most immediate and personal perceptions fuse with

about evolution are subordinated today to the dialectical moment we have reached between civilization and the primitive experience.

By studying primitive peoples through the screen of our civilization, by plunging into history, we learn that, although human nature as a system of interlocking potentials remains constant, specific, mutually exclusive types of realization along with what we are obliged to consider distortions, occur. The vision of Man that resolves out of close study of primitive society is clearly the antithesis of Man in maximally politicized civilizations, such as our own. We may put the matter as follows—differential social existence actualizes certain potentials of being and nullifies others. Moreover, each quality has its negative. Where we, as noted, no longer ritualize our cultural existence, except through the residual, passive-defensive and compulsive means metaphorically documented by Freud, they, the primitives, symbolize their personal perception and mastery of their environment through rituals that renew human, social, and natural existence. The potential negative in the primitive experience is the denial of nature as a paradigm of processes of which Man is a manifestation, but perhaps not the center. The negative of our notions of science is in Man splitting himself into object and observer, and the concomitant loss of the person as an integrated subject, as a partner in a universe of persons.

In examining such complementarities, one is struck by the possibility of synthesis; but for complementarities, in the areas that interest us, to develop beyond the condition of paired opposites and to confront each other as antitheses to theses, foreshadowing synthesis, requires, as it did for Socrates, a concretely political transformation of intellectual insight. Social reconstruction based upon historical considerations of human nature, and the thus far segregated expressions that have dominated the successive eras of man can be programmatic only to a limited degree. It is not, and cannot be, a question of grafting primitive forms on civilized structures or, need it be said again, of "retreating" into the primitive past. It is not a question of

---

the archetypal and ritual relationships of human society to the universe. Poetry made from here is not "automatic," but it is often effortless; and it does not exclude the pleasure of occasional intellectual ingenuity and allusion. My best poems flow from such a state; they have . . . a tendency . . . toward exploring the architecture of consciousness.

regaining lost paradises or savage nobility, neither of which ever existed in the manner imputed to their authors; they were merely straw constructions to be blown down by the kind of easy and baseless irony which Voltaire addressed to Rousseau. The problem, and it remains the central problem of anthropology, is to help conceptualize contemporary forms that will reunite man with his past, reconcile the primitive with the civilized, making progress without distortion theoretically possible, or, at least, enabling us to experience the qualities that primitive peoples routinely display. This, in turn, demands innovation of the highest order, even if nourished on despair, innovation equivalent to the genius that one detects, for example, behind the kinship paradigms of primitive people. What better place is there to begin than with the rational devolution of bureaucracy, the common ownership and decentralization of the basic means of production, for which we have the techniques at hand and for which we must develop the apposite social imagination. Human beings have lived in analogous circumstances before, we learn from anthropology, and it seems essential that we learn to do so again, albeit on a higher level and in different forms. Reflexive, merely determined behavior, condemns us to the destructive course of our civilization, to the irresponsibility of our fate.

5

PLATO
AND THE DEFINITION
OF THE PRIMITIVE

The origin and nature of the state is a subject peculiarly appropriate to cultural anthropology, for states first arise through the transformation and obliteration of typically primitive institutions. Thinkers of the most diverse backgrounds and intentions have throughout history grasped this cardinal fact of state formation. Lao-tzu, Rousseau, Marx and Engels, Maine, Morgan, Maitland, Tonnies and many contemporary students of society have understood that there is a qualitative distinction between the structure of primitive life and civilization. Moreover, they have, more or less explicitly, sensed the contradictions inherent in the transition from kinship or primitive society, to civilized or political society. This momentous transition, this great transformation in the life of man, this social and cultural trauma, has led to a passionate and ancient debate about the merits of primitive existence as opposed to civilization. The debate has frequently been waged in utopian terms. Some utopias face backward to a sometimes fantastic image of the primitive, others face forward to the complete triumph of the rational state. Although I have no intention of engaging in this debate, it seems to me that it is the opposition to the primitive which lies at the root of Plato's utopia,[1] and that is the theme I intend to pursue

---

Throughout this chapter, I have used the term *God* metaphorically, since Plato's notion of the deity is, historically and technically, somewhat different from ours. But Plato's meaning is nonetheless conveyed, and the implications of my argument are in no way affected. Similarly, the definition of the essence as an idea in the *mind of God* is neo-Platonic, most notably developed by Malebranche.

here. In opposing the primitive, Plato helps us define both it and the state.

The Opposition to the Primitive

The *Republic* can be considered a projection of the idealized, total city-state, conjured out of the ruins of fourth-century Athens and influenced by the Spartan oligarchy. But in its perfection, it transcends these local boundaries and becomes a classic model of the state to which Western scholars have turned for centuries in debating the good life and its relation to political society. This tension between the local and the universal is evident in all utopian constructs, whether merely literary, or socially realized; it is preeminently true of the *Republic*. Plato maintains certain landmarks of the city-state, but he takes us on a "journey of a thousand years." This span of time is reckoned, perhaps, too modestly, for all subsequent political societies commanded by a permanent, self-proclaimed, benevolent élite, and all élitist social theory, are adumbrated in the *Republic*.

The *Republic*, of course, is more than a political tract. It is also a psychology, an esthetics and a philosophy, but it is all these things within a political context. There is hardly any facet of Plato's vision, however abstruse, nor any action he believed imperative which is not colored or dictated by political considerations. The *Republic* is, in short, a work of enormous scope, but it is saturated with politics, with ideology. This point deserves emphasis because Plato has traditionally been considered the very image of the pure philosopher, and the *Republic* has been extolled as the masterwork, in which most of his major ideas appear, impressively interwoven. As Emerson put it, "Plato is philosophy and philosophy Plato...." The New England Platonist goes further, ceding to Plato Omar's "fanatical compliment" to the Koran: "Burn the libraries, for their value is in this book."[2] The phrase sticks—it is an appropriately Platonic sentiment, and it is a political remark.

What then are the political assumptions underlying the *Republic*? To begin with, Plato's personal political bias is clear. He was an aristocrat who experienced the decay of the Athenian "democracy." He was a philosopher in a society that put Socrates to death. He avoided the rough-and-tumble of politics and shrank from any actual political role in his own society for which his birth and training may have qualified him. Yet he seems to have been obsessed with the idea of politics; the political problem for Plato seems to have consisted in how to abolish politics.

It is possible, therefore, to view the *Republic* as the idealization and rationalization of Plato's personal motives. His ideal state is, after all, a utopian aristocracy, ruled by philosophers who have become kings, and the political problem has ceased to exist. But this is too close an exercise in the sociology of knowledge. Plato's personal motives are unquestionably important; they help fix the precise form of the republic, but they do not determine its broader cultural-historical meaning. In Cornford's words:

> The city-state was a frame within which any type of constitution could subsist; a despotism, an oligarchy, or a democracy. Any Greek citizen of Plato's day, rich or poor, would have been completely puzzled, if he had been told that he had no interest in maintaining the structure of the city-state. The democrat, in particular, would have replied: "Do you really think that an oriental despotism, where all men but one are slaves, is a higher and happier type of society? Or would you reduce us to the level of those savages with all their queer customs described by Herodotus?"[3]

Plato's oligarchic inclinations, then, cannot be considered contradictory to the basic structure of the city-state; the exact form of his republic is less significant than its over-all statism. The political assumptions underlying the *Republic* are simply the assumptions of political society, of the state, writ large and idealized. We must remember that classical Greece could look back to its own archaic and primitive past; moreover, it lived on the fringe of a "barbarian" Europe. Thus, the forms and usages of primitive society, even when these were being transformed into organs of the state or abolished in favor of state institutions, were by no means strange to the Greeks, as Fustel de Coulanges, Engels, Morgan, Bury and others have emphasized. Bury, for example, in tracing the early history of Greece, speaks of the authority of the state growing and asserting itself against the comparative independence of the family, and he remarks further that "in the heroic age . . . the state had not emerged fully from the society. No laws were enacted and maintained by the state."[4]

It seems likely then that Plato had ample opportunity to react against concrete primitive elements in Greek society and cultural tradition while envisioning his utopian state. Only the classical scholars, with the aid of a more fully developed classical anthropology, can establish the degree to which this was possible, but it is not essential to my argument. Plato could have been acting out of sheer political instinct, logically constructing the perfect political society and rejecting those institutions and modes of behavior which could not be coordinated with it, that is, the primitive modes. In any case, the fact of opposition to the primitive is clear in the *Republic*, as is Plato's sure sense of the strategy of political society. And this, I believe, is the larger cultural-historical meaning of his work, conceived, as it was in the morning of European civilization. Indeed the Heavenly City may be viewed as that essence of which all realized polities are inadequate reflections.

DENYING THE FAMILY

Although the themes that will concern us in the *Republic* are very subtly interwoven and sometimes lack precise definition, I shall consider them separately without trying to reconstruct Plato's full argument.

There is, first of all, the suggestion that Socrates makes about the initiation of the republic:

> They will begin by sending out into the country all the inhabitants of the city who are more than ten years old, and will take possession of their children, who will be unaffected by the habits of their parents; these they will train in their own habits and laws, I mean in the laws which we have given them: and in this way the State and constitution of which we were speaking will soonest and most easily attain happiness, and the nation which has such a constitution will gain most.[5]

The republic is to begin, then, by severing the bonds between the generations and by obliterating the primary kinship ties. This is, of course, an extreme statement of the general process through which states arise, which is by releasing the individual from kinship controls and obligations and thus making him subject to the emerging civil laws. There is, however, a remarkably exact parallel to Socrates' suggestion in native Dahomean usage as reported by Norris, one of the early chroniclers of the Slave Coast. In the Dahomean proto-state, "children are taken from their mothers at an early age, and distributed to places remote from their village of nativity, where they remain with little chance of being ever seen, or at least recognized, by their parents afterwards. The motive for this is that there may be no family connections or combinations, no associations that might prove injurious to the King's unlimited power."[6]

But we must never forget that Plato has no intention of outlining the process of state formation per se; he is, in our view, idealizing that process, hence the purpose of setting up the republic in the manner described is seen as beneficent.

I might add, parenthetically, that the attempt to weaken or sever the ties between the generations is also a typical utopian and quasi-revolutionary aim. The most recent instance is the Israeli kibbutz, where the collective rearing of children is motivated by the desire to produce a generation quite different in character from the parental image of the Shtetl Jew.[7] As a matter of fact, wherever a massive shift in political power and structure is contemplated or wherever a radical rearrangement of public loyalties is demanded, the family, the psychic transmission belt between the generations, tends to be attacked not merely in terms of any particular form but as a primary social unit. This is evident in rather different ways in the work of many reformists, among a number of so-called Marxists, and in Nazi theory and practice.

Plato's modest proposal for initiating the republic, then, can be seen in both a revolutionary and a cultural-historical perspective. The *Republic* begins, appropriately enough, in opposition to the antecedent kin and generational ties. And we shall see that this imperative is extended to the rearing of the guardians within the republic. That is, state and family, echoing the old antagonism between political and primitive organization, are seen to be antithetical, even after the establishment of the ideal polity.

THE DIVISION OF LABOR AND CLASS

Primitive societies that are not in transition to one or another archaic form of the state (that is, that are not proto-states) may function through rank and status systems and always function through kin or transfigured kin units, the latter being associations whose members are not necessarily reckoned as kin but which pattern themselves on kin forms. They are, however, devoid of class or caste. Further, primitive societies do not manifest the highly specialized division of labor which is one of the major aspects of the rise of class and caste systems. In these related respects, Plato's republic represents the reverse of primitive usage and is the state brought to its highest power. To clarify, let us begin with his vision of an absolute division of labor.

In the republic, no man is to engage in more than a single task. Indeed, the ultimate definition of justice, which Socrates pursues as perhaps the major aim of the entire dialogue, consists in each person doing the work "for which he was by nature fitted" within the class to which he constitutionally belongs. And "at that [occupation] he is to continue working all his life long and at no other."[8] Later on, Socrates elaborates this point as follows: "in our State, and in our State only, we shall find a shoemaker to be a shoemaker, and not a pilot also, and a soldier a soldier, and not a trader also, and the same throughout." He emphasizes: in "our State . . . human nature is not twofold or manifold, for one man plays one part only."[9]

In other words, it is imagined that the identity of the individual is exhausted by the single occupation in which he engages. The occupational status, so to speak, becomes the man, just as his class position is, in a wider sense, said to be determined by his nature. In this way, the existence of the state is guaranteed, but the life of the person is constricted and diminished. The division of labor is, of course, an expression of the socially available technology. The point is that Plato not only sensed the congruence of the elaborate division of labor with state organization, but carried it to its furthest reach and then gave it the name of justice.

The contrast with primitive usage could hardly be more striking. Primitives learn a variety of skills; a single family unit, as among the Nama, Anaguta or Eskimo, may make its own clothing, tools and weapons, build its own houses, and so on. Even in a transitional society such as the Dahomean proto-state it is expected that every man, whatever his occupation, know three things well: how to cut a field, how to build a wall and how to roof a house.[10] Moreover, the average primitive participates directly in a wide range of cultural activities relative to the total available in his society, and he may move, in his lifetime, through a whole series of culturally prescribed statuses. He plays, in short, many parts, and his nature is viewed as manifold. The relevance of this to Plato's conception of the drama will be considered below, but it is first necessary to examine the class structure of his republic and its implications.

The republic is to be divided into three classes: the guardians, or ruling élite; the auxiliaries, including the soldiers; and the lowest class, consisting of all those engaged in economic production, particularly the artisans and farmers. We see at once that the manual laborers are at the base of the social hierarchy, being considered constitutionally unfit to rule themselves. This is of course a quite typical attitude, however rationalized, and we find it associated with the rise of civilization almost everywhere. In early states, the intellectual gradually emerges from the class of scribes or priests; his connections with the ruling groups are primary. The artisans and farmers grow out of the submerged primitive community, which is transformed into a reservoir of workers for the state through direct conscription of labor, taxation, slavery, or related means.

But whatever the details of the process, and they vary in different areas, the subordination of primitive artisan and cultivator is a function of state formation. An Egyptian document dating from the New Kingdom is pertinent, in that it reflects this state of affairs, long consolidated:

> Put writing in your heart that you may protect yourself from hard labor of any kind and be a magistrate of high repute. The scribe is released from manual tasks; it is he who commands. . . . Do you not hold the scribe's palette? That is what makes the difference between you and the man who handles an oar.
>
> I have seen the metal worker at his task at the mouth of his furnace with fingers like a crocodile's. He stank worse than fish spawn. Every workman who holds a chisel suffers more than the men who hack the ground; wood is his field and the chisel his mattock. At night when he is free, he toils more than his arms can do; even at night he lights [his lamp to work by]. . . . The stonecutter seeks work in every hard stone; when he has done the great part of his labor his arms

are exhausted, he is tired out. . . . The weaver in a workshop is worse off than a woman; [he squats] with his knees to his belly and does not taste [fresh] air. He must give loaves to the porters to see the light.[11]

This process and the attendant attitudes are, I believe, ideally reflected in the *Republic*. They develop in Plato's cave, in the turmoil of history, but they are presented to us in a purified, philosophic and ultimate form.

Now the classes in the ideal state are relatively fixed; they tend to be castes, rationalized on a eugenic basis. But Plato provides for both a modicum of social mobility and the predominant freezing of the entire structure through the medium of a "royal lie," that is, through propaganda, a term that Cornford considers more appropriate,[12] and a condition which we shall take up in connection with the exile of the dramatist. Socrates states:

Citizens . . . God has framed you differently. Some of you have the power of command, and in the composition of these he has mingled gold, wherefore also they have the greatest honor; others he has made of silver, to be auxiliaries; others again to be husbandmen and craftsmen he has composed of brass and iron; and the species will generally be preserved in the children. But . . . a golden parent will sometimes have a silver son, or a silver parent a golden son. And God proclaims as a first principle to the rulers, and above all else, that there is nothing which they should so anxiously guard . . . as the purity of the race . . . if the son of a golden or silver parent has an admixture of brass and iron, then nature orders a transportation of ranks and the eye of the ruler must not be pitiful towards the child because he has to descend in the scale and become a husbandman or artisan, just as there may be sons of artisans who having an admixture of gold or silver in them are raised to honor, and become guardians or auxiliaries. For an oracle says that when a man of brass or iron guards the state, it will be destroyed. Such is the tale; is there any possibility of making our citizens believe in it?[13]

The class structure of the republic then, is based on a theory of human nature, assimilated to Plato's doctrine of essences.[14] Here we confront a perfect example of the convergence of characteristic Platonic concepts to an immediate political issue, a technique that weaves throughout the dialogue and accounts in part for its great dialectic density. The final nature of the individual is viewed as unambiguous, since human nature is a matter of distinct and single higher and lower essences, subdivided further into occupational essences. That is to say, the division of labor and class in the *Republic* is reflected in the division into essences or vice versa, if you will. The important point is that the whole structure is guaranteed by human nature, watched over by the guardians, justified by philosophy and sanctified by God, as the allegory states.

At the peak of the pyramid stand the guardians. They are said to have a pure intuition of the good; they live in the place of light above the cave and are, in a sense, divine; or at least they have intimations of divinity. Shall we call them divine kings? It matters little, for all kings have been considered holy since the primary differentiation of the king from the local primitive chief. The holiness of the king is the sanctification of civil power, as opposed to the common traditions which are symbolized in the person of the local chief and may thus render *him* sacred. The ultimate other-worldliness of the guardians or philosopher kings is, I believe, a reflection of the process through which civil power was first sanctified as the primitive community was transformed into political society. We should recall that Plato was impressed by the Egyptian theocracy and may have visited Egypt, where the concept of divine rule was as old as the state itself. In any event, the elite tradition of the guardians is the opposite of the communal tradition of primitive peoples.

Yet neither the divinity of the kings, who shape the end of the republic, nor the sterling quality of their auxiliaries is sufficient to ensure their devotion to the state. This can be achieved most readily through a completely collective life and training. Socrates says: "the wives of our guardians are to be common, and their children are to be common, and no parent is to know his own child, nor any child his parent."[15] The children are to be reared collectively by special nurses who "dwell in a separate quarter." The mothers will nurse them but "the greatest possible care" will be taken that no mother recognizes her own child nor will suckling be "protracted too long." The mother will "have no getting up at night or other trouble, but will hand over all this sort of thing to the nurses and attendants."[16]

Further, the guardians and their helpers, under a regime of

spartan simplicity, are to live in common houses, dine in common and hold no property; and they are not to engage in economically productive work. The obvious aim is to disengage them from all connections and motives which might diminish their dedication to the state. Plato clearly sensed the antagonism between state and family, and in order to guarantee total loyalty to the former, he simply abolished the latter. Moreover, his distrust of kin ties in the ideal state leads him to invoke the aid of a "royal lie," possibly the first half of the propaganda-myth quoted above. Socrates, simulating embarrassment, says:

> I really know not how to look you in the face, or in what words to utter the audacious fiction, which I propose to communicate gradually, first to the rulers, then to the soldiers, and lastly to the people. They are to be told that their youth was a dream, and the education and training they received from us, an appearance only; in reality during all that time they were being formed and fed in the womb of the earth, where they themselves and their arms and appurtenances were manufactured; when they were completed, the earth, their mother, sent them up; and so their country being their mother and also their nurse, they are bound to advise for her good, and to defend her against attacks, and her citizens they are to regard as children of the earth and their brothers.[17]

This is, of course, a direct statement of the conflict between kin and political principles. The territorial state is to receive the loyalty previously accorded the kin group, and this can only be done by personifying the state, an essentially impersonal structure. Plato remarks that the fiction is an old Phoenician tale of "what has often occurred before now in other places."[18] Certainly, the myth is precisely of the type we would expect in societies in transition from kin to civil structure, that is, in societies engaged in a primary kin-civil conflict.

There is a peculiar parallel with Dahomean usage here, not in the form of myth but in actual social convention. In Dahomey, every important official in the emerging state structure had a female counterpart within the king's compound. This woman, termed his "mother," had precedence at "court," acting as a sort of buffer between the official and the king and personalizing the purely material relationship involved.[19] The bureaucrats were mustered from the local villages, the conquered and subordinate areas; they had no kin ties with the royal clan or dynastic lineage. The system of "civil mothers" thus symbolized the new connections that had begun to develop in distinction to the old kin loyalties. The idea of the motherland, or fatherland, although expressed in kin terms, seems coincident with the rise of the state, at the point where the problem of political loyalty begins. This, I believe, is the meaning of Plato's fiction, concretely revealed in Dahomean usage.

It should be noted that Plato confines the fiction of the "earth-born heroes" to the guardians and auxiliaries. The ordinary people, composed of brass and iron, are to live under ordinary family circumstances. No extraordinary behavior of any kind is expected of them, certainly no unusual loyalty to the state. Their worldly concerns, their emotional ties and their inferior natures are conceived as making such behavior impossible. The soldiers guard the city, the guardians rule it; acquiescence and temperance, a living up to their own limited possibilities, are the demands made on the mass of people. That, and the labor which supports the upper classes. The economic producers are, of course, deprived of political means; in the ideal state this was visualized as the solution to the political problem. Yet Plato seems uncertain. He speaks of the soldiers selecting a spot "whence they can best suppress insurrection, if any prove refractory within,"[20] and also of their maintaining "peace among our citizens at home ... [that they may not] have the power to harm us."[21]

One further point is worth consideration. The selectively bred but family-less upper classes are to refer to all peers as brothers and sisters and to the members of the older generation as father and mother, seemingly congruent with extended family or clan usage. However, the upper classes represent what can be technically termed a collective, not a community; the relational forms are retained, but the substance is lacking.[22] What we confront here is a rather interesting politicization of kin terminology, as in the case of the Dahomean "civil mothers," in direct opposition to primitive behavior. The latter is always based on concrete and complex family relationships which may then be extended outward to include remote relatives, strangers or even natural phenomena. But as we have seen, the mothers of the upper classes are not to know their own children.[23] They are to be relieved of all domestic and maternal responsibility and thus converted into ideal instruments of the state, fully equal, in this respect, to the men.

The above is a rough outline of class structure and function in the *Republic*. In general, it is the antithesis of what Kroeber, for one, has called "primitive democracy."[24]

CENSORSHIP OF THE DRAMATIST

There is, I believe, a keystone in the soaring arch of Plato's argument, an imperative on which it must inevitably rest. In this imperative, the statism of the republic culminates, as does its opposition to the primitive.

The dramatists, the makers of tragedy and comedy, the "imitative poets," as Plato calls them, are to be exiled and their works abolished or heavily censored. Socrates says:

When any one of these pantomimic gentlemen, who are so clever that they can imitate anything, comes to us, and makes a proposal to exhibit himself and his poetry, we will fall down and worship him as a sweet and holy and wonderful being; but we must also inform him that in our State such as he are not permitted to exist; the law will not allow them.[25]

Plato has already given us a reason for this, quoted above in connection with the division of labor: "[in] our State human nature is not twofold or manifold, for one man plays one part only." The "pantomimic gentlemen," Homer or Aeschylus, for example, have no place in the class and occupational structure of the republic, assimilated, as it is, to the doctrine of essences or ultimate forms. Socrates makes this clear to Adeimantus: "human nature appears to have been coined into yet smaller pieces, and to be as incapable of imitating many things well, as of performing well the actions of which the imitations are copies."[26]

But before pursuing Plato's theory of art, which emerges so logically out of the dialogue, let us examine some of the simpler reasons for establishing a "censorship of the writers of fiction"[27] and the implications thereof.

The poets are perceived as impious and corrupters of youth. They misrepresent the nature of God, which is absolutely good, by spinning tales of rage and ribaldry in heaven. If at all possible, children in the ideal state should be told that conflict is unholy and has never existed among the gods or between citizens. The wicked must always be represented as miserable, "because they require to be punished, and are benefitted by receiving punishment from God," but God must never, in verse or prose, be considered the author of evil, for such a fiction would be suicidal in "any well-ordered commonwealth." The poets, such as Euripides, must not be permitted to say that suffering is the work of God, or if it is of God, they "must devise some explanation . . . such as we are seeking." The task of the poet, then, is to justify the ways of God to man, to buttress morality in the republic. And the ultimate impiety is to speak, with Homer, of "Zeus, who is the dispenser of good *and* evil to us."[28]

Moreover, the poets are inappropriately emotional. They portray death and the underworld in lurid terms; they lament the fallen warrior and rail against fortune, whereas, in the republic, "the good man . . . will not sorrow for his departed friend [or son, or brother], as though he had suffered anything terrible, [since he] is sufficient for himself . . . and therefore is least in need of other men."[29] What is worse, the poets portray famous men, heroes, even the gods themselves, in undignified postures of grief or frenzy. Nor can Homeric laughter, whether indulged in by men or gods, be tolerated; in men it leads to "violent reaction[s]," and it is a falsification of the nature of God. Hence, such verses from the *Iliad* as "inextinguishable laughter arose among the blessed gods, when they saw Hephaestus bustling about the mansion," must be excised.[30]

Finally, the heresy of the poets is expressed in the conception of God as a magician, "and of a nature to appear insidiously now in one shape, and now in another—sometimes himself changing and passing into many forms, sometimes deceiving us with the semblance of such 'transformations.'"[31] For, "the gods are not magicians who transform themselves, neither do they deceive mankind in any way."[32]

Thus far, then, there are three related reasons for Plato's antagonism to the poets. First, they ascribe a dual nature to the gods—the gods are the authors of good *and* evil. Second, they portray the gods as extravagantly emotional, sometimes obscenely so, as in the case of Zeus, who, at the sight of Hera, "forgot . . . all [his plans] in a moment through his lust."[33] Third, they present the gods in a variety of shapes and deceptive appearances.

I submit that Plato's objections betray a direct antagonism against the transformer, or trickster, image of the gods; that this image is "one of the oldest expressions of mankind," has been conclusively shown by Paul Radin.[34] The Trickster is an authentically primitive figure, appearing in his sharpest form among primitive peoples—a bestial, human and divine being, knowing "neither good nor evil, yet ... responsible for both." Trickster "is at the mercy of his passions and appetites," is devoid of values, "yet through his actions all values come into being." At the same time, all figures associated with Trickster, for example the "various supernatural beings" and man, possess his traits. Thus, Plato says the poets must not be permitted to "persuade our youth that the Gods are the authors of evil, and that heroes are no better than men; for "everybody will begin to excuse his own vice when he is convinced that similar wickednesses are always being perpetrated by 'the kindred of the Gods, the relatives of Zeus.' " He gives as an example "the tale of Theseus, son of Poseidon, or of Peirithous, son of Zeus, [who went forth] to perpetrate a horrid rape."[35]

In his never ending search for himself, Trickster changes shape and experiments with a thousand identities. He has enormous power, is enormously stupid, is "creator and destroyer, giver and negator." Trickster is the personification of human ambiguity. He is the archetype of the comic spirit, the burlesque of the problem of identity, the ancestor of the clown, the fool of the ages, the incarnation of existential absurdity.

This existential absurdity is the converse of what can be termed "political" absurdity. The latter is the result of the effort to train men to respond on command, in terms of signals rather than symbols. So, for example, hazing at a military academy or in any other bureaucracy systematically conditions a recruit *not* to inquire into the meaning of the absurd act which he is compelled to perform. He obeys without question, and it is assumed he will do so in the future when appropriately stimulated. The absurdities which define conventional bureaucratic behavior do not, of course, originate in existential reflection on the absurdity of life—which is a source of creative energy—but in the reduction of men to reflexes in a system, which is the death of the creative instinct. The image of the wooden soldier fits precisely here. Political structures which manipulate persons hardly generate loyalty, skill or initiative. That first and most basic bureaucracy, the "regular" army, dominated by career officers, predictably fails when confronted with the spontaneity and inventiveness of the guerrilla band, functioning on a higher symbolic level, stimulated by the immediacy of their associations and the consistencies of their goals. Plato was correct in assuming that the guardians would need rigorously trained auxiliaries to "suppress insurrection" in the ideal state; he was wrong in assuming they could succeed.

Inevitably, Trickster must be banished from the republic, wherein identity is a matter of pure, ideal, unambiguous forms and where men are to be totally and strategically socialized. The poets who have created or inherited Trickster's image of the world are, it follows, to be silenced. Once again, Plato's opposition to the primitive is clear, if not necessarily conscious.

It would be possible to claim that Plato's negative image of the poets themselves is that of the Trickster, for has he not called them "pantomimic gentlemen" and "imitators"? And may we not add that Plato sensed and distrusted the old connection between art and magic? This is a sensible, if superficial, interpretation; to deepen it we must explore Plato's theory of art and its implications.

Plato regarded the art of the tragic and comic dramatists, along with that of the painters, as essentially imitative, as dealing with appearances only. The painter, for example, paints a bed, but this image is "thrice removed" from the truth. The ideal form or essence of the bed is created by God; this is the eternal bed which the philosopher kings can intuit; it is the bed in truth and goodness, of one nature, essentially inimitable and complete. At a second remove from the truth is the tangible bed created by the artisan, the particular bed, which is a "semblance of existence," but not existence entire as manifested in God's bed.[36] But the bed of the painter is sheer imitation, being neither useful nor ideal. In no sense can it be considered a *creation*. Further, all artists, save those who echo the needs of the state by composing "hymns to the Gods and praises of famous men,"[37] are deceivers who, in effect, presume to create but cannot.[38] The painter, for example, does not know how to make a bed nor does he know anything of the work of the cobbler or carpenter whom he may represent. Socrates states: "the imitator has no knowledge worth mentioning of what he imitates. Imitation is only a kind of play or sport, and the tragic poets, whether they write in Iambic or Heroic verse, are imitators in the highest degree."[39] Nor can the artist-imitator have any knowledge of good or evil "and may be expected, therefore, to imitate only what appears good to the ignorant multitude."[40] Plato seems to mean here that the intuition into pure existence aided by the study of mathematics, a basic subject for the guardians, is also the apprehension of the good, or at least a prerequisite to it. The artist reproduces appearances only, and these vary; pure essence cannot be reproduced, only intuited. Since the artist has no knowledge of the good, he can have no knowledge of evil, nor does he possess any understanding of the useful, for he is once removed from the particulars that he copies and hence thrice removed from the truth. A perfectly antithetical view of the artist is Goya's statement in the catalogue to *Los Caprichos*: "Painting, like poetry, selects from the universe the material she can best use for her own ends. She unites and concentrates in one fantastic figure circumstances and characters which nature has distributed among a number of individuals. Thanks to the wise and ingenious combination, the artist deserves the *name of inventor and ceases to be a mere subordinate copyist*" (italics added).

The absolute, reciprocal antagonism of the true artist and Platonism could not be more pertinently expressed. But this antagonism, it must be said, is not necessarily directed against a belief in God or religious passion as such, only against the removal of God from the concretely human, that is, against the turning of God into an abstraction. All religious art of any stature and all religious artists worthy of the name, from the Byzantines and Giotto through Michelangelo to Blake and Rouault (confining the example to a fragment of the Western tradition), inscribe their vision in the flesh and see God either as an aspect of man's nature or as a perception to which every man is capable of attaining, usually out of his agony. Hence, God may be apprehended by the artist as objectively real, yet always in the most ordinary, unexpected, various but human guises. The institutionalized and abstract God of the church and the philosophers is never the God

191

of the artist, though called by the same name. The human distance between Plato's God and Blake's is infinite.

But whether or not we accept the terms in which it is couched, Plato's argument has extraordinary power and beauty. The philosopher expressed completely what many who have subsequently shared his attitudes have only dimly perceived; the artist is dangerous, as life is dangerous; he sees too much, because that is all he desires to do, and he presumes to create, to erect man into the role of the creator. But his vision is incomplete, he cannot penetrate to the objective order of the universe, the handiwork of God. And to men of Plato's temperament that objective order, the pure anatomy of reason, is as essential as breathing. Yet if the artist would accept the eternal order and thus learn humility, if he could convert his art into a public strategy in behalf of an abstract idea of the good, the state would find a place for him. Let the protagonists of Homer and of poetry in general prove their worth, and they will be returned from exile. Moreover, there is a passionate tie between the artist and the "ignorant multitude." The artist does not believe in abstract systems; he deals with felt and ordered emotional ideas and believes that order is attained through the contradictions, the tense unities of everyday experience. Thus, the artist himself may be unstable, a changeling, and this is a threat to any establishment. Plato is entirely consistent. He was, it seems, a man of a certain type, incapable of tolerating ambiguity, positive in his conviction of an objective, superhuman good. He believed in God with the cool passion of a mathematician, and he believed at least abstractly that the perfectly just city could be established through perfectly rational and perfectly autocratic means. He began as a poet, and so he must have understood in his own being the old argument between poetry and philosophy to which he occasionally refers. In evicting the dramatist, Plato reveals himself, the nature of the republic and the functions of art; his motives, of course, are above suspicion.

The poets, then, are to be exiled from the ideal state. There is simply no room for them; they are the first superfluous men. The philospher kings intuit the universal, ultimate forms, God creates them, and the multitude lives among and constructs their particular manifestations. Hence, the class structure of the republic reflects the doctrine of forms or essences. It descends from the superior, from the abstract, created by God and grasped by the guardians, to the inferior, to the particular, grasped by the craftsmen and ordinary citizens, who live in a world of ordinary, useful, sensuous things. Here we encounter Platonism enthroned, a political hierarchy perfectly mated to a conceptual one. The "fleshy" Homer, who also presumes to create, is a threat to this structure, and cannot be tolerated.

The class division between the universal and particular, between the institutionalized intellectuals and the economic men reflects a condition that develops with ancient civilization as opposed to primitive civilization. This is not to say that temperamental distinctions do not exist among primitives, for they do, as Radin has brilliantly shown in his analysis of the thinker and man of action.[41] The point is that among primitives such distinctions complement each other, the concrete and the abstract interpenetrate, "thinker" and "man of action" are tied together; sometimes, as Radin points out, they meet in the same individual, and in any case, such differences are not politicized. Just as soon as the latter occurs, in early states or as idealized in the *Republic*, there is both an impoverishment and a denial of the sources of human creativity. Further, in early states in the real world, the differential worth often ascribed to people in the various occupations within the broader classes is a political rationalization, generated from the top down. For not only did accidents of birth and training determine social fate, but the point of view from which evaluations were made was that of the scribes, the priests, the nobility. In the *Republic*, in the ideal world, Plato's division of labor and conceptual capacity is said to be genetically determined. The social accident is nullified, yet the division remains artificial because it isolates the abstract from the concrete, the intellectual from the emotional, and considers the craftsman and the farmer useful but inferior beings, not from the perspective of the priest or noble, but from that of Plato's philosophy.

I submit, further, that the Platonic definition of the abstract has become so entrenched in Western thought that the frequently encountered attitude toward primitives, that they are incapable of or deficient in this capacity, is a manifestation of it. Conversely, the attempt to prove that primitives are capable of abstracting too often centers on the types of abstraction emerging out of the history of Western culture, which would seem quite irrelevant. While it is true that no primitive group is made up of Platonists in the technical sense of that term (for primitives tend to live, as Radin has put it, "in a blaze of reality") and the various politico-conceptual divisions generic to the state have not yet been established, this does not mean that they do not think abstractly. In the basic sense, every linguistic system is a system of abstractions; each sorting out of experience and conclusion from it is an abstract endeavor; every tool is a symbol of abstract thinking. Indeed, all cultural convention, all custom, is testimony to the generic human capacity for abstracting. But such abstractions are indissolubly wedded to the concrete. They are nourished by the concrete, and they are, I believe, ultimately induced, not deduced. They are not, in short, specifically Platonic abstractions, and they do not have the politicized psychological connotations of the latter.

For Plato there is an order in the universe that escapes the human eye. That order is, as we have seen, composed of forms or essences which must ultimately be conceptualized; they cannot be perceived by the senses. There is a radical split between perceptions and conceptions in Platonic discourse, a split that has been elaborated endlessly in Western science to the point of morbidity and at the expense of the senses. Reality has become increasingly reified and, at the same time, thrown into question; the conceived object has been detached not only from the perceiving subject, but from itself. When a Platonist looks at an object, the reflection in his eye represents an inferior order of reality; he has no faith in either the perception or the object realized in the world. The object exists only as the shadow of a conceptual meta-reality, *as an instance of a class*, an analytic construction. The majority of civilized men, it is assumed, see only superficially (they are not "seers"), and they look at the object in a utilitarian, unthinking way. Being incapable of probing more deeply into, analyzing, the nature of their experience, they see but do not *see*. Therefore, they are compelled by their limited conceptual capacity to follow those who can *see*.

The expectation of a superior interpretation of what we apprehend is built into the use of our everyday language. That anticipation is an imperative of neither vocabulary or syntax, but of the cultural arrangement of meaning generic to the civilizational process, as Plato understood so well.

Tylor is equally acute although his evolutionary enthnocentrism is insupportable:

It may be said in concluding the subject of Images and Names, that the effect of an inability to separate, so clearly as we do *The external object from the mere thought or idea of it in the mind, shows itself very fully and clearly in the superstitious beliefs and practices of the untaught man* ... between our clearness of separation of what is in the mind from what is out of it, and the mental confusion of the lowest savages of our own day, there is a vast interval ....[42]

Most broadly defined, then, the language of theoretical science is also the language of political society. The ordinary man, it is imagined, bears witness only to the ordinary object. The priest or scientist—or being more rigorously Platonic, the priest trained as a scientist—conceives a metaphysical or theoretical construct, and that construct constitutes the specifically Platonic definition of the abstract. When we talk about the object in our usual Platonic mode, then, we are talking either metaphysics or theoretical science (not technics); and we are also talking politics, the latter because of the presumed inaccessibility of ultimate reality to the mass of civilized men, except through the conceptual mediation of their perceptions by statesmen, priests and scientists.

For the Platonic abstraction is, above all, the basis of the deductive, theoretical proposition which serves as the ground of what we call science. The notion of systematic forms (or, alternatively put, of underlying formal systems *governing* perceived reality, that is, the notion of logically deducible, conceptual meta-realities) dominates our definition of science, of *knowing.* In the Platonic view, these conceptions are eternal. They do not enter directly into the perceived world; they are the unmoved scources of all process, dialectic or otherwise; and they have no history. They are the ultimate structures, regularities, laws governing the universe; and they find their analogue in the laws governing the Republic.

But there is another way of relating to the object. Looking, for example, can be an intensely perceptual experience. The object may be seen in its absolute singularity through, let us say, the eye of a Vermeer. It erupts as a unique thing in the world, irreducible to an exclusive, a priori class, yet subject to a variety of relationships, a thing which may have been made, used, exchanged and which nonetheless may reveal different aspects according to the quality of light, position among other objects, meaning to those who relate to it. Or it may exist as a thing in nature, its being contained in its existence.

The uniqueness of the object inheres in the immediate, concentrated response of the unaided, humanly experienced eye. The object is *connotative*. Through the structure of analogy and metaphor that defines discourse among primitive people, it reveals a manifold and spontaneous reality. No decisive denotative statement can be made about the object, no mathematical or metaphysical statement can define it. This heightened perception is, of course, an aspect of the definition of art and commands a focus on the singularity of the object to such a degree that everything seems at once marvelous, strange, familiar and unexpected. No category can exhaust such an object; it saturates the perceiving subject. That is what William Blake, who despised Plato, meant when he said that he could look at a knothole in a tree until he became terrified. This existential perception, which is also that of the artist and the mystic, cannot be trimmed to fit a metaphysical class, and it is the converse of a theoretical construct.

Yet all three ways of looking—the utilitarian, the Platonic, and the poetic—are abstract and relational. What is at stake is the type of abstraction involved. The non-Platonic or "concrete" abstractions comprise the customary mode of primitive thinking,* not generically but culturally, and also define the mode of the artist who has been politically alienated from the ordinary man. Yet, despite everything, the artist is more closely aligned with the ordinary man, now differentiated from his primitive estate than he is with the priest, scientist or statesman. Like the ordinary man, he ambivalently perceives his dependence on the structures the priest, scientist and statesman command. Like the ordinary man, he focuses on the object; but for him the object has become incandescent. He is perpetually recovering his primitivism.

---

* Robert Redfield understood this as follows: The patterns of thinking of a city man where a multitude of unfamiliar experiences are dealt with by relating them to convenient classes are different from those of a remote rural dweller, whose social objects are all unique and known by their individual characters.[43]

Plato's theory of cognition is, therefore, not only an aspect of his esthetics, but logically defines his sense of justice or rather, demonstrates once again how astonishingly integrated, how final his thinking is. Justice, the aim of the *Republic*, confined one man to one vocation; that principle of esthetic and political order is extended to assume single "realities" behind a multitude of "appearances." Indeed, Plato's ontological ethic inheres precisely in this: for a man to engage in many jobs is to deny his essential nature, for men to concentrate on the uniqueness of things in this world is to deny their essential natures, and for men to presume above their natural stations is to deny the essential nature of the State. Justice in the *Republic* inheres in the given structure and indivisibility of essences.

This is not only a reflection of the political imperatives of civilization—it is, at the same time, the basis for a definition of evil (violation of the order) and an affirmation of the meaning of virtue (appreciation of the order). In the Platonic order, we discover the link between political, metaphysical and scientific classification and, therefore, the significance of the Platonic abstraction, the essence of civilized modalities of thought.

PRIMITIVE RITUAL DRAMA

Plato's opposition to the drama and the dramatist is directly associated with the class and ideational structure of the *Republic*. At its root, this is also an opposition to the primitive, not merely with reference to the old tie between artist and magician but, more comprehensively, in connection with the form and meaning of the primitive ritual drama.

In the ritual drama, art and life converge; life itself is seen as a drama, roles are symbolically acted out, dangers confronted and overcome and anxieties faced and resolved. Relations among the individual, society, and nature are defined, renewed, and reinterpreted. I am, of course, defining the primitive ritual drama in the broadest possible way, that is, as comprising those ceremonies which cluster around life crises or discontinuities, either of the individual or of the group at large. Generally speaking, the latter are concerned with crises arising from the group's relation to the natural environment, while the former are concerned with personal crises, that is, with the individual's relation to himself and the group. In all ritual dramas, however, despite the relative emphasis on the group or the individual, there is an apparent continuity from the individual's setting in the group to the group's setting in nature. Moreover, the problems of identity and survival are always the dominant themes, and it is for this reason that we can, I believe, term these primitive ceremonials dramas.

To clarify, let us consider those ceremonials which devolve upon personal crises, such as death, marriage, puberty or illness. These can be considered "existential" situations; that is, people die, marry, sicken, become sexually mature and economically responsible in all societies. In primitive societies, such ordinary human events are made meaningful and valuable through the medium of the dramatic ceremonies. Here we confront man raising himself above the level of the merely biological, affirming his identity and defining his obligations to himself and to the group. The ritual drama, then, focuses on ordinary human events and makes them extraordinary and, in a sense, sacramental.

At the same time, the ceremonials we are speaking of enable the individual to maintain integrity of self while changing life roles. The person is freed to act in new ways without crippling anxiety or becoming a social automaton. The person discharges the new status but the status does not become the person. This, I believe, is the central psychological meaning of the theme of death and rebirth, of constant psychic renewal, which is encountered so frequently in primitive ceremonials. It is an organic theme; what one is emerges out of what one was. There is no mechanical separation, only an organic transition extending over a considerable time, often crowded with events and never traumatic, but modulated and realistic in its effects.[44]

Hence, the ceremonies of personal crisis are prototypically dramatic in two related ways. They affirm the human struggle for values within a social setting, while confirming individual identity in the face of ordinary "existential" situations such as death or puberty. These ceremonial dramas constitute a shaping and an acting out of the raw materials of life. All primitives have their brilliant moments on this stage, each becomes the focus of attention by the mere fact of his humanity; and in the light of the ordinary-extraordinary events, his kinship to others is clarified. Moreover, these ritual dramas, based on the typical crisis situations, seem to represent the culmination of all primitive art forms; they are, perhaps, the primary form of art around which cluster most of the esthetic artifacts of primitive society—the masks, poems, songs, myths, above all the dance, that quintessential rhythm of life and culture.

Ritual dramas are not automatic expressions of the folk spirit. They were created, just as were the poems, dances and songs that heighten their impact, by individuals moving in a certain cultural sequence, formed by that tradition and forming it. Whether we call these individuals "poet-thinkers," "medicine men" or "shamans," (terms used by Paul Radin[45]) seems unimportant. Plainly, they were individuals who reacted with unusual sensitivity to the stresses of the life cycle and were faced, in extreme cases, with the alternative of breaking down or creating meaning out of apparent chaos. Let us call them primitive dramatists. The meanings they created, the conflicts they symbolized and sometimes resolved in their own "pantomimic" performances, were felt by the majority of so-called ordinary individuals. There was, of course, magic here too; but, more deeply, there was a perception of human nature that tied the group together. The primitive dramatist served as the lightning rod for the commonly experienced anxieties, which, in concert with his peers and buttressed by tradition, the primitive individual was able to resolve. This is not to say that the primitive dramatist simply invented meanings promiscuously. It was always done within a given socio-economic and natural setting. But he shaped dramatic forms through which the participants were able to clarify their own conflicts and more readily establish their own identities.

There was an organic tie, then, between the primitive dramatist and the people at large, the tie of creation and response, which is in itself a type of creation. The difference was that the dramatist lived under relatively continuous stress, most people only periodically so. Thus the dramatist was in constant danger of breakdown, of ceasing to function or of functioning fantastically in ways that were too private to elicit a popular response. In this prototypical primitive situation, we can, I think, sense the connection that binds the psychotic to the shaman whom we have called a dramatist and the dramatist to the people at large. The distinctions are a matter of degree. The very presence of the shaman-dramatist is a continuous reminder that life often balances on the knife edge between chaos and meaning and that meaning is created or apprehended by man coming, as it were, naked into the world.

THE INEVITABILITY OF GREEK DRAMA

The Greek drama is the direct heir of the primitive ritual drama, as Cornford, Murray, and Harrison have helped establish. Indeed, it retains various technical ritual elements: the chorus, the conscience of the play, was a vestige of group participation. The plays of Sophocles were watched with an air of "ritual expectancy," Aristophanes was performed at the Dionysiac festivals, and the themes of Greek drama had the style of ritual.[46]

Thus we can begin to apprehend why Plato found it necessary to exile the dramatist, as the very prototype of the artist, from the republic. The dramatist is tied to the "ignorant multitude," he presumes to create meanings and reveal conflicts, he senses in his own being the ambiguity of man, and he is concerned with the ordinary-extraordinary things, with values as a problem and the common human struggle for personal identity. Such men are dangerous precisely because they view life as problematical in the best of states; they clarify what others feel. Hence, they must either be confined to composing "hymns to the Gods and praises of famous men" or exiled.

We must remember that in the *Republic* the problem of identity is presumably solved in terms of a political interpretation of higher and lower human natures. Such an institutionalized human identity is entirely contrary to the dramatist's perceptions; it is equally foreign to the mind of primitive man. The dramatist, as a dramatist, cannot believe in such stark and ultimate separations between men or within the individual man. When Shakespeare writes his tragedies of kings, he plays out their conflicts against a specific socio-economic background, but in the end he tells all of us about ourselves, and the "multitude" in the pit responds. And was not Shakespeare, in a sense, all the characters he constructed, what Plato would call a gross "imitator"?

Nor can the dramatist deny the sensuous, earthy things, since his plots are based on the "existential" situations: marriage, death, the coming to maturity, sickness of mind and body, the recurring issues in the inner relations among men, the very themes that served as the occasions for the primitive drama of personal crisis. Let me put it as plainly as I can. In the end, the dramatist must either become an antagonist to Plato's perfectionist God, or he must cease being a dramatist. Within his own lights, the philosopher was right.

If the dramatist is a tragedian, then he is grimly concerned with the problem of identity, self-definition, integrity; for tragedy is no more than the dissolution of personal identity and social value through behavior to which the hero is compelled and of which he is, sooner or later, aware. And by that awareness, he transcends himself in one final blinding moment, as did Oedipus at Colonus. The civilized tragic drama is, then, a free elaboration on the theme of identity, celebrated in the primitive ritual.

If the dramatist is a comedian, then he burlesques the problem of identity, he laughs it out of court, he stands aside and lets men make fools of themselves; men, he tells us, with Aristophanes, are everything but what they presume to be. The civilized comic drama, then, is based on the trickster's primitive image of the world, on identity, as it were, turned inside out. It is a celebration of the failure of identity.

Among primitives, the most serious rituals (those ancestral to the modern tragedy) and the ancient comic spirit of the trickster are often mingled. In Wintun, Pueblo, and Kond ceremonials, for example, "in nearly every instance it is the very thing which is regarded with greatest reverence or respect which is ridiculed," as Steward states.[47] The Dionysiac tradition of the satyr (or trickster) play following the tragic trilogy echoes this primitive usage.

It should be clear, then, that on every major count Plato's exile of comedy and tragedy was inevitable; for the dramatist, in his elemental—or, better, primitive—nature, would have worked havoc with the structure of the ideal state and its ideology of identities.

But if one exiles or diminishes the artist, then who helps discover and dramatize the people to themselves? And if the people are considered incapable of attaining to real understanding, a view obviously not held here but essential to the *Republic*, then how are value and meaning to be transmitted to them? Plato answers this question, although he does not ask it. The royal or noble lie, the manufactured or applied myth filtering down from above, that is, official propaganda, is to provide the popular *raison d'être* of the republic. The youth are to be told, in morality tales, that they live in the best of all possible worlds. We have already quoted the fictions which justify the class structure. These lies, these political myths as opposed to primitive myths are the means for fixing personal and social identity for the majority of people in the ideal state in the absence of the artist, both as a specialized figure and as an inherent aspect of the personality of every man.

But if the philosopher kings can lie in the name of the public good and in the interests of a higher truth accessible only to them, the common people cannot. Socrates says: "It seems that our rulers will have to administer a great quantity of falsehood and deceit for the benefit of the ruled."[48] And further, "for a private man to lie to them in return is to be deemed a more heinous fault than for the patient or the pupil of a gymnasium not to speak the truth about his own bodily illnesses to the physician or to the trainer, or for a sailor not to tell the captain what is happening about the ship and the rest of the crew."[49]

Plato was a sober, shrewd, sometimes witty, but hardly comic, idealist; he constructed his heavenly city, brick by brick, with great care and impeccable intentions. When he has finished—and what a craftsman he was—we confront a shining, impervious structure, a luminous monolith, a society with no problems, no conflicts, no tensions, individual or collective. As the *Republic* approaches its end of perfect justice and harmony, it becomes perfectly inhuman. It is so abstractly and ruthlessly wise, so canny and complete an exercise in statecraft, that were we to disregard Plato's temperament, we should have to consider him one of the most skilled totalitarian thinkers in history, the first state utopian, as opposed to the primitive utopians. His historic fault, which speaks to us across millennia, is not merely in his anthropology, it is not in his intoxication with God, abstract though that was, but rather that he, who so fastidiously shunned politics, should have insisted upon the politicization of his faith. Even Cornford, an eloquent defender of Plato,[50] sees him finally as president of the Nocturnal Council, an inquisitor. His prisoner, of course, is Socrates.

6
THE USES
OF THE PRIMITIVE

The concept of the primitive is as old as civilization because civilized men have always and everywhere been compelled by the conditions of their existence to try to understand their roots and human possibilities. But the converse does not hold. Primitive societies, so far as I know, have not generated any systematic notion or idea, certainly not any vision, of civilization. This I believe to be an odd and revealing circumstance. How are we to explain it? May we say that primitive people have no conception of progress or development nor any sense of history and thus no basis for projecting an image of civilization? I think not. In the first place, primitive peoples have strong canons and perceptions of personal growth. The concrete *idea* of personal development saturates primitive society. Second, primitive cosmologies are often developmental in the broadest, metaphorical sense. Primitives do not lack a general capacity to conceptualize development or change in form over time; their perceptions are not static. Nor do they ignore simple chronologies; the memories of primitive people are, in the absence of writing, unusually efficient. But history to them is the recital of sacred meanings within a cyclic as opposed to a lineal perception of time. The merely pragmatic event, uninvolved with the sacred cycle, falls outside history, because it is of no importance in maintaining or revitalizing the traditional forms of society. So it is true, I believe, to state that primitives have no *secular* sense of history and no lineal *idea* and hence no prophetic *ideal* of social progress. Moreover, progress as an abstraction has no meaning for them.

Obviously, this is not the result of a lack of imagination but of a lack of need. Primitive myths, folk tales, legends, oral traditions generally, abound in the most vivid and trenchant symbolic comments on the human condition, but their content, in no case of which I am aware, foreshadows that level of social structure and quality of cultural being which we call civilization. The civilized human condition is *inconceivable* to primitive peoples. It is not even imagined as a mythological alternative, since civilized behavior is so critically different in actuality from primitive behavior—as different as the differences between the sexes. Nor is this the result of a lack of contact between any given primitive people and civilization. For example, no American Indian tribe, moving on the expanding margins of civilization, fighting for the room to breathe, proved willing or eager to "civilize" itself after the model of the Europeans.

In fact, acculturation has always been a matter of conquest. Either civilization directly shatters a primitive culture that happens to stand in its historical right of way; or a primitive social economy, in the grip of a civilized market, becomes so attenuated and weakened that it can no longer contain the traditional culture. In both cases, refugees from the foundering groups may adopt the standards of the more potent society in order to survive as individuals. But these are conscripts of civilization, not volunteers. Thus, the idea of civilization is among primitives determined after the fact of contact; and then the conceptions seem negative, fragmented, uncommitted to any grandiose notion of civilization as such. They are often uncomfortable caricatures of our cheapest desires. Pertinently, among the more significant political leaders of the emerging ex-Colonial states in areas where primitive cultural characteristics still remotely exist, one gets no sense of any deracinated and secular belief in progress. Rather, there is always the conception of a *return* to the communal ethos and disciplined expressiveness, of the primitive community, achieved through a new technology and more broadly based social forms. As we shall see, this was a typical Enlightenment attitude. Strangely enough, as the last phase of the French Revolution reaches Africa, the leadership looks to the spirit of the past of its own people, to those "savage tribes" that caught the fancy of certain *philosophes* and which they used to exemplify certain truths, as a guide and catchword for the future. If Old Europe and the New World are to survive their own hardening civilization, it may be to those "savage tribes" now emerging that we must look. Torn by the Western world, still free of most of our vested interests and archaic capital equipment, more disordered but not so civilized and sick as we are, they may, were they to control their resources and technics, yet prove the case for the Enlightenment, which is also our case. That, at any rate, is what their best leaders, speaking in the idiom of our eighteenth-century forefathers, imply. But their polities are no longer primitive; they trade on memories and on the inherited richness of the apolitical human associations in the localities. No primitive society has gone to civilization as to a greater good—in the emerging areas it is simply a question of using whatever primitive resources remain.

The fact (startling as it may seem to a civilized mentality) is that the majority of men for the greater portion of human history and prehistory have found primitive societies economically, socially and spiritually (or, as we would say, ideologically) *viable*. The absence of revolutions and reform movements; the nativistic opposition that arises when primitive cultures are under assault, with doctrines that turn the unacculturated state into an Eden and chiefs into prophets, preaching that civilization is but the wrath of God which may be exorcised by penance and right living, the spontaneous, marked distaste (despite the selective borrowing of potent instruments) when the primitive culture retains a base from which to view civilization, and the absence of any alternative mode of life as a systematic element in primitive oral tradition— these are all symptomatic of the human adequacy of primitive institutions. The passionate notion of death and rebirth through ritual; the linking of the deceased to the living and the unborn; the projected kinship of the society with nature and the person with society, in creative correlation with traditional subsistence techniques; all these set primitive perceptions against the idea of progress. Even when a relatively integrated and defiant primitive society borrows from civilization a superior tool for a specific purpose, the effort is made to incorporate the new element into the preexistent structure of belief and action. It is not imagined that the tool may have other consequences. How often primitive persons have lost their way in civilization because they could not anticipate the responses expected of them in a novel environment! How often they have misconstrued intention, misread sign or symbol, or looked for brothers where only strangers lived! To mistake the city for a compound, the European for an elder or a peer, or money in the hand for the capacity to live alone—such little soul-destroying errors need only be committed once.

The cyclic sense of time in accord with natural and human rhythms and the absence of the idea of progress and of any vision of civilization are, of course, related phenomena; they are further correlated with the nature of primitive as opposed to civilized technology. When we examine archaic civilizations (Egypt, Babylonia, Greece, China, Rome) or contemporary commercial-industrial civilizations, we find that the life pace set by the demands of the market, the civil authority or the machine increasingly displace human and natural rhythms. In both slave- and machine-based societies, the expressive, musical movements of the primitive, communal work group have been abandoned. The primitive work group is traditional and multifunctional; labor is, of course, utilitarian but it is also sacred—a sport, a dance, a celebration, a thing in itself. In civilization, group labor becomes a compulsive means. In an archaic society, slaves may work under overseers in large, uniform groups, constructing public utilities by brute labor; or they may work under extreme pressure, using rationalized, mechanical motions to produce as many agricultural or commercial products as possible within a given period of time, in order to maximize profit to masters.

In machine-based societies, the machine has incorporated the demands of the civil power or of the market, and the whole life of society, of all classes and grades, must adjust to its rhythms. Time becomes lineal, secularized, "precious"; it is reduced to an extension in space that must be filled up, and sacred time disappears. The secretary must adjust to the speed of her electric typewriter; the stenographer to the stenotype machine; the factory worker to the line or lathe; the executive to the schedule of the train or plane and the practically instantaneous transmission of the telephone; the chauffeur to the superhighways; the reader to the endless stream of printed matter from high-speed presses; even the schoolboy to the precise periodization of his day and to the watch on his wrist; the person "at leisure" to a mechanized domestic environment and the flow of efficiently scheduled entertainment. The machines seem to run us, crystallizing in their mechanical or electronic pulses the means of our desires. The collapse of time to an extension in space, calibrated by machines, has bowdlerized our natural and human rhythms and helped dissociate us from ourselves. Even now, we hardly love the earth or see with eyes or listen any longer with our ears, and we scarcely feel our hearts beat before they break in protest. Even now, so faithful and exact are the machines as servants that they seem an alien force, persuading us at every turn to fulfill our intentions which we have built into them and which they represent—in much the same way that the perfect body servant routinizes and, finally, trivializes his master.

Of such things, actual or possible, primitive societies have no conception. Such things are literally beyond their wildest dreams, beyond their idea of alienation from village or family or the earth itself, beyond their conception of death, which does not estrange them from society or nature but completes the arc of life. There is only one rough analogy. The fear of excommunication from the kinship unit, from the personal nexus that joins man, society and nature in an endless round of growth (in short, the sense of being isolated and depersonalized and, therefore, at the mercy of demonic forces—a fear widespread among primitive peoples) may be taken as an indication of how they would react to the technically alienating processes of civilization if they were to understand them. That is, by comprehending the attitude of primitive people about excommunication from the web of social and natural kinship we can, by analogy, understand their repugnance and fear of civilization.

Primitive society may be regarded as a system in equilibrium, spinning kaleidoscopically on its axis but at a relatively fixed point. Civilization may be regarded as a system in internal disequilibrium; technology or ideology or social organization are always out of joint with each other—that is what propels the system along a given track. Our sense of movement, of *incompleteness*, contributes to the idea of progress. Hence, the idea of progress is generic to civilization. And our idea of primitive society as existing in a state of dynamic equilibrium and as expressive of human and natural rhythms is a logical projection of civilized societies and is in opposition to civilization's actual state. But it also coincides with the real historical condition of primitive societies. The longing for a primitive mode of existence is no mere fantasy or sentimental whim; it is consonant with fundamental human needs, the fulfillment of which (although in different form) is a precondition for our survival. Even the skeptical and civilized Samuel Johnson, who derided Boswell for his intellectual affair with Rousseau, had written:

> when man began to desire private property then entered violence, and fraud, and theft, and rapine. Soon after, pride and envy broke out in the world and brought with them a new standard of wealth, for men, who till then, thought themselves rich, when they wanted nothing, now rated their demands, not by the calls of nature, but by the plenty of others; and began to consider themselves poor, when they beheld their own possessions exceeded by those of their neighbors.

This may be inadequate ethnology, but it was the *cri de coeur* of a civilized man for a surcease from mere consumption and acquisitiveness, and so interpreted, it assumes something about primitive societies that is true, namely, predatory property, production for profit does not exist among them.

The search for the primitive is, then, as old as civilization. It is the search for the utopia of the past, projected into the future, with civilization being the middle term. It is birth, death, and transcendent rebirth, the passion called Christian, the trial of Job, the oedipal transition, the triadic metaphor of human growth, felt also in the vaster pulse of history. And this search for the primitive is inseparable from the vision of civilization. No prophet or philosopher of any consequence has spelled out the imperatives of his version of a superior civilization without assuming certain constants in human nature and elements of a primitive condition, without, in short, engaging in the anthropological enterprise. A utopia detached from these twin pillars—a sense of human nature and a sense of the precivilized past—becomes a nightmare. For humanity must then be conceived to be infinitely adaptable and thus incapable of historic understanding or self-amendment. Even Plato's utopia presumes, at least, a good if no longer viable prior state, erroneously conceived as primitive by the refined Greek when it was merely rustic; and the *Republic* was, after all, founded on a theory of human nature that was certainly wrong. Nevertheless, it was a saving grace, for Plato believed that his perfectly civilized society would realize human possibilities not merely manipulate them.

Even the most brilliant and fearful utopian projections have been compelled to solve the problem of the human response, usually with some direct or allegorical reference to a prior or primitive level of functioning. In Zamiatin's *We*, a satirical work of great beauty, the collective society of the future is based on, and has become a maleficent version of, Plato's *Republic*. The people have been reduced to abstract ciphers, their emotions have been controlled and centralized (as in the Republic, mathematics is the most sublime language; but it is not a means of human communication, only an abstract dialogue with God); and history has ceased to exist. Zamiatin documents the growth of the internal rebel who is gradually educated in the experience of what the regime defines as love. When the revolt against this state of happiness occurs, the civil power uses two ultimate weapons: one is a method of instantaneously disintegrating the enemy. Since the enemy is legion, the other method is the "salvation" of the person, as an eternal civil servant, through a quick, efficient operation on the brain that results in a permanent dissociation of intellect and emotion without impairing technical intelligence. Zamiatin's description of the rebel rendered affectless, lucidly describing the changes on his beloved coconspirator's face and feeling nothing as she dies, anticipates Camus and transmits in its terrifying, poignant flatness a psychological truth about our time that has become a dreadful cliché. Zamiatin informs us that such a materialist, secularized and impersonal utopia can function only by altering human nature itself. And, outside the glass wall of his utopian city which had arisen out of the ruin of the "final" war between the country and the city is a green wilderness in which primitive rebels live off the land, alive to their humanity, and seek to free the ultimately urbanized brother within.

The point is (and it applies equally to the lesser works of Huxley, Orwell, and others) that where the utopian projection is conceived as a nightmare, as a mere extension of the shape of contemporary industrial society, and where the intent is to protest rather than to create a vision of a more viable future, even in such cases the author finds himself rediscovering the flaw in the monolith—human nature—and the necessity of a more existential realization through a more primitive expression.

Contemporary civilization everywhere tends toward collectivization, whether upon a "public" or "private" basis; it is not the devil of any particular system. Thus, contemporary states forge or ignore history; create political myths which propagate the official version of human nature and an inevitable past that wholly justifies the present. The capacity to create primitive myths that explore the ambivalence of man, and the incessant struggle for a common human identity simply withers like an unused human muscle.

Established party and church ignore the existential perspective on history; they are concerned with making history conform to their ideologies, to the achievement of their ideal reflections of themselves. They deny real history, which would deal with how their realities came to be. This bowdlerizing of history to satisfy ideology is the converse of reading the past as a potential, as a dynamic, and then by self-transforming acts, creating what is only *intimated* in the past rather than making the past conform to a static image of the present. The historical heresy, which exalts the present by arbitarily inventing the past and does away with the need for continuous action and reaction, is the culmination of the opportunism of a traditionless civilization. In the end therefore, there is no past, only two dovetailing projections, that of the rationalized past and that of the idealized present. Neither party nor church demands of men that they confront themselves or the institutions with which they are affiliated; indeed, to do so is the greatest crime.

In the face of these civil compulsions, the Soviet authors Mayakovsky, poet, and Olesha, novelist, conceive a "conspiracy" of *ambivalent* emotions, which holds all society in ransom for the chance at social expression. In *The Bedbug*, Mayakovsky resurrects, in a more perfectly collective future, a "vodka-soaked, guitar-strumming vulgarian of a party member, with a proletarian ancestry." He is displayed in a glass case as a zoological curiosity with certain superficial similarities to man. At the close of the play, this "insect" shouts: "Citizens! Brothers! My own people! Darlings! How did you get here? So many of you! When were you unfrozen? Why am I alone in the cage? Darlings, friends, come and join me! Why am I suffering? Citizens! . . . " But this vulgarian of the late twenties, who, Mayakovsky prophesied, would be a hero of human feeling before the century was out, is led back to his cage by an armed guard. In his "Letter from Paris to Comrade Kostrov on the Nature of Love," Mayakovsky instructs a literary bureaucrat in the complex meaning of that emotion: "Love has inflicted/ on me/ a lasting wound . . . / Love will always hum—love/ human and simple. Hurricane/ fire/ water/ surge forward, rumbling. Who/ can/ control this? Can you?/ Try it. . . . "

Similarly, in "Conversation with a Tax Collector about Poetry," he ridicules the Philistine standards of the state: "Your form/ has a mass of questions:/ 'Have you traveled on business/ or not?'/ But suppose/ I have/ ridden to death a hundred Pegasi/ in the last/ 15 years?/ And here you have—/ imagine my feelings!—/ something/ about servants/ and assets./ But what if I am/ simultaneously/ a leader/ and a servant/ of the people/ . . . Citizen tax collector/ I'll cross out/ all the zeros/ after the five/ and pay the rest. I demand/ as my right/ an inch of ground/ among/ the poorest/ workers and peasants."

With their roots in a more tragic view of life than our own and confronted with a blunter, more clearly demarcated style of collectivism, the Russian literary conspiracy against utopia merges with a critique of the modern industrial state that is universal.

The idea of the primitive is, then, as old as civilization, because civilization creates it in the search for human identity. This was already evident in the works of Herodotus, Tacitus, Ovid, Horace, Hesiod, and other poets and scholars of Western classical antiquity; they tried to grasp the nature of their own ancestry and conceptualize the barbarian strangers who thronged the borders of their archaic states. I say "conceptualize," not merely "describe," because any act of historical understanding is a reading of systematic meaning into the behavior of others. In seeking to understand the primitive world from which they descended and which echoed all around them, these early chroniclers, themselves the product of political societies, also had to sound the depths of their own actual or potential experience. That is, the task was not only conceptual in the abstract but perceptual, and demanded that quality of introspective imagination that moved Terence to write, *Nil humani a me alienum puto ergo sum* ("Nothing human is alien to me; therefore, I am a man"). It is a remark that any historian and any anthropologist (for anthropology is in the field of history) must be able to make, or they should remain silent. Yet such a conviction cannot be empirically validated. No anthropologist has had experience in more than a few societies; no historian can live in the time about which he tells us.

The point is that the absolute prerequisite of historical consciousness is an unrelenting exploration of the self as it exists and may be imagined to exist. The facts of other cultures, the artifacts, mentifacts and sociofacts, are the external phenomena, the indirect evidence which must be tracked down to their human sources. The conceptualization of another culture or of another period in history (the problem is the same) is the result of the interaction of the sense of self with the artifacts of another time and place. The idea of the primitive is, then, a construct. But this is merely to acknowledge that all historical thinking is "constructive," which does not render historical knowledge merely subjective. Rather, the assumption is that, as members of the same species, human beings are capable of interpreting the inwardness of the acts of others. Historical knowledge is, therefore, a form of *communication*, analogous to immediate human transaction in vivo. Both share an a priori component. When communicating with other people, we assume that they are as we are. That is, we feel sure that common meanings can be understood and expressed through an unexpressed agreement about the meaning of the symbols involved. This process includes the idiosyncratic and highly personal use of symbols as, for example, when one reads and understands a novel or a poem whose language may be symbolically richer and subtler than that of ordinary communication. But the author of the novel or poem, or the person with whom we communicate directly, is no more accessible to us than is an actor in another time or place. We interpret his consciousness on the basis of symbolic acts. *What the other is*, if that makes any sense at all, is inaccessible; his acts speak for him. The paradigm of historical knowledge, then, is in direct human communication: we approach an understanding of people of the past or of other cultures through an appreciation of the meaning of their emotions as expressed in signs, which constitute direct physical evidence, or symbols. It is our consciouness, as a species, that enables us to empathize with what we do not directly share. The authentic historian may thus be said to have attained, by training and talent, a very high pitch of speciational consciousness. He approaches other societies in other times with the confidence that his humanity is equal to the task of registering differences. And that, though not the only element, is the critical one in all human communication.

The anthropologist must be such a historian. In conceptualizing a primitive society, he interprets signs and symbols by exchanging places with the actors in the system under study. The mere cataloguing or even systematic linking of institutions and artifacts

is meaningless unless the effort to reproduce the social consciousness, the cultural being of the people who live and produce in their
modality, is made. Every technique available must, of course, be
used in these efforts, but the techniques may not become ends in
themselves. If we detach the social forms and tools from persons
and arrange and rearrange them typologically in the service of this
or that method or as abstract, deductive models, we lose touch
with concrete social reality, with the imprecisions of human
behavior and with its actual meaning at a particular time. The
merely logical elaboration of kinship cosmological and linguistic
structures that we may impose upon a people does not necessarily
reflect the consciousness of the actors and may, in fact, lead to a
grotesque notion of behavior if translated into behavioral
equivalents. The abstract concern with the evolution of the forms
of energy, which represents no encountered historical sequence, is
similarly irrelevant, as opposed, for example, to a description of
what it means to make and use and control a primitive tool in
contrast to pushing a button on an automatic lathe or working in a
coal mine. The study of cultural apparatus finds its basic meaning
in the attempt to understand the social consciousness that it both
reflects and creates. Otherwise, the study of man is not the study
of man but the study of social, ideological, economic or technical
forms, a sort of cultural physics. The end, however, does not lie in
technique but in the effort to understand those who are different
from ourselves by virtue of what they have created, responding as
we know we would in their circumstances. As Daniel Foss wrote
sometime ago in criticizing Parsonian and related systematics:
"They failed to touch upon an entire vast realm of the industrial
experience, horror; they failed to comprehend either the collective
horrors or the personal horrors which certain features of industrial
society almost necessarily involve. What may be needed is a
'sociology of horror' in which social science tries to be honest with
the industrial world and with itself."

The possibilities of conceptualizing a primitive society (indeed
any society anywhere) are inexhaustible. The intent and position
of the observer are constant variables. Their portraits may differ in
emphasis, but if they are faithful to the data they examine and if
their purposes are clear they will not be contradictory but
complementary. For example, nineteenth-century anthropology
hardly deals with the problem of war, whereas in the last decade,

we have become increasingly fixed on the nature, definition and extent of war and thus, of human conflict generally. This is surely correlated with the fact that the nineteenth century, although marked by a few civil and colonial struggles, was, relatively speaking, an era of international amity in the Euro-American purview. The critical problem of the twentieth century has further directed our attention, as anthropologists, to primitive warfare, and one concludes (Malinowski had made the point a generation ago) that is is qualitatively distinct from the modern species; abstract, ideological conflicts and mass secular means of extermination are unknown in primitive society. Primitive war consists of heavily ritualized skirmishes (Malinowski refused to define them as "war"), except where the life of a culture is at stake. It seems clear that, as human society develops, the intricacy and pertinence of our images of past societies increase rather than decrease. The distinctions in these images of primitive society are, in a broader sense, instrumental; we describe the system with a continuous redefinition and refinement of problems as they exist in our own time. Of course, incompetence and dishonesty can assume the guise of historical knowledge, but the reference here is to serious work, by students who possess no more than the usual complement of human foibles and who learn to know themselves as they learn to perceive others. "Of all human sciences," wrote Rousseau in the preface to his *Discourse On the Origin of Inequality*, "the most useful and most imperfect appears to be that of mankind: and I will venture to say, the single inscription on the Temple of Delphi contained a precept more difficult and more important than is to be found in all the huge volumes that moralists have ever written."

There is, then, no final or static or exclusively objective picture of primitive society. *We* snap the portrait, using film of different sensitivity for different purposes. Moreover, there is no "definitive" portrait of primitive society that can be transmitted to us by an actor from within the system, precisely because it is our experience of civilization that leads to questions that the primitive person is unlikely to ask about his culture and to recognize problems (for us) where he perceives routine. The difficulties, for example, that beset direct human communication in contemporary industrial society (as opposed to the multiplication of mechanical means of communication) are foreign to primitive cultures. Lacking experience in civilization, they are probably beyond primitive conception. Therefore, it is only a representative of our civilization who can, in adequate detail, document the differences and help create an idea of the primitive, which would not ordinarily be constructed by primitives themselves. We *need* such ideas of the primitive, but that does not make them any the less "objective" or valid. The complementarity of systems, the possibility of different yet independently consistent, purposive interpretations, faithful to the data, is in the very nature of historical knowledge. Indeed, as Neils Bohr indicates, it is in the very nature of our knowledge of physical systems.

The more immediate modern origin of the idea of the primitive is in the European Enlightenment. The collapse of feudalism had, of course, destroyed many fixed medieval assumptions about the nature of man, the position of man in society and the position of the earth in the cosmos. Two intricately connected traditions, which have since polarized the thinking of anthropologists yet never completely divided it and which can therefore be described as ambivalent, began to emerge clearly in the eighteenth century, notably in France but throughout Western Europe. Rousseau above all, as well as Monboddo, the early Herder, Schiller and others represent the *retrospective* tradition, that is, the conscious search in history for a more deeply expressive, permanent, human nature and cultural structure in contrast to the nascent modern realities that were being generated by the revolutionary bourgeoisie. The preceding "Age of Discovery," discovery in the European purview, had introduced the West to an "exotic" world, and this became the fulcrum for the effort to understand the contemporary scene in a Europe that had been growing increasingly civilized and "enlightened" through the late Renaissance and the Reformation, even before the Enlightenment itself. The Age of Discovery held a constant image of another aspect of humanity before a Europe that was beginning to break out of medievalism and free itself of the dogmatic Catholic cosmology, looking "back" to its own primitive roots. In the sixteenth century, Montaigne, was a universe in himself; and Camoëns, later Dryden and then Pope responded with a more or less sentimental, more or less sophisticated but always arresting primitivism. More systematic and balanced formulations were to succeed theirs. The direction and the purpose were clearly marked by Rousseau, who in questioning the credentials of missionaries as chroniclers of savage tribes ("for the study of man there are requisite gifts which are not always the portions of the saints") called upon "the scientific academies to send expeditions composed of trained and genuinely philosphical observers to all savage countries, that they might compose at leisure, a natural, moral, and political history of what they have seen. By such a study a new world would be disclosed and by means of it, we should learn to understand our own."[1]

The Age of Discovery, which was also the origin of colonialism, provided the opportunity for direct scrutiny of radically different peoples, the forerunner of field work and participant observation. This latter technique, the basic methodological contribution of anthropology, is an extension of the notion of the romantic historians that sympathy with "the object of study" was essential to historical understanding. The majority of subsequent historians of any stature, whether or not technically associated with the romantic tradition, have accepted this principle as a necessary prerequisite of historical knowledge. As Marc Bloch put it: "Behind the features of landscape, behind tools or machinery, behind what appear to be the most formalized documents, and behind institutions, which seem almost entirely detached from their founders, there are men, and it is men that history seeks to grasp."[2]

The mere pursuit of forms obscures, also, our understanding of functional equivalents, to which diverse forms may be assimilated. Hence, our broader sense of historical levels suffers, and we fail to report, for example, in our formal work, *what it is like* to move in a human and natural world of kinship as opposed to a technical stratum of civilized society. The study of the fantastic array of irreducible culture forms that men have invented may serve as the grist for a critical esthetics; they are also the reason for the existence of museums, those repositories for the loot of the world and testaments to imperial power. But the deeper contemplation of esthetic forms demands the human context; there is no substitute for the functional sense from within.

Despite their formal and abstract preoccupations, the majority of anthropologists continue to record, with the left hand, deep affection and respect for their primitive informants. In *In the Company of Man* a number of anthropologists, representing a broad spectrum of areal and topical interests, coverge to a single opinion about the extraordinary character of their informants; they are portrayed as expressive, insightful, brave, dignified, deeply individuated, and so on. In other works, Colin Turnbull, Elizabeth Marshall, Laura Bohannan, Monica Wilson, Knut Rasmussen and Peter Freuchen, to name a few, document the multi-dimensional humanity of primitive peoples. Frequently, as noted, this is in sharp contrast to the more technical aspects of such work. That is, the forms of the society studied are not integrated with the state of cultural being described in more personal statements.

In undertaking participant observation, anthropologists are, then, in the romantic tradition of historical knowledge, in turn based upon the retrospective tradition of the Enlightenment, which found its reflection in the Age of Discovery. The eagerness with which most anthropologists accept the canons of participant observation in small communities testifies to something beyond mere pride of technique. It is, I believe, the symptom of an attitude that anthropologists, as civilized individuals, share about the inadequacy of civilized human associations. The anthropological temperament is, after all, marginal. It is historical. We take the deep past seriously. We try to speak for societies that have been prevented from speaking for themselves, and we esteem the things men make. We are preservers, not destroyers. We are specialists in tradition in an age that is growing traditionless, and still largely self-selected to study people off the mainstream of contemporary civilization. We think enough of such people to live among them, to learn from and to respect them and in their light to examine ourselves and our society. Another, a positive way of expressing our marginality, is our search for a culture to which we can commit ourselves. We should not be confused with the adherents of an abstract and legal concept of world government. In this perhaps final phase of the era of imperial states, not of nations or nationalities, that can be a dangerous frame of mind. We are sharply aware of the narrowing chances of cultural variation in the modern world, of the loss of customs and languages. We worry about such matters, and we are not easily taken in by political propaganda or advertisements for progress. A slogan such as "Progress is our only product," repels us, and most of us would agree with Lévi-Strauss when he writes, "Civilization manufactures mono-culture like sugar beet."[3] That at any rate is our image of ourselves and the *ideal* position we represent.

When anthropologists (or people in related disciplines, who learned the method from us just as we learned it from the romantic historians) undertake participant observation in their own societies, we may interpret this as both a professional and a personal effort to create human ties that are highly restricted, attenuated or specialized in contemporary industrial milieus. The very *need* for field work among people of our own society is, of course, a symptom of dissociation, which we confuse with "social complexity," since field work among the middle class is done, for example, by middle-class intellectuals. More often than not they are shocked by what they learn, as were Seeley, Sims and Loosely in their investigation of Crestwood Heights. This implies a degree of social and human ignorance about ourselves (I do not mean that pejoratively; we all share it) that is unimaginable among primitive persons. The proliferation of psychological counselors of every conceivable type—not shamans, not dramatists, not creators of meaning, but adjusters, those fragile safety valves for the emotional underground of our rationalizing civilization—is a parallel symptom of the hardening and formalization of human associations. Rousseau, the parent of our retrospective tendency, had already complained of this, as Lovejoy indicated when he spoke of "the elaborate structure of pretense and accommodation, the keeping up of appearances, the tribute which the vanity of one leads him to pay to the vanity of another, in order that he may receive a return in kind,"[4] that mark the emotional life and behavior of civilized men. The "savage," wrote Rousseau, "has his life within himself;" civilized man, " ... in the opinion of others."[5] We may reformulate this: in contemporary civilization, the person tends to dissolve into the status or role; among primitives, new statures are assimilated to the person, who grows to encompass them through crisis rites, ritual dramas that may be psychologically and physically painful but give him a series of brilliant moments in a living drama on a social stage in a chorus of kinsmen. Henry James understood the modern situation also. In *The Private Life*, he dissects a character who, "though a master of all the social graces, had *no* private life; he ceased to exist altogether when not in society—when no longer an object of the admiring attention of others."[6]

Participant observation is, in our society, an effort to get behind this infinite regression of social masks that hypercivilized sociologists, lost in a reified maze of role and status studies, mistake for personal reality and a sort of eternal human truth. Just as anthropologists, as representatives of civilization, have a need to construct an idea of the primitive, so they *participate* in primitive societies in order to tell us what it is like to encounter a human situation and, when engaging in field work in our own society, what it means simply to seek a human encounter. Success in either of these latter ventures may even negate professional success, for the anthropologist may choose to remain silent.

The Enlightenment generated a mature version of the primitive (as distinct from the earlier "primitivism"), defined by Rousseau and necessarily related to his severe criticism of nascent modern culture; correlatively, it initiated a modern vision of an evolving secular civilization. Reinforced by the new techniques that seemed to be at hand for the control of the natural environment and flushed by the possibilities of a new science, rooted in Newton, Bacon and Locke, the English forerunners of the Enlightenment, the Encyclopedists in general sought an empirically derived, rational and logical periodization of the laws of nature and society and the revelation of a new man, freed from all past superstitions and prejudice. This *prospective* trend in Enlightenment thinking, this evolutionary thrust into the future, was related to its apparent opposite: the retrospective concern with a more permanent definition of the nature of the species and of the realization of human needs in an appropriate social environment. As I have pointed out in the instance of the fictional utopias, Enlightenment thought plunged into the past to develop a more viable sense of the future. However, Enlightenment thinkers tended to move in one or another of its major streams. Rousseau, alienated by the rising bourgeoisie, the new urbanism, the pervading commercialism and acquisitiveness, the droning bureaucracies and the estrangement of men from natural and human rhythms, devoted most of his energies to the retrospective search for the means of uniting technical education and a more fully human socialization; and he addressed himself to the role of human volition in the formation and acceptance of government. But it is important to recall that this was a matter of emphasis. Despite the epigrammatic Voltaire, Rousseau never counseled a return to any historically specific "state of nature," such a return he dismissed as impossible; although he did wonder that men should have abandoned that relatively creative life which we would probably designate as early neolithic, a problem that is far from solved. But he answers his question with surprising adequacy, foreshadowing in general outline the work of the evolutionary prehistorians, Gordon Childe, Graham Clark, and others. There is no doubt that the *Discourse on the Origins of Inequality* is the earliest systematic modern effort of any consequence to build a grand theory of human and cultural evolution; and it is the first outline of a general text in anthropology.

Rousseau spoke consistently of the "perfectability" of man; he believed in the possibility of progress; progress for him was the result of a human dialectic between past and present, not a blind plunge into novelty, not a mechanistic compulsion. But he recognized that certain human possibilities had been creatively realized in an *inimitable* way in the viable societies of primitive people. In contrast, Condorcet, Quesnay and most of their fellow philosophes were primarily in the prospective mode—Condorcet wrote his *Sketch for a Historical Picture of the Progress of the Human Mind* while in hiding from the Terror, and probably committed suicide in Robespierre's prison; he was not progressive *enough*, having fought against the death penalty for the deposed King. Did any major philosophe ever wholly lose the dialectic sense of return that renders the future livable and is the hallmark of the authentic historian?

Modern anthropology, then, is the natural heir of the Enlightenment, the axial age of contemporary civilization. Our basic concern with primitives springs from the use to which Rousseau and others wished to put the Age of Discovery (or, Incipient Conquest). Participant observation, that further refinement of field work, is rooted in the sense of history, in the effort to penetrate the consciousness of past actors, to evaluate our social being against theirs. Our progressive, evolutionary, lawful, materialistic, and secular interpretations of human development tie us to the prospective Encyclopedists. Our wrestling with the problem of human nature, with its variety and unity, our appreciation of cultural variation, distrust of civilization, and preoccupation with the contrasting values of primitive society place us in the retrospective tradition.

But there is one Enlightenment inheritance that we have lost: the theoretical-instrumental unity of thought and action. No Enlightenment thinker felt that he was talking into the wind; they all spun out their ideas in an experimental, dangerous, and changing environment. For better or worse, a sheltered scholasticism was conceived as the medieval antagonist. The thinkers of the Enlightenment spoke to the ordinary citizen on the one hand (the Encyclopedia had a wide popular sale in France proportionate, of course, to the extent of literacy—the papers of the American Revolution were breakfast reading) and worked as revolutionaries, ministers of state and teachers (but independent teachers) of kings on the other. No Enlightenment thinker could have concluded with Ralph Linton that

> the signs are plain that this era of freedom is [also] drawing to a close, and there can be little doubt that the study of culture and society will be the first victim of the new order. The totalitarian State has no place for it. In fact, for men to take an interest in such matters is in itself a criticism of the existing order, an indication that they doubt its perfection. Unless all history is at fault, the social scientist will go the way of the Greek philosopher. However ... [he] will leave a heritage of technique for investigation and *of discerned but unsolved problems*; a new frontier from which free minds will sometime press forward again into the unknown. When this time comes, perhaps after centuries of darkness and stagnation, men will look back to us as we look back to the Greeks.

Here, then, is an anthropologist expressing his frustration at being socially and politically impotent and thus acknowledging his desire to be otherwise, to be in the Enlightenment mode. The only practical echo of the Enlightenment imperative to action is in the ambiguous milieu of applied or action anthropology, which has no force in the formative social decisions of our time but, rather, reflects them. If our eighteenth-century forbears discharged their revolutionary impulses in a variety of ways, they did not, however, create a revolutionary discipline, although that was clearly Rousseau's intention.

As with their major Enlightenment ancestors, no contemporary anthropologist is wholly committed to the retrospective or prospective undertaking. The profession looks backward and forward at the same time, while uncomfortably straddling the breach between knowledge and action. But there are relatively distinct types. Radin, Redfield and Sapir are significant figures in the retrospective tradition. We may take Sapir as characteristic. His distinction between genuine and spurious cultures readily transforms itself into a primitive-civilized historical sequence. The affective-cognitive-instrumental unity of many primitive activities serves as a basis for Sapir's critique of civilization (see, for example, his analysis of the affective isolation of the telephone operator); yet Sapir's purpose is to understand and amend the modern condition.

Typical ambivalence is expressed by Redfield and Lévi-Strauss. In concluding his *Primitive World and Its Transformations*, Redfield finds it necessary to become prospective. He tries to define progress objectively, more or less following Kroeber's problematical criteria, although Kroeber had been skeptical about the subjective validity of the notion of progress as such. There is no need to examine Redfield's indexes of progress (he was a brilliant retrospectivist at heart), for they are not impressive; the important thing is to note the ambivalent and unresolved Enlightenment inheritance.

Lévi-Strauss, in his summary of his life thus far as an anthropologist, concludes that all human efforts can be reduced to the arrangement and rearrangement of elements, forming transient structures; eventually man and his works will sink back without a trace into the flux of matter. This is as close as Lévi-Strauss gets to a *prospective* statement, and, even if it is a rather negative statement of the ideas of the physiocrats, particularly those of Baron d'Holbach, it is linked to those ideas. However, we can understand this view logically, not only historically, if we recall that Lévi-Strauss is a structuralist with a certain respect for primitive society, in the French tradition. Since the primitive is, presumably, beyond recall and since Lévi-Strauss is profoundly skeptical of the possibilities of civilization, (not, however, of the reified civilized mind, the disintegration of human effort in the future, as in the past, is all that he cares to anticipate.

Julian Steward, Leslie White, Gordon Childe and one of their progenitors, Tylor, are primarily *prospectivists*. Tylor, the Quaker, defined anthropology as the "reformer's science," a didactic nineteenth-century echo of the Enlightenment with retrospective overtones. White, despite his mechanical materialism (which is adumbrated among the physiocrats), assumes that a primitive level of integration is a historical reality; he has managed to refrain from an enthusiastic assessment of the present condition of civilization, and he has written empathically of a primitive world view, even if in the vein of a *post mortem*, in the ethnological custom. Steward's evolutionism has been similarly tempered; at one time in his career he was interested in the position of the clown in primitive societies, thus implying but never pursuing an essential difference with civilization—the way in which socially ambiguous and personally ambivalent attitudes are structured in primitive cultures.

Most anthropologists, however, have been less consciously committed to either Enlightenment tradition. Kroeber, Benedict, Boas and Linton, among others, indicate more randomly both retrospective and prospective tendencies. Benedict's relativism is particularly interesting in this context. It seems, on the one hand, to have been motivated by the desire to reflect the state of social consciousness signaled by the structure of a culture, in accord with the romantic notion of historical knowledge. On the other hand, by trying to reveal the multifarious human expressions in primitive society, it in effect denies the inhumanity of primitive peoples and the irrelevance of studying them. Perhaps we can reformulate Benedict's impulse, which is far more important than her achievement, as the effort to establish the value of studying primitive societies by a close scrutiny of their *values*. But despite obvious criticisms, which need not be discussed here, the most striking thing about Benedict is her use of anthropology as a weapon for culturally criticizing modern civilization. Her work can be taken as a metaphorical critique of her own time—of the position of women, of our acquisitiveness, our popular culture, ethnic prejudices, the inadequacy of our educational system, our misconceptions of liberty, and so on—all done with high style and verve but with no resolution. This variety of relativism must be seen, then, as an attempt to educate a chaotic and narrowing society to a more spacious view of human possibilities, and for that reason alone it proved more provocative and popular than orthodox work. Benedict came to the study of culture with a sense of problem; but that, of course, is only the *first* step in the construction of faithful and significant histories or of a critique which must go beyond relativism if it is to have any integrity or lead to action in the world.

There are other indications of the traditional ties of this middle group. Kroeber writes very sensitively of the character of folk culture, contrasting it with civilization, and reprimands the Soviets for being among the most ardent proponents of a universal, progressive, industrial state and thus of an alienating collectivism in contrast to the communal values, the personalism and the full participation of the person in folk society. Linton proposes that the decay of the local group in contemporary society, that is, of the sense and reality of community, is the fundamental problem of modern man—since it is through the local group that people learn to realize their humanity. This is a critical anthropological concept, and it is drawn from experience in the primitive locality, composed of reciprocating persons, growing from within, as opposed to the imposed, technically estranging, modern collective. Lowie found it appropriate to write a book entitled *Are We Civilized?*, and his portrait of the Crow world view is deeply sensitive and respectful. Boas constructs objective criteria of progress, roughly anticipating Kroeber's, but throughout his work, particularly in the area of art, runs an appreciation of the achievements of primitive peoples and also an explicit effort to understand their varieties of esthetic consciousness, which he believes to be more intense than is ordinarily the case in civilization. His active concern with the condition of modern society, his struggle against the anthropological establishment and its acquiescence to the imperialist uses of the discipline, hardly need documentation. Malinowski shared that concern and drew up a kind of model of primitive social functioning—which he characterized as protodemocratic and nonexploitative—in order to illuminate, by contrast, the nature of, the political state and to express his opposition to it and to modern totalitarianism. Can we doubt that his "functionalism" is the reflection of that circular, institutionally integrated (but not conflict-free) process that binds economic, social and ideological aspects of behavior into single irreducible acts in primitive society? Functionalism is a synthetic rather than analytic concept—it does not segregate causes and effects but deals with self-sustaining systems—in which the idea of progress is irrelevant because institutional disequilibrium is never severe enough to generate dramatic types of internal change. Functionalism may be a sophisticated outsiders' view of the primitive system from within, a system to which Malinowski paid the highest tribute. But his initial error, was in assuming that functionalism was a tool of general social analysis rather than a theory based on human experience on a particular level of history. Later, he realized that his functionalist attitudes, which took the legitimacy and human adequacy of primitive societies for granted, could not be mechanically applied to civilized, increasingly totalitarian states; that is, the latter were not necessarily good or viable merely because they seemed to function. This position is explored in his last book, *Freedom and Civilization*. In a similar vein, most prominent British social anthropologists have indicated their respect for the institutions of primitive society and the customary values of primitive life, about which they generalize.

It is clear, then, that anthropologists somehow manage to combine both Enlightenment perspectives in their attitudes and, to a lesser degree, in their work—even if unselfconsciously, and without resolution. But conscious efforts at synthesis, at the confrontation and transcendence of our historically derived ambivalence are rare. Lewis Henry Morgan is almost unique in this respect. His hand in Rousseau's, he concludes *Ancient Society* as follows:

Since the advent of civilization, the outgrowth of property has been so immense, its forms so diversified, its uses so expanding, and its management so intelligent in the interests of its owners, that it has become, on the part of the people, an unmanageable power. The human mind stands bewildered in the presence of its own creation. The time will come, nevertheless, when human intelligence will rise to the mastery over property, and define the relations of the state to the property it protects, as well as the obligations and the limits of the rights of its owners. The interests of society are paramount to individual interests, and the two must be brought into just and harmonious relations. A mere property career is not the final destiny of Mankind, if progress is to be the law of the future, as it has been of the past. The time that has passed away since civilization began is but a fragment of the past duration of Man's existence, and but a fragment of the ages yet to come. The dissolution of Society, bids fair to become the termination of a career of which property is the end and aim—because such a career contains the elements of self-destruction. Democracy in Government, brotherhood in society, equality in rights and privileges, and universal education foreshadow the next higher plane of society to which experience, intelligence, and knowledge are steadily tending. It will be a revival, in a higher form, of the liberty, equality, and fraternity of the ancient Gentes.

This is the most effective summary statement in Morgan, deriving logically from his view of the Iroquois and his conception of the rise of civilization traced through the early phases of the Greek and Roman states. The statement is libertarian in intent and interestingly enough, dialectic in form, thus sharing a common Enlightenment ancestry with the German romantic culture historians climaxed (albeit in a Platonic mode) by Hegel. The early Marxists, who were intellectual cousins of Morgan and involved with anthropological problems, similarly tried to resolve the Enlightenment ambivalence by prophesying a future in which the state apparatus would wither away and the new technology would be wedded to the principles, in higher form, of the primitive commune, thus looking backward with Rousseau and forward with Condorcet and company. Marx found Morgan's work congenial because each had reached a complementary conclusion in working over parallel materials with commonly inherited cultural tools.

Morgan's effort to synthesize our Enlightenment inheritance was significant, but we need superior efforts. I believe it is necessary for us to develop a more precise and subtle idea, an inductive model of primitive society, informed by the problems of civilization—as Morgan was concerned with the problem of property and Malinowski with war and totalitarianism—resulting in complementary conceptions of primitive society that place critical aspects of *our* civilization in critical perspective.

In seeking to speak for man, not for states and systems, anthropology will have to assume a comprehensively critical role, based on our respect for and knowledge of human nature and the "irreducibly" human, I would say the primitive, past—the past that we have reduced to the past by the imperial machines that civilizations are, most particularly those of the Euro-American world of the last 500 years.

7

SCHIZOPHRENIA AND CIVILIZATION

At the 1972 meeting of the National Academy of Sciences, the Chief of the Psychology Laboratory of the National Institute of Mental Health (NIMH) estimated that 60 million Americans[1] would be classifiable as ambulatory schizophrenics if the methods of his research team in Denmark were extended to the United States.[2] This statistic would include about one-half the population, if one excluded children under ten and adults over 65. Nonetheless, he obviously finds the extrapolation appropriate.

Certain serious questions, some of which are acknowledged by the author, are raised by this imaginary statistic and its assumed cosmic definition. How, for example, does one define schizophrenia and differentiate it from border-line schizophrenia, or isolate the schizoid personality and distinguish that from normality? And how are we to respond to categories such as "cold, distant and inadequate" or, "odd and eccentric," terms used to define schizophrenia in the report. What do these adjectives mean? If every family in the United States has managed to create at least one officially diagnosable locus of a schizophrenic spectrum disorder—a fair deduction from the imaginary statistic—what are we to think about the "normal" members of such families? What role did they play in the creation and selection of the patient? Are we dealing with a familial dynamic, a so-called genetic entity or both? Was the announcement in question a desperate attempt to recognize a social reality, even if within the confines of a clinical language, or was it the sound of the mental health establishment reducing itself to absurdity? Or does the report reflect exactly the opposite of its intention, namely, that schizophrenia is a social process of such dimensions that it cannot be reduced to a clinical entity.

This essay is an attempt to answer these questions. Certain

observations can be made at once. Schizophrenia is the most prevalent, malignant and intractable of mental illnesses; officially designated schizophrenics occupy one quarter of all hospital beds in the United States, approximately 250,000. Just as one infers, for example, potential or undiagnosed heart cases from the actual incidence, it follows that there are many times the official number of potential schizophrenics in the population. But these projections could hardly justify an estimate of 60 million. Therefore, one must take into consideration the current theoretical tendency to assimilate psychopathology in general to the spectrum of schizophrenic or potential schizophrenic reactions; schizophrenia, usually qualified by the term paranoid, shows every sign of becoming a synonym for mental illness in our society. It certainly defines the basic process as Harry Stack Sullivan was perhaps the first to understand. But this theoretical tendency contradicts the established and orthodox diagnostic categories of custodial psychiatry. Therefore, the actual commitment or prevalence figures for schizophrenia are no indication of the opinion of the more theoretically inclined, research-oriented mental health establishment.

The figure of 60 million is an extreme manifestation of the contradiction between custodial orthodoxy and theoretical speculation. But in the latter case, the impulse to diagnose schizophrenia as a clinical entity is no less conventional than in the former; the implication that schizophrenia is subject to clinical analysis, definition and handling remains constant. And it is, I believe, tragically wrong. What is the source of this impulse?

One must recognize that the mental health establishment, which the National Institute represents, assumes (a conventional assumption in this society) that the expenditure of vast sums of money on so-called research will eventually reveal the "causes of mental illness"—that money in research can reveal the cause and cure of anything. This is not merely a scientific idea, but is deeply related to the fact that the tragic contradictions of life have little or no standing in our society. We seek to cure people of everything; we tinker with the machine. All the ills that the flesh and spirit of man are heir to are reduced to abstractions. We are dedicated to the proposition that pain can be eliminated. An instrumental, hyper-civilized, consumer and clinically oriented culture such as ours generates, and simultaneously avoids acknowledging the contradictions that are the occasions for tragedy. Moreover, we are led to confuse the merely pitiful with the tragic. We perceive the crack-up of the individual in society as we would an automobile accident: hardly as a struggle for awareness that is at once moribund and transcendent. In the broadest sense, schizophrenia is the process through which the inadequacy of the culture is concretized in the consciousness of individuals; and that inadequacy may be as deeply sensed, without being named, as it is reflected in "pathological" behavior. Yet the tragic struggle for awareness remains a catastrophic, insurmountable challenge because it cannot be located in a culture which fails to serve as the ground for the development of the self. But it is precisely the tragic experience which is the hallmark of the healthy culture, where persons have not been converted into objects, and where the struggle for meaning is a drama enacted and re-enacted in the decisions confronted during the ordinary course of life.

In reducing schizophrenia to a problem for research, one must assume that its essence can be analyzed (that it is an "it"), that knowledge is attainable, and, above all, that the problem can be confined in a laboratory or quasi-laboratory environment. Converting schizophrenia into a research problem, while indentifying it with psychopathology in general (which the report quoted does by the sheer magnitude of its figures) has the effect of converting all psychopathology into a series of discoverable essences. By calling something or other schizophrenia we conspire linguistically to establish an entity, a mental construct that pre-judges, *presumes* the "reality" (actually *multiple* realities) to which we seek to address ourselves. NIMH and the mental health establishment generally, is a latter-day Platonic academy enfranchised by the society it represents to search out the essences that are hidden behind what are taken as the signs of mental disease. Thus, NIMH is symptomatic of civilization's investment in the expert, who, segregated in specialized institutions, works on problems that are necessarily isolated from the contexts that generate and define them. Such problems inevitably take on the character of reifications.

More specifically, bureaucratic research manufactures the idea of research as a product; that product is then falsely concretized in a series of objects, "the objects of research." These objects— "schizophrenia," "juvenile delinquency," "aging"—are further subdivided, and have the ultimate effect of justifying the continued existence of the bureaucracy. At the same time each bureaucratic sub-division struggles to make the object of its research primary by converting it into a major problem of society at large. But in fact the bureaucracy becomes the custodian, not the resolver of such problems; converted into entities, the problems are somehow administered or researched out of existence without the basic changes in society having been achieved. For, above all, the bureaucracy must not be self-liquidating. Its latent function is to freeze the society from which it has emerged and on which it depends. Therefore, not only is the bureaucracy incapable of solving the problems generated by the society, but it *must* not solve them; the logic of the culture forbids it. It is in this sense that all professions, linked through the particular bureaucratic establishment to the bureaucratic structure of civilization as a whole, maintain a stake in the very afflictions they are supposed to heal. The medical profession, for example, has a stake in disease; the average physician is under great pressure to become a pill-pusher for the pharmaceutical industry, a pressure increased by the expectations and demands of the patient. Thus, the average physician knows and cares little or nothing about preventive medicine, or, if he does, his approach to it is inevitably restricted. He is bounded by the limits of his society and must adapt both himself and his patient to its structure; the reactionary character of the American Medical Association amply reflects these cultural compulsions on a broader scale.

Similarly, the mental health establishment is a pathological symptom of the society that created it; it is part of a fragmented social process within which the alienated study the alienated. Theoretically one might learn from a reified and academic social science which examines both itself and the object of study, and transforms the results into politics, but that is precisely what is not being done. On the contrary, the conventions of our civilization conceal our social fragmentation while supressing the insights that might conceivably be generated by it exposure. It is only in such misconceived but understandable statements as that of the Chief of Psychology Laboratory of the NIMH that one gets a sense of the frustrated effort to move beyond the artificial boundaries of the research object and, perhaps unwittingly, include the observer among the alienated.

But the fact remains that after decades of research, the behavioral science experts in the mental health establishment, including the NIMH, have failed to discover either the cause or the cure of schizophrenia. Nor have they defined the elusive essence which they have been committed to understand. Every approach that can be adopted within a laboratory or simulated within an experimental or quasi-experimental setting continues to be pursued. Latitudinal and longitudinal studies of intrafamilial phenomena ranging from birth trauma to birth order have failed, or generated so many possible interpretations that even a clear-cut statement appears as an infinitely regressive possibility. The manipulation of crosscultural data in the effort to identify and determine the cause and rate of incidence of schizophrenia has been inconclusive; the same holds for involved statistical formulations of presumed genetic continuities. The scrutiny of schizophrenic patients and their families through one-way mirrors while in group therapy, the endless tapes of patients speaking to psychiatrists, of psychiatrists speaking to each other, and of the latter being further analyzed by panels of behavioral scientists have created endless activity but accomplished little. A whole industry has arisen in pursuit of schizophrenia. But the artifacts it has produced, the recordings, the papers, the books, the lectures, only make work for the archivist. No research scientist could possibly familiarize himself with the vast store of available information, but it is just that possibility which keeps the research mills grinding toward their infinitely regressive goal. And periodically we are informed that the problem of schizophrenia (not to speak of the incidence) is greater, more prevalent and more subtle in the clinical sense than ever before.

The problem is indeed so great that a crisis in what is called the "management" of mental illness has developed proportionately. The predictable reflex in our culture when faced with a person identified as mentally ill is to commit him to a custodial institution. This may be a mental hospital; as psychiatrists know, it may also turn out to be a jail. In the ordinary course of events there is simply no place for such persons in a class-structured, urban society, cross-sected by a highly technical subdivision of labor. Nor can the shrunken nuclear family or its quasi-kin network accommodate people who make extraordinary demands upon their day to day resources. Custodial commitment of the mentally ill is, therefore, socially expedient, while the compulsion to commit is fully in accord with the nature of our culture. Commitment may even be aided and abetted by the patient in search of shelter, care and community.

And that defines the paradox. Despite the expectations of an occasional, naive patient, or the nominal intentions of psychiatrists, the mental hospital cannot be turned into an authentic community. It cannot rise above its source; it must eventually replicate the problems and patterns of the society that sustains and populates it. Since the mental hospital cannot be turned into a community of reciprocating, autonomous, working and loving persons, the alternative, adopted by the mental health establishment, is to convert the wider society into a mental hospital through the expanding list of psychoactive drugs. In the psychoactive drug, research literally finds a product, an analyzable object and a proven result. Therefore, one understands why their discovery, synthesis and sale is widely considered as the most fruitful and pragmatic sign of the advance of psychopathology during the past several decades.

By means of these drugs, patients are released into society at large, while using the hospital and other out-patient centers as clinics. This seems progressive. But it marks the failure to achieve authentic community in our society. On the one hand, the number of patients in mental hospitals is drastically reduced while those remaining are rendered malleable by the use of drugs. Thus the hospital's function as a rehabilitation center seems to have been discharged, or as is sometimes said, "The revolution in drugs has rendered the hospitals obsolete." On the other hand, the patient is returned to the society, to his web of relationships, sufficiently immobilized by drugs to give the impression that society's resources are being constructively used to alter the sorrowful trajectory of his life. But the latent function of the drug-based community mental health movement is economic, in the broadest use of the term. That is, the society generates more breakdowns than its institutions can handle, more "inadequacy" than it can absorb. The mental health movement has the paradoxical effect of deflecting attention from the source of the problem in the society itself, while it solves the economic dilemma of the over-crowded, inadequately staffed, and costly custodial institution. Of course, the mental health movement appeals to the resources of the "community" continuously, giving the impression that a real effort at therapy has actually been made; but that effort, is merely ameliorative, particularly when it focuses on limited aspects of what are called "interpersonal relationships." But no analysis of the deep structure of the society is, or can be undertaken.

Moreover, the drug-based mental health movement masks the rate of breakdown, so that in any given year the admissions for this or that clinically defined syndrome may shift relative to another, while the official rate of admission may fluctuate without reflecting the reality of overall social pathology. Finally, the drug-based mental health movement also stops custodial institutions from replicating themselves to the point at which they would represent, in their numbers and archaic nature, an indictment of the society which created them. Thus, the whole system of mental care becomes a self-reinforcing social loop, a cultural feedback which leads us to deny social reality. We seem to be controlling mental illness, but our social pathology deepens.

Although the achievement of pseudo-community through the artificial raising, lowering or dulling of consciousness was systematically resorted to by the psychiatric establishment for a generation prior to becoming an alternative for the disaffected, the dependence upon drugs or their equivalent is a growing and general characteristic of modern civilization. It is not a specific, bounded, researchable "social problem," confined to a particular segment of the population. Just as people in revivalistic movements whose cultures have been shattered by imperial civilizations may acquire a related dependence on drugs in order to stimulate fantasies of the past and future, pursue lost dimensions of experience,* and to make cultural defeat bearable in the

---

* "Mescaline," wrote the distinguished French poet, Henri Michaux, after systematically experimenting with the drug, "is the enemy of poetry, of meditation, *and above all of mystery*.... Images completely stripped of the pleasant fur of sensation ... purely mental ... abstract ... [were] imposed on me by the drug ... [I could] take no liberties with them [there were] no possible variations ... [my] imagination was completely paralyzed. [Mescaline] elaborates stupidity" (p. 32). And further "to the amateurs of one-way perspectives who might be tempted to judge all my writings as the work of a drug addict ... I regret, but I am more the water drinking type. Never alcohol. No excitants.... [a little] wine. All my life, in ... food or drink moderate.... Fatigue is my drug. The most unspeakable of all [is] alcohol" (p. 89).[3]

Baudelaire would concur. And most recently Carlos Castenedra seems to have reached a similar, if less autonomous and esthetic conclusion.

present, so chronic use of drugs is one way of achieving parallel ends for people who have been blocked by vicarious experience, and civilized associations inadequate in range and depth. Drugs literally cool the victim. It is, therefore, in accordance with the logic and limitations of our culture that methadone, almost as destructive a drug as heroin, be substituted for another, in a tautological therapeutic effort. Drugs have become a surrogate for the experience of culture itself; the culture is reduced to the drug ("the drug culture")* and the person is converted into a physical/chemical object, an irresponsible system of responses. This passivity and this complex of illusions have the effect of adapting the person to any social arrangement which ensures the gratification pursued. The dialectic between the person and society is broken: a creative politics becomes less and less possible.

It is, of course, difficult to locate the source and locus for a failure of such dimensions directly in our own society; we are too involved in its dynamic, too much the product of our cultural shortcomings. We can only understand ourselves through cross-cultural contrast, by learning to perceive another society or another cultural situation which resonates with our own. That is what defines the anthropological perspective. And it is, I believe, the only way that we can penetrate to the social origins, the definition of pathological behavior. But I prefer to be as concrete as possible.

In pursuing this problem further, then, I shall use as an example the paranoid schizophrenia diagnosis of a patient who was the subject of a cross-cultural case conference in which I participated several years ago at the Upstate Medical Center, Syracuse, New York. The person involved was identified as an "immigrant alien"

---

* According to the state-commissioned Fleischman report of October 1972, 45 percent of all high school students in New York City used one drug or another; the suburban rate was 25 percent. The figure estimated for junior high school students in the city was also 25 percent. But this sort of statistic is misleading. It divides the "psychotherapeutic" and socially sanctioned from outlawed drugs, reflecting the distinction between classes and ethnic groups. Yet social reality blurs the line; marijuana is so commonly used that it may become as legal as alcohol; tranquillizers are used by street gangs. In any case, drug control, whether permissive or restrictive, is one way of politically controlling a "drug society." This has the effect of evading the underlying reality; the drug becomes the focus of concern; "rehabilitation" of the victim becomes the presumed goal. And that poses no challenge to the existent social order—in fact, reinforces it.

from an exotic society, Laos. Actually, he turned out to be South Vietnamese, a fact which was less important in 1963 than it would be now. Nonetheless, the fact that he was an exchange student, necessarily middle class, from a country torn with conflict would have further sharpened the conflicts that could ordinarily have been anticipated in his career in the United States. When first invited to participate in the conference, I composed, for my own benefit, a list of questions of the following order:

1. What was the social and economic background of the patient? Was he born and bred in an urban or rural area? This is particularly significant in relating to people from archaic civilizations in economically disadvantaged areas.

2. How fluent was he in English? What were the details of his formal education? What was his capability, for example, in French?

3. How traditional was the family structure? How severe, relatively, was the conflict between tradition and the drive toward modernity? What were the cultural signals and concrete metaphors of this conflict?

4. What was the class and occupational status of the critical members of the family and their friends?

5. What was the cultural significance of birth order and of other relationships within the immediate family?

6. Had the patient traveled before and under what conditions?

Before inquiring into the available details, I then drew up a list of circumstances conducive to a reaction that could be interpreted as schizophrenic in a person undergoing certain kinds of cultural experience.

First, the visiting Vietnamese was a member of a darker race among a white majority. Residual feelings of inferiority or disadvantage would be deepened in the race-conscious American milieu. There might also be a shift from a feeling of cultural inferiority (or disadvantage) vis-à-vis the European generally and the French in particular, to the new problem of racial division; or rather, the old problem presented itself in a novel and nuanced form. The strategy of race relations in an American city would have had to be absorbed rather quickly by this Oriental patient. It should be noted that no matter how good his intentions, a white American physician would have great difficulty in exploring this area.

Second, the patient's native language was considered exotic and was rarely encountered in his new environment.

Third, the patient found himself in a Western urban situation, one which was mechanized, impersonal and elaborated beyond the archaic market-ceremonial-commercial towns that he experienced in his homeland.

Next, his extended family orientation, with particular reference to status expectations of aid and support, routine duties and rights, was not being fulfilled. The configuration of the "anarchic," less cohesive family encountered in the United States was unfamiliar to him. Relationships between the sexes and between the generations were particularly bewildering.

Forms of public deference and service, including terms and modes of address, were underdeveloped or not apparent in the culturally (but not socially) egalitarian American society.

Women probably were inaccessible, or, if accessible, did not take the patient seriously. He was not considered really a man, even by the women who did sleep with him, since his command of the environment was inept and they could anticipate no future with him. This led to the practical impossibility of relating either sex and tenderness or sex and social obligations. Sex became a segregated, obsessive, detached and, in both reality and fantasy, autistic activity. It is in this phase of his journey to the hospital that the patient might appear to be a severe "psychoneurotic."

He encountered a minimum of familiar cultural landmarks, either in the form of artifacts or signs and symbols. Everything, from food and clothing to the significance of yellow as the color of caution and cowardice was strange to him.

He experienced a physical climate that is peculiar and harsh. The responses of his body may be unexpected (an actual example turned out to be the flow of mucous in his nose, about which he became obsessive). Ordinary routinized activities, such as dressing properly required a careful effort.

Finally, his knowledge of the United States was probably gleaned from the cinema, assorted popular books and gossip.

In sum he felt like a visitor from another planet; he lived in a dream projected by an unknown author; he split into subject and object or object-subject-object, he monitored himself very carefully and may even have mediated his various selves. These effects would have been intensified, of course, if the patient were a man in transition in the first place, that is, if he were not firmly grounded in his native milieu.

The anticipated result of the patient's experience was traumatic cultural shock, not the tourist's malady celebrated by the anthropologists, but an acute identity crisis. In such a situation suicide is possible, and might be threatened (*as in the instance of a "psychopathic" personality*), resulting from a turning inward of hostile feelings in the service of their ultimate social expression (*at which point the patient might give the appearance of a "depressive"*). But the likely result, then, is a chain of related "schizophrenic" responses that exhaust the definition of psychopathology. These would probably include the following:

—Cultural depersonalization: the patient feels himself to be a thing, a mere category in someone else's system. Obsessive-compulsive maneuvers might signify an evasion of conflict.

—Uncanny feelings, including the feeling of personal, physical dissociation.

—Withdrawal and a desire to be cared for or the paranoid transformation of the latter, the certainty of being under attack.

—Privatization of language and probably a relapse into the mother tongue, including related cultural gestures.

—Hallucinations, auditory or visual or both.

These general responses did, in fact, constitute the paradigm of the patient's illness; they were clinically defined as his symptoms.

But a cross-cultural or situational perspective dissolves the clinical diagnosis. For example, a hallucination may be understood as a visualized (heard) and interpreted (projective) memory or anticipated happening based on past experience, cunningly constructed from personal or cultural symbols or both. Hallucinations are dream work; in moments of severe stress, perhaps following on prolonged sleeplessness, the "repressed" material may burst into consciousness in a new form, as the organism seeks a creative resolution. But we all, so to speak, *see* (hear) what is in our brains. When a Blake sees a tree full of angels, he does it as a transcendent artist. It cannot be reduced to a clinical symptom. When a painter sees a painting he is about to paint this is also in a sense a hallucination.

On the cultural level, when New Guinea natives in the area of Port Moresby *see* a spirit witch in a tree, the phenomenon is not psychopathological. When an Anaguta of the Northern Nigerian plateau says that whirlwind is a spirit, we cannot make a clinical interpretation. As a matter of fact, among primitives generally, spirits are concretized, individuated; they are persons and they *exist*. Even death, among certain people of the lower Niger, is a person and exists. This is not psychopathological, nor is it the same as a Freud postulating unconscious forces.* Of course, if a New Guinea native saw a pig jumping over the moon his people would look askance, since the vision would be idiosyncratic, not culturally anticipated. But, and this is the important point, they would not necessarily consider him crazy, only privy to a type of information inaccessible to others. Such a person might, indeed, become a shaman.

One could go on in this vein trying to illustrate the danger of assuming that certain phenomena are *ipso facto* psychopathological or somehow qualitatively removed from our ordinary human experiences. The point is that the predictable symptoms in the schizophrenic reaction constitute an effort at adaptation to a series of experiences that are perceived as discontinuous and absurd, contrary to expectations and destructive of hope; the future disappears. On the esthetic level, these discontinuous experiences destroy the sense of life as a drama of meanings, as a tragedy that can be endured. This is equivalent to a failure of socialization, a failure which can probably be modified within fairly inflexible cultural boundaries, given great effort throughout the life cycle. The experience of culture shock is, then, a schizophrenic or, if you will, a schizoid reaction. In either case, it exposes the schizophrenic process both within our society and cross-culturally—process, not essence; for schizophrenia is a dynamic, not a category. Let me put it this way: the schizophrenic reaction among ourselves is a type of home-grown experience of culture shock. There is, of course, this difference: the "exotic" patient may have the memory, at least, of an alternative life pattern to which he may return or perhaps just the knowledge that such an alternative has existed. For this reason, the expression "schizoid reaction" may be appropriate in that the process it describes may be readily reversible.

---

* Although the psychoanalyst, following the Greeks, personified love and death, he hardly considered love and death persons; they remained abstract, stereotyped conceptions.

The analogues to the traumatic cross-cultural experience in our own society are inadequate socialization both instrumentally, relative to sparsity, trivialization and overspecialization in development of skills; and affectively, relative to the separation between the generations or the inertness of interaction between the generations and the resultant mechanical quality of peer interaction, and the failure to celebrate the person at critical psycho-physiological points in the culturally derived life cycle.

The result is the tendency to reduce the person occupationally and emotionally, in work and love, to a category or function based upon a principle of mechanical performance in an increasingly secular milieu. Therefore, affective, cognitive and instrumental functions are separated from each other, in turn related to the extreme division or subdivision of labor. It is only in this context that schizophrenia can be labled a cognitive disorder, an impairment in thinking: for on the one hand, cognition stripped of affect or work in the world must be distorted, and on the other hand, the social fragmentation of the person leads to partial and alienated conceptions of reality. The self is not only split, it is subdivided and hardly has the chance for organic development through a life cycle of normal range, and work of a socially integrating character.

Thus the ordinary psychopathology of everyday life in our society is, on the deepest and broadest levels of our personalities, a series of alienating reactions to social imperatives reflected in, and in turn reflecting the structure and function of the family. This familiar condition makes all of us some of the time and some of us most of the time feel like visiting Vietnamese drifting through a world full of strangers, a world without landmarks, in which we endlessly reify ourselves and others. In other words, schizophrenia, as we know it, gives every indication of being a protest against and a response to the problem of learning how to be human in contemporary society. Two complementary aspects of that response can be isolated. The first is exemplified in the "underachieving," socially thwarted and therefore "mock-creative" person, who makes redundant efforts to control the environment by complex symbolic evasions. But the goals of our society are not consciously questioned; the manipulation of persons is substituted for the command of things. The structure of suffering, which inheres in the manipulation of persons, can be glimpsed in the case of a schizophrenic family that served, on the obvious assumption that familial dynamics are implicated in schizophrenia, as the object of research for a number of years in a project at the National Institute of Mental Health.*

In these pilot studies schizophrenic families were, without their knowledge, observed during group therapy through one-way mirrors by interdisciplinary teams. The family member who had been officially designated as a schizophrenic was a voluntary patient in the elite, custodial unit of the Institute, an experimental hospital. At the inception of the program, the families of patients were also quartered in the clinical center, all expenses paid, but this practice was eventually discontinued because of economic and other difficulties. Moreover, certain families tried to convert the experiment into a way of life, thus generating intolerable tensions among the staff. The therapeutic sessions were conducted by at least one therapist, usually an analyst, together with a psychiatric social worker who served as a resource for background and day to day information about the patient's behavior. The sessions included as many members of the immediate biological family as could be gathered on a given occasion. The group observing them through the mirrored windows of darkened observation booths consisted of psychoanalysts, psychiatrists, psychologists, and in this particular instance, myself, an anthropologist, serving as the cultural anchor for the psychodynamic team. From time to time external consultants—sociologists, philosophers, a novelist—were invited to join. The weekly sessions of the family in therapy and the elaborate discussion that took place directly afterwards were recorded. After each session, the observers subjected each therapist to a searching critique of his performance, suggested alternative interpretations of family behavior, argued endlessly, ventilated their prejudices and sometimes their pathology, in the tautological attempt to penetrate to the essence of schizophrenia. The therapist being observed was under extraordinary pressure— every aspect of his relationship to the patient and the patient's relatives was explored. Each involution of transference, counter- transference, projection, introjection, and rejection was traced, noted and analyzed. Several analysts could not stand this sort of exposure. One deeply experienced senior analyst, for example,

---

* In the narrative that follows, I have changed names, dates and identifying details in order to protect those involved.

began to arrive late or miss appointments completely. He finally conceived the family as conspiring against him, a conclusion that resonated with certain critical aspects of his then current personal life. But there were grounds for his suspicion. For several months, he had been trying to penetrate the individual and group defenses and reach what he assumed were the repressed feelings of family members towards each other and also towards himself. The more persistent he became the more evasive was their response. They handled him with an almost exquisite finesse, passing him along the circuit from husband to wife to son and back again, deflecting his attention from any reaction that seemed promising, baiting him. There were moments when the analyst under observation simply stopped dead in his tracks, surrendering in confusion to the false cue, the contradictory signal employed to throw him off the scent. Occasionally, father and son might exchange an identical smile across his line of vision, or the mother would look down, modestly amused at some *riposte* of her husband. Gradually, unable to bear the isolation, the analyst began to ally himself with this or that member of the family in specific situations. Alternately, his hostility focused on the father and he found himself wooing the mother. This contest for dominance, which was rationalized by the analyst as necessary to establish his credibility, that is, his authority, culminated in a frank outburst (beginning in the therapy room, and finishing in the observation booth) to the effect that "the old son-of-a-bitch was exactly the kind of man my father was—incorrigible, dishonest, impossible to relate to." Shortly thereafter he resigned from the project.

In the perspective of the analyst shuttling between therapy room and observation booth, the project provided no exit into reality, not much material compensation, and no apparent progress in the presumed condition of the patient. In private practice, or in an ordinary mental hospital, such negative consequences can be masked or diffused. Even if under supervision the therapist is not subject to such direct observation and wide-ranging analysis; his link with the patient is partial, he is usually paid well, and, above all, he is not obliged to define theoretically a pathology or to question assumptions, but to alter or confine behavior. He is, therefore, less subject to paranoid or depressive reactions.*

* But it should be noted that even in the ordinary course of events the suicide rate among psychiatrists is higher than among other professional groups.

In the course of the project it became clear that unless the psychotherapist can attain a commanding position vis-à-vis the patient, he is likely to lose confidence in himself very quickly. If he cannot define himself as representing normality, reality, competence, the world, in sum, the establishment—and the patient as seriously inadequate, his professional armor disintegrates. A split develops between the professional ego, or "status personality" and the self. The analyst may then become nakedly manipulative in order to maintain his status as he and others conceive of it. The self is revealed as underdeveloped and conflicted. The research project then had the unintended consequence of revealing a basic social dynamic of schizophrenia: investment in and pursuit of the chimerical status ego at the expense of the potential self, a dynamic as evident among the psychiatrists as among the patients. The pragmatic, self-reinforcing distinction between these two categories of persons was that the patient had little or no status, and had become habituated to the notion that he was incompetent in critical respects.

No matter how modest the therapist, the patient was obliged to orient his sanity vis-à-vis the assumed health of the other, that is, the psychiatrist is officially defined as the custodian of health. His personal characteristics were as irrelevant as a surgeon's. Moreover, the psychiatrist had the real world and his position in it as retreat. His habitual, reflexive competence, his ego saved him from "breakdown," that most deeply personal of protests against the throttling of self. The responses of the psychiatrist were not related to his manifest convictions or public temperament. He might be liberal, even radical in his view of mental illness, and sceptical of his own omniscience, but if relating to the family undermined his sense of his status in society, threatening what he took for granted, he would seek to evade, manipulate, and finally lose interest, that is, dissociate from the situation.* The deeper one plumbs the psyche of the other, the more interchangeable we become. Individuation is the result of acting in the world.

The tactics of the psychiatrists, were also used by the patient

---

* For an official conception of the risks run by the psychiatrist in a mental hospital see a report on legitimate defense from the *Annales medico-psychologiques*, in *Manifestos of Surrealism*, Andre Breton, (Ann Arbor: University of Michigan Press, 1972), pp. 119-123.

and his relatives. In the particular family under consideration, whom we shall call the Dixons, the father was something of an adventurer, an odd job man, a distinguished looking hobo in the American grain. He was glib, apparently poised, knowledgeable about the inequities and iniquities of the system. In other times and places he had been a surveyor and a river boat pilot but had not found work for years, busying himself with schemes for getting rich quick. His wife, a meek-mannered, beautiful woman with a decaying body, was a generation younger than her husband (then past 70, he looked 50), and supported the family by working as a saleslady in a boutique. Her family of origin was southern, prestigious but money poor, and one had the impression that she had been swept off her feet by the energetic and plausible roustabout that her husband had been. When other impulses ran counter to her loyalty to her husband—or her fear of offending him—she became more passive, and her manner even more graceful, than usual.

They had three children. The oldest, a son, was at college in another state, the youngest, a daughter, was completing high school. The third, a young man in his early twenties was the patient. He had been introduced to that role in his late teens when conflict with his father over his lack of interest in school work and his penchant for motor bikes culminated in an attack by the son on the older man. His father, with the presumed consent of the mother, called in the police; they recommended a psychiatrist who referred the youth to a state hospital. There was no record of the severity of the attack on the father, and there were no witnesses except the mother. Nonetheless, the young man, whom we shall call Tom, was admitted to the hospital, and after brief observation was diagnosed as a paranoid schizophrenic.

Tom was tall, rangey, obviously intelligent. His tentative smile conveyed a certain distrust of self and others, and seemed to seek validation for his sense of the world as absurd. His career in the hospital, which lasted for more than six months, was undistinguished. Presumably, he discharged the role of paranoid schizophrenic with such force and clarity that the initial diagnosis persisted. That is, he may have hallucinated, proved hard to handle, acknowledged a peer group, and conspired with the staff to maintain his status. By the time the family had been admitted as an experimental case to the clinical center, the record of his previous hospitalization had largely "disappeared." The welcoming staff had little information about the initial diagnosis, the events leading up to it, or his first hospitalization. But it seems unlikely that a consistent case history was in the first instance even available. Such a history is always something of an illusion; psychiatrists come and go, "diagnoses" are complex and over-lapping, individual perspectives differ, and the generic culture of the mental hospital must also be taken into account, along with the specific social personality of the given institution.* But it was no illusion that the identification of Tom as a paranoid schizophrenic, his apparent compliance in the state asylum and his family's acceptance of his condition recreated him as a social being.

This resolution was by no means uncongenial to the parties concerned. The removal of Tom from the scene served the needs of his father, since a myth, in accord with family politics, had been invented concerning Tom's special relationship to his mother. Only his mother was said to be able to handle Tom, which meant, in reality, that she was permissive, gracious and, in contrast with her husband, never obviously punitive. Though Tom had no vocation he had an elaborate interest in automobile engines, intimating a creative interest in commanding things. Jobless, he was frequently at home and was the only immediate male competitor for his mother's affective energies; she was not much older than Tom than she was younger than her husband. It was also clear that Tom's unconventional manner reminded the father of himself; thus any crisis in his self-esteem was translated into hostility towards Tom. When the conflict between them became, in the father's view, insupportable, exiling Tom in the service of curing him was conceived as a sensible alternative. Of course, the negative identification between Tom and his father never became visible to either.

As far as the mother was concerned, by considering Tom a patient, that is, as a hopelessly dependent and irresponsible person, she reconverted him into an infant, she *reconceived* him. She could then safely deal with him, express her deep concern and

---

* For an independent confirmation of this point see the remarkable article by D.L. Rosenhan on "Being Sane in Insane Places," in *Science*, vol. 179 (1973) pp. 250-258.

sympathy, and act out the role of the mother without risking the displeasure of her husband. As a working woman in the retail trade, always mildly ill, under the thumb of her bosses, having to genuflect to customers and exhausted most of the time, she was in no position to act independently at home. Moreover, she valued the curiously courtly, almost chivalric relationship that she maintained with her husband, since it echoed the society in which she no longer moved and gratified her "romantic" longings. She appreciated her husband's "sense of humor," which must really be defined as *Schadenfreude*, wit or amusement at the obvious expense of others while exempting oneself from the other's predicament. Therefore, the removal and labelling of Tom could be readily rationalized by his mother.

So far as Tom was concerned, assuming the role of the patient was a logical alternative to the conflicts he faced at home and school. His new identity made him the center of ineffectual familial concern, and permitted him a latitude which would have been inappropriate in a normal situation. Tom had opted for the role of a literally "institutionalized deviant" in the civilized sense of the term, a deviant who had no standing in society at large, but was permitted to act out his problems and play with his identity, as a child is supposed to have the right to play, in a custodial situation. Society having failed him, he permitted the specialized institutions to take over. And in the logic of our civilization, the specialized institution crystallizes the negative aspects of society at large; they are, so to speak, the caricatures of our ordinary functions. Maximum "security" is, for example, attainable in a jail.

If Tom had felt that he was incapable of living conventionally, he was nonetheless able to shape his new environment to certain uses of his own. He was relieved of ultimate responsibilities for himself and avoided the necessity of making a conventional commitment to job, wife and so on. At the same time he was entitled as an institutionalized schizophrenic, to explore in fantasy other possibilities that the person sealed in some partial, ego-based identity in "normal" society, repressed, avoided or learned to condemn.

In Tom, then, this family was able to identify a pathological process. The family's anxieties, fears and conflicts were focused, personified, in a sense exorcised, in a being who was simultaneously of them yet alienated from them. Tom had become a willing sacrifice, analogous to what the Igbo-speaking people of southeastern Nigeria call an "Osu" slave—a holy, or *untouchable* person burdened with the guilt of his normal counterparts and therefore detested, dreaded, excluded from society at large, yet living invulnerably within an exclusive circle of his own. He was also a secular personification of the customarily sacred insane.

Tom's diagnosed schizophrenia enabled his family to find a place for him; having created him out of their own needs, Tom became the living reification of their conflicts. And, perhaps, for the first time they—father, mother, siblings—really felt connected to this creation of theirs, while reserving the right, because of his illness, to disengage when the situation became intolerable. On such occasions, in turning away from Tom, they evaded themselves, "understandably," and with full official sanction. Tom's symbolic rebirth was the negation of the primary misconception into which his life had been converted. But his illness was not only a victimization, it was also a confession that no other resolution for his family through its network of associations and possibilities was feasible. For Tom, his parents, and his siblings accepted the society in which they were embedded. His father's sophisticated griping did not deflect him from his hope of the main chance, or change his conventional standards of success and failure. His mother's fatigue did not lead her to look for immediate personal alternatives. His siblings, on the other hand, pursued only the most limited personal alternatives, moving cautiously away from home, watching their words, and preparing themselves for safe careers. To the extent that they could, they sought to adapt to society at large by manipulating each other to that end. Therefore, their schizophrenia can be defined as an adaptation mediated by a protest. It was a flight into an institution, an abdication of autonomy, a surrender to a social designation.

As a family, then, they were preadapted to the clinical experiment undertaken at the NIMH. The research interests of the NIMH coincided with their emotional and economic needs and resources. The Dixons were in search of maximum security and understanding; and the NIMH needed raw material. The tautology came full circle in the closed environment of the observation room, which obscured both the social dimensions and the potential of these experimental "objects," the people involved. Suspended in a laboratory situation, they could now be conceived as timelessly and essentially schizophrenic.

As the experiment progressed, the manipulation of people, including oneself, as a means of survival and fulfillment, intensified and became more visible. Two related events, one intermediate, the other final, epitomized this situation. The intermediate event (intermediate in a developmental, not a chronological sense) occurred several years after the family had been introduced to the project. And it consisted of a critical therapeutic session which Tom, the paranoid schizophrenic, completely controlled. Tom was usually withdrawn, but relatively attentive, and his appearance was characteristically unkempt. He had been for some months prior to the critical session engaged in finger painting as a combined therapeutic-vocational activity under the guidance of a psychiatric social worker. This, however, did not absorb or structure his energies. He had begun a flirtation with a fellow patient, a young woman from a "good" Washington family. His tentative and necessarily surreptitious attentions were not unwelcome and on one occasion Tom and the young woman were found in her room in a tete á tete that was interpreted as sexually compromising. The response of the staff was immediate. Tom was forbidden to go near the girl again, the rationalization being that his behavior would disrupt the routine and betray the function of the institution, not to speak of the damage he might do to himself and the girl. She, after all, could become pregnant; moreover, Tom would certainly be unable to channel his impulses in a conventional way, ("we can't have screwing in the halls," said one psychoanalyst-administrator) and should such behavior spread, the primary aim of the experimental unit, namely, directed family therapy would be subverted. It was also tacitly assumed that the hospital remained responsible to the girl's relatives, and they would hardly have sanctioned a liaison with Tom. Thus Tom developed a reputation for being hard to handle. (On one occasion he had struck a nurse who had suggested that he get out of her right of way, and it was reported that he often made threatening gestures to the staff at large.)

Some weeks after the "sexual" episode, Tom's family, on his birthday, presented him with a black suit and a new pair of shoes. Tom made an unexpected use of them. When the critical therapeutic session began, he appeared exactly on time (he was usually late), immaculately dressed in black suit, appropriate tie, white shirt and polished shoes. His posture (usually slouched) was erect, his step certain, and his manner confident. As he entered the room he nodded graciously to his parents, held out his hand to the therapist, acknowledged the presence of the psychiatric social worker and took his accustomed seat. At first he said very little, but closely followed the questioning and counter-questioning between the therapists and his parents. Then, at a certain point, he began to speak quietly, with conviction, yet never completely focussing on the person to whom his remarks were addressed. But what he said was taken as nonsense.

On other occasions, Tom had "lapsed" into idiosyncratic sounds or words, sometimes repeating them to himself, at other times contributing them to the general conversation. This was language moving toward poetry—but not yet iconic, not yet a world in itself, still a reification. But now, he strung together whole blocks of unfamiliar syllables, just sufficiently interspersed with other parts of speech, in a syntatically logical sequence, to hold the attention of the other people in the room. When he was asked to explain what he meant, he seemed even more eager to make himself understood, and would either continue to talk in his private pidgin or pause, apparently pondering the difficulties of human intercourse.

The analyst was particularly intrigued by this performance, and, by gesture and word, kept trying to elicit a consistently meaningful statement or at least an interpretation of his remarks from Tom. Now and then the analyst became impatient, even angry, but Tom remained cool, either falling silent, or lowering his voice further while making no effort to avoid the analyst's gaze. In the background, Tom's mother smiled continuously, bewildered but also pleased at her son's manicured appearance. The father was quiet and actually nodded his head at one or two of Tom's indecipherable remarks. Towards the close of the session, the analyst, truculent, made it clear that he considered such language meaningless. Tom responded with a graceful, non-commital sound.

It was Tom who terminated the session. He rose from his chair with obvious dignity, kissed his mother lightly on the cheek, shook hands with his father, wished him well, and thanked him for the gift of the black suit. He then turned to the analyst, encircled his shoulder with a patronizing arm, made it clear that he had enjoyed the session immensely, hoped that the analyst had also, and looked forward to seeing him the following week. Without further comment, looking straight ahead, and striding briskly, he left the room to return to his quarters as if to an important meeting.

The initial comment by the civil servants in the observation booth following this performance was that Tom "ought to be dismissed from the hospital or promoted." He had, of course, been playing with his identity; he had used the suit, the analyst's air of authority, the easy, endless and circular flow of language in the therapeutic sessions, his mother's mild manner, his father's courtly gestures and manipulated them to fit a momentary identity of his own. At the same time he had inverted his typical social presence—formerly untidy, withdrawn, passive, explosive, he had become immaculate, cooperative, active, controlled. This transformation, this easy exercise in the adoption of a status ego, not only caricatured role playing, but revealed the dilemma of both the psychiatrist and the family. Tom had finally permitted himself the luxury of revealing himself as the mediating and mediated schizophrenic, a field for cultural distortions. At the same time, the link between the psychopathic actor and the schizophrenic problem of the self (those two presumably polar syndromes) become evident; they are shown to be no more than arbitrary perspectives on a single basic process.

Shortly therafter a new therapeutic tactic was adopted by the project because of both a change in research personnel and the therapeutic stalemate that had been reached. Tom was encouraged to leave the hospital and live at home while efforts were made to find him some kind of unskilled work. Therapeutic contact was maintained but members of the family were seen individually, the assumption being that with privacy, more intimacy and candor, deeper "communication" would become possible. However, it quickly became evident that relating to one member of the family implied relating to all the others, whether or not they were physically present. The alternative, namely, shattering the inverted integrity of the family and dispersing its members was obviously out of the question, and if attempted, would have been tautological; the family already reflected society.

It was not possible to find Tom a steady job, but he helped in shopping, cleared the lawn, assisted around the house in other ways, and worked on his bike. It was no surprise when after several months an argument between Tom and his father led to another outburst. This time the father knocked Tom unconscious with a baseball bat, inflicting a severe wound in his scalp. The parents called in the police, who called in a psychiatrist, and following surgical treatment Tom was admitted to a state hospital, where, so far as I know, he remains.

If the mock-creative, manipulative aspect of the schizophrenic process (investment in the status ego at the expense of the self) is epitomized in the Dixon family and revealed in the psychiatric milieu, the authentic schizophrenic is linked with artists and criminals, and may, in our society, be an artist or a criminal. In the archetypal, contemporary instance of Genet, whose inverted dramas ring every conceivable change on the problem of split consciousness, the artist and the criminal fuse; they become facets of an esthetic unity. The ordinary goals of the culture are flatly rejected and a creative alternative composed of personal and social meanings is constructed. After the disintegration of the civilized consciousness, after the social suicide of the artist, a reconstitution may take place, which, if achieved, is a devastating cultural critique. The self emerges, inevitably at the expense of status egos; the struggle is towards another reality.

Hans Arp, the surrealist poet, illuminates this arduously reintegrated consciousness in his own way.

life is the goal of art, art can misunderstand its means and merely reflect life instead of creating it. Such means are then illusionist descriptive academic. i exhibited along with the surrealists because their rebellious attitude toward "art" and their direct attitude toward life were as wise as dada. more recently the surrealist painters have been using illusionist descriptive academic means which would warm the cockles of rop's heart.

neoplaticism is direct but exclusively visual it lacks all relationship to the other human faculties.

but finally i feel that man is neither a parasol nor a para-la-si-do nor a paramount for he is made up of two carnivorous cylinders one of which says white when the other says black.

assuring you of my very pressed dishes i remain
sincerely yours[4]

And further:

i was born in nature, i was born in strasbourg. i was born in a cloud, i was born in a pump, i was born in a robe.

i have four natures. i have two things. i have five senses. sense and nonsense. nature is senseless. make way for nature. nature is a white eagle. make dada-way for dada-nature. i model out a book with five buttons, artis-tree of sculpture is a dark stupidity.

Finally:

you know no one can prove to me that i am not an eagle, the eagle works hard at life, you know the eagle has *five lives* and *four natures*, you know the eagle also has a title. you know the general has five titles five buttons on his two senses and four holes in his joys. but nature and i are against these joys and things that are born, nature works hard at life whether sitting or standing. the black cloud in the white robe joyfully gives birth to a bird-thing.

It was the day of the Nativity, the first day of the month of May. Snowmen and tuns of thunder were falling from the sky. The last three caulked hearts were drifting across the world: Liberty, Equality, Fraternity. It was the last day of the new year. The tree of idealism, that sentimental tree in which the nests of materialist philosophers sway, came crashing down in one single stroke of helium thunder.

Men had changed into boiled onions, each with a toothpick clutched in his toes and the banner of sacred colors in the righthand buttonhole of the left trouser leg. ten minutes later, all men had vanished and the last woman was munching her Oriental pills while sitting on the extreme tip of the highest mountain on earth. She bore a certain resemblance to Noah's Ark, although her beard was slightly longer and her male dove slightly shorter. However, the nose of her perfidious gaze bore a lovely olive branch (today, the olive tree it came from has become the tiepin of specialized short circuits).

As the reader must have realized by now, man has disappeared from the face of the earth, and in his place we can see the *hermaphrometallic globule*, svelte and elegant, no larger than half the ear of the evening angelus, no longer than the Greenwich meridian at 6:40 a.m.

This svelte and elegant creature is perfectly standardized, and anyone can obtain it for two and a half francs in any well-stocked store. Its living space is never more than 25 cubic centimeters. As soon as its respiration develops the slightest bit beyond that, the globule folds it in half or even in thirds, depending on the circumstances.[5]

As noted, the mock-creative and creative reactions overlap to such an extent that they can be considered two dialectically related aspects or phases of a single process. In the first instance, the self diminishes; in the second, the civilized position in the world collapses. In neither instance, is primitive integration possible.[7] The manipulative aspect signifies the struggle with persons, including oneself. It exposes the need to dominate, control, to put the other and oneself in their places, to locate them, and, therefore, to solve the problem of the self. This endless struggle, this constant rearrangement of people vis-a-vis oneself cannot, of course, work. It does not represent an exploration, but a mechanical exploitation, the objectification or reification of self and others. Manipulation inevitably ends in frustration because its ulterior motive and goal, the search for an authentic and creative connection, cannot be achieved by the means adopted. The "art" of manipulation is a distortion of the creative process, so understood we can situate both the source of the process and its negation in the relations of society at large. And that permits us to understand why artists must live through, comprehend and finally transcend civilized associations if they are fully to realize or develop their gifts. Thus the modern (nonacademic) artist is likely to share certain aspects of the consciousness of the criminal—at the very least he will sympathize with the criminal who, like himself, is an outcast and a victim who refuses to be victimized.

The more general point is that the schizophrenic reaction is no more and no less than the ultimate pathology of modern society; that pathology may be seen in its actuality as a society-wide dynamic manifested in varying degrees and combinations in all individuals according to their temperaments, their talents and their precise circumstances.

But the unfortunate person who for one reason or another becomes publicly exposed may then be defined as a schizophrenic. This vicious, if unwitting, clinical habit of reducing the person to a class or category, mirroring the mechanisms of social identity generally, not only limits the possibilities of relating to the patient, but also makes it possible to locate the problem in our organization of society, articulated in the language of our cultural assumptions. This means, among other things, that although the episodic character of all psychosis may be recognized, it cannot be taken into account. Thus, when Antoine Artaud states that psychoanalysis was invented in order to destroy the visionary in man, he confuses a purpose with a consequence, or at least with a consequence that has not yet been intended; but his insight concerning the social functions of psychiatry remains sound. We are obliged to acknowledge that we have created the clinical entity that we have named. We have hypostatized, reified and converted it into a diagnostic category, reflected as a disease of the individual, genetic or otherwise. And we close the circle finally by claiming that schizophrenia is statistically predictable in its distribution at a rate of say 1 per 100 throughout the civilized world, and increasing in frequency. That, of course, is one way of defining society as fate and is perhaps our cruelest evasion of social reality, and human possibility.

This brings us to the ultimate cross-cultural question of whether schizophrenia exists among primitive people.* I believe that as an essence it does not, but the *process* is identifiable. That is, schizophrenia as a diagnostic category is irrelevant in authentically primitive societies. The reasons for this are as follows:

1. The rights to food, clothing and shelter are completely customary; each person learns as an organic part of the socialization process the requisite variety of skills. *Functionlessness* is not a problem in primitive society.

2. Rituals at strategic points in the bioculturally defined life

---

* In 1939 George Devereaux observed: "Schizophrenia seems to be rare or absent among primitives. This is a point on which all students of comparative society and of anthropology agree."[6]

cycle permit the person to change roles while maintaining, and expanding, identity. His ordinary humanity is celebrated in an extraordinary way. The life-cycle is a normal curve; it does not collapse in the middle, leaving the aged without wisdom, work or honor, their only alternative being the dissimulation of youth.

3. Rituals and ceremonies permit the expression of ambivalent emotions and the acting out of complex fantasies in a socially prescribed fashion. It is customary for individuals or groups of people to "go crazy" for self-limiting periods of time without being extirpated from the culture.

4. The ramifying network of kinship associations sets the developing person firmly in a matrix of reciprocal rights, obligations and expectations. *Social alienation* as we experience it in civilization is unknown.

The fact that there are no mental hospitals or asylums in primitive societies or, to my knowledge, any institutional equivalents, testifies to the social use and containment of the schizophrenic process, which is a generic human process. It does not become a clinical entity until a society which can erect no boundaries to the process and no creative channels for its expression, exiles those who are as a result incapacitated to specialized institutions, or otherwise immobilized. One may fairly conclude that although the schizophrenic process is identifiable, the structure, function and the psychodynamic character of primitive societies set cultural limits to the process and prevent it from becoming a diagnostic entity. Primitive cultures realize the major function of culture which is to make men human, and at the same time to keep them sane. That is what civilization, as we know it, is failing to do. Schizophrenia, then, is no less and no more than the subjective aspect of the socio-economic dynamic of alienation.

8

THE RULE OF LAW VERSUS THE ORDER OF CUSTOM

Creon: *Knowest thou the edict has forbidden this?*
Antigone: *I knew it well. Why not? It was proclaimed.*
Creon: *But thou didst dare to violate the law?*
Antigone: *It was not God above who framed that law,*
              Nor justice, whispering from the underworld,
              Nor deemed I thy decrees were of such force
              As to o'er ride the sanctities of heaven;
              Which are not of today or yesterday.
              From whom—whence they first issued, no one knows.
              I was not like to scant their holy rites
              And brave the even justice of the gods
              For fear of someone's edict.

—Sophocles

The lowest police employee of the civilized state has more "authority" than all the organs of gentilism combined. But the mightiest prince and the greatest statesman or general of civilization may look with envy on the spontaneous and undisputed esteem that was the privilege of the least gentile sachem. The one stands in the middle of society, the other is forced to assume a position outside and above it.

—Engels

There's too much due process of law. The electric chair is a cheap crime deterrent to show these criminal elements that law and order is going to triumph.

—Detective Sergeant John Heffernan,
1971 vice-president of the
International Conference of Police
Associations and head of the
New Jersey State Police Benevolent Association

We must distinguish the rule of law from the authority of custom. In a recent effort to do so (which I shall critically examine because it is so typical), Paul Bohannan, under the imprimatur of the *International Encyclopedia of the Social Sciences*.[1] contends that laws result from double institutionalization. He means by this no more than the lending of a specific force, a cutting edge, to the functioning of customary institutions: marriage, the family, religion. But, he tells us, the laws so emerging assume a character and dynamic of their own. They form a structured, legal dimension of society; they do not merely reflect, but interact with, given institutions. Therefore, Bohannan is led to maintain that laws are typically out of phase with society, and it is this process that is both a symptom and cause of social change. The laws of marriage, to illustrate Bohannan's argument with the sort of concrete example his definition lacks, are not synonymous with the institution of marriage. They reinforce certain rights and obligations while neglecting others. Moreover, they subject partners defined as truant to intervention by an external, impersonal agency whose decisions are sanctioned by the power of the police.

Bohannan's sociological construction does have the virtue of denying the primacy of the legal order and of implying that law is generic to unstable (or progressive) societies, but it is more or less typical of abstract efforts to define the eternal essence of the law and it begs the significant questions. Law has no such eternal essence; it has a definable historical nature. Thus, if we inquire into the structure of the contemporary institutions which, according to Bohannan, stand in a primary relation to the law, we find that their customary content has drastically diminished. Paul Radin made the point as follows:

> A custom is, in no sense, a part of our properly functioning culture. It belongs definitely to the past. At best, it is moribund. But customs are an integral part of the life of primitive peoples. There is no compulsive submission to them. They are not followed because the weight of tradition overwhelms a man ... a custom is obeyed there because it is intimately intertwined with a vast living network of interrelations, arranged in a meticulous and ordered manner.[2]

And "what is significant in this connection," as J.G. Peristiany indicates, "is not that common values should exist, but that they should be expressed although no common political organization corresponds to them."[3] V.C. Uchendu, writing about the Igbo, claims: "the use of force is minimal or absent . . . there are leaders rather than rulers, and . . . cohesion is achieved by rules rather than by laws and by consensus rather than by dictation. In general, the Igbo have not achieved any political structure which can be called a federation, a confederacy, or a state."[4]

No contemporary institution functions with the kind of autonomy that permits us to postulate a significant dialectic between law and custom. We live in a law-ridden society; law has cannibalized the institutions which it presumably reinforces or with which it interacts. Accordingly, morality continues to be reduced to or confused with legality. In civil society, we are encouraged to assume that legal behavior is the measure of moral behavior. It is a matter of some interest that a former Chief Justice of the Supreme Court proposed, with the best of intentions, that a federal agency be established to advise government employees and those doing business with the government about the legal propriety of their behavior. Any conflict of interest not legally enjoined would thus tend to become socially or morally acceptable; morality becomes a technical question. Efforts to legislate conscience by an external political power are the antithesis of custom: customary behavior comprises precisely those aspects of social behavior which are traditional, moral and religious—in short, conventional and nonlegal. Put another way, custom *is* social morality.[5] The relation between custom and law is basically one of contradiction, not continuity.

The customary and the legal orders are historically, not logically related. They touch coincidentally; one does not imply the other. Custom, most anthropologists agree, is characteristic of primitive society, and laws are characteristic of civilization. Robert Redfield's dichotomy between the primitive moral order and the civilized legal or technical order remains a classic statement of the case. William Seagle writes:

> The dispute whether primitive societies have law or custom, is not merely a dispute over words. Only confusion can result from treating them as interchangeable phenomena. If custom is spontaneous and automatic, law is the product of organized force. Reciprocity is in force in civilized communities too but

at least nobody confuses social with formal legal relationships.[6]

Parenthetically, one should note that students of primitive society
who use the term "customary law" blur the issue semantically, but
nonetheless recognize the distinction.

It is this over-all legalization of behavior in modern society
which Bohannan fails to interpret. In Fascist Germany, for
example, laws flourished as never before. By 1941, more edicts
had been proclaimed than in all the years of the Republic and the
Third Reich. At the same time, ignorance of the law inevitably
increased. In a sense, the very force of the law depends upon
ignorance of its specifications, which is hardly recognized as a
mitigating circumstance. As Seagle states, law is not definite and
certain while custom is vague and uncertain. Rather, the converse
holds. Customary rules must be clearly known; they are not
sanctioned by organized political force, hence serious disputes
about the nature of custom would destroy the integrity of society.
But laws may always be invented and stand a good chance of being
enforced: "Thus, the sanction is far more important than the rule
in the legal system ... but the tendency is to minimize the
sanction and to admire the rule."[7]

In Fascist Germany, customs did not become laws through a
process of double institutionalization. Rather, repressive laws,
conjured up in the interests of the Nazi Party and its supporters,
cannibalized the institutions of German society. Even the residual,
customary authority of the family was assaulted: children were
encouraged to become police informers, upholding the laws
against their kin. "The absolute reign of law has often been
synonymous with the absolute reign of lawlessness."[8]

Certainly, Germany under Hitler was a changing society, if
hardly a progressive one, but it was a special case of the general
process in civilization through which the organs of the state have
become increasingly irresistible. It will be recalled that Bohannan
takes the domination of law over custom to be symptomatic of
changing societies. But the historical inadequacy of his argument
lies exactly here: he does not intimate the over-all direction of
that change and therefore fails to clarify the actual relation
between custom and law. Accordingly, the notion that social
change is a function of the law, and vice versa, implies a dialectic
that is out of phase with historical reality.

Plato understood this well enough when he conceived the problem of civilization as primarily one of injustice, which he did not scant by legalistic definition. Whether we admire his utopia or not, the *Republic* testifies to Plato's recognition that laws follow social change and reflect prevailing social relationship, but are the cause of neither. (The best laws, of course, would reflect the divine order.) Plato's remedy was the thorough restructuring of society. Curiously, this view of the relationship between law and society accords with aspects of the Marxist perspective on the history of culture. Customary societies are said to precede legal societies, an idea which, semantics aside, most students of historical jurisprudence would accept. But Marxists envision the future as being without laws as we know them, as involving a return to custom, so to speak, on a higher level, since the repressive, punitive and profiteering functions of law will become superfluous. Conflicts of economic and political interest will be resolved through the equitable reordering of institutions. Law for the Marxists and most classical students of historical jurisprudence, is the cutting edge of the state—but Marxists, insisting on both a historical and normative view of man, define the state as the instrument of the ruling class, anticipating its dissolution with the abolition of classes and the common ownership of the basic means of production. Sir Henry Maine equates the history of individual property with that of civilization:

> Nobody is at liberty to attack several property and to say at the same time that he values civilization. The history of the two cannot be disentangled. Civilization is nothing more than the name for the ... order ... dissolved but perpetually reconstituting itself under a vast variety of solvent influences, of which infinitely the most powerful have been those which have, slowly, and in some parts of the world much less perfectly than others, substituted several property for collective ownership.[9]

In the words of Jeremy Bentham: "Property and law are born together and die together."

Thus, law is symptomatic of the emergence of the state; the legal sanction is not simply the cutting edge of institutions at all times and in all places. The double institutionalization to which Bohannan refers needs redefinition. Where it does occur, it is a historical process of unusual complexity and cannot be defined as

259

the simple passage of custom into law. It occurs, as we shall see, in several modes. Custom—spontaneous, traditional, personal, commonly known, corporate, relatively unchanging—is the modality of primitive society; law is the instrument of civilization, of political society sanctioned by organized force, presumably above society at large and buttressing a new set of social interests. Law and custom both involve the regulation of behavior but their characters are entirely distinct. No evolutionary balance has been struck between developing law and custom, whether traditional or emergent.

ARCHAIC LAW AND LOCAL CUSTOM

The simple dichotomy between primitive society and civilization does not illustrate the passage from the customary to the legal order. The most critical and revealing period in the evolution of law is that of archaic societies, the local segments of which are the cultures most often studied by anthropologists. More precisely, the earlier phases of these societies, which I call proto-states, represent a transition from the primitive kinship-based communities to the class-structured polity. In such polities, law and custom exist side by side; this gives us the opportunity to examine their connections, distinctions and differential relationship to the society at large. The customary behavior typical of the local groups—joint families, clans, villages—maintains most of its force; the Vietnamese, for example, still say: "The customs of the village are stronger than the law of the emperor." Simultaneously, the civil power, comprising bureaucracy and sovereign, the dominant emerging class, issues a series of edicts that have the double purpose of confiscating "surplus" goods and labor for the support of those not directly engaged in production, while attempting to deflect the loyalties of the local groups to the center.

These archaic societies are the great historical watershed; it is here that Sir Henry Maine and Paul Vinogradoff located the passage from status to contract, from the kinship to the territorial principle, from extended familial controls to public law. For our understanding of the law, we need not be concerned with the important distinctions among archaic societies, or with the precise language or emphases of those scholars who have recognized their centrality. The significant point is that they are transitional. Particularly in their early phase, they are the agencies that transmute customary forms of order into legal sanction. Here we find a form of double institutionalization functioning explicitly. We can witness, so to speak, what appears to be the emergence of a custom, in defense of the kinship principle against the assault of the state, and the subsequent shift of the customary function into its own opposite as a legal function. The following example from the archaic proto-state of Dahomey, prior to the French conquest in 1892, will make this process clear.

Traditionally in Dahomey, each person was said to have three "best" friends, in descending order of intimacy and importance. This transitional institution, a transfiguration of kin connections, of the same species as blood brotherhood, reinforced the extended family structure, which continued to exist in the early state, but was being thrown into question as a result of the political and economic demands made by the emerging civil power. So for example, the best friend of a joint-family patriarch would serve as his testator and, upon the latter's decease, name his successor to the assembled family. It seems that the ordinary convention of succession no longer sufficed to secure the family's integrity, since the central authority was mustering family heads as indirect rulers. In this instance, the institution of friendship was assimilated to the form and purpose of customary behavior. On the other hand, the best friend of a man charged with a civil crime could be seized by the king's police in his stead. However, these traditional friendships were so socially critical, so deeply held, so symbolically significant that the person charged, whether or not he had actually committed a civil breach, would be expected to turn himself in rather than implicate a friend in his punishment. Whether or not he did so, the custom of friendship was given a legal edge and converted by the civil power into a means of enforcing its will. This example of double institutionalization has the virtue of explicitly revealing the contradiction between law and custom. But there are other examples in which the law appears as a reinforcement of customary procedure.

In eleventh-century Russia, for instance, Article 1 of the codified law states:

> If a man kills a man ... the brother is to avenge his brother; the son, his father; or the father, his son; and the son of the

brother (of the murdered man) or the son of his sister, their respective uncle. If there is no avenger (the murderer) pays 40 grivna wergeld. . . .[10]

Similarly, circa A.D. 700, the law of the Visigoths states: "Whoever shall have killed a man, whether he committed a homicide intending to or not intending to (volens aut nolens) . . . let him be handed over into the potestas of the parents or next of kin of the deceased. . . ."[11] In these instances, a custom has been codified by an external agency, thus assuming legal force, with its punitive character sharpened. Such confirmation is both the intimation of legal control and the antecedent of institutional change beyond the wish or conception of the family. "Whatever princes do, they seem to command," or, as Sir Henry Maine put it, "What the sovereign permits, he commands." Maine had specifically in mind "the Sikh despot who permitted heads of households and village elders to prescribe rules, therefore these rules became his command and true laws, which are the 'solvent' of local and domestic usage."[12] Simpson and Stone explain this apparent reinforcement of custom by the civil power as follows:

> Turning then to the role of law in the emergent political society . . . it is true that political institutions, independent of the kin and the supernatural, had risen to power; yet these institutions were young, weak and untried. Their encroachment on the old allegiance was perforce wary and hesitating. Social cohesion still seemed based on nonpolitical elements, and these elements were therefore protected. It is this society which Pound has perceived and expressed when he says that the end of law envisaged in his period of strict law, is the maintenance of the social status quo. In modern terminology this means *the primacy of the interest in the maintenance of antecedent social institutions* (italics added).[13]

This sort of confirmation, which betrays the structural opportunism of early civil power, inheres in the limitations of sovereignty and is further apparent in the sovereign's relation to the communally held clan or joint-family land. In Dahomey, for example, where the king was said to "own" all property, including land, it is plain that such ownership was a legal fiction and had the effect of validating the pre-existent joint-family tradition. That is, the king "permitted" the joint families, by virtue of his fictional ownership, to expand into new lands and continue transmitting their property intact, generation after generation. The civil power could not rent, alienate or sell joint-family property, nor could any member of a joint family do so.[14] This is borne out by A.I. Richards, who informs us that "in Northern Rhodesia [Zambia] the statement that 'all the land is mine' does not mean that the ruler has the right to take any piece of land he chooses for his own use. . . . I have never heard of a case where a chief took land that had already been occupied by a commoner."[15] The same point is made by Rattray about the Ashanti[16] and by Mair about the Baganda.[17] Civil validation, then, expresses the intention but not yet the reality of state control. We might more realistically formulate Maine's epigram as: What he cannot command, the sovereign permits.

Ultimately, local groups have maintained their autonomy when their traditional economies were indispensable to the functioning of the entire society. They could be hedged around by restrictions, harassed by law or as we have seen, they could be "legally" confirmed in their customary usage. But so long as the central power depended on them for support, in the absence of any alternative mode or source of production, their integrity could be substantially preserved. This certainly seems the case during the early phases of state organization in the classic nuclear areas (Egypt, Babylonia, Northern India) before the introduction of large-scale irrigation and analogous public works, and it was true of precolonial Africa. But in all archaic societies, whether incipient (as in sub-Saharan Africa) florescent (as in the ancient peasant societies of the Middle East or China) or in cognate contemporary societies which probably still embrace most of the world's population, the extensive kin unit was more functional, in spite of varying degrees of autonomy, than the family in commercial and industrial civilization.

As the state develops, according to Maine, "the individual is steadily substituted for the family as the unit of which civil laws take account."[18] And in Jhering's words, "The progress of law consists in the destruction of every natural tie, in a continued process of separation and isolation."[19] That is to say, the family increasingly becomes a reflex of society at large. The legal stipulation that spouses may not testify against each other appears as one of the last formal acknowledgements of familial integrity and the exception that proves the historical case. Clearly, the nuclear family in contemporary, urban civilization, although bound by legal obligations, has minimal autonomy; obviously, the means of education, subsistence and self-defense are outside the family's competence. It is in this sense that, given the absence of mediating institutions having a clearly defined independent authority, the historical tendency of all state structures vis-à-vis the individual may be designated as totalitarian. Indeed, the state creates the disaffiliated individual whose bearings thus become bureaucratic or collective; the juridical "person," who may even be a corporation doing business, is merely the legal reflection of a social process. If "totalization" is the state process, totalitarianism cannot be confined to a particular political ideology but is, so to speak, the ideology, explicit or not, of political society.

This étatist tendency has its origins in archaic society. We can observe it with unusual clarity in the proto-states of sub-Saharan Africa. In East Africa, pastoralists, competing for land, and in West Africa, militaristic clans, catalyzed by the Arab, and, later, the European trade, notably in slaves, conquered horticulturalists, thereby providing the major occasions for the growth of civil power. Since the basic means of exploiting the environment in these polities remained substantially unchanged, and, to some extent, survived under colonialism, we can reconstruct through chronicles extending back for centuries and by means of contemporary field work, the structure of early state controls, which evolved in the absence of writing and the systematic codification of law. The absence of writing should relieve the scholar from that dependence on official records that has so thoroughly shaped our sense of European history; unfortunately, rubbing shoulders with the upper class in a nonliterate state creates equivalent distortions.

In such societies, Rattray tells us, referring to Ashanti:

the small state was ever confronted with the kindred organization which was always insidiously undermining its authority by placing certain persons outside its jurisdiction. It could only hold its own, therefore, by throwing out an ever-widening circle to embrace those loyalties which were lost to it owing to the workings of the old tribal organization which has survived everywhere.... [Further] the old family, clan and tribal organization survived in the new regime which was ever striving to make territorial considerations, and not the incidence of kinship, the basis of state control. . . . "corporate responsibility for every act was an established principle which survived even the advent of a powerful central public authority as the administration of public justice."[20]

Concerning the Islamized Nupe of the Nigerian Middle Belt, Nadel saw "a much more subtle development and a deeper kind of antagonism [than interstate warfare], namely, the almost eternal antagonism of developed State versus that raw material of the Community which, always and everywhere, must form the nourishing soil from which alone the state can grow."[21] And Engels refers to the "irreconcilable opposition of gentile society to the state."[22]

I have documented this conflict in detail in a study of the Dahomean proto-state. There, as elsewhere, it is apparent that the contradictory transition from customs to specified laws, double institutionalization if you will, is by no means the major source of law. Whether the law arises latently in confirmation of previous usage or through the transformation of some aspect of custom which the law itself may have provoked, as in the ambiguous example of the "best friend," neither circumstance brings us to the heart of the matter. For we learn, by studying intermediate societies, that the laws so typical of them are unprecedented; they do not emerge through a process of double institutionalization, however defined. They arise in opposition to the customary order of the antecedent kin or kin-equivalent groups; they represent a new set of social goals pursued by a new and unanticipated power in society. These goals can be reduced to a single complex imperative: the imposition of the census-tax-conscription system. The territorial thrust of the early state, along with its vertical social entrenchment, demanded conscription of labor, the mustering of an army, the levying of taxes and tribute, the maintenance of a bureaucracy and the assessment of the extent, location and numbers of the population being subjected. These were the major direct or indirect occasions for the development of civil law.

The primary purpose of a census is indicative. Census figures provide the basis on which taxes are apportioned among conquered districts and on which tribute in labor is exacted from kin units. The census is also essential for conscripting men into the army. This information was considered so important in Dahomey that each new king, upon his enstoolment, was escorted by his two leading ministers to a special hut in the royal compound and there admonished as he knelt: "Young man, all your life you have heard Dahomey, Dahomey, but you have never until today seen the true Dahomey, for Dahomey is its people and here they are."[2][3]

With this declaration, the two elders pointed to sacks of pebbles, each pebble representing a person, each sack representing a sex or age group (thus in a nonliterate society are records kept, with pebbles for counters). The young king was then told that he must never allow the contents of the sacks to diminish and that every year the pebbles would be counted to see whether their number had increased or declined. He was then given an old gun (in earlier times a hoe handle) and advised, "Fight with this. But take care that you are not vanquished."[2][4]

The census figures represented the potential power of the state and were carefully guarded; perhaps they were the first state secret. The act and intent of the census turned persons into ciphers and abstractions; people did all they could to avoid being counted. Suspicion persists; even in the United States the authorities during the period of census taking find it necessary to assert that census information will not be used to tax or otherwise penalize the individual and in fact, to do so is said to be against the law.

The double meanings of certain critical terms in common English use—"custom," "duty" and "court," reveal this conflict between local usage and the census-tax-conscription system of the early state. We have been speaking of custom as traditional or conventional nonlegal behavior, but custom also refers to a tax routinely payable to the state for the transportation of goods across territorial borders. All such taxes are clearly defined legal impositions, frequently honored in the breach, and they do not have the traditional command of custom. In Dahomey, the "Grand Customs" held at the unveiling of a new king, presumably in honor of his ancestors, were the occasion for the payment of taxes, the large-scale sentencing and sacrifice of criminals and the prosecution of other state business. Camus has Caligula describe such an event in a passage that could have been extrapolated from a Dahomean chronicle:

> It's only the Treasury that counts. And living is the opposite of loving . . . and I invite you to the most gorgeous of shows,

a sight for gods to gloat on, a whole world called to judgment. But for that I must have a crowd—spectators, victims, criminals, hundreds and thousands of them. Let the accused come forward. I want my criminals, and they are all criminals. Bring in the condemned men. I must have my public. Judges, witnesses, accused—all sentenced to death without a hearing. Yes, Ceasonia, I'll show them something they've never seen before, the one free man in the Roman Empire."[25]

Along with the annual customs, the Grand Customs paralleled the form of local ceremonies, but the substance had entirely changed. Fiscal or legal coercion and political imposition were not the purpose of these ancestral ceremonies which ritually reenacted reciprocal bonds. The customs of the sovereign were laws, the ceremonies of the kin groups were customs.

Similarly, the term *duty* implies a moral obligation on the one hand and a tax on the other. Naturally, we assume that it is the duty of citizens to pay taxes: the paradox inherent in the term becomes more obvious as we examine archaic civilizations.

The term *court* is analogously ambivalent. On the one hand, it refers to the residence or entourage of the sovereign; on the other, to a place where civil justice is dispensed, but at their root the functions fuse. The prototypical juridical institution was, in fact, the court of the sovereign where legislation was instituted, for which no precedent or formal analogue existed on the local level. Peristiany, speaking of the Kipsigis, sharpens the latter point: "One of the most significant differences between the . . . council of elders and a European judicature is to be found in the relation between officer and office. The Council elders do not hold their office from a higher authority. They are not appointed . . ."[26]

The contrast is noted by V.C. Uchendu: "Under a constitution like that of the Igbo, which does not provide for a specialized court, judicial matters are ad hoc affairs. The injured party takes the initiative. He may appeal to the head of the compound of the offender or to a body of arbitrators. . . . Since the arbitrators have no means of enforcing their decision, for it to be respected it must be acceptable to both parties."[27]

As Seagle, among others, indicates, the court is the first, the most important and perhaps the last legal artifact. In Montaigne's words, "France takes as its rule the rule of the court."[28] Put another way, the court is a specialized legal structure, and it embraces all those particular and determinate legal bodies which are peculiar to civilization.

Clearly, the function of the court was not primarily the establishment of order. In primitive societies, as in the traditional sectors of proto-states, there already existed built-in mechanisms for the resolution of conflict. Generally speaking (as Max Gluckman, among others, has shown), in such societies conflicts generated by the ordinary functioning of social institutions were resolved as part of the customary ritual cycle integral to the institutions themselves. With regard to more specific breaches, we recall Rattray's observation on the Ashanti: "Corporate responsibility for every act was an established principle which survived even the advent of . . . the administration of public justice."[29] That is to say the kin unit was the juridical unit, just as it was the economic and social unit. Furthermore,

> Causes which give rise to the greater part of present "civil" actions were practically nonexistent. Inheritance, ownership of moveable and nonmoveable property, status of individuals, rules of behavior and morality were matters inevitably settled by the customary law, with which everyone was familiar from childhood, and litigation regarding such matters was . . . almost inconceivable. Individual contract, moreover, from the very nature of the community with which we are concerned, was also unknown, thus removing another possible, fruitful source of litigation."[30]

The primary purpose of the historically emerging court, the sovereign's entourage and habitation, was to govern. The distinguished British jurist Sir John Salmond has observed, "Law is secondary and unessential. . . . The administration of justice is perfectly possible without law at all."[31] And Sir William Markby writes, "Tribunals can act entirely without law."[32] The perhaps unintended point here is that justice, commonly defined, is not deducible from the law, nor was the legislation of the court a measure of justice, but of the political thrust of the early state, and that flowed from the implementation of the census-tax-conscription system.

In the census-tax-conscription system, every conceivable occasion was utilized for the creation of law in support of bureaucracy and sovereign. We observe no abstract principle, no impartial justice, no *precedent*, only the spontaneous opportunism of a new class designing the edifice of its power. It should be re-emphasized, however, that in certain instances formal analogues for civil imposition existed on the local level, but no formal or functional precedents. Civil taxation, for example, can be rationalized in the context of reciprocal gift-giving in the localities, but such gift-giving was not confirmed by law or specifically used by the sovereign; similarly, corvée labor is a political analogue of local cooperative work groups. But such evolutionary and dialectical relationships are most important for their distinctions.

Stubbs writes about the Norman kings that "it was mainly for the sake of the profits that early justice was administered at all."[33] Burton relates that at Whydah in Dahomey in the event of a financial dispute, the Yevogan, the leading bureaucrat in the district, sat in judgment. For his services, he appropriated half the merchandise involved, in the name of the king and another quarter for various lesser officials. The remainder presumably went to the winning contestant in the judicial duel.[34] Among the Ashanti, the central authority relied on the proceeds of litigation as a fruitful means for replenishing a depleted treasury. Litigation, Rattray notes, came actually to be encouraged.[35]

Tolls were an important source of revenue. In Ashanti, the king had all the roads guarded; all traders were detained until inquiries were made about them, whereupon they were allowed to pass on payment of gold dust.[36] W. Bosman writes that in early eighteenth century Whydah, "in proportion to his country, the king's revenue is very large, of which I believe, he hath above one thousand collectors who dispose themselves throughout the whole land in all market roads and passages, in order to gather the king's toll which amounts to an incredible sum, for there is nothing so mean sold in the whole kingdom that the king hath no toll for it. . . ."[37]

The punishment for the theft of property designated as the king's was summary execution by kangaroo courts organized on the spot by the king's agents.[38] This is echoed in the code of Hammurabi: "If a man steals the property of a god [temple] or a palace, that man shall be put to death; and he who receives from his hands the stolen [property] shall also be put to death."[39] Where the king's property was concerned, no judicial duel was possible. In these instances, which could be endlessly multiplied, we witness the extension of the king's peace as the primary form of the civil "order"; actually, this order grew from the invention and application of sumptuary law through the subsidiary peaces of highway and market. In Maitland's words, "the king has a peace that devours all others." If in these proto-states, the sovereign power is not yet fully effective, it nonetheless strives to that monopoly of force which characterizes the mature state.

The purpose and abundance of laws inevitably provoked breaches. The civil authority, in fact, continually probed for breaches and frequently manufactured them. In Dahomey, for example, a certain category of the king's women were distributed to the local villages and those men who made the mistake of having intercourse with them were accused of rape, for which, following a summary trial, the punishment was conscription into the army.[40] Thus, rape was invented as a civil crime. If rape had occured in the traditional joint-family villages (and such an occurrence would have been rare, as indicated by the necessity of civil definition), the wrong could have been dealt with by composition (the ritualized giving of goods to the injured party), ritual purification, ridicule and, perhaps for repeated transgressions, banishment; the customary machinery would have gone into effect automatically, probably on the initiative of the family of the aggressor. Such examples as this only sharpen the point that in early states crimes seem to have been invented to suit the laws. The latent purpose of the law was punishment in the service and profit of the state, not prevention or the protection of persons, not the healing of the breach. As Seagle indicates, "The criminal law springs into life in every great period of class conflict," and this is most obviously the case during the initial phases of state formation.

In its civil origins then, a correlation existed between law and crime, which partook of entrapment. One may even state that the substantial rationale for law developed after the fact of its emergence. For example, civil protection of the market place or highway was certainly not necessary to the degree implied in the archaic edicts at the time they were issued. Joint-family markets and village trails were not ordinarily dangerous places, if we are to believe the reports of the earliest chroniclers as well as those of more contemporary observers. More significantly if trouble had developed, the family, clan or village was capable of dealing with it. But, in an evolving state, the presence of the king's men would itself be a primary cause of disruption. Indeed, as Quénum, a descendant of Dahomean commoners, informs us the soldiers were referred to as bandits and predators who victimized many people. Sometimes their forays were confined to a compound, where someone, whether man, woman or child, resided who had spoken badly of the sovereign or whom the king suspected. In common parlance, the very names of the elite army units became insults; one meant "nasty person," another "arrogant person," and one would say of a tragic event that it was worthy of a particular military cadre. It is, therefore, understandable that the peace of the highway became an issue.[41]

As the integrity of the local groups declined, a process which, in the autochthonous state, must have taken generations or even centuries, conditions doubtless developed which served as an ex post facto rationalization for edicts already in effect. In this sense, laws became self-fulfilling prophecies. Crime and the laws which served it were, then, co-variants of the evolving state.

Just as entrapment was characteristic of early civil law, the idea of protection, in the sense of a protection racket, was also an early development. In Dahomey, we are told by Norris and others, prostitution was encouraged by the civil power and prostitutes were distributed through the villages, the price of their favors being set by civil decree. They were obliged to offer themselves to any man who could pay the moderate fee, and once a year they were convened at the annual customs where they were heavily taxed.[42] Skertchly notes that the prostitutes were licensed by the king and placed in the charge of the Mew, the second leading bureaucrat, who was entrusted with the task of "keeping up the supply."[43] Bosman observes at Whydah that "for every affair that can be thought of, the king hath appointed a captain overseer."[44] *What the king permits, he commands; what he "protects," he taxes.*

The intention of the civil power is epitomized in the sanctions against homicide and suicide; indeed, they were among the very first civil laws. Just as the sovereign is said to own the land, intimating the mature right of eminent domain, so the individual is ultimately conceived as the chattel of the state. In Dahomey, persons were conceived as *les choses du monarque*. Eminent domain in persons and property, even where projected as a fiction, is the cardinal prerequisite of the census-tax-conscription system. We recall that Maine designated the individual the unit of which the civil law steadily takes account. Seagle stated the matter as follows: "By undermining the kinship bond, they [the early civil authorities] made it easier to deal with individuals, and the isolation of the individual is a basic precondition for the growth of law."[45]

Homicide, then, was regarded as an offense against the state. In Rattray's words, "The blow which struck down the dead man would thus appear to have been regarded as aimed also at the . . . central authority."[46] In Ashanti, homicide was punishable by death in its most horrible form as customarily defined, in Dahomey, by death or conscription into the army. There is a nuance here which should not be overlooked. By making homicide, along with the theft of the king's property, a capital offence, the sovereign power discouraged violent opposition to the imposition of the civil order. An act of self-defense (ordinarily, a war) thus becomes a crime. As the state develops the externally sanctioned becomes internally enjoined. The military becomes the police, and this identity is echoed in the universal modern institution of the military police.

Traditionally, murder in a joint-family village was a tort—a private, remediable wrong—which could stimulate a blood feud, not to be confused with the *lex talionis*, until redress, though not necessarily injury in kind, was achieved. But a breach was most often settled by composition. As Paul Radin put it: "The theory of an eye for an eye . . . never really held for primitive people. . . . Rather it was replacement for loss with damages."[47] And this is echoed by Peristiany: "they claim restitution or private damages and not social retribution."[48] In any case, the family was fully involved. "The family was a corporation," said Rattray, and "it is not easy to grasp what must have been the effect . . . of untold generations of thinking and acting . . . in relation to one's group. The Ashanti's idea of what we term moral responsibility for his actions must surely have been more developed than in peoples where individualism is the order of the day."[49] This more or less typical anthropological observation makes it clear that the law against homicide was not a "progressive" step, as if some abstract right were involved which the state, the moral idea coming of age, finally understood and sought to establish. "Anti-social conduct

[is] exceptional in small kinship groups," writes Margery Perham of the Igbo.[50] Crimes of violence were rare, Richard Burton reported of Dahomey, and "murder virtually unknown."[51]

Acts of violence, of course, must be distinguished from crimes of violence. The incidence, occasion for, and character of violence in primitive societies is a subject of the utmost importance. But the question here has to do with crimes in which violence is used as a means to an end, such as the theft of property. In contemporary societies, unpremeditated acts of personal violence that have no ulterior motive, so-called crimes of passion, may not be penalized or carry minor degrees of guilt, that is, their status as legally defined crimes is ambiguous. This would certainly seem to reflect a historically profound distinction between crime and certain types of violence; in primitive societies violence tends to be personally structured, nondissociative and thereby self-limiting. As with other crimes defined by civil law, crimes of violence may have increased as the social autonomy, economic communalism and reciprocity of the kin units weakened. But this is much less important than Dalzel's observation that in Dahomey "many creatures have been put to death ... without having committed any crime at all," thus exemplifying the power of the sovereign literally to command the lives of his citizens.[52] The threat and example of summary execution, especially but by no means exclusively evident at the mortuary celebrations or the "Grand Customs" on the enstooling of a king, encouraged obedience to civil injunctions.

The law against suicide, a capital offense, was the apotheosis of political absurdity. The individual, it was assumed, had no right to take his own life; that was the sole prerogative of the state, whose property he was conceived to be. The fanatical nature of the civil legislature in claiming sole prerogative to the lives of its subjects is conclusively revealed among the Ashanti, where, if the suicide was a murderer, "the central authority refused to be cheated thus and the long arm of the law followed the suicide to the grave from which, if his kinsmen should have dared to bury him, he was dragged to stand trial."[53] This contrasts remarkably, if logically, with the behavior of the more primitively structured Igbo, as reported by Victor Uchendu, an anthropologist who is himself an Igbo:

Homicide is an offense against *ala*—the earth deity. If a

villager is involved, the murderer is expected to hang himself, after which ... daughters of the village perform the rite of ... sweeping away the ashes of murder. If the murderer has fled, his extended family must also flee, and the property of all is subject to raids. When the murderer is eventually caught, he is required to hang himself to enable the [daughters of the village] to perform their rites. It is important to realize that the village has no power to impose capital punishment. In fact, no social group or institution has this power. Everything affecting the life of the villager is regulated by custom. The life of the individual is highly respected; it is protected by the earth-goddess. The villagers can bring social pressure, but the murderer must hang himself.[54]

It can hardly be argued that the purpose of the civil sanction against suicide was to diminish its incidence or to propagate a superior moral consciousness. Dare we say, as with other crimes, that attempts at suicide increased as society became more thoroughly politicized? The law against suicide reveals, in the extreme, the whole meaning and intent of civil law at its origins. In the proto-state, the quintessential struggle was over the lives and labor of the people, who, still moving in a joint family context, were nontheless conceived to be *les choses du monarque*.

LAW AND DISORDER

If revolutions are the acute, episodic signs of civilizational discontent, the rule of law, from Sumer or Akkad to New York or Moscow, has been the chronic symptom of the disorder of institutions. E.B. Tylor stated: "A constitutional government, whether called republic or kingdom, is an arrangement by which the nation governs itself by means of the machinery of a military despotism."[55]

The generalization lacks nuance, but we can accept it if we bear in mind what seems to be Tylor's point of reference: "Among the lessons to be learnt from the life of rude tribes is how society can go on without the policeman to keep order."[56] When he alludes to constitutional government, Tylor was not distinguishing its ultimate sanction from that of any other form of the state: all political society is based on repressive organized force. In this he was accurate. For pharaohs and presidents alike have always made a public claim to represent the common interest, indeed to incarnate the common good. Only a Plato or a Machiavelli in search of political harmony, or a Marx in search of political truth, has been able to penetrate this myth of the identity between ruler and ruled, of equality under law. The tradition of Plato and Machiavelli commends the use of the "royal" or "noble lie," while that of Marx exposes and rejects the power structure (ultimately the state) that propagates so false a political consciousness. On this issue, I follow Marx.

Tylor distinguishes the civilized from the primitive order. Such a distinction has been made at every moment of crisis in the West but nowhere so pertinently as in Montaigne's contrast of a primitive society with Plato's ideally civilized republic:

> This is a nation, I should say to Plato, in which there is no sort of traffic, no knowledge of letters, no science of numbers, no name for a magistrate or for political superiority, no custom of servitude, no riches or poverty, no contracts, no successions, no partitions . . . no care for any but common kinship. How far from this perfection would he find the Republic he imagines![5 7]

The issue of law and order implicit in Montaigne's contrast between primitive and civilized societies has been a persistent underlying theme for the most reflective and acute minds of the West. The inquiry into the nature of politics probably demarcates most accurately the boundaries of our intellectual landscape. The evolution of the state toward what Max Weber called maximally politicized society, the unprecedented concentration of bureaucratic and technological power, which economically and culturally dominates the rest of the world, creates a climate in which all problems cast a political shadow. We may flee from the political dimension of our experience or we may embrace it in order to do away with it, but we are obsessed by politics. It was perhaps Plato's primary virtue that at the very origin of the Western intellectual tradition, he understood that, in civilization, all significant human problems have a political aspect; and he insisted upon the solution of a political problem as a coefficient of the creative resolution of the human problem. The *Republic* is the first civilizational utopia, and it maintains its force both as a model of inquiry and as antithesis to all projections of the nature of primitive society. Any contrary view of the possibilities of human association must take the *Republic* into account.

The legal order, which Plato idealized, is as Tylor maintained and Marx understood, synonymous with the power of the state. "The state," writes Paul Vinogradoff, "has assumed the monopoly of political co-ordination. It is the state which rules, makes laws and eventually enforces them by coercion. Such a state did not exist in ancient times. The commonwealth was not centered in one sovereign body towering immeasurably above single individuals and meting out to everyone his portion of right."[5 8] And Engels, reflecting on the origins of the state, asserts: "The right of the state to existence was founded on the preservation of order in the interior and the protection against the barbarians outside, but this order was worse than the most disgusting disorder, and the barbarians against whom the state pretended to protect its citizens were hailed by them as saviors."[5 9] Moreover, "The state created a public power of coercion that did no longer coincide with the old self-organized and (self) armed population." Finally, in a passage that epitomizes the West's awareness of itself, Engels writes:

> The state, then, is by no means a power forced on society at a certain stage of evolution. It is the confession that this society has become hopelessly divided against itself, has estranged itself in irreconcilable contradictions which it is powerless to banish. In order that these contradictions, these classes with conflicting economic interests may not annihilate themselves and society in a useless struggle, a power becomes necessary that stands apparently above society and has the function of keeping down the conflicts and maintaining "order." And this power, the outgrowth of society, but assuming supremacy over it and becoming more and more divorced from it, is the state....[6 0]

In a word, the state is the alienated form of society; it is this process which has fascinated the Western intellect and which may in fact have led to the peculiar intensity of the reflective, analytic and introspective consciousness in the West, to our search for origins and our inexhaustible concern with secular history. A knowledge of one's present, as Montaigne maintained, implies not only a knowledge of one's past but of one's future.

However we project, imagine or reconstruct the past, we

recognize the division, the objective correlate of the division within ourselves, between primitive and civilized society, between moral and civil order, between custom and law. Interpretation of the nature of the primitive and the civilized has, of course, not been uniform. But most theorists tend to see civilization as a kind of fall from a "natural," or at least more natural, to a legal or more repressive order. No matter how the virtues of civilization are weighed, the price exacted is inevitably noted. This is as true of Plato as of Freud or Engels. Plato notes, however inadequately, a condition of existence prior to the city-state, a type of rusticity which he views nostalgically and whose destruction he maintains was socioeconomically determined. I suspect that even the great majority of anthropologists, despite professional illusions of dissociated objectivity, sense that primitive societies are somehow closer than civilized societies to the realization of "natural" law and "natural" right. I believe this emphasis in the Western tradition to be the sounder, and it serves as the basis of my own thinking. There is, as Montaigne noted, an "amazing distance" between the primitive character and our own. In the contrast between these two sides of our historical nature, which we existentially reenact, we come to understand law as the antonym and not the synonym of order.

THE RESPONSE TO CIVIL LAW

I agree with Nadel that in the transition from primitive to political society the means of control and integration employed were, in a wider sense, "all . . . deliberately conceived and [executed]: they are agencies of an assimilation conscious of itself and of the message which it carries."[61] Finally, we are led to ask, as did Nadel about the Nupe:

> What did the tax-paying law-abiding citizen receive in return for allegiance to king and nobility? Was extortion, bribery, brutal force, the only aspect under which the state revealed itself to the populace? The people were to receive, theoretically, on the whole, one thing: security—protection against external and internal enemies, and general security for carrying out the daily work, holding markets, using the roads. We have seen what protection and security meant in reality.

277

At their best, they represented something very unequal and very unstable. This situation must have led to much tension and change within the system and to frequent attempts to procure better safeguards for civil rights.[62]

The struggle for civil rights, then, is a response to the imposition of civil law. With the destruction of the primitive base of society, civil rights have been defined and redefined as a reaction to drastic changes in the socioeconomic structure—the rise of caste and class systems, imperialism, modern war, technology as a means of social exploitation, maldistribution and misuse of resources, racial hatred. The right to socially and economically fruitful work, for example, which did not come into question in a primitive society or in a traditional sector of an early state (and therefore was not conceived to be a stipulated right) becomes an issue under capitalism. The demand implies a need for profoundly changing and, if not changing, discarding the system and indicates that our sense of the appropriately human has very ancient roots indeed. However, the struggle for civil rights reminds us that legislation alone has no force beyond the potential of the social system that generates it. From the study of proto-states we also learn that the citizen must be constantly alert to laws which seek to curb his rights in the name of protection or security. Restrictive legislation is almost always a signal of repressive institutional change but, of course, is not the cause of it.

The major focus of the defense of the citizen as a person can only be on procedure or, as we call it in our own society, due process. Quénum reports of the early state of Dahomey: "There was no penal code promulgated ... punishment had no fixity ... the Miegan [leading bureaucrat, chief judge and executioner] would become restive if capital punishment would be too long in coming."[63] In the words of Dalzel, "There was a vast disproportion between crimes and punishments."[64] And in early states, most if not all civil breaches were what we would define as crimes, just as in primitive societies "civil crimes" were considered, where they were not unprecedented, private remediable wrongs. As every intelligent lawyer knows, the substance of the law can hardly be assimilated to morality. It is clear, therefore, why Jhering insisted that "Form is the sworn enemy of unlimited discretion (of the sovereign power) and the twin sister of freedom."[65] The degrees of theft or homicide, the question of double jeopardy, habeas corpus, the right to counsel, the question of legitimate witness, trial by jury and the selection of jurors, protection against summary search and seizure, the very division between civil and criminal law—these intricacies of procedure are the primary, but far from the absolute, assurance of whatever justice can be obtained under the rule of law.

For example, the only way dissidents in the Soviet Union can defend themselves against summary punishment and make their cases understood to the rest of the world is by calling attention to abuses of procedure. The spirit of the laws, mummified in the excellent constitution of 1936, is irrelevant, abstract. The tribunal that discharges the intentions of the state can discard, suspend, reinterpret and invent laws at will. The court, not the constitution, is the primary legal reality. And the politically inspired charge of insanity, which can remove dissidents from the body politic altogether, is the ultimate étatistic definition of the person—a nonbeing incapable of autonomy. And that, I should note, is foreshadowed in the consummate anti-Socratic Platonism of the *Laws*, the heavenly city brought to earth, wherein the ordinary citizen is "to become, by long habit, utterly incapable of doing anything at all independently."

Procedure is the individual's last line of defense in contemporary civilization, wherein all other associations to which he may belong have become subordinate to the state. The elaboration of procedure is a unique if fragile feature of more fully evolved states, in compensation, so to speak, for the radical isolation of the individual; procedure permits the individual to hold the line, while working toward associations designed to replace the state. In the proto-states, the harshness of rudimentary procedure was countered by the role of the kinship units which, as we recall, retained a significant measure of functional socioeconomic autonomy and, therefore, of local political cohesion. But "law has its origin in the pathology of social relations and functions only when there are frequent disturbances of the social equilibrium."[66] Law arises in the breach of a prior customary order and increases in force with the conflicts that divide political societies internally and among themselves. Law and order is the historical illusion; law versus order is the historical reality.

In the tradition of Rousseau, Lévi-Strauss in a moment of candor declares: "We must go beyond the evidence of the injustices and abuses to which the social order gives rise, and discover the unshakable basis of human society.... Anthropology shows that base cannot be found in our own civilization, ours is indeed perhaps the one furthest from it."[67] The progressive reduction of society to a series of technical and legal signals, the consequent diminution of culture, that is, of reciprocal, symbolic meanings, are perhaps the primary reasons why our civilization is the one least likely to serve as a guide to "the unshakable basis of human society."

9

JOB AND THE TRICKSTER

The Book of Job, generated by an archaic civilization, a society no longer primitive, symbolizes the converse of the primitive notion of the trickster and also represents the origin of our own conceptions of good and evil. It is, so to speak, an ideological pillar of our civilization. This is implied in *Primitive Man as Philosopher*, where Paul Radin contrasts an African folk tale with the Book of Job.

In this tale, the heroine is trapped in an analogue of Job's dilemma:

> She was an old woman of a family with a long genealogy. Leza [the high God of the Ba-ila], "the Besetting-One," stretched out his hand against the family. He slew her mother and father while she was yet a child, and in the course of years all connected with her perished. She said to herself, "Surely I shall keep those who sit on my thighs." But no, even they, the children of her children, were taken from her. She became withered with age and it seemed to her that she herself was about to be taken. But no, a change came over her; she grew younger. Then came into her heart a desperate resolution to find God and to ask the meaning of it all. Somewhere up there in the sky must be his dwelling. She began to cut down trees, joining them together and so planting a structure that would reach heaven. Finally she gave up in despair, but not her intention of finding God. Somewhere on earth there must be another way to heaven! So she began to travel, going through country after country, always with the thought in her mind: "I shall come to where the earth ends and there I shall find a road to God and I shall ask him: "What have I done to thee that thou afflictest me in this manner?" She never found where the earth ends, but

though disappointed she did not give up her search, and as she passed through the different countries they asked her, "What have you come for, old woman?" And the answer would be, "I am seeking Leza." "Seeking Leza! For what?" "My brothers, you ask me! Here in the nations is there one who suffers as I have suffered?" And they would ask again, "How have you suffered?" "In this way. I am alone. As you see me, a solitary old woman; that is how I am!" And they answered, "Yes, we see. That is how you are! Bereaved of friends and husband? In what do you differ from others? The Besetting-One sits on the back of every one of us and we cannot shake him off!" She never obtained her desire: she died of a broken heart.

The point of the tale, as Radin indicates, is that one must come to terms with the realities of the world; anything short of this invites spiritual destruction, symbolized by the death of the old woman. Thus, a "broken heart" is equivalent to a deeply moral (not merely ethical) failure. Among primitive peoples, the belief in God or the "supernatural" is not connected with the hope of other-worldly reward; "heaven" is the double of earth. Religion never functions as a means of evading the moral contradictions that must be confronted in this world. Radin contrasts the integrity of the primitive tale with the embarrassing denouement felicity of the Book of Job—Job restored to health, property and domestic felicity over and above his original affluence. Radin has in mind, of course, a primitive culture in which the peculiar delusions and pathologies of civilization have not yet become evident.

Radin does not discuss the substance of the Book of Job at all, nor does he elaborate on the curiously civilized failure of the old woman. That failure may be defined as the refusal to understand and accept the relationship between good and evil, and its expression in human ambiguity. The principle of ambivalence is incorporated into the myths and rituals of primitive peoples to an extraordinary degree and in a variety of ways which need no explication here. Radin himself has provided us with endless examples of the theme. That principle or rather *personification* of ambivalence (since we are dealing with primitive perceptions and not abstract conceptualizations) is most directly realized in the figure of the trickster, as Jung, Kerényi and Radin have sufficiently indicated. With the appearance of civilization, the concrete and ramifying image of the trickster becomes a segregated and vicarious aspect of human experience, acted out by the clown as an entertainment. At the same time, it is epitomized abstractly in the civilized assumption that evil, reified, befalls good men. Put another way, the concrete image of the trickster is suppressed and simultaneously transformed into the problem of injustice. The circus that surrounds and depends upon the clown is therefore the diminished setting for a moral struggle. The grotesque inversions of the clown, the defiance of death, the terrifying reality that seems to overflow the ring itself only to recede to a totally alien experience the next moment, and the superhuman skill of the actors—these are serious matters indeed. Laughing at a circus demands the capacity to laugh at oneself, to identify with the reversals and risks of identity that take place before our eyes. Wit, laughing at the other, does not work. And this laughing at oneself means accepting the ambivalence of the human condition, for which civilization gives us very little instruction or structured opportunity. Hence, the strange gravity of audiences, particularly the expressions on the faces of children, encountered at circuses.

The Book of Job, like Plato's *Republic* which was composed at roughly the same time, is bent upon denying human ambivalence and social ambiguity. Thus Job and Plato insist upon the obliteration of injustice. Plato tells us that the Republic is conceived for one major reason: in this world as we know it, there is no remedy for injustice. As Socrates says, many a blackguard goes to his grave with a reputation for virtue and many a virtuous man dies a scoundrel in the public eye. (There is a perfect parallel in Ecclesiastes: "There is a vanity which takes place on earth, that there are righteous men to whom it happens according to the deeds of the wicked, and there are wicked men to whom it happens according to the deeds of the righteous.") Therefore Plato constructs a heavenly city in which the divine and the human reflect one another in complete harmony. Evil is eradicated for God cannot be the author of evil, and the principle of ambiguity is denied. In the Book of Job, there is a parallel effort to understand and come to terms with the blind injustice of the world. If Plato represents the civilized consciousness projected as a utopia and brought to its highest pitch, Job represents the religious conscience of western civilization, more nakedly expressed than is the case with Plato and with no effort at a social prescription. Plato and Job must be understood with reference to each other; together they explicate the root of western ethics.

In both Plato and Job the relationship between the human and the divine is no longer played out in dramatic form, but is orchestrated in imposing intellectual dialogues which rationalize the very basis of our civilization. The one important difference, apart from the distinctions inherent in the cultural styles of Greek and Hebrew, is that Plato will reform the state by making it more perfect in the technical sense of the term, more complete and more omniscient; in Job society is not questioned. But correlatively, the Plato of the *Laws* has abandoned utopia, and obedience to the mundane dictates of society (whose ultimate sanction is divine) is now considered the mark of piety. Job would have made an exemplary citizen of the polity put forward in Plato's *Laws*. In order to understand this more fully, it is necessary to consider the Book of Job in greater detail.

To begin with, Job is rich, blessed and upright—as near perfect a father, husband, and subject of his society and his God as can be imagined. Satan challenges God, claiming Job is good because his life is easy and successful. God accepts the challenge and permits Job to be tormented by the devil in order to test his loyalty to Him. There then follows the first series of manipulated misfortunes. Job's family, excluding his wife, is exterminated. Job's response is, "the Lord gave, and the Lord has taken away; blessed be the name of the Lord."

Satan then argues further that as long as Job's skin is saved, he will remain loyal to God. This second challenge is also accepted, and God puts Job completely in Satan's hands—the sole *caveat* being that his life be spared. At this point, and for the first time in the work, the relationship between good and evil is obscured, perhaps deliberately. For God apparently commands Satan, but is distinguished from him, just as evil is becoming segregated as a principle from the principle of good. At the same time, since God can ultimately control Satan, He is omnipotent but not responsible for the evil that men choose to do through the mediation of the devil as Calvin formulated. At the beginning of the Book of Job, then, the concrete ambivalence of the human condition is denied; good and evil have a dual rather than a single source as in the complex unity of the primitive consciousness. In the Book of Job integrated acts have been disintegrated into contrasting ideas; human behavior is now seen as representing and being driven by principles that are abstracted from the reality of actual behavior. Actual behavior is never wholly good nor wholly evil; such purity is never encountered, least of all in primitive societies. It is only with the civilized reversal of principles and persons that such an attitude becomes conceivable; the abstraction becomes a weapon against the person.

Satan afflicts Job from head to foot. As he sits in agony, his wife commends him:

> Do you still hold fast your integrity?
> Curse God, and die.

She demands, in effect, that Job must bow neither to God nor the devil; one is obliged to remain faithful to the knowledge of oneself. If man is fated to die in misfortune, and if God is responsible for the world as we know it, then die, she admonishes, but curse that kind of God. If one finds it impossible to change one's faith, she implies, then one should have the grace to die—and here we are reminded of the old woman in the Ba-ila tale. Job, of course, dismisses his wife:

> Shall we receive good at the hand of God,
> and shall we not receive evil?

This sounds like the recognition of ambivalence, but in his continued agony Job pleads for death, wishes that he had never been born and curses *himself*. In so doing, he disavows responsibility for his life, and the insight hinted at is revealed as an abstraction. It should also be noted that Job actively pleads for death, whereas in the Ba-ila tale the old woman inevitably dies of moral ("natural") causes while still denying the ambiguity of life.

The advice of his wife, who represents a totally different, a more primitive perception of reality, is rejected. In western theology, when not ignored, she has been despised as a second Eve. The Book of Job, then, is best understood as the theological reflection of a patriarchal and theocratic state. The order of society is never seriously put to question; the resolution of the tale is fully in accord with the status quo. Not a sparrow has to move from its place in order to insure the primacy of God, the structure of society and the piety of the subject. Whereas the Greeks spoke of utopia, the patriarchs guarded the structure of the world as it was; they only wished to clarify its ethical order. But both Greeks and Hebrews were guardians of an order with which we are fully capable of identifying.

After the disappearance of Job's wife, his three friends appear on the scene and, after a preliminary expression of sympathy, engage him in the conversation that carries most of the tale and has caught the attention of the conventional commentators. The pattern of the dialogue is exceedingly simple: each of the friends insists that Job has sinned, for God is just and punishes only for sin. Job is also told that if he bears up, all will end well. God will reward him. Moreover, he is suffering for his own good. As one of them says, "Man is born to trouble as the sparks fly upward." Has not Job similarly advised afflicted people?

But Job considers this hypocrisy. Since his friends are not suffering, they lack compassion. He again begs for death:

What is man, that thou dost make so much of him

. . . and test him every moment?

The second friend, and one must note that the friends are interchangeable, asserts that Job is being dealt with justly, for God deals with men according to their works. But Job's attention is elsewhere. He is reaching for another rationalization, and responds that God is so much more powerful than man that man's perfection and innocence, even when they exist, must be insufficient, unimpressive and even perverse. Therefore God destroys both the innocent and the wicked, not because that is the nature of the world, but because in the eyes of God all are wicked. This expression of cosmic piety leaves Job in an insoluble dilemma. If he were wicked, he says, then God would certainly punish him. If he were righteous, then he dare not proclaim it because God's judgments are inscrutable. Yet, God made him, and might show him a little mercy before his death because He knows Job is not wicked in the human sense. But this casuistry cuts no ice. Job's third friend repeats the refrain: Job is vain to consider himself a just man, only God knows good and evil and when He punishes it must be for a good reason. Only the wicked hope to die in the face of adversity—the good will live through affliction and be rewarded.

Job again defends himself in front of his friends: he has as much wisdom as they, and it is easy to speak when one is not suffering.

God, says Job, is omnipotent, He creates and destroys for reasons beyond human comprehension. Here again one catches a glimpse of God as a trickster, that is to say, of the principle of ambivalence and of the relationship between good and evil, perhaps even of their personification. That is the primitive substratum in the consciousness of Job. In the words of Radin, the trickster is "creator and destroyer, giver and negator" knowing "neither good nor evil yet . . . responsible for both."

But this perspective is too dizzying, and Job reverses himself. He begs God to reveal the nature of his iniquity; though God slay him, he will trust in Him and, moreover, he will maintain his own ways before Him. That is, he will argue his innocence before God. He will argue that he has been obedient to the spirit and the letter of the law. But his friends reply that man is by nature wicked, an idea that has also occurred to Job; therefore, how can Job insist on his innocence, which is no more than his lack of knowledge of having sinned. Job scorns them for their lack of mercy and continues to claim that he is innocent in his own eyes. His friends reply that he is presumptuous and impatient. Job then despairs of them along with, in the passion of his suffering, his family. God is torturing him for unknown reasons, he replies. (And this is truer than he is ever to be permitted to understand.) His friends, he continues, desert him when they insist that he is undergoing a just punishment, and he warns them of retribution.

But they prove relentless, and Job finally responds that the wicked often go unpunished in this world, giving many examples of this state of affairs. In so doing, he not only unwittingly questions his own implicit conviction of the connection between piety and worldly reward, but his more recently stated belief that God punishes the wicked only. He also asserts what the Book has ostensibly set out to question: Why do the just suffer and the wicked flourish? And so the dialogue comes to a close, Job seeking sympathy and defending his behavior, his friends accusing him of impudence, perfidy, hypocrisy and self-righteousness.

There are two related observations that should be made about the role of Job's friends. They are not only interchangeable, but are interchangeable with Job himself. In the first instance, they comprise an intellectual chorus revealing different aspects of the same argument, constantly reinforcing each other and representing, as a chorus, the conscience of the dialogue, which is no more than the conscience of Job. The structure of the argument is almost musical: Job makes a point and his friends make the counterpoint. They then reverse the contrapuntal progression from a necessarily limited repertoire of logical possibilities. For there is nothing that Job's friends say that Job himself has not said. They have, for example, advised him to endure, assured him that God is just and predicted that all good men are eventually rewarded. They have also made the subtle point that in God's eyes even the just among men are unjust, thereby excusing Job by rendering his misinterpretation of his own behavior inevitable. They have suggested, finally, that he walk more humbly before God, anticipating the argument of Elihu. It is, therefore, a curious theological mistake to distinguish Job from his friends. They are in opposition not on principle, but only because of an "accidental" reality.* It is exactly here that their lack of freedom, individuality and humanity is evident. And that leads to the second observation. In a society such as that reflected in the Book of Job, men could no longer spontaneously turn to their friends and peers and confront the acknowledged absurdities of life as members of complexly related, reciprocating kin or quasi-kin groups. Job's relationship to his friends is one of classic alienation. They are his friends only in the sense that they are of equivalent status and class. The paradox is that the common values that motivate Job and his friends make it impossible for them to rely on each other or even to understand each other in their extreme moments even though, or rather because, they speak the same language. The friends of Job must adopt the attitudes they do in order to rationalize their own positions, which are equivalent before his disaster and potentially equivalent following his disaster. For how

---

* Even so advanced a critic as Morris Jastrow—by now himself a classic—insists upon interpreting Job's contradictions as priestly distortions of an "original" text. He would, therefore, deny the paradoxical structure, which is the real esthetic strength of the work, and the sources of its terrifying honesty. For it thereby stands as a faithful expression of the spirit of the times. One should approach a text such as the Book of Job head on—its meaning for us is a deeper question than the issue of texual "authenticity," which can never be established, perhaps not even in the minds of the "original authors." Certain critics seem to be more interested in creating their own Job than in listening carefully to what the "standard" Job has to say—and considering the pattern of the whole work relative to that.

else can they maintain their faith in the correctness of their ways?

Contrast this with the institution of *best friend* in indigenous Dahomey, which is a protostate or early archaic civilization in West Africa. Each Dahomean had three best friends, arming him against the restrictions imposed by the civil power in this transitional society. The function of best friend is clearly revealed in the following folk tale: It seems that a man was asked to help work the fields of his diviner, his father-in-law and his best friend on the same day. Faced with this dilemma, since aid could hardly be refused anyone, he went out into the bush. There he killed an animal. He then went to his father-in-law's house and told him he had killed a man. The father-in-law shouted, "I don't want to hear about it! I don't want to hear anything about it! You killed one of the king's men and now you want to hide here? I don't want to hear anything about it!" So the hunter left and went to the house of the diviner, where he repeated his story. The diviner said, "Ah, we can have nothing more to do with each other. Today you killed a man belonging to the king, and now you want to come here to hide. Go! You cannot hide in my house!" Now the hunter went to the house of his best friend and told him, "I wanted to kill an antelope for you . . . but as I shot at it I shot a man." The best friend asked him if he had told anyone. Then they left the house, the best friend carrying his bow, and went out into the bush to hide the body. Of course, the best friend soon discovered that it was not a man at all, but an antelope. So he asked the hunter why he had claimed to kill a man. And the answer was, "I wanted to know which of the three—friend, father-in-law, diviner—one could follow into death." Then they both went to work in the best friend's field, the dilemma solved. That is why, the Dahomeans say, a man must be always closest to his best friend.

The key to an understanding of the Book of Job, then, is in the triumph of orthodoxy; the work is an awe-inspiring rationalization of God's ambivalent nature. And the abstract recourse to principle, punishment, reward and God-as-a-concept reflects the patriarchal, theocratic polity—as the antithesis of the classless, ambivalently structured cultures of primitive peoples.

Almost as an afterthought, and it may well have been that, the conclusion of the Book of Job emerges. Whether or not it was an afterthought, the climax of Job is the inevitable outcome of the thrust and conception of the work as a whole. A young man

(Elihu) appears and lectures Job on the omnipotence of God. God is not to be approached on the human level. Why should Job demand to know his sins? God must be approached in humility. Although Elihu sympathizes with Job, in contrast to the increasing harshness of his (Job's) friends, his intellectual differences from them are trivial. The Lord approves and, speaking out of a whirlwind, reveals the scope of His achievements; He made the world, creation is His, can Job question such power? Can Job dare to measure his notion of justice against all this? But again, the propositions of the Lord are not substantially different from conclusions reached by Job's principled friends, by Elihu and by Job himself.

Job now abhors himself; he prostrates himself before God and asks forgiveness for his blasphemy which originated, it would appear, in his all too human pride. In response, God humbles the friends of Job for their hypocrisy and their presumption in claiming to know His ways, and for their lack of confidence in Job. For Job, in the judgment of the Lord, never lost faith in a humanly understandable justice. This apparent contradiction aside, the theological "tragedy" ends happily. Job lives for another 140 years, and so on. In both Plato and Job, it should be noted, the abolition of injustice depends on the obliteration of ambivalence, and the obliteration of ambivalence is the death of tragedy. The Book of Job is in no sense a tragedy but something very different, a theodicy, an apology for the projection of a certain concept of God.

One can readily understand why Radin preferred the African folk tale. It is harder to decide whether or not Satan won his argument, for at its critical moments the basically civilized tale of Job depends on a *deus ex machina*—the evil that has befallen Job is simply assumed to be the work of the devil and in the end Job is redeemed from on high. Both God and the devil are at an infinite and dissociated remove from human experience, and this reflects the structure of civilization. Conversely, among primitive peoples, all antinomies are bound into the ritual cycle. The sacred is an immediate aspect of man's experience. Good and evil, creation and destruction—the dual image of the deity as expressed in the trickster—are fused in the network of actions that define primitive society. Therefore moral fanaticism, based as it is on abstract notions of pure good, pure evil and the exclusive moral possibility or fate of any particular individual—what may be called moral exceptionalism—is absent among primitive people. In primitive perspective, human beings are assumed to be capable of any excess. But every step of the way, the person is held to account for those actions that seriously threaten the balance of society and nature.

Even while creating their myths and ceremonials, their meanings and their insights, primitive people are aware of the reality that they mold. Radin tells us that a Maori witness before a native land-court in New Zealand stated in the course of certain testimony:[1]

"The God of whom I speak is dead."

The court replied:

"Gods do not die."

"You are mistaken," continued the witness. "Gods do die, unless there are *tohungas* (priests) to keep them alive."

And in a Maori myth, one God advises another:

"When men no longer believe in us, we are dead."

That reflects the existential, the created reality of the primitive world. There can be no deeper antithesis to the Book of Job, which represents the determinism of civilization.

10

THE INAUTHENTICITY
OF ANTHROPOLOGY:
THE MYTH
OF STRUCTURALISM

Somewhere there must be primordial figures the bodies of which are only images. If one could see them one would know the link between matter and thought; what being consists of.
— The Temptation of Saint Anthony *(Flaubert)*

Following paths that are reproached for being too exclusively intellectual, structuralist thought recovers and brings to the surface of consciousness profound and organic truths. Only those who practice it know, through intimate experience, that impression of plenitude its exercise brings, through which the mind feels it is truly communicating with the body.

— L'Homme Nu

In fragments of ice he makes out efflorescences, imprints of bushes and shells—not knowing if they are the imprints of these things or the things themselves . . . .
Finally he perceives small globular masses, as big as the head of a pin and encircled with lashes.

— The Temptation of St. Anthony

When we make an effort to understand, we destroy the object of our attachment, substituting another whose nature is quite different. That other object requires of us another effort, which in its turn destroys the second object and substitutes a third—and so on until we reach the only enduring Presence, which is that in which all distinction between meaning and the absence of meaning disappears: and it is from that Presence that we started in the first place.

— A World on the Wane

I would like to have wings, a carapace, a bark, to bellow smoke, to possess a trunk, to twist my body, to divide myself into everything, to be in everything, to be in the emanation of perfumes, to grow like plants, flow like water, vibrate like sound, to shine like light, to crouch in all forms, to penetrate each atom, to descend to the depth of matter—to be matter.
—The Temptation of St. Anthony

History, politics, and the social and economic universe, the physical world, even the sky—all surround me in concentric circles, and I can only escape from those circles in thought if I concede to each of them some part of my being. Like the pebble which marks the surface of the wave with circles as it passes through it, I must throw myself into the water if I am to plumb the depths.
—A World on the Wane

The temptation of Saint Anthony seems to have become the intellectual passion of Claude Lévi-Strauss. The anthropologist even conjures with the "chilling alternative" of monasticism, although with reference to Buddhism, rather than Christianity. These cosmological reflections aside for the moment, Lévi-Strauss is emerging as the exemplary thinker and the paradigmatic anthropologist of the second half of the twentieth century. This implies a good deal about the intellectual milieu of our time and of anthropology in particular. It represents the reabsorption of the discipline into the mainstream of Western ideas since, through Lévi-Strauss, anthropology is reestablished as an intellectual undertaking, a profession of the intelligentsia, rather than a specialized vocation with its own peculiar language, corpus of data and theory, and technical focus.

This implicit redefinition of anthropology, of which anthropologists seem unaware, explodes certain of their basic assumptions, while realizing the destiny of the profession—a paradox that I shall confront in due course. Lévi-Strauss admits to the relative poverty of his own ethnographic experience. His field work has been episodic and can be counted in months, rather than years; he has never lived in any primitive or archaic society for an extended period of time. Nor does this linguistically-oriented thinker make any claim to competence in linguistics (or languages, for that matter), but rather states the contrary; and there is no evidence that he has made any serious effort to record or interpret texts in a native language. In *L'Homme Nu*[1] Lévi-Strauss argues against the conventional ethnological canon; his argument is important for what it reveals of the author's methodological casuistry. He reasons as follows: since no primitive myth is generic to any given culture, all myths are, in essence, translations from one culture to another and therefore constitute a series of linked but shifting perspectives. Thus, the focus of mythological inquiry (the essence of the science of man) is on the articulations between cultures. The ethnologist has just as much right to translate a primitive myth into his (the ethnologist's) perspective as does the member of the indigenous society who reworks the myth in his native language. They are, it seems, performing parallel operations.

Where Does the Ethnologist Stand?

But this ingenious logic is not acceptable. The point of Lévi-Strauss's argument cannot be confined to myth; it applies to the whole of culture, since in no case have the majority of a culture's constituent elements, including the mythological, been invented. In the ethnological tradition, the study of culture is the study of the specific integrations of cultural elements, invented or diffused, among a given people in a given place. It is this particularity which Lévi-Strauss evades. But it is not only the particularity of the people concerned which is at stake; it is also the particularity of the "ultimate" observer in his own—that is, Western—culture. For if Lévi-Strauss's avoidance of the concrete cultural language of myth is to be rationalized by the argument that the perspective on any given myth is that of its latest translator (who inevitably conceives of it in terms of his own culture), then one must conclude that Lévi-Strauss has not admitted to the cultural context of his own interpretations. He has preferred to consider them "final," or thus far final, which is basically to make the same claim, since he has frequently expressed his faith in the universality and inevitability of his method, despite intermittent and disarming modesty concerning his specific findings.* Put another way, Lévi-Strauss denies the possibility that recent interpretations of primitive myths reflect the categories and the mode of cognition of modern Western civilization. His commitment to an abstract, metalinguistic paradigm, combined with his disinterest in particular languages, has here led the anthropologist into an impossible situation, which can only be understood on grounds other than those he has himself proposed. That situation can be defined as the avoidance of the particularity of self and other. Ethnology becomes an exercise in an infinitely regressive series—neither the observer nor the observed can be located relative to each other; they can only be reduced to a common denominator: "For if the final aim of anthropology is to contribute to a better knowledge of objectified thought and its mechanisms, it is in the last resort immaterial whether . . . the thought processes of the South American Indians take shape through the medium of my thought, or whether mine take place through the medium of theirs."[3] Peeling his infinite onion, he continues, attempting to embrace, to penetrate the reader. "It follows that this book on myth is itself a kind of myth. [The myth of mythology] . . . . If it has any unity, that unity will appear only behind or beyond the text and, in the best hypothesis, will become a reality in the mind of the reader."[4]†

---

* He is, for example, capable of stating, with reference to his analysis of the Oedipus myth, that

> I am well aware that the Oedipus myth has only reached us under late forms and through literary transmutations concerned more with esthetic and moral preoccupations than with religious or ritual ones, whatever these may have been. But we shall not interpret the Oedipus myth in literal terms, much less offer an explanation acceptable to the specialist. We simply wish to illustrate—and without reaching any conclusions with respect to it—a certain technique, whose use is probably not legitimate in this particular instance, owing to the problematic elements indicated above. The "demonstration" should therefore be conceived, not in terms of what the scientist means by this term, but at best in terms of what is meant by the street peddler, whose aim is not to achieve a concrete result, but to explain, as succinctly as possible, *the functioning of the mechanical toy which he is trying to sell to the onlookers* (italics added).[2]

† This can be translated as follows:

This book [*The Raw and the Cooked*] does not exist in any ordinary sense or in any manifest system of meanings. It is a myth. But it is not a concrete myth; more importantly, it is an abstract revelation of how a myth is formed. It is the paradigmatic process of creation. Yet as a process it has no

One must not permit oneself to be overwhelmed by the apparent range and detail of Lévi-Strauss's work. It is doubtful whether any living anthropologist could stand up to such a crescendo of minute observations and evaluate their legitimacy. Still, one must bear in mind that error compounded exponentially remains error—"facts," like Scripture, can be quoted to fit almost any systematic hypothesis. In marshalling so many details, Lévi-Strauss pays ironic tribute to empiricism, while proving that the data never speak for themselves. It is the organization of Lévi-Strauss's ideas that creates his facts—as a cyclotron creates subatomic particles.

Lévi-Strauss is, in short, a successful iconoclast who has violated both the most romantic and the most technical demands of his colleagues. Yet, despite the criticism to which his work is subjected, his reputation among anthropologists remains exalted—a symptom of the unwitting reorientation of the profession. Of course, one may say that journeymen anthropologists are pleased to have such a distinguished representative at court, one who gives the impression of being able to think for them, while they spend their time collecting data, dealing with conventional problems, and shuttling to and from the field. Who can doubt that Lévi-Strauss is a more distinguished representative than the handful of other claimants to world attention among his American and British colleagues? Moreover, he is French—actually Franco-Belgian (also Jewish, a fact I shall reflect on later)—and the daring, deceptively lucid, French intellectual tradition, still basking in the glow of the Enlightenment, maintains a certain international prestige. The force of Lévi-Strauss's ideas has propelled him into a contest with Sartre which has little to do with personalities; or, rather, the personality and the idea have become so fused that the truth of one being is pitted against another, each claiming to represent the truth of the world, and of man in the world. These intellectual contests, if not peculiar to France, assume a particular

systematic unity or final form. The latter can only be realized in relation to the mind of the reader. But if the reader admits to this or not—"in the best hypothesis" the myth becomes a unified structure by being fitted into the mold which shaped it, the universal mind to the mind of the reader.

Lévi-Strauss thus presumes to reach into the minds of others, in order to grasp a truth beyond particularity. This seems to me to be condescension, more seriously, *hubris*, and because of its violation of the person, sinister *hubris*.

form and intensity there; it often seems that the destiny of the species is at stake. One recalls the struggle of Pascal against Descartes, of Rousseau against Diderot and Voltaire. Now, in a somewhat diminished arena, Lévi-Strauss challenges Sartre for the undivided attention of France and, perhaps, of all Western intelligentisia. For structuralism, epitomized in Lévi-Strauss, is the intellectual ideology, and the immanent logic, of a new, technocratic totalitarianism.

What Does the Ethnologist Believe?

Yet, the position of Lévi-Strauss as so far outlined is hardly sufficient to explain his preeminence in anthropology. One has to examine not only his anthropology, but also his existence, his attitude, his social location, his situation. To begin with, he has taken an intellectual position, and the act of taking this position is far more important than the evidence he uses in its support. His position is also consistent, although the arguments for it may be contradictory. The point is that, at a time in the history of anthropology when most of the data has been gathered, when the possibilities of work in the field (now the Third World) have narrowed considerably, and when anthropologists are under great pressure to make political commitments at home and abroad, Lévi-Strauss's position becomes a charismatic, and a near-utopian solution to the universal anthropological dilemma. He is utterly detached; an admittedly alienated personality who insists on the objectivity of his observations. He gives the impression of having sacrificed himself to his own objectivity: "And yet I exist. Not in any way, admittedly, as an individual: for what am I, in that respect, but a constantly renewed stake in the struggle between the society, formed by several million nerve-cells which take shelter in the anthill of the brain, and my body, which serves that society as a robot."[5] *

Lévi-Strauss is avowedly not interested in the search for meaning, the imperatives of action, or the dialectic between the idea and the act, except in the Buddhist sense: "what is the use of action, if the thinking which guides that action leads to the

---

* This is Durkheim writ small, in a neuro-physiological metaphor.

discovery of meaninglessness. But that discovery cannot be made immediately: it must be thought, and I cannot think it all at once."[6] The end of the structuralist enterprise is no less than the destruction of culture.

Opinions, for Lévi-Strauss, must be meaningless in the technical sense, since they are mere data assimilated to the underlying structures which determine the functions of the brain—and, more than that, such structures are the sign, the revelation of order in the universe. He frees himself, therefore, to make apparently outrageous comments about our civilization and man in general without risking his status in society (unlike his chosen ancestor, Rousseau), because such statements are divorced from action and are also of no ultimate substantive importance; or, as Lévi-Strauss might put it, they are of merely substantive importance. He is quite capable of telling us that the immediate reasons for studying ethnology do not reveal the underlying function of the discipline, namely, to contribute to the fundamental understanding of how the human mind works. To do this he nullifies all intentionality but his own.

Thus Lévi-Strauss emerges as a cold humanist, a man without technical scientific training, who defines himself as a natural scientist of great purity. In his work the scientific attitude, as distinguished from the inductive aspects of the scientific method, matures and turns to the question of man, turning man into an object. His passion is to uncover the patterns of "objectified thought." His central metaphor is music, which he considers the most basic of all art forms precisely because it is wordless, hardly cognitive, a pristine syntax of sounds, of harmonic and rhythmic contradictions and progressions—structuralism incarnate. One is reminded of the music of the spheres and of Plato's choice of mathematics, gymnastics and music as related and essential subjects in the training of his philosopher kings. Indeed, he seems as suspicious as Plato of poetry, of its iconic language, unpredictable tensions, immediate and transcendent meanings—and its extraordinary ordinariness.

The Esthetic Hierarchy

Lévi-Strauss's esthetic attitudes are worth exploring here, because they reveal his actual historical situation, along with his sense of the proper focus of social science. In *The Raw and the Cooked*, we are told that both mythology and music "bring man face to face with potential objects of which only the shadows are actualized . . . ."[7]

The implications of this sort of conceptual realism are further elaborated:

> We do not understand the difference between the very few minds that secrete music and the vast numbers in which the phenomenon does not take place, although they are usually sensitive to music. However, the difference is so obvious, and is noticeable at so early an age, that we cannot but suspect that it implies the existence of very special and deep-seated properties. But since music is a language with some meaning at least for the immense majority of mankind, although a tiny minority of people are capable of formulating a meaning in it, and since it is the only language with the contradictory attributes of being at once intelligible and untranslatable, the *musical creator is a being comparable to the gods* [Lévi-Strauss quotes Mallarmé on Wagner to that effect] *and music itself the supreme mystery of the science of man, a mystery that all the various disciplines come up against and which holds the key to their progress* (emphasis added).[8]

I believe that this statement is critical to the understanding of Lévi-Strauss. In the first place, it is ethnocentric; Lévi-Strauss is obviously referring to the Western tradition of classical music, and he seems to feel that the ultimate composers are Wagner and Debussy. But improvisation by musicians themselves, as in the folk-jazz tradition, which has always been at odds with academic music, is ignored. Moreover, there is no consideration of the meaning of the widespread manufacture, distribution and use of musical instruments among a given tribal people in, let us say, West Africa. Among such peoples a drummer, either alone or in combination with others, may create extremely complex contrapuntal rhythms which disappear at the moment of invention, as they are not fixed in any system of musical notation. The number of themes may be relatively limited, but the elaboration upon them is rich, and everyone seems capable of musical invention. Indeed the distinction between theme and elaboration becomes trivial, merely academic under such circumstances.

But in Lévi-Strauss's perspective, the musical creator is comparable to a god. Since he also believes that the language of mythology is closest to that of music and that myths are a kind of music, it is clear that the organization of society, signified by myths, is here being mystified; the majority of men are reduced to ciphers. The elite is free only insofar as it reflects the human essence. The supreme mystery essentialized in music is the ultimate, inescapable anthropological problem. Lévi-Strauss is obviously referring to a final principle of order underlying all cognition and communication, a principle, one should add, that he believes may one day be reducible to mathematical formulation. The conclusion one is compelled to draw is that the "mystery" projected creatively in only a few structurally endowed minds should be guarded and nurtured. And we find ourselves only one step from the intellectual politics of Plato.

It is significant, then, that Lévi-Strauss in defining the critical role of anthropology, namely, to confront and penetrate the mystery of music and, by analogy, that of myth, avoids all mention of social processes such as exploitation, alienation, the extreme division of labor, modern war and the character of the state. His thirst for the ultimate evades our realities or, perhaps, takes them for granted as mere contingencies. There is, moreover, a certain naïveté in Lévi-Strauss's exalted view of music. "Civilized" musicians or composers are by no means as impressive in their capabilities, judgments, wisdom or even their esthetic appreciation outside their chosen field as they may be within it. As Marx might have put it, that is a penalty in the division of labor, and the deformation of character by civilization.

Poetry, Painting and Politics

But Lévi-Strauss at least helps us understand why Plato exiled poets while institutionalizing music. In arguing that poetry is not a reflection of the essential realities represented by music and mythology, he states that poetry is "common property," merely "articulate speech . . . subject to certain restrictions." He contrasts this with music, which "has its own vehicle"—and here again he seems to disregard the music of pre-literate peoples. He then concludes that, because of the lack of a particular vehicle, "an adequately educated man could write poems good or bad."[9]

The error grows in complexity. First of all, a bad poem is not a poem; a poem is something that happens beyond, despite, or sometimes in opposition to mere formal restrictions. As Sartre and so many others have known, a poem is iconic, the incarnation of another reality, a world created. Lévi-Strauss appears to sense this also: only poets, he says elsewhere, understand that words were once values.[10]* Nor do poems have to be written; children who cannot write can create poetry. Moreover, the oral literatures of primitive peoples are fundamentally poetic; a growing number of modern poets have been influenced by, while interpreting, such traditions. Vico, it may be recalled, described the language of primitive peoples as naturally "poetic"—connotative, meta-phorical, yet concrete. And this remains closer to the opinion of most artists, and I dare say, of those anthropologists who continue to concern themselves with such matters, than is Lévi-Strauss's assimilation of myths to music. To adopt Lévi-Strauss's criteria, if any adequately educated person can write poems, any person trained in musical composition can write music, "good" or "bad."

But Lévi-Strauss does not linger on these esthetic judgments which provide us with the key to his notion of science. He turns his attention to painting, which he also considers inferior to music, because it imitates colors that preexist in nature, whereas he feels that sounds—bird calls, for example—do not similarly preexist, or are merely noise. That claim aside, it seems obvious that the colors used by painters can be, but are not necessarily, imitations of colors in nature. This Platonic notion of painting (not to speak of poetry) as inherently mimetic, which is the sense of Lévi-Strauss's argument despite the nuances is, of course, eloquently denied by Goya in his introduction to *Los Caprichos.* Thus, what is central to an understanding of Lévi-Strauss is his notion that "the congenital subjection of the plastic arts to objects results from. . . . the organization of forms and colors within sense experience."[11] In other words, the highest achievements of which only a few men are capable—the creation, for example, of Western music—must bear no relationship to the object and cannot be dependent upon

---

* But here as elsewhere, Lévi-Strauss's "understanding" is no indication of his convictions.

the senses. Lévi-Strauss's conceptual realism awaits only its political fulfillment. It is tempting to speculate that the deeper impulse behind Lévi-Strauss, as he himself has hinted, may not be philosophic at all, but rather that of the artist, the composer-musician manqué, in which case he becomes the ultimate academic critic, rationalizing and policing, rather than creating, the world.*

The Complementary Scientific Hierarchy

Thus, for one reason or another, Lévi-Strauss assumes a position of personal privilege within the generally privileged context of an objectifying Western science. Put another way, Lévi-Strauss is a relativist in every sense but the most critical. He maintains his adherence to "abstract abstractions," to the Western canon of logical-deductive scientific conceptualization,† which he transforms into an esthetic. Moreover, this implies an indirect, if nonetheless absolute, acceptance of the society (his own) which has fetishized that mode of cognition. For example, in *Structural Anthropology*, Lévi-Strauss objects to certain practices of psychotherapy, which he distinguishes from the theory of psychoanalysis,[13] since the former constitute what he calls a form of magic. Whatever form of therapy is practiced, the human context mediates. Therefore, he implies, the underlying deformation of structure, which he is confident is the source and locus of "mental illness," is obscured. It seems that science is the examination of the underlying structure, whereas human associational understanding is magical, meaningful, superficial, merely ameliorative and misleading. Here, as in so many other instances, Lévi-Strauss aligns himself with Western essentialistic science, in opposition to the "magical" surface of action in the world, that magic having both a historical and a contemporary reference.†

---

* One recalls here Plato's abortive identity as a poet.

† He believes that: "The ethnologist ... does not feel obliged to take the conditions in which his own thought operates, or the science peculiar to his society and his period, as a fundamental subject of reflection in order to extend these local findings into a form of understanding. ..."[12]

‡ Yet Lévi-Strauss appears to "understand" this also; in a typical passage which indicates how he continuously embraces and thus attempts to nullify

Similarly, when alluding to certain alterations affecting the principle of parity in the physicists' view of the cosmos he claims, in *L'Homme Nu*,[15] that their discovery is an authentication of his structuralist perspective which, presumably, reflects the very substructure of the universe. He is hard to follow here, even if we admit the far-fetched analogy between phenomena on such vastly different levels of operation, analogies that philosophically-minded physicists such as Schrodinger explicitly deny. One thing is certain: the complexity of relationships between microcosm and macrocosm, between matter and antimatter, or right-handed and left-handed spin cannot be assimilated to the antinomies of Lévi-Strauss. It is important to point out such things, not to discredit Lévi-Strauss, but to reveal the off-hand certainties of his style and, as we shall see, the goal of his thought. The deterministic and reductionistic character of the latter is evident.

A number of critics have made this observation about Lévi-Strauss's approach to the universe of experience. There is, obviously, an inconsistency in the presumably highly symbolic categories of structuralism and the reductionism inherent in its explanatory principle. Lévi-Strauss's effort to bridge the gap, in a recent lecture[16] is not convincing. He states that the ensemble of human receptor organs prestructure or predetermine reality—thus, cognition is already abstract on a microcosmic level. This is true, but trivial. Descartes probably made the point first in the Western academy, but it more explicitly echoes Liebnitz, who concluded that there is nothing in the intellect except what was first in the senses—nothing that is, except the intellect. This also represents the Kantian movement from sensations through perceptions to conceptions, the organizing principle being conceptual. But such abstractions have nothing to do with the history of culture, with the particular abstractions represented by cultural forms; they are symbolic inventions no more reducible to the ground out of which they spring than a tree is reducible to the molecular system of

---

all contradictions except those which he chooses to recognize, he states, in agreement with Koehler "the freedom to be mistaken has been lost.... Language along with scientific civilization has helped to impoverish perception and to strip it of its affective, esthetic and magical implications, as well as to schematize thought."[14] But note that he considers the esthetic, the magical and the affective as the freedom to be mistaken. In short, the more correct we are, the more determined we are.

earth and seed. In fact, in another context this notion contradicts Lévi-Strauss's own effort to distinguish the "concrete" (inductive, experiential) abstractions of primitive cognition from the "abstract" (deductive, propositional) abstractions of modern science.*

Yet Lévi-Strauss's instrumental ambiguity is evident here also. In order to make his particular notions about the universal functioning of the human mind consistent, he is obliged to say that primitive modes of thought are identical to civilized modes, the difference being in the object. Among primitive peoples, the mind is directed to myth; among civilized peoples the mind is directed to science.[18] This would seem to imply that myth is the science of primitive peoples and science is the myth of civilization. In turn, that leads to the conclusion, more frankly arrived at by Spengler, that the scientific worldview must be understood as an ideology. But for Lévi-Strauss science represents a superior myth; it not only presumes to be, but actually is closer to the truth, since science can reveal myth, but myth cannot explicate science. Thus, at one stroke Lévi-Strauss rationalizes myth and mystifies rationality. He has tried to modify this position on a number of occasions, but he is always forced to conclude, as did Husserl, that his civilization provides him with a superior form of understanding. By making abstract conceptual thought a human constant, he universalizes a process which the Western academy epitomizes. What he is basically attempting, then, is to assimilate conceptions to perceptions,† an assault on the primacy of the senses and the autonomy of perceptual cognition, whether practiced in our own or in primitive cultures. And this reductionism further reflects Lévi-Strauss's evasion of historical reality.‡

---

* The definition of primitive and civilized modes of cognition presented in *The Savage Mind* would seem to make other conclusions reached by the author, both earlier and later, ambiguous. But the book is quite properly regarded by Lévi-Strauss as a "pause" in the trajectory of his work.[17]

† An inadmissable undertaking, as I have pointed out elsewhere.[19]

‡ Correlatively, he is capable of saying: "As he moves forward within his environment, Man takes with him all the positions that he has occupied in the past, all those that he will occupy in the future. He is everywhere at the same time, a crowd which, in the act of moving forward, yet recapitulates at every instant every step that it has ever taken in the past." This, of course, further negates the meaning of action in history, in fact negates history.[20]

Reductive Scientism

One can also locate Lévi-Strauss's reductionism within the classical framework of the idealist-mechanical materialist split. Engels, for example, classified idealism and mechanical materialism as obverse aspects of a single view. The idealist constructs theories out of abstractions that seem to have a life of their own. In the Platonic or even Hegelian sense, the universe is a pattern of ideas, and they are viewed as both the spirit and cause of social and cultural phenomena. Conversely, the mechanical materialist reduces the symbolic invention to an exclusively material imperative—for example, technology or population pressure. Leslie White is particularly skilled in this duality; he posits "culturology" as, literally, the highest of the sciences, dealing with the symbolic systems of human groups, and then reduces explanation in history to a kind of energetics or technological determinism. Lévi-Strauss's straddling of idealism and mechanical, or biological, materialism is curiously similar, and runs the full range of Engels's definition of each. For between these two spheres, the symbolic and the materially determined, there is no specific historical mediation, no dialectic evident between man and culture, but only a system of eternal polarities, which continuously reflect each other. Here again one senses the Cartesians (particularly Geulincx), and their complementary mental and material clocks, calibrated in the mind of God. In any event, the significance of human action is read out of existence.[21]

Reductionism=Alienation

Therefore, in Lévi-Strauss, we witness the anthropologist's transformation of marginality to a recognized and prestigious immunity. He is mandated to understand everything but himself, and that, in turn, relieves his colleagues of the need to engage in a serious critique of themselves or of their society. Thus, realizing their fantasies, they convert weakness into strength. The position of Lévi-Strauss becomes decisive; he demonstrates how the Western intelligentsia can make imposing careers out of their alienation. And we can understand why a distinguished anthropologist, a member of the most alienated of all professions, should now occupy a central position in the intellectual life of the West.

Lévi-Strauss's theoretical position is itself a definition of alienation. Sartre's insight, in *Réflections sur la question juive*, is strangely appropriate—as if in 1946, he had anticipated the emergence of a Lévi-Strauss: "We must understand this world of extremes, this humanity cut in two. . . . there is a basic doubling of Jewish sensibility concealed beneath the exterior of a universal humanism."[23] As I shall argue, it is because both the doubling and the universal humanism are evident in Lévi-Strauss, that he is initially so difficult to understand.* But more immediately, if one subordinates concrete meaning to underlying structures, as does Lévi-Strauss, if the structure is said to determine the logic through which ideas present themselves to consciousness, and if the specifics of meaning are little more than random or superficial data—conceits, in the basic sense of the term—then it seems we are in the presence of the ultimate rationalization for alienated and dissociated behavior. What we are faced with is a separation of the abstract principles said to underlie behavior from the behavior itself. Thus, these principles are conceived to have a life of their own and are used to interpret the more or less integrated, "merely" phenomenal behavior of persons in terms of an essential polarity.

It should be noted, because of current efforts to link structuralism and Marxism, that this separation of reality from appearance does not resemble Marx's formulation of the problem and cannot be assimilated to a Marxist perspective. Marx denied that essence precedes or lies behind existence. For example, one recalls his delightful distinction between the abstract peach—the peach of the philosophers—and the only peach that he agreed to recognize, with its skin, pit, pulp and, one might add, its worm. Marx insisted that social conditions distort the sense of social

---

* Durkheim, Lévi-Strauss's real predecessor, had written:

It is true that we are doubles, that we are the realization of an antinomy. In connection with this truth, however, a question arises that philosophy and even positive psychology cannot avoid. Where do this duality and this antinomy come from? How is it that each of us is . . . 'a monster of contradictions' that can never completely satisfy itself. And certainly, if this odd condition is one of the distinctive merits of humanity, the science of man must try to account for it.

Lévi-Strauss has tried to "account for it," but in a direction that is the reverse of Durkheim's.[22]

reality. If alienation is to be overcome, these underlying conditions can and must be made conscious. They are, therefore, the reverse of Lévi-Strauss's unconscious structures.

Moreover, for Marx, social conditions form reality, "social existence determines consciousness"; whereas for Lévi-Strauss, biological being may be said to determine the social unconscious, and therefore the behavior of men.*

Methodological Reductionism: The Trickster

Lévi-Strauss describes the process this way:

> The layered structure of myth. . . . allows us to look upon myth as a matrix of meanings which are arranged in lines or columns, but in which each level always refers to some other level, whichever way the myth is read. Similarly, each matrix of meanings refers to another matrix, each myth to other myths. And if it is now asked to what final meaning these mutually significative meanings are referring—since in the last resort in their totality they must refer to something—the only reply . . . is that myths signify the mind that evolves them by making use of the world of which it is itself a part. *Thus there is simultaneous production of myths themselves, by the mind that generates them and by the myths, of an image of the world which is already inherent in the structure of the mind.*
>
> By taking its raw material from nature, mythic thought proceeds in the same way as language, which chooses phonemes from among the natural sounds of which a practically unlimited range is to be found in childish babbling. For, as in the case of language, the empirical material is too abundant to be all accepted indiscriminately or to be all used on the same level. Here again, it must be accepted as a fact that *the material is the instrument of meaning*, not its object. For it to play this part, it must be whittled down. . . . [By Lévi-Strauss, one presumes] *Only a few of its elements are*

---

* For Lévi-Strauss it is not men who think myths, but myths that think men. This is the reverse of Marx's reflection; man makes religion, religion does not make man, and further, "religion is the sigh of the oppressed."[23]

retained—those suitable for the expression of contrasts or forming pairs of opposites (emphasis added).[24]

In one effort to explicate this method, Lévi-Strauss proposes his solution to the problem of the Trickster in American Indian mythology, which, it seems, had hitherto been insoluble. Why, he asks, referring to one aspect of the problem, is the Trickster personified as "coyote" or "raven" throughout North America?[25] To understand this we must "keep in mind that mythical thought always progresses from the awareness of opposites towards their resolution. . . . And we need only assume," he tells us, "that two opposite terms with no intermediary always tend to be replaced by two equivalent terms, which admit of a third one as a mediator; then one of the polar terms and the mediator (are) replaced by a new triad, and so on." (Note the fugue-like progression.)

The two polar terms Lévi-Strauss begins with are "life" and "death." But one must observe at once that in a primitive culture "life" and "death"—which the secular mind conceives as irreconcilable—may not be perceived as polar at all, but rather as aspects of a single condition, the condition of existence. In Radin's words "The Indian does not make the separation into personal, as contrasted with impersonal, corporeal with impersonal, in our sense at all. What he seems to be interested in is the question of existence, of reality; and everything perceived by the senses, thought of, felt and dreamt of, exists." Nonetheless, following, for the moment, Lévi-Strauss's construction which presumably reflects "the unformulated argument" of, let us say, the Pueblo,* "life," a concept which cannot be mediated, is transformed into agriculture. "Death," the other unmediated concept in the initial pair, is transformed into warfare. Between agriculture and warfare, mediation becomes possible; and that, we are told, is hunting, for hunting provides food while using the techniques of warfare. This first triad now must undergo a second transformation before we can discover why "raven" and "coyote" are salient figures in American mythology. Agriculture must be personified as "herbivorous animals"; correlatively, hunting is personified as "beasts of prey." Maintaining this logic, the mediators in the second

---

* It is the mythological process that interests Lévi-Strauss, not the specific people.

triad—between herbivorous and carnivorous animals—are, of course, scavengers, animals who eat the flesh of others but do not kill them. Therefore, while they are carnivorous and thus resemble beasts of prey, they also resemble food producers in that they do not kill what they eat. We can now conclude that "raven" and "coyote" mediate the binary opposition life—death, and thus represent the image of the Trickster who, as is well known, is both good and evil, both creator and destroyer.

On the analogy of this inherent, logical progression which Lévi-Strauss attributes to the universal structure of the mind, a series of other mediators can be constituted. These mythic terms include mist (between sky and earth); scalp (between war and agriculture, since scalp is a war crop)*; clothing (between nature and culture); ashes (between roof—sky—and hearth—ground), and so on. This method, according to Lévi-Strauss, illuminates whole areas of North American mythology; for example, it explains why scalps are mist-producing; why the Spirit of the Dew (between sky and earth) may be correlated with the Keeper of Game (between hunting and agriculture) and may also be the Giver of Fine Garments (between nature and culture). And we are finally able to understand why the Spirit of the Dew may be personified as an Ash-Boy (soot and ashes being between sky and ground) and why Ash-Boy is generically but not historically related to Cinderella. In this latter instance, the nominal mediation has been transformed into a social mediation—lower class marries into higher class which, pursuing his logic, Lévi-Strauss would have to claim is an intellectual resolution of class conflict. The exemplary mythic terms, "coyote," "raven," "mist," "scalp," "clothing," and "ashes" are, then, equivalent because of their analogous positions in the mythic structure. It is this relational equivalence, signifying the basic process which underlies all apparent meaning, that concerns Lévi-Strauss, not the integrity of the word itself, nor any other association or connotation that it may have. In this endgame of stereotyped metaphors (read illusions)† which Lévi-Strauss

---

* But two questions arise here: would scalping have the same distribution as the coyote and raven myths; and what of the disparity between the late development of scalping on the one hand, and the historical depth of the Trickster myth on the other?

† In the structuralist lexicon "illusion" may be defined as the reality within the reach of "ordinary" people in the world.

plays with endless virtuosity, the goal is the revelation of the structure, that is, of the specific juxtaposition of the opposing elements involved.

The Method and Conclusion Criticized

Yet if we examine the initial pair, "life" and "death," there seems to be no compelling reason, even if we accept their binary character (which the ethnological evidence by no means compels us to do) to maintain the first triad as the expression of an inherent logic. For Lévi-Strauss is assuming a necessary progression from the concept "life"; to an activity "agriculture"; to a personification "herbivorous animals"; paralleled by the analogous transformation from "death" to "warfare" to "beasts of prey." It would be just as logical and more parsimonious to argue directly from "life" to "herbivorous animals" and from "death" to "beasts of prey," in the latter instance, without the mediating term "hunting." In so doing we would be personifying both life and death more immediately; in fact, the direct personification of death is commonplace among primitive peoples. In any event, the personifications which one encounters among such people are irrelevant to the specific sequence of Lévi-Strauss's "unformulated [Pueblo] argument." For it is the personification, or concretion, that represents ethnological reality; it is what we start with. But Lévi-Strauss only gives the impression of arguing inductively from particular personifications to unmediated abstract concepts, which are then said to represent basic assumptions of the culture under scrutiny and are, therefore, translatable into universal assumptions, ultimately to the polarizing principle of nature itself. Actually, Lévi-Strauss has not reasoned inductively at all, but has argued backwards from the supposed evidence (the Trickster as a sign) to the *a priori* unmediated concepts* ("life" and "death" as the signified). He presents this method as follows: "empirical categories. . . .categories of the raw and the cooked, the fresh and the decayed, the moistened and the burned, etc., which can only

---

* For Lévi-Strauss the concept seems to be the signified of the concrete sign, a particular and arbitrary form of experience, and, at the same time, a sign of the underlying structure of reality.

be accurately defined by ethnographic observation and, in each instance, by adopting the standpoint of a particular culture—*can nonetheless be used as conceptual tools with which to elaborate abstract ideas and combine them in the form of propositions*" (italics added).[26] These empirically determined binary oppositions are, then, no more than the cultural names designating the formal dichotomies that define the functioning structures of nature and mind; and these, it appears, are both universal and a priori propositions. Lévi-Strauss's method is, in this representative instance, tautological.

But the Trickster can be grasped more fully as the personification of human ambiguity, on a directly perceived level of meaning; a concrete human ambiguity, subject to transcendence in everyday life. This is quite different from Lévi-Strauss's notion that "mythical thought always progresses from the awareness of oppositions towards their resolution"; for his mythological resolution is curiously undialectical, and emerges as a mere clarification of certain formal antinomies. Moreover, as Lévi-Strauss must and does acknowledge, the kind of mediation (read resolution) that he postulates has no bearing on the real contradictions encountered in society or lived by persons.

One should also add that the Trickster names "raven" and "coyote" which Lévi-Strauss explains can be arrived at with greater economy on the basis of, let us say, the cleverness of the animals involved, their ubiquity, elusiveness, capacity to make mischief, their undomesticated reflection of certain human traits. But even on its own terms, Lévi-Strauss's argument is questionable here. For example, bears, who are not here presented as Tricksters, may act as scavengers, while coyotes are not only scavengers, but may kill prey directly; and ravens are known to act as beasts of prey. Moreover, Jane Goodall has pointed out that the coyote (like the hyena), develops scavenging habits in a changing environment where he is outranked in the competition for game. Goodall refers to Africa, but the historical soundness of the mythological argument is, nevertheless, called into question, and the structuralist finds himself haunted by history on a rather elementary level. Finally, spiders, mantises and hares* (not

---

* Arguing in Lévi-Strauss's mode, one could say that the hare is hunted as animal food but lives on plant food and is thus an "inverted mediator." One could go on with these inversions, conversions and reversals indefinitely. But

buzzards or hyenas) typify the Trickster in other parts of the world and one would be hard put to account for such personifications in Lévi-Strauss's logical terms. What emerges from an examination of one aspect of the Trickster myth is a much more rewarding question, the question of personification,* which helps us to understand certain historical distinctions between primitive and civilized modes of cognition.

Binary Oppositions: A Civilized Interpretation

A useful way to approach this relative difference in cognition, which further reveals Lévi-Strauss's procedure, is to consider the radical separation between good and evil, and their transformation into concepts, a symptom of archaic and modern civilizations. Lévi-Strauss does not come to grips with this particular polarity, but it is of some importance. The point is that in the actual behavior of persons, good and evil are rarely abstracted as such. But we selectively project their pure forms as external forces, ordering or disordering the behavior of the person. We may speak abstractly of evil befalling a man, or of his good luck; correlatively

---

what do we do with spiders and mantises? Lévi-Strauss claims that different Trickster figures outside North America are arrived at by other "unformulated arguments." If so, the process which they represent could not be one of universal logical mediation which, he tells us, both defines the Trickster and reflects the specific nomenclature. His argument, then, has an inescapable internal paradox. Either his "proof" of the Trickster being named as mediator is universal but obvious in only a few cultures, or it is culturally specific and, therefore, not universal. That is, the basic unmediated concepts "life" and "death" either need universal mediators or they do not. Since "spider," "mantis," and "hare" are mythological analogues of "raven" and "coyte," Lévi-Strauss would have to explain the irrelevance of his "unformulated argument" with reference to them.

* The term personification is here used to represent a mode of cognition opposite to that epitomized in deductive abstractions. The phenomena referred to need not be obviously definable as persons, but the process of personification is always evident. Mana, the Polynesian term for the power of the universe is, for example, the essence of a deity, residing in an object or a human being. Both the Maori and the Dakota typically claim that every object reflects a spirit. Alternatively, mana is that which works, has activity, has an effect. The personal (being) and the active or existential are always related aspects of primitive perception. Therefore, personification seems a perfectly acceptable shorthand term for the process I am discussing.

in politically structured societies we may also consider a person to be inherently good or evil, just as we would reduce his humanity to his occupation, class or status in society. In both instances—external and internal—the human agency hardly exists or appears in grossly alienated form as a reified fate. If, on the other hand, we visualize a situation in a primitive society where principles are subordinated to persons, where what we reduce as principles are "personifications"; then real, integrated behavior in the world becomes the basis for analysis—rather than the structural, or any other species of principle said to underlie behavior. This primitive sense of a dialectical reality is even extended to the behavior of the gods; Laura Benedict reports, for example, with reference to the Bagobo:

> Before the world was made, there was Tagamaling. The Tagamaling is the best buso, because he does not want to hurt man all of the time. Tagamaling is actually buso only a part of the time; that is, the month when he eats people. One month he eats human flesh, and then he is buso; the next month he eats no human flesh, and then he is a god. So he alternates, month by month. The month he is buso, he wants to eat man during the dark of the moon; that is, between the phases that the moon is full in the east and new in the west. . . .[27]

And Lowie tells us:

> The two great deities of the Ekoi are no more consistently conceived than the Sun or Old-Man-Coyote of the Crow. Neither is uniformly good. [Their designs can be frustrated.][28]

Heaven and Hell, in a further example, are civilized inventions; neither the projection nor the abstract polarity of these two concepts exists among primitive peoples. These polarities, developing with civilization, can be located in religious, legal or other institutional codes; they tend to reduce the behavior of persons and thus the persons themselves to essential binary characteristics. Thus, we are led to refer to rich and poor (an economic division), we and they (a political division), and then demand that a person identify himself as, say, a carpenter or a plumber (an occupational division).

The reification of the discontinuity between "young" and "old" is a further case in point. We speak of the young and the old as if they were separate populations that had no relationship to the rest of us. They appear as the extremities of a human condition which we abstract, and somehow make alien to ourselves. That is, we do not perceive ourselves in terms of an integrated life cycle incorporating a period of youth, resolved and transformed during maturity. Rather, we try—in a so-called "progressive effort"—to create homes and activities for the aged, and marginal solutions for the problems of "restless" youth. This socially determined reduction of the life cycle leads us to conceptualize the binary division between young and old and, consequently, to reify them as distinct populations. That, in turn, is a political process. For the young and the old—that is, ourselves, in different, and radically discontinuous phases of growth— represent surplus populations that cannot be assimilated into the system. Disenfranchisement and, perhaps most obviously, special dispensations given to the young and the old, help to fix the rest of us in the established structure, since the young and old are a reservoir of potential competitors.

The young and the old are therefore reified as antagonistic to the self in society; we are immobilized by the threat of competition with ourselves. The binary opposition "young" and "old," abstractions standing over and against the "real" person, reduces the latter to an abstraction, the alienated form of the self at the disposal of civilization. Our logic, isomorphic with our society, is exclusive and bipolar; if a phenomenon is one thing, it cannot at the same time be another. Dorothy Lee understood this as follows: "Wintu philosophy in general has no law of contradiction. Where we have mutually exclusive dualistic categories, the Wintu have categories which are inclusive."[29]

In civilization, then, there is the sense of acting in accord with or in violation of absolute principles which take no account of the actual complexity of human behavior. There is, therefore, the alienating sense of being driven by forces beyond one's control. Analogously, Marx refers to the fact that "separate individuals have, with the broadening of their activity into world-historical activity, become more and more enslaved under a power alien to them (a pressure which they have conceived of as a dirty trick on the part of the so-called Universal Spirit), a power that has become more and more enormous and, in the last instance, turns out to be the world market."[30] Society itself is hypostatized as an antagonist to the individual; this is the antithesis of the primitive conception of the person in the community. The metaphors of command and responsibility that define primitive ritual, while reflecting both the natural division and the inherent unity of labor, are the opposites of what Durkheim termed, the "organic," linked functions to which persons are reduced in modern society. Therefore, Lévi-Strauss has explored for us the landscape of alienation and has, with a certain despair, finally tracked it to the deep structure of the brain—determinative of, while inaccessible to, the human actor.

But interestingly enough, Lévi-Strauss does not subject the myths of his own society, which he properly defines as political, to structural analysis; he claims that the myths of civilization have been subject to so much dislocation and reinterpretation by generations of mandarins that they no longer reflect the underlying structures. It is, of course, likely that primitive myths have been interpreted as much as our own. This is the position, it will be recalled, which Lévi-Strauss also seems to take in rationalizing his right to be at least one step removed from the myth under scrutiny. Moreoever, it is clear that Lévi-Strauss's avoidance of our regnant ideologies effectively isolates the observation platform into which he has converted his society. This is regrettable, because closer examination of Western ideology would, I think, reveal that the determining structures to which Lévi-Strauss refers are cognitive, in the broadest sense political, and symptomatic of the sharp and ramifying social contradictions reflected in the superstructure of civilization. At the same time they represent the most banal dichotomies that can be abstracted from any situation, event, structure or idea. Therefore, Lévi-Strauss's determinism and bipolar theorizing can be defined as both a projection of civilized cognition into primitive culture, and as the strategy of a reductive universalism. By locating the process neurodynamically, either directly or analogously, he avoids that confrontation with his own culture which Rousseau perceived as the goal of trying to understand others. It seems that Lévi-Strauss has reversed Rousseau's dictum and seeks to understand primitive cultures through the unexamined assumptions of our own civilization.

Thus, when Lévi-Strauss claims that primitives, along with

ordinary people in our own society, cannot understand the real basis of their own behavior (since they cannot simultaneously act and analyze*), he is perhaps admitting that he imposes his explanations on them in more ways than he is willing to concede. A recent essay by the Korean anthropologist, Kang[31] deserves to be noted in this connection. Kang outlines the well-known dualisms that charaterize the traditional Chinese world-view. But his point is that these oppositions are dialectically resolved and continually transcended. This is a reflective and cognitive process, a cultural exploration of infinitely subtle meanings that define the traditional Chinese human universe; they are not the determined, unconscious, and quasi-mathematical polarities which Lévi-Strauss constructs.

Here is another example of not imposing explanations along rather different lines. When I was engaged in fieldwork in North Central Nigeria, I was indentified as both a spirit of a certain type and as a man. No binary opposition was evident; I was understood simultaneously as both. One might say, in this case, that the synthesis had taken place in the minds of the Anaguta, but that would be reading an a priori opposition into the matter. The point was that the view of the Anaguta was integrated, and there was no need to disintegrate it for the sake of a fetishized Western logic of polarities.[32] As the Salish say: "imitate the spirit of the animal or thing inside you" [which may be seen as a synthetic statement rather than an oppositional imperative].[33] Still another example is with reference to the division between black and white magic. This definition, as many anthropologists have pointed out, shifts relative to the subject and object of the magic; the division can be defined as situational, that is, as a shifting perspective on a single event, and not as abstractly polar. Of course, Lévi-Strauss will continue to find ways to resolve such difficulties by distinguishing between primary and secondary levels of reality (the transformations having taken place) or by ignoring the social context of the division by attributing it to a "fundamental process of the human mind." It is in this way that one could begin to construct a countermodel to Lévi-Strauss.

---

* —any more than the anthropologist can, which is probably why he has chosen to analyze.

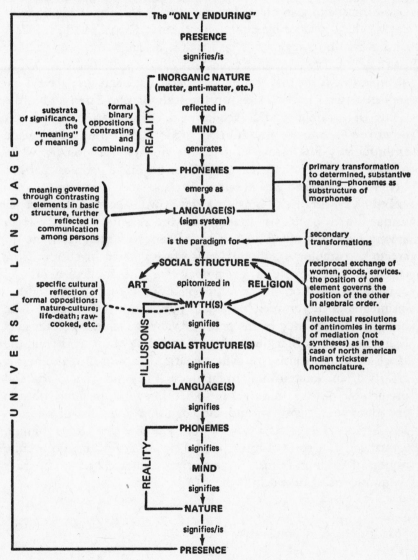

Fig. 1 The Cosmos According to Lévi-Strauss

The "ONLY ENDURING"

PRESENCE

signifies/is

INORGANIC NATURE
(matter, anti-matter, etc.)

reflected in

MIND

generates

PHONEMES

emerge as

LANGUAGE(S)
(sign system)

is the paradigm for

SOCIAL STRUCTURE

ART   epitomized in   RELIGION

MYTH(S)

signifies

SOCIAL STRUCTURE(S)

signifies

LANGUAGE(S)

signifies

PHONEMES

signifies

MIND

signifies

NATURE

signifies/is

PRESENCE

REALITY

UNIVERSAL LANGUAGE

ILLUSIONS

REALITY

substrata of significance, the "meaning" of meaning

formal binary oppositions contrasting and combining

meaning governed through contrasting elements in basic structure, further reflected in communication among persons

specific cultural reflection of formal oppositions: nature-culture; life-death; raw-cooked, etc.

primary transformation to determined, substantive meaning—phonemes as substructure of morphones

secondary transformations

reciprocal exchange of women, goods, services. the position of one element governs the position of the other in algebraic order.

intellectual resolutions of antinomies in terms of mediation (not syntheses) as in the case of north american indian trickster nomenclature.

LEGEND: TIME ELAPSED = ILLUSIONS = HISTORY = HUMAN MEANING

The Cosmological Impulse

While digging a new niche for anthropology in its society of origin, Lévi-Strauss has also created and deployed a considerable body of data in the service of his underlying theory. This has had the effect of further intensifying his reputation as an anthropologist, for there now exists an embarrassing surplus of presumably empirical information at the disposal of anthropologists, and they have done very little with it. An effort on the scale of Lévi-Strauss's has the virtue of organizing and accounting for information that might otherwise seem useless. In that sense, Lévi-Strauss has made anthropology interesting to the professional anthropologist while helping to satisfy that curiosity about primitive peoples that has been so pronounced within our civilization since Montaigne.

But Lévi-Strauss's sense of his own accomplishment, as distinguished from his strategy, or the reasons for his esteem among his colleagues is, I believe, of another order. He wants to create a cosmology, and this must always be an invention. How can one man create a cosmology for the modern world, a cosmology based on the analytic spirit, when that spirit itself has disintegrated the universe he would put back together again? The obsessive consistency of his point of view, which raises contradictions only to smother them; the sheer volume of his work; and the range of his concerns are symptomatic, in a sense, of the heroic efforts of an isolated modern intellectual to conceive a logical and predictable order in nature and society, beyond meaning, illusion and disappointment, beyond the cognition and control of men. Lévi-Strauss emerges as a type of philosophic and religious thinker, a theologian in spite of himself, who cannot accept an apocalyptic notion of God, and thus adopts an anthropological stance in order to ground his argument in "reality."

The Cosmological Imperative

This accounts for his effort to incorporate the major intellectual traditions of our time into his work. His structuralism, like any other cosmological enterprise, must be inclusive or it will appear as just another point of view. Hence, Lévi-Strauss acknowledges his debt to Marx, Freud, Kant, Rousseau, modern physicists and empirical American anthropologists, among others. By allying himself with them, he makes them partially responsible for his vision; that is, he interprets them as determinists, universalists and reductive or analytic rationalists. Structuralism is thus rationalized as the ideology of our time, the logical denouement of Western reflection on self, society and nature,[34] until Lévi-Strauss sounds like Spengler, a predecessor to whom he acknowledges no claim. But there is no trace, for example, of a Marxist analysis in his ethnological work. And there is a basic divergence from the principles and purposes of Marx. Marxism, Lévi-Strauss tells us, is the first step, the last of which represents the Buddhist "no" to meaning.*[35] Of course, he does not tell us what comes in between.

The analogy with Freud's undertaking is no more than an analogy; Lévi-Strauss's search for an ethnological unconscious has a Freudian appearance, but the closer one gets to Freud's theory of drives, his metaphorical sense of history and his practice, the further away one gets from Lévi-Strauss. Perhaps, then, Lévi-Strauss is a nontranscendental Kantian, as Ricoeur called him. I take this to mean that the anthropologist believes in the preexisting categories of cognition (in the curious absence of a

---

* A further example of Lévi-Strauss's effort to neutralize, by embracing, as much opposition as possible, is evident in his essay on "The Place of Anthropology in the Social Sciences."[36] After setting forth a program in what amounts to applied anthropology for colonial servants, he then dismisses it in a footnote (it seems that he really doesn't care for applied anthropology). But he then attempts to defend the principle of applied anthropology by quoting Marx, to the effect that English factory and public health inspectors in the nineteenth century provided useful information about the exploitation of the proletariat. Lévi-Strauss points out that these applied anthropologists of the time were "servants of the established order yet Marx did not censure them."

It so happens, however, that applied anthroplogy is counter-revolutionary and, to my knowledge, has never supplied facts which could be used by revolutionary social scientists. Apart from the effort simultaneously to associate and disassociate both himself and Marx from applied anthropology, he avoids the reality of applied anthropology as it is actually practiced—namely, as an effort to adopt subordinate peoples at home and abroad to the dominant power structures.

One recalls Lévi-Strauss's philosophy of history: "As he moves forward within his environment, Man takes with him all the positions which he has occupied in the past, etc." One might say that as Lévi-Strauss moves forward,

transcendental subject).* He has certainly been influenced by Kant's speculative, nondialectical antinomies. But as one approaches Kant's concern with ethics, his reticence on the ultimate nature of nature, or the issue of final truth, one abandons Lévi-Strauss. The claim to kinship with Rousseau is equally tenuous, although Rousseau, as a model builder, can be used to rationalize Lévi-Strauss's handling of ethnological material. But Rousseau's unqualifiedly revolutionary critique of modern civilization, linked to his consistent respect for the primitive and, above all, his refusal to consider the study of man on the analogy of the natural and physical sciences—that is, his denial of a mechanical or physical determinism in human affairs—remove him from significant affiliation.

The Ultimate Rationalization

It is not possible, therefore, to understand Lévi-Strauss as he would wish us to. As a cosmologist, he is more readily understood as an eclectic descendent of Plato, Descartes and Spinoza. He is a system builder, a civilized man driven to ask basic questions, who accepts his condition as the inevitable consequence of scientific reflection. Using that mode of cognition, he tries to turn it against itself in order to make the universe habitable. He emerges as a domestic, a social metaphysician; for him the cosmos replicates itself in the organization of subatomic matter, the genetic code, the nature of the brain, and it is finally revealed in the structure of society.†

His debt to Durkheim and Mauss is clear enough: "Logical

---

he takes with him all the positions that he has occupied in the past. There is in this "expansion of meaning" the danger of bursting, and Lévi-Strauss is aware of it: "an expansion conducted inwards from without and pushed home to explosion-point."[37]

* "Neither psychology, nor metaphysics, nor art can provide me with a refuge; for one and all are myths subject, within and without, to that new kind of sociology which will arise one day and treat them as severely as has our earlier one. *Not merely is the first person singular destestable:* there is no room for it between 'ourselves' and 'nothing' " (italics added).[38]

† As he puts it: "As early as 1945 I applied transformational laws to facts of social life and things of art without thinking of deviating in the slightest from a structuralist linguistics called by some out of date without their even

relations," they claimed, "are in a sense domestic relations. . . . and the unity of knowledge is nothing else than the unity of the collectivity extended to the universe."[40] Society was not simply a model which classificatory thought followed: "it was its own divisions which served as divisions for the system of classification. The first logical categories were social categories."[41] Lévi-Strauss, however, has converted the sociological metaphor into a conceptual reality. Society is no longer the mediator of human logic; it is a reflex of the objective order of the universe. This reversal puts Lévi-Strauss closer to Frazer, who claimed (as Durkheim and Mauss point out), that "the social relations of men are based on the logical relations between things."[42] Yet Lévi-Strauss only makes the claim; his evidence is not persuasive. It seems clear that his cosmology is a reflection of his sociology, and thus too contingent and relative to realize his metaphysical ambitions. Simply turning Durkheim and Mauss around cannot change the historical root, nor the direction, of Lévi-Strauss's dilemma. One is reminded of Sartre's uncanny statement of a generation ago: "The disquietude of the Jew is not metaphysical, it is social. . . . He does not dream . . . of considering the *condition of man in its nudity.** He is the social man par excellence, because his torment is social" (emphasis added).[43]

Within the teleological universe that Lévi-Strauss has so painstakingly invented, his social situation finds its reflection. Human freedom and authenticity lose their definition. No self-defining choice, hence no authenticity is possible in such interlocking, isomorphic structures of reality. Freedom becomes

---

realizing that it has acquired a natural and objective status with the discovery and deciphering of the genetic code: that universal language used by all forms of life, from micro-organisms to higher mammals, passing through plants, in which one can see the absolute prototype of which, on another level, articulated language repeats the model; namely, in the beginning a finite ensemble of discrete units, chemical bases, or phonemes, without significance themselves but which, diversely combined in units of a higher rank—words of language or triplets of nucleotides—specify determined meaning or chemical substance. Similarly words of language or triplets of the genetic code combine in their turn into "phrases" which life writes in the molecular form of the ADN, itself a vehicle also for a differential meaning whose message specifies such and such a protein of a given kind."[39]

* One reflects on the title of the fourth (the last) volume of the Mythologiques: *L'Homme Nu.*

no more than the recognition of a total, but unrecognized necessity; man is the instrument of an externally determined order or, in theological terms, man is free only to obey the dictates of God. In this world which Lévi-Strauss has been constructing during his whole professional career, no ultimate risk is possible. There is no uncertainty, no impenetrable question, no uniqueness, no human particularity. Hence, there is no identity and, finally, no persons. The local, the concrete, is only an instance of a process reduced to a structure.*

Lévi-Strauss feels that since the person is a psychological-social-biological reflex, human meaning is and must be illusory. This monolithic vision is the logical abreaction to bourgeois atomization; it represents a pseudo-order, a collective deriving from the mechanical association of isolates and that, in turn, reflects the evolved bourgeois consciousness examining the wreckage of contemporary society. Once again we encounter Durkheim in grotesque form.

The Conflict With Sartre

In this totalitarian world, which is a result, if not the intention, of the anthropologist's work (and to which Lévi-Strauss has thus far not opposed the binary principle of total disorder), an existential

---

* There are certain obvious parallels with Spinoza's beliefs:
  1. The primacy of an eternal substance or order—all existence, all particulars are secondary;
  2. The structure of the world is beyond human judgment, esthetic or otherwise;
  3. Freedom of action is an illusion.

Moreover, Spinoza declared his intention to "write about human beings as though [he were] concerned with lines, planes and solids." Thus, he conceived "the order and connection of ideas as being the same as the order and connection of things." Lévi-Strauss uses very similar terminology: "Since the laws [of the human mind] governing its operations are not fundamentally different from those it exhibits in its other functions, *it shows itself to be of the nature of a thing among things*. The argument need not be carried to this point, since it is enough to establish the conviction that if the human mind appears determined even in the realm of mythology, *a fortiori* it must also be determined in all its spheres of activity" (italic added).[44]

One might say that just as Lévi-Strauss is a Kantian without a transcendental subject he is also, consciously or otherwise, a Spinozan, who

view of man is simply absurd. For this reason, although Lévi-Strauss can afford to be condescending towards phenomenology (he seems to consider its concern with superficial phenomena "real," if of an inferior order of reality) and finds it possible, to selectively incorporate so many other perspectives, he is obliged to reject existentialism; and the ground is cleared for the struggle between himself and Sartre,* a struggle that is itself indicative of a division in the consciousness and conscience of the West. It is at this juncture that we must inquire into the identity of Lévi-Strauss, which cannot be considered a fixed and unassailable point representing the evolution of human consciousness in general, however much he might wish it to be.

The Basis of the Conflict:
The Situation of Lévi-Strauss

No one has done this with greater acumen than Sartre, although Sartre could hardly have had Lévi-Strauss in mind in 1946, when he published his courageous *Réflections*. In this work, Sartre sets out to examine the dialectic between anti-Semite and Jew.[45] The anti-Semite is hollow, and inauthentic to the core; a coward incapable because of time, circumstance and will, of engaging in the struggle to become a person, specifically a cultured (in the anthropological sense) Frenchman. Anti-Semitism, the hatred and exclusion of the Jew, serves to make the anti-Semite feel accomplished, affiliated, alive. By depriving the Jew of identity, he achieves his own false identity, his own false particularity, but passively, without pain or effort. The Jew pays a terrible price for the inauthenticity of the Gentile, for the latter's failure to achieve his own particularity. But the Jewish response, Sartre maintains (implying no moral blame), can also be inauthentic. "What is astonishing," says Sartre, "is certainly not that there are

---

never quite assimilates nature to God. He has not struggled directly with the major issues in the history of philosophy, as did Spinoza in his time but, rather, has chosen to transmit his message through his interpretation of the mythology of primitive peoples.

* Sartre defines existentialism as an "enclave in Marxism"—a perspective with which I fully agree.

inauthentic Jews ['those who do not live to the full the condition of being Jewish, in fact deny it and attempt to escape from it']; it is rather that, in proportion, they are fewer than inauthentic Christians."

Thus the inauthentic* Jew, however understandably, has evaded the particularity of his situation. But Sartre does not confine inauthenticity to certain Jews or to anti-Semites. He is attempting to lay bare a general aspect of modern man, who refuses to be himself. Therefore, he speaks of the liberal, the democrat who chose once and for all in the eighteenth century "the analytic spirit,"† who has no eyes for the concrete synthesis with which history confronts him. He recognizes neither Jew, Arab, Negro, bourgeois nor worker, but only man—man always the same in all times and places. . . . "To him," and here Sartre could have been addressing himself directly to Lévi-Strauss, "a physical body is a collection of molecules; a social body, a collection of individuals." By individuals he means "*the incarnation in a single example* of the universal traits which make up human nature"† (emphasis added). Further, the democrat, like the scientist, "fails to see the particular case; to him the individual is only an ensemble of universal traits." Thus the democrat, like the inauthentic Jew, "wishes to destroy" the Jew as Jew, "and leave nothing in him but the man, the abstract and universal subject of the rights of man, and the rights of the citizen." The anti-Semite reproaches the Jew with being Jewish; the democrat reproaches him with willfully considering himself a Jew.

The Overdetermined Rationalism of the Inauthentic Jew

But it is necessary to interrupt the flow of Sartre's argument here

---

* The term "inauthentic" is the existential equivalent of the Marxist "alienated"—it is not, of course, deployed as a personal, characterological attack—but as a mode of understanding.

† It is necessary to point out that there were other choices available in the eighteenth century—as in the instance of Rousseau.

‡ Says Lévi-Strauss: "We . . . have the hope of overcoming the opposition between the collective nature or culture and its manifestations in the individual, since the so-called "collective consciousness" would, in the final

and to observe that there are certain nuances of the connection—liberal-democratic-inauthentic-Jew-rationalist that understandably escape him, while concretizing, in a Jewish context, the universalist response to the false particularities of anti-Semitism. For that response is also against the fossilized particularities of the orthodox Jewish community (e.g., the relentless logic of the Talmudic code) which had absorbed so much intellectual energy, and had been the conventional sign of Jewish reverence for the mind. The *Haskalah*, the Jewish form of the Enlightenment (associated with Moses Mendelssohn), struggled with the orthodoxy of Jewish life in Western Europe and, diffusing eastward, transformed the culture of the traditional Jewish community which was, of course, ripe for the assault. In instance after instance, Jewish scholars became champions of the rational, analytic and universalistic aspects of the Enlightenment, both as a defense against anti-Semitism and as a rebellion against the archaic synthesis of Jewish culture. The Talmudic mind, so to speak, made a direct leap into *Haskalah* modernism, transforming theological rationalization into a new secular religion of reason. This break in the content of consciousness was sudden and traumatic, generated from the outside and spread by secularized Jewish missionaries. There was no mediating Renaissance, and hardly any Reformation, although the traditional Jewish respect for the ordered life of the mind was retained. Hence the conversion of many Jews to universalistic rationalism and related conceptions of the ascendent European bourgeoisie which Sartre seeks to explain, is not only determined, but over-determined.

Yet these new prophets were quickly reduced to priests because of the reductive character of their ideas. The descent of reason to rationality is, after all, one of the achievements of the late nineteenth century, and it was more or less coincident with the diffused and thus chronologically later Jewish Enlightenment in Central Europe. This tension between priests and prophets in Jewish history, a tension which cannot be confined to Jewish culture alone, nonetheless adds dimension and specificity to Sartre's argument. The prophet is perpetually attempting to break through into freedom, personal meaning and socially lived faith.

---

analysis, be no more than the expression, on the level of individual thought and behavior, of certain time and space modalities of the universal laws which make up the unconscious activity of the mind."

The priests defend, interpret and fall back on the compulsively ritualized codes. The prophetic sense has always been existential, concrete, liberating, focusing on the uniqueness of self and others, of all phenomena. Eighteenth-century Hassidism, the modern interpretations of Heschel, the derivative, yet Jewish* theology of Buber may therefore be said to represent forms of Jewish authenticity, although in a religious context that Sartre would deny. At the same time it remains possible to contrast them with the priestly inauthenticity of Lévi-Strauss in Sartrean terms.

Sartre's Definition

What, then, are some of the qualities of the inauthentic Jew, qualities that he shares with the democrat and the scientist? Sartre's description is as follows: He has "an almost continuously reflective attitude. . . . He absorbs all knowledge with an avidity which is not to be confused with disinterested curiosity. He hopes to become a man, nothing but a man, a man like all other men, by taking in all the thoughts of men and acquiring a human point of view of the universe. He cultivates himself in order to destroy the Jew in himself [the particular man in himself] as if he wished to have applied to him—but in modified form—the phrase of Terence: *nil humane a me alienum puto ergo homo sum*."

Rationalism, the passion of the last two centuries, the root of "the sciences and their practical application . . . tried to bring men together by uncovering for them universal truths on which they could all reach agreement. The rationalism† of Jews is such a passion—the passion for the universal. . . . Of all things in the world, reason is the most widely shared: it belongs to everybody and nobody; it is the same to all. If reason exists, then there is no French truth or German truth, there is no Negro truth or Jewish truth. There is only one truth, and he is best who wins it. In the

---

* In form, if not in content; in intention, if not in result.

† Sartre does not distinguish between the "sweet reason" of the eighteenth century, and the functional rationality of the nineteenth, but one assumes that he has in mind the former, despite his use of the term "rationalism." Of course, as noted, eighteenth-century reason had the potential to—and did—harden into functional rationality in the context of industrial capitalism.

face of universal and eternal laws, man himself is universal. There are no more Jews or Poles, there are men who live in Poland, others who are designated as of "Jewish faith" on their family papers, and agreement is always possible among them as soon as discussion bears on the universal."

"Recall," says Sartre, "the portrait of the philosopher that Plato sketches in the Phaedo: how the disembodied philosopher, pure lover of abstract and universal truth, loses all his individual traits in order to become a *universal look of inquiry*.*

It is precisely this sort of disincarnation that certain Jews seek. The best way to feel oneself no longer a Jew is to reason, for reasoning is valid for all and can be retraced by all. There is not a Jewish way of mathematics; the Jewish mathematician becomes a universal man when he reasons and the anti-Semite who follows his reasoning becomes his brother, despite his own resistance" (emphasis added).

"Thus the rationalism to which the inauthentic Jew adheres so passionately is ['the royal road to flight'], an exercise of asceticism and of purification, an escape into the universal.... On a superior level he realizes that accord and assimilation which is denied him on the social level. The choice of rationalism is for him the choice of a human destiny and a human nature." The inauthentic Jew "has a taste for pure intelligence ... he loves to exercise it with reference to anything and everything.... There is in the Jew a sort of impassioned imperialism of reason: for he wishes not only to convince others that he is right; his goal is that there is an absolute and unconditional value to rationalism. He feels himself to be a missionary of the universal.... He asserts the 'catholicity' of the rational, an instrument by which to attain to the truth and establish a spiritual bond among men. It is not by chance that Leon Brunschvicg, a Jewish philosopher [and once again Sartre could have been speaking directly to Lévi-Strauss] brings together in his writings the progress of reason and the progress of *unification* [unification of ideas, unification of men]."

The defense of the Jew against the irrational powers arrayed against him—tradition, race, national destiny, instinct—is to make

---

* For an explicit, if unwitting, confirmation of Sartre's characterization of this kind of inauthenticity, see the concluding chapter of *World on the Wane*.

them vanish; "magic, unreason, everything that cannot be explained on the basis of universal principles, *everything that betrays a tendency to the singular and exceptional*" is challenged by the Jew. "He is distrustful on principle of those totalities which the Christian mind from time to time produces. . . " (emphasis added).

"What the Jew wishes to destroy is strictly localized." [In this context Lévi-Strauss's universalistic pessimism should be noted, along with his fascination with the primitive which he nonetheless believes has been destroyed]. "It is the ensemble of irrational values that present themselves to immediate cognition without proof. . . . "

"Before any debate he wishes agreement on the principles with which the disputants start; by means of this preliminary agreement, he offers to construct a human order based on the universality of human nature." So, deduces Sartre, "the Jew has a marked inclination to believe that the worst difficulties can be resolved by reason; he does not see the irrational, the magical, the concrete and particular nuance; he does not believe in singularities of sentiment. By a very understandable defense reaction this man who lives by the opinion that others have of him tries to deny the value of opinion. He is tempted to apply to men the reasoning which is suited to objects; he moves toward the analytic rationalism of the engineer . . . " not because he is formed or attracted by objects, but because he is rejected by men. *And the analytic psychology he constructs permits him readily to reduce the synthetic structures of consciousness to a play of interest, to the composition of appetites, to the algebraic sum of tendencies*"* (italics added).

But all this, says Sartre, is infused with a naïveté, a faith in sweet reason, a mildness of temperament, a passion against violence, "a sense of justice . . . which they put up as their sole defense against a hostile, brutal, and unjust society, [and] is perhaps the best part of the message they bring to us and the true mark of their greatness." Moreover, "completely given over to rationalizing the world," this understandably inauthentic Jew, this

---

* Recall the title of the first volume of the *Mythologiques: The Raw and the Cooked*, and note also Lévi-Strauss's method which involves us in an algebraic play of interests.

rationalist to the bitter end, "is constantly overwhelmed by a fresh and powerful mass of passions and emotions. . . . There is a sincerity, a youth, a warmth in the manifestations of friendship of the Jew that one will rarely find in a Christian, hardened as the latter is by tradition and ceremony." "This," concludes Sartre, "is what gives such a disarming character to Jewish suffering, the most overwhelming of sufferings." Hence the paradox between Jewish feeling, on the one hand, and the Jew who, in fleeing from himself, "*conceives of psychological processes as mechanical functionings. . .* " (emphasis added).

Sartre's Alternative

Yet, for Sartre, there is an alternative to what I would call the "creative" inauthenticity of the rationalist Jew, an inauthenticity which, he tells us, the Gentile world is responsible for stimulating, and which the Gentile has no right to criticize. The Jews may choose to be authentic, although that is not the business of the Gentile; the latter is no less guilty for that. Jewish authenticity consists in choosing oneself as Jew, and abandoning "*the myth of the universal man.*" Thus the Jew knows himself and wills himself into history as a historical and damned creature. "*He understands that society is bad*; for the naïve monism of the inauthentic Jew he substitutes a social pluralism. He knows that he is one who stands apart, untouchable, scorned, proscribed—and it is as such that he asserts his being. At once he gives up his rationalist optimism [or pessimism] . . . for he accepts the obligation to live in a situation that is defined precisely by the fact that it is unlivable; he derives his pride from his humiliation. . . " (emphasis added).

"The authentic Jew *makes himself a Jew*, in the face of all and against all . . . at one stroke the Jew, like any authentic man, escapes description. The common characteristics that we have attributed to the inauthentic Jews emanate from their common inauthenticity. We shall encounter none of them in the authentic Jew; he is what he makes himself, that is all that can be said. In this isolation to which he has consented, he becomes again a man, a whole man, with the metaphysical horizons that go with the condition of man" (emphasis added). But, Sartre states finally, this cannot solve the social and political problem of the Jews as a group; only the moral problem of the individual. And here one may disagree, for the solution of the moral problem is only one phase of the dialectic, the other phase being the working towards the solution of the political and social problem; they cannot be resolved independently.

The Implications for the Understanding of Man

This lengthy consideration of Sartre's argument of 1946 which, I repeat, is directed against all hyperrational, analytic, abstract, reductive and scientistic modes of conceiving the world, throws into brilliant relief, anticipates the philosophical antagonism between himself and Lévi-Strauss. And it bears directly on the decisive situation of Lévi-Strauss among the Western intelligentsia. As an anthropologist, he represents the observer incarnate, disengaged, realizing our society's catastrophic assumption that man can be totally objectified by man. This is the denouement of the positivist potential of eighteenth-century thought: the detached, academic scientist classifying a disintegrating phenomenon—an atom, a primitive people.

Sartre understood this also: "they (the structuralists) will not have any transcendence or at least any transcendence made by men. We have returned to positivism but it is no longer a positivism of facts, but a positivism of signs. There are totalities, structural ensembles, constituted through man whose unique function it is to decipher them."[46]

For Lévi-Strauss to have achieved this so completely represents a triumph of inauthenticity. In his work he has presented us with the gift of his being, an unwitting autobiography. It is perfectly understandable then why so little of Lévi-Strauss exists in his "confession," *Tristes Tropiques*, and why so much of him intrudes into his "scientific" construction. We should honor his work, understand the circumstances of its creation, marvel at its consistency, and accept the sacrifice, but finally we must reject the claims made for it.

Authentic anthropologists will not make careers out of their alienation, but will understand it as a specific instance of a pathological condition, demanding political commitment and action; that is, they will reject the reified identity: "anthropologist." Yet, anthropology has given us the contrast between primitive and civilized peoples, which a Marxist will take as the root of the socialist possibility; and anthropology has led us to appreciate the subtle variety of cultures. It remains for us, under the imperative of Rousseau, to use our insights, and oppose the critical potential of our intellectual heritage to the structuralist command of its academic themes. We will understand ourselves and our world only by seeking to change ourselves and our world—concretely, historically, dialectically. Man cannot be known abstractly as man; man is a constitution, a creation, and the revolution that our civilization demands, demands our full attention. We are impelled to this revolution by the recognition of our inauthenticity, that lies like a shadow upon black and white, Jew and Gentile, male and female; obscuring identity, denying self, objectifying thought and reducing the universe to an equation.

11

WHAT HISTORY IS

To know in the scientific sense means, ultimately, to-have-power-over. To the degree that human beings are authentic persons, unique and self-creating, they cannot be scientifically known.

—W.H. Auden

Everything that happens in nature or society, happens as history. More specifically, all human events are fundamentally historical. But I must acknowledge at once that these events are not of equal importance; human affairs are often trivial, or apparently chaotic. The patterns are there but they are so intricate and private that it demands a divine eye to sort them out; they crisscross through our daily lives; they happen as history but they have no historical gender. No socially critical turn of events hinges upon them, but this is not, as we shall see, because the behavior of "mere" individuals is involved.

A convenient point of departure is the following individual analogy. Should citizen X be killed crossing the street, the event would be called an "accident," a "chance" occurrence; and it would be historically irrelevant, although a sad business for all concerned. But in what sense is the fate of citizen X an accident? And why is it historically irrelevant? I shall consider these, in a sense related, questions separately.

First, the event may be viewed as an accident descriptively, in the sense of being a casualty. The fact that it is "unexpected" or "unpredictable" does not, on that account alone, lead us to classify it in any particular way. Many events are equally unforeseen, but we do not call them "accidents." If we did, then most of the future would have to be regarded an accident of the present. In such a view the life of the individual or the group would be almost wholly determined and equally unpredictable, an attitude that is untenable, and a point to which I shall return. Moreover, the manner of citizen X's dying is not without precedent; it is less unpredictable than a good many other events. Traffic fatalities are relatively common; rather intricate rules and regulations operate in order to prevent them; and so on. Nor is the death of citizen X an accident in the sense that it is isolated, intrusive or merely random, without immediate "cause." On the contrary a superhuman eye could detect its position in a marvelously involved, if apparently meaningless, pattern. Citizen X and the automobile may be said to have collided at a particular time and place, at the intersection of a practically infinite sequence of events, to which the accident provides a "nonsensical" climax.

All this is simple enough. Why then, supposing that citizen X did not commit suicide, that he and the driver were obeying regulations and that both were exercising reasonable judgment— for to suppose anything less would be to introduce the element of responsibility, and thus, volition—why then do we persist in defining the death of citizen X as an "accident?" The answer has already been implied. It is an accident, first and foremost, because it was *beyond human control* not because it seemed random or may have been more or less unpredictable or unexpected. Citizen X's accident falls into that class of events which seems always and everywhere to have been designated "acts of God." This does not mean literally that no human decisions preceded the death of citizen X; on the contrary, an infinite number of decisions is implicated. But the climax of these decisions was involitional, although, in this case, well within the category of what is known to be possible. Citizen X knew that he conceivably *could* be killed crossing the street, and the driver of the automobile was aware of the possibility of striking a pedestrian. In retrospect, then, the accident became part of a patterned series of historical occurrences. Indeed, one is tempted to state that the accident *created* the pattern, that is, the last event made everything immediately preceding it and connected with it significant and visible within a small social radius.

But the aspect of citizen X's accident that interests us most is that it was inevitable. This may sound a paradox, but all true accidents are inevitable (that is, literally unavoidable) and thus, to the human consciousness, nonsensical or absurd, the conclusion of a sequence of hidden events beyond human control. Accidents can be most broadly defined, then, as unintended, inevitable events which affect or determine the existence of individuals and the fate of groups. Of course, it does not logically follow that because all accidents are inevitable, everything that is inevitable is an accident. But I am not arguing in terms of a perfectly abstract logic; the human perception is decisive and there is a fundamental sense in which we perceive the accidental and inevitable as coterminous. That is, we apprehend both accidents and inevitabilities as fated and, either metaphorically or literally, as "acts of God," thus echoing the ancient attribution of intent to caused but incomprehensible occurrences.

This brings me to a brief consideration of natural history. All natural events are, of course, historical events. Natural history overlaps with, interpenetrates and is often experienced in the same way as, but cannot be equated with, human history. Natural history, to the extent that it is not mastered or negated by human history, is perceived as inevitable. Birth, death, hunger, the rotation of the earth, fatigue, the weather—all those natural or physical conditions which remain beyond human control are normally accepted as aspects of our fate. From the standpoint of the human will, the world of nature may be enjoyed, accepted or adapted to, but it remains a vast accident, unintended (except by God for those who believe in God) and inevitable. For us, the imperatives of nature have the drastic inevitability of accidents. This, of course, is precisely the opposite of saying that natural history is in itself a question of chance. For chance conventionally denotes the property of being undetermined. In the more radical Peircian sense, chance being a cause itself is itself uncaused, while accident is absence of intention linked to the impossibility of control and is thus wholly determined. Even Cournot's conservative conception of chance (following Aristotle) as a coincidence of two causally determined series of events, permits us to distinguish it from accident, since in accident, the "coincidence" must itself be seen as completely determined, or caused. In short, chance is the antithesis of accident, although the two words are commonly used synonymously.

Because we have proposed that the death of a pedestrian is a perfect accident (perhaps the driver suffered a minor stroke, perhaps sunlight reflected on metal blinded both), it assumes the aspect of an event in natural history although it occurred in human history. That is, citizen X's mishap is experienced as an inevitable event, as, say a sudden change in the weather would be, in the face of which all concerned are helpless. For, to extend the analogy, the manner of citizen X's dying is as absolutely uncontrollable as the rising or the setting of the sun. There is, of course, this objective difference between certain inevitable events happening in nature and perfect human accidents: many (by no means all) natural events are, in the particular case, repetitive and, within a small margin of error, predictable. They occur in cycles that occur as history but which may fluctuate only slightly over a given period of humanly scaled time. And once we admit that the universe has a history, we must recognize that none of its laws can be absolute. However, similarities and distinctions of this character could be pressed indefinitely; for example, general classes of accidents are predictable; specific accidents are not. On the other hand, even the cyclic movements of the stars are not exactly predictable. The major point has already been made; on the critical score of inevitability (more precisely lack of human intention plus lack of control), accidents can be assimilated to natural history. They are, so to speak, "given."

This perception is expressed in ordinary idioms. Soldiers during the First World War were supposed to have said that if a bullet had your name on it you were done for—so why worry? Thus they merged the accidental and the inevitable; in trying to convert a human event, which is always in some degree contingent, into a purely natural event, which is inevitable, they perhaps succeeded in reducing anxiety. That is, from the soldiers' point of view, the event might just as well have been a natural one. The diminution of anxiety was a normal accompaniment of an authentically felt denial of responsibility.

Similarly, romantic lovers characteristically say that it was "fated" or inevitable that they should have met; the greater the insistence on inevitability, the more "accidental" the meeting is likely to have been, until we reach the point of the absolute inevitability of the perfectly romantic "chance" encounter, experienced as an imperative of natural history. In the same vein, the recourse to astrology literally recognizes the identity of accident and inevitable event, both for individuals and groups and then invokes, aptly enough, a psuedo-natural historical argument, the conjunctions of the planets, in order to advise men or explain what they do.

THE SUPER-ORGANIC AND OTHER ILLUSIONS

On a more sophisticated level, students of society who perceive human history as fate and history as accident, are retailing identical conceptions. Kroeber, for example, argued that cultural history must be studied as if it were an extension of natural history.[1] It follows that the fact of human volition is one that Kroeber struggled with throughout his life, never reaching any coherent conclusion. For Kroeber, culture was a cumulative accident, a sort of vast coral structure exuded by individual polyps (to use his well known analogy), who have little sense, and less control, of the whole.[2] The human person is free, Kroeber believed, only in that he can choose between "alternatives provided by the culture," as one chooses a vocation. The reification of culture seems here a plausible metaphor, but the view is at once too historically restricted, and too relativistic. It is too restricted because it does not give sufficient weight to the human decisions which create the alternatives that are open to choice; it is too relative because it does not grasp the recurrent decisions which men have had to make in all cultures. And it gives no credence to the capacity of the human mind to stand outside of its particular tradition, to be skeptical or passionate. Nor, of course, does Kroeber's attitude adequately account for the dynamics of groups, particularly of the decisive relationships between individuals who have been members of conflicting classes and estates since the rise of civilization, of political society.

Even the familiar argument about the "inevitability" of a language relative to its individual speakers becomes ambiguous on closer inspection. Any given language may be spoken with great flexibility; words, idioms and dialects are constantly being invented and then lost again. Each speaker shapes the language in a subtly personal way; rhythm, volume, pitch, juxtaposition of words, style, vary widely and significantly from person to person. All they share is a code that appears the more flexible, the more closely we scrutinize it. Speech is not only a broadly societal but a familial and personal series of experiences and symbols. Language itself is an invention; what could be more arbitrary, more *decisive* than the association of a particular sound with a particular thing or event. Such an invention, such a group of specific correlations is the very opposite of an accident; it is hardly inevitable.

More generally, to suppose that language *had* to be developed because it was something that men were *capable* of doing is to indulge in an obvious teleology. Culture as accident, as inevitability and as teleology, these comprise a single condition. It must be acknowledged, of course, that this *may* be the human condition but, if so, the human race has been living in a vast solipsistic illusion. Social science would then be a more sectarian source of amusement and a simpler discipline than even its enemies imagine. Moreover, dramatic art would not exist, and meaning lack any human dimension, for both comdey and tragedy emerge from the publicly consequential and volitional struggle for identity; they are historical and existential phenomena. I conclude that history is and always has been a matter of experiment and choice, even when unwitting. In human history there are no absolute imperatives; even at those points where it cross-sects with natural history, the problem of how we meet our fate defines our freedom. But who can determine the precise moment in the life of the person or of the society when the realm of necessity passes into the realm of freedom.

Just as Kroeber seems to have adopted the influential position that culture is an aspect of natural history, in effect, an accident, the trajectory of Leslie White's approach is even more extreme, in the same direction. But the immediate sources are different. White's work either converges to or results from two major movements. The first is eighteenth century mechanical material- ism, which was the logical extension of the hyper-rationalistic theme in the European and American Enlightenment. The second, a complex elaboration of the Enlightenment, is mechanistic materialism, a major postlude of Marxism, one variant of which persisted throughout the late 1920s in the Soviet Union in opposition to the reigning dialectician, Deborin, who was himself eclipsed in 1930.³ After 1930, whatever significance philosophy may have had was wholly reduced by Stalinism. The mechanists, as they were called, inherited the vulgar materialist idea of rigid determinism, which is a form of diabolism, since it denies human dignity and makes of man a brief particle created and obliterated in a social cyclotron. The mechanists also tried to erase all philosophic thought, which they derided as pre-scientific, while attempting relentlessly to apply the analytic methods and concepts of the natural and physical sciences to human affairs. For them, the sum of the findings of the positive sciences equalled the human view of the universe, but this was a mechanical sum, disconnected from any integrated view of the whole, which demands intelligent traffic with metaphysics. Naturally, their conception was marked by an unconcern with the "human agency" which they considered some kind of a constant amenable to endless social manipulation, a theoretical idea with obviously sinister practical implications, no matter the intent of the theorists. For the mechanistic materialists, as for the mechanical materialists that preceded them, social and cultural inquiry had become a branch of natural science, that is, it had been assimilated to natural history. This seems identical with the implications of White's position, except that White maintains a convenient category of the "historical" conceived as the realm of the "accidental." Formally put, for White culture is inevitable, history is accidental. This assumes, of course, that the inevitable and the accidental are quite distinct categories. But, as we have seen, each can be assimilated to the other; thus if White's definition of history is to mean anything at all, it would have to embrace the "random" or "uncaused" in the Peircian sense in which he patently does not believe. Or alternatively, he would have to confine history to the personal-volitional, that is, to the very opposite of the accidental, as here defined, which contradicts his systematics as a whole. In other words, White's definition of history is, in the perspective of this paper, no more than a logical and formal imperative of a system sprung from a mechanically materialistic root; it is an insubstantial, and radically inconsistent definition (if convenient) under which all that is distinctively human can be filed and forgotten.

For White, then, culture is an abstraction, functioning through laws of its own in which the human agency can be considered a relatively passive and predictable participant or vehicle.[4] As Marc Bloch said of Durkheim, social theorists of this type "Shut up the human facts which they condemn as the most superficial and capricious of all." They, and their epigones, operating on what they choose to call a high level of abstraction, in pursuit of what may be more fruitfully termed an irresponsible objectivity, create "homo-religiosus, homo-economicus, homo-politicus and all that rigmarole of Latinized men, the list of which we could string out indefinitely [and we are] in grave danger of mistaking them for something else than they really are; phantoms, which are convenient providing they do not become nuisances. The man of flesh and bone, reuniting them all simultaneously is the only real being."[5] Or, as Marx put it: "History does nothing, it possesses no colossal riches. It fights no fight. It is rather man—real, living man, who acts, possesses and fights in everything. History is nothing but the activity of man's pursuit of his ends."[6]

The current concept of culture which finds its logical level in the idea of culturology is merely an imprecise and arbitrary way of looking at history. It has no dynamic of its own; to confuse it with reality is to ignore what Bloch terms the "interrelations, confusions and infections of human consciousness." It is a bowdlerization of Tylor, who never reified culture but merely sought to chart the components and explore certain of their relationships.

But above all it is an academic way of reflecting the abstractionism and mechanism of our time, of getting around the risk and decision of the human condition. For history is decision. Every act is first and foremost an historical event; only after it is living history can it become a frozen specimen, categorically subsumed and subject to abstract analysis—in short, material for the culturologists. Indeed, history is not a category at all but an *attribute* of events. It is the state of being of events and cannot be dissociated from them.

A social structure is, for example, a series of repetitive acts, a repetitive process functioning in a certain direction. Or, it might be more elaborately defined as a culturally learned and structured sequence of acts to which human beings become more or less accustomed in the effort to achieve economic, social and psychological viability. By exchanging terms in appropriate places in this cumbersome statement, we might similarly define economic structure, cultural pattern or psychological syndrome. That is to say, social and economic structures, cultural patterns, and psychological syndromes represent levels of abstraction which are reified and then divorced from each other by academic specialists for analytic purposes. But any synthetic attempt must return to the whole act or event, from which the various abstract categories are distilled; it must consider the problem of volition, of contingency; it must return, in short, to history, either consciously to affect the course of events or to understand them and it may well be that one effort depends upon the other.

History is both the study and the actual occurrence of events—of their initiation and resolution and their concrete connections. Moreover, history is never merely predictable, which may be one reason why social scientists prefer to study "something else," as if there were something else to study. It is an embarrassing truth that the most exhaustive and abstract analyses do not enable us to look into the future with any precision, because the future, within the limits set by natural history, is a matter of choice. For this reason, most prophets, who understand and celebrate human decision, have been closer to an appreciation of the human condition than most scientists. The future is always the realization of one possibility among many; it is never certain. But this is not to deny that there may be insights that are, as Paul Radin put it, ultimate for man, and, of course, there are subtle imperatives in man's nature (in addition to the obvious ones) which demand social expression, and are frustrated at the risk of destroying society itself.

Only if we regard the future as accident could it take on that character of inevitability which would make it the proper field of abstract science; and if the future is determined, past and present are also. In short, the only perfect social science would be a science of perfect accidents. And that is not merely a nominal contradiction but an actual impossibility.

Even the past in many of its aspects is never wholly past, except for the actors who have created it in the first place. Our behavior in the present, our making of immediate history, conditions our reading of more remote history; and, of course, this statement has its obverse. Our present acts affect our interpretations of the past not only by changing our opinions but by changing the total context in which past events now exist. This is what Marc Bloch implied, when he argued that history is a landscape whose unity exists only in the mind of the beholder. In a sense then, the past is always waiting to be recognized and completed by us. To grasp the meaning of any happening anywhere, any time, requires a reconstructive act of the imagination, simultaneously true to our stated purposes and faithful to the spirit of the object with which we are actively engaged, that is, which is in accord with the "facts." In the end, we live in the history we choose to make and that is salvation, or punishment, enough.

White, then, along with Kroeber, views culture as man's collective fate, as sui-generis, as the growing edge of natural history and therefore, as an *accident*. While Kroeber seemed to have been an idealist, White is a mechanical or mechanistic, as opposed to a dialectical materialist. This latter distinction, which is, of course, familiar to students of the history of thought, warrants a brief recapitulation. The major difference between the varieties of materialism is that the dialecticians emphasize the person in his interaction with the world of nature and the inheritance of history; therefore, they deny the validity of the separation between theory and practice. We can see at once that this is an existential perception. Put another way, human beings not only reflect cultural events but synthesize experience and have the capacity to react in creative and unexpected ways. Or, as Peirce might have expressed it, human groups are capable of creating their own chances. Indeed, the potential for spontaneous action—action that is emergent, rather than merely reactive, determined or conditioned and not reducible to one or more discreet, preceding events, but flowing from their creative clash or combination—is a quintessentially human process. Marx seemed to be aware of this process, and for that reason alone, White, although obviously influenced by Marx, is not a Marxist in the traditional sense at all.

As an *ethnocentric* evolutionist, White is led, wittingly or not, to an expedient standard of moral and scientific "success" in presenting us with the major outlines of cultural development. Morally, he makes no serious effort to distinguish viability, or mere power, from worth. Progress must then be identified with evolution, since we are left with no alternative definition, and the result is a species of social Darwinism wedded to the second law of thermodynamics.

Scientifically, White refuses to recognize that an apparently lawful evolutionary "stage" may be no more than a construct based on the diffusion of a single successful historic case, as Tylor pointed out. But candor compels us to acknowledge that there are insufficient independent cases to make a scientific proposition out of any special theory of social evolution; any special theory must remain a working hypothesis. Nor may we suspend, without becoming prisoners of a shrunken interpretation of the past, our critical inquiry into the nature of "success" in history. As Irving Goldman observed: "Differentiation by variation ... is the very heart of evolutionary doctrine."[7] And that, I would add, demands a constant refinement of our sense of history, including a fully human respect for the triumphs and failures of the past, for its unrealized potential. Such a view cannot be accommodated to any teleological interpretation of cultural development.

Interestingly enough, both Marx and Engels argued time and again against the doctrine of mechanical materialism, equating it with philosophical idealism because of its teleological character; for them, Marxism remained a working hypothesis not a dogma. Moreover, Marx and Engels devoted most of their efforts to the social dynamics of historical change, more exactly to the human groupings (classes) which, they supposed, decided the course of events in conflict or cooperation. But White and his epigones, while acknowledging the priority of Ostwald, and hardly mentioning Marx, seem to reduce this social dimension to the level of material energetics, to one or more laws of cultural thermodynamics.[8] Although they argue for new emergent levels of phenomena, they are, in fact, reductionists.

But the types of determinism implicit in the work of Marx and Engels are of a different order. They all, perhaps, converge in the Hegelian doctrine that freedom lies in the recognition of necessity. In the broadest sense, as adopted by Marx, this can be taken to mean that, in order to be free and desiring to be free, men must act with the fullest possible consciousness of the consequences of their behavior in a world which is assumed to be composed of orderly processes, that is, to have an orderly structure. The latter point signifies no more than that the intention of any given actor may be realizable within the classic framework of cause and effect; it is rather soberly assumed that the world plays no tricks and that things are what they seem.

The first step toward freedom, then, in the Marxist view, is the recognition of a dialectically rational order in nature and society and based on that, the attainment of accurate knowledge of the effects of any given sequence of socially significant acts. The second step is the employment of efficient, revolutionary means to eradicate what are assumed to be the sources of exploitation of man by man, by bringing them into the consciousness of the majority of people through historical analysis of social causation; exploitation is conceived to be fundamentally economic but ramifies through, and interacts with all major phases of cultural activity. The third step is to establish a technically advanced, communist society which, lacking classes and no longer requiring political power or an elaborate division of labor, is presumed to be both good and desirable. In the classic Marxist view, it should be noted, "premature" anarchistic and individualistic expressions are opposed as ineffective, desperate or antisocial. Nature and society are conceived as structures composed of complexly interacting parts, which must be understood in order to be reorganized and reorganized in order to be mastered. The first prerequisite of freedom consists in the acceptance of this total necessary effort; freedom is in this sense the recognition of necessity, and finally, freedom is the actual state of social mastery and individual creativity which inevitably emerges when man emancipates himself from the negative burdens of history. It is worth re-emphasizing that this future condition is conceived to be apolitical, and in a certain sense, ultimately anarchic. But to a thorough and consistent Marxist, anarchism as both a means and an immediate end, is equivalent to bondage, since the anarchist is at the mercy of the social forces which he seeks to escape or ineffectually to control by terroristic or self-isolating methods. Both anarchism and its apparent opposite, the submerging of the person in the collective, are perceived as contrary sides of the same coin and are rejected as equally impotent, since both, in effect, substitute the possibility of real social mastery for an illusion of absolute individualism, in the first instance by the denial of tension between self and society, by personalizing the collective and dehumanizing the person, and in the second instance, by creating a static, theoretically false antithesis between man and society, thus hopelessly exposing the individual to the full force of organized society and crippling any significant effort toward social change.

For Marx, as Tillich has emphasized, and of course for Hegel, the world structure is also of a moral nature.[9] Ultimately, for Marx in particular, freedom could not be divorced from history, precisely because history was conceived as the arena of an active material struggle, in moral form. But he considered the whole history of civilization as predominantly natural history or at best only partially human, since most men, in all strata of society, made choices in what they conceived as personal or group (class) interests, alienated by the exploiting, exploited or pecuniary character of civilized labor from society at large and from themselves. Thus the era of a fully human history initiated, so Marx imagined, by a new organization of the most alienated class—the industrial workers, who had the least to lose—an era in which man freely and consciously directs his behavior toward the social good through the development of individual qualities, has not yet arrived. Nor are there any indications that workers, who are shrinking in number and function, in the "advanced" industrial countries have decided or shall decide to fulfill the Marxist imperative; regimes that define themselves as communist and revolutionary have been established, from 1918 to the present, in "backward," predominantly peasant, areas. Marx believed that an age of freedom beckoned but he did not conceive of it as preordained, that is, inherent in a sequence of cultural events of which man is either the neutral medium or in which he is, in crisis, a predictable actor. Marx made a tremendous effort to reconcile a natural scientific view of history with an existential view of history, primarily through the application of the idea of alienation as a phase in the growth of the civilized human consciousness. This attempt alone divorces his work from that of all vulgar materialists, whether of ancient or modern vintage, and leads also to some very important anthropological questions.[10] Just as Marx was not a reductive materialist, he was not a mechanical behaviorist. Nonetheless, one frequently encountered definition in Marxist anthropology is that man (human nature) is the "ensemble of social relations."[11] This interpretation, which can lead directly to behaviorism, has been the major canon of academic and instrumental psychology in the Soviet Union; and it is entirely likely that a similar definition of man elicited from the work of George Herbert Mead, who was influenced by Hegel, has reinforced the growth of behaviorism in both its social and experimental aspects in the United States. The point is that the sinister use of behavioristic political techniques by the Soviet establishment is not only an immediate imperative of power but is also "substantiated" by a positivistic interpretation of Marx.

However, Marxism is not behaviorism. The definition referred to above must be amended: man is "the ensemble of social relations *and* possibilities." Obviously, the Marxist notion of alienation as social pathology flows from the assumption that there is a nucleus of possibilities in human nature which "the ensemble of social relations" in modern civilization distorts. There is, in short, a normative base in Marxism, what may be called a normative ontology; the morality of Marxism is built into its conception of being. This matter can be put quite simply:

1. All social arrangements are expressions of "human nature."
2. But some social arrangements are better than others.
3. The question is where does that "better" come from.
4. The schematic answer is that it is not fantasized, but has both a historical and an existential source.

Irving Fetscher made a similar point: "Technological thought penetrates even the historical concept itself—and substitutes the notion of infinite progress for Marx's and Engles's notion of the final form of human community which could be achieved in this world."[1 2]

Such a community, I submit, can properly be called a natural society. Its adumbration is primitive society prior to the rise of the state. But there is more to be said on this issue of Marxist ontology. In his third thesis on Feurbach, Marx wrote: "The materialistic doctrine concerning the changing of circumstances and education forgets that the circumstances are changed by man and the educator himself has to be educated."[1 3] And in another place: "It is not history as if she were a person apart that uses men as means to work out her purposes, but history itself is nothing but the activity of men pursuing their purposes."[1 4]

In short, men make circumstances, and as they become more conscious of their positions in society, they are likely to make revolutionary circumstances. This imperative has an impulse, the content of that impulse is Marx's normative notion of human nature. Its result is Marx's normative notion of human society.

In essential respects, then, White's attitude to history is closer to Kroeber's than it is to that of Marx and Engels. Indeed, White and Kroeber, especially White in the critical sense already noted, are closer conceptually to Teilhard de Chardin than they are to other contemporary anthropological theorists. De Chardin was a frank idealist and an extraordinarily subtle evolutionist, to which Julian Huxley has attested, but he avoided history as assiduously as White, fulfilled the promise of the superorganic more richly than Kroeber and adopted a curiously un-Christian view of man, although he was as moral as Hegel.[15] For de Chardin, God, Omega, was the beginning and the end of organic and inorganic evolution; evolution runs a determined course, which de Chardin insisted could be charted scientifically, in terms of emergent cosmic principles. He was, as a theorist, remarkably disinterested in the concrete or existential aspects of human experience. Hence, neither history as act or form nor the inner lives of men, their immediate spiritual lives as distinguished from their ultimate spiritual destinies, seemed to mean very much to him, despite his splendid and abstract imagination, his cosmic piety.

Superorganicists and evolutionary determinists, whether they seize on matter or spirit as a guiding principle, avoid history, avoid men and thus form an awkward brotherhood. White, Kroeber and de Chardin are among its currently eminent members in contemporary anthropology, though minor revisionists can be found in profusion. But the genealogy can be traced back through Hegel to Plato, that is, to the beginnings of our civilization, and the rise of church and academy. Dialectical materialism and existentialism, Marx and Kirkegaard, can be more readily accommodated to each other than can either to the spiritual or material mechanists. It should be remembered that both Kierkegaard and Marx attacked Hegel on different but complementary grounds. Kierkegaard abandoned the abstract system and insisted on spiritual action.[16] Marx maintained the system, while changing its emphasis, but he also insisted on action, although in a political and scientific context, which Kierkegaard would probably have considered irrelevant and may even have denied.

In any event, contemporary American anthropology, faced with the disappearance of primitive peoples and having rationalized the concept of the primitive out of existence, will have to create some new trembling vision of humanity as a metaphysical grounding for the science it supposes itself to be, that is, if it is to assume a virile part in civilized men's search for himself. In this new structure of assumptions, or first principles, the conceptions of history as matter and history as spirit, each within a contingent human context, must somehow be adapted to each other. Or perhaps we shall always have to hold them separate, as antitheses, within a single framework. And certainly we shall have to return to the great modern originators who asked the seminal questions about man from the Renaissance through the end of the nineteenth century (and whose descendants have grown so specialized and withered), in order to reinterpret their insights and rivet them on the human situation. They were more literally anthropologists than most of us who sail under the name.

PARTICULARITY

The death of citizen X is, as we have seen, unavoidable, an accident. It is, therefore, in the perspective of a fully human history an absurd or irrelevant occurrence. But the irrelevance of the event is not a function of the fact that it happens to an individual, nor that it is, in itself, a trivial or major (in this case terminal) occurrence in the life of a person. Citizen X's death is historically irrelevant because it does not affect the lives of enough people in a way which could shift the shape of society at large. In short, the demise of citizen X is an historically neuter accident, but not for the reasons and not in the sense characteristically advanced by culturologists.

Obviously, superorganicists and culturologists, along with most cultural anthropologists, overlook the individual event and actor in the attempt to delineate overall patterns and structures. These are, of course, legitimate efforts, but once they become surrogate for the need to confront the living flux of people making events they are mere academic exercises. The failure to confront the meaningful particular is a reflection of academic pathology, of a falsely objective social science that seeks merely to report or to build some theory which generalizes all human responsibility out of existence and, more seriously in our presently complicated world, helps prevent us from understanding the critical and contingent nature of certain sequences of events.

This echoes Kierkegaard's attitude that Hegel was a buffoon, not, I would add, a conscious clown, a knowing celebrant of human absurdity, but a buffoon, an unconsciously failed identity, because of the obvious discrepancy between his philosphy and the actual mode of his life. And Ortega y Gassett has written of Goethe in a similar vein.[17] Ortega's Goethe was a genius, but he was nonetheless a security-seeking stuffed shirt, the caretaker of an overpowering talent that, had it risked and had it prevailed, would have made him the authentic European artist of modern times rather than the not quite universal man. This breach between the abstract intention and the actual act is, of course, the occasion for modern existentialism; civilization provides these occasions with increasing frequency and the accompanying philosphy is the truest indication of our condition. Contemporary existentialism is the converse of philistinism, of the bourgeois spirit; and only in a philistine civilization, whether capitalist or socialist, could existentialism have developed as a formal and urgent self-conscious mode of thought. For existentialism asks questions that shock and surprise us, questions that modern man everywhere has put aside in the press of commercial and industrial progress, questions of the simplest kind that are the basis for the folklore of all other human cultures.

HISTORY AS CONTINGENCY

Just as the future is the realization of one alternative among many, so the past is only one of many possible pasts. For we must regard each past as the future of its own receding present. Because the past is what it was, does not imply that it had to be that which it became. But to understand such an attitude requires a closer scrutiny of the significance of individuals and of individual events; it demands, in short, that "social science," and anthropology especially, must begin by being interpretive, sophisticated history.

This is what Maitland meant when he predicted that by and by anthropology would have to choose between being history or nothing at all.

The significance of the individual and of the individual event in determining the course of history (and thus the more abstract morphology of culture which interests many anthropologists) can be readily established.

Let us assume that Germany had not been permitted to remilitarize the Rhineland in 1936. Such a prohibition was easily within the power of France and England. Indeed, French diplomats were, at that time, vigorously opposed to the Nazi action. Had they carried the day with their West European allies, especially the British, some other resolution than that of World War II might have been found. Or suppose that Roosevelt, who had the respect and affection of the American people, had decided to assist the Spanish Republicans. A Germany restrained from expanding and thus experiencing an increasing internal pressure, might have descended into a civil conflict in which the socialists rather than the Nazis, deprived of their easy victories on the international front, might have succeeded. And the aggressive character of German Fascism, which precipitated the war, would never have been at issue. Indeed, the omission or change of any critical event in the pattern completed by World War II (and retrospectively, appearing inevitable because of World War II) could have shifted the climax from the war to some other series of happenings. Had the French general staff, for example, been more alert to the superiority of mobile offenses to entrenched defenses, it is even possible that Germany would have been contained and Hitler defeated by 1941. The more minutely one looks into events in France, England, Germany, Russia and the United States from 1914 to 1939, the more apparent it becomes that a decision which might reasonably have been made, could have saved the world its penultimate agony. It would not be difficult to devise a series of charts reconstructing alternative possibilities dependent upon decisions taken during that critical period, but for intelligent readers such an effort would be redundant.

As for the significance of the individual in history, let us regard Hitler. It was not necessary that Hitler be an anti-Semite for him to be a Fascist (Peron, for example, was friendly toward Jews; Mussolini's anti-Semitism was borrowed). The intensity of Hitler's anti-Semitism was both idiosyncratic and a socioeconomic strategy. Such a demoniacal personality could have had other idiosyncratic traits, and he and his government might have devised other socioeconomic strategies than that of making the Jews scapegoats, confiscating their property and thus forging the link between the most debased elements in modern society, a scatalogical shock-troops, and the Nazi Party. Of course anti-Semitism is latent wherever Christians who resent their faith congregate; they tend to project their guilt onto the Jews, who are held responsible for initiating Christianity and then subverting it, thus imposing an intolerable burden on Christians which they themselves have supposedly escaped by being Jewish. The Jews thus become convenient foils for any purpose. But this does not mean that anti-Semitism is inevitably a social disaster.

The significance of Hitler as an individual was for the Jews, critical and catastrophic. Obviously it shifted the morphology of Jewish and European culture.

Or, let us assume that Roosevelt had not died before Leo Szilard's memorandum advising against the use of the atomic bomb on Japan had reached the White House. It was at least possible that Roosevelt's decision would not have been the same as Truman's. The bomb may never have been dropped in anger; and there is a growing body of evidence that it was never a military necessity. The resultant change in the present international atmosphere might be reasonably expected to have been radical indeed. "Co-existence" may have begun a decade or more ago, in a different mood, and without the nuclear threat.

Or let us suppose that Stalin had died and Lenin had lived to designate another heir and perhaps to pursue another policy against the background of a more moderate and helpful attitude by the Allied powers toward revolutionary Russia; Plekhanov, one of Lenin's elders, it should be remembered, had been opposed to Bolshevik extremism and rigidity from the beginning. Any combination of these happenings in several countries could have prevented the present impasse or made it less sinister and put us more constructively in touch with ourselves and each other.

The point is that history is a thread of contingencies, woven by decisions into cultural forms. Moreover, since the rise of civilization, history has grown progressively more universal in its effects, concentrated on specific decisions which now echo instantaneously around the world. Official histories, more precisely, histories conceived by the establishment within a single political society, are no longer possible. Whatever sense may once have been contained in them is now delusive and merely flattering to political vanity. For example, in this perspective the modern world, through the interaction of the major states, may be viewed as responsible for Stalinism, not the evil genius of the Russian people, not domestic Soviet events alone, nor the abstract compulsions of a particular version of "Marxism." In the same way, our civilization is responsible for Nazism, not the constitutional perfidy of the Germans, etc. To begin to be sane, each state must recognize the effects of its actions on every other state. This does not absolve us as individuals, for we are all confronted with existential choices in almost every aspect of our lives in a world which has become a village in circumference, if not yet in substance. Today the actions of any state, in the name of its people, *are* the actions of its people, with their consent or by their default. Thus, should there be a nuclear war, we shall, every last one of us in society who has not risked whatever demands to be risked in the struggle against the many forms of fascism, be responsible. The imperatives of modern history are cruel and perhaps, as Freud indicated, more than we can bear.[18]

These things I learned, once and for all, from observing and associating with the Anaguta, for they have decided not to join the modern world. They move like ghosts on the outskirts of civilization on the high plateau of Northern Nigeria and say *Anaguta mini ma gehri*, "The Anaguta are a basket of water." Their culture crumbles, their population declines, their lands shrink, and as an ethnic entity they change only disintegratively. They accept, they pursue their decline; for them the world ends. We are obliged to ask why have similar, even adjoining, peoples responded differently—although not uniformly—to the stimuli of new conditions? This is a historical question but most significant is the spectacle of a people forming out of their natural, material and spiritual resources, their "fate." That is what history *is* .

EPILOGUE

Kierkegaard, the revolutionary Christian, the most immediate and intimate of critics, defines the present age as the "negative unity of the negative reciprocity of all individuals." In other words, he feels that the present age is a "public" age. In theory, he distinguishes the public from the social, but in actuality he believes that any society formed by unemancipated men would quickly deteriorate into a public. Kierkegaard does not imagine that deformed people could create a community worth caring about: "an association of individuals who are themselves weak is just as disgusting and harmful as the marriage of children." The individual has first to cease being an integer: "only after he acquires an ethical outlook in the face of the whole world . . . can there be any suggestion of really joining together."

This is reminiscent of Nicola Chiarmonte's observation made some years ago, that we leave the cave one by one, or else we do not leave it at all. Kierkegaard, however, is simply not interested in the social dimension of revolution. For him, a society that worked would have to be transparent; men would have to be able to look through it to God. For Kierkegaard, a personal movement is implied in the progression from a public to a social to a sacred existence. This complements the historical sequence from sacred to public societies, which in one form or another has been a salient anthropological, sociological, psychological and theological assumption in the Western tradition. The basis of Kierkegaard and Marx's preoccupation with the concept of the primitive lies in the social, personal and historical meaning of this movement. As

Lawrence Krader has reaffirmed, Marx conceived of primitive society as *the* critique of civilization—the theme of this book.

But what concerns us here is the conservative definition of the situation. The God-intoxicated conservatives believe that a society which permits its members fully to express the ambiguity of despair and faith while exploring the limits of human association does not need to bother very much about culture in the ordinary use of the term, that is, the artifacts of culture, which they dismiss as commodities. For faith, culture as communion, can dispense with culture as commodity; the signs and symbols of faith are spiritual, ineffable, and faith is, if not the enemy, at least the inquisitor of change. The road from spiritual conservatism to the index, Plato's road, is both direct and logical.

The first and final argument for *conventional* cultural conservatism which reflects but does not embody such spiritual absolutism —is that it leans toward the existing Establishment, not as the vessel of faith, but because it provides a certain room for sacred behavior relative to any immediately apprehended alternative. When T.S. Eliot wrote that human needs cannot be fully realized in human relations, he seemed to share the cryptic notion of the young Marx that communism, the ultimate form of society, is not the goal but the means for man's further understanding of society itself. But Eliot, of course, was expressing a conventional skepticism towards contemporary social programming.

In our present age, a century after Kierkegaard, cultural conservatism is drawing its energy from its ambivalence, is gaining momentum. It is the salient mood of both the counterculture and its most principled antagonists, the critical cultural conservatives on the near side of the Establishment. It is precisely this split between the two types of conservatism that needs to be understood, if we are to grasp the present dilemma. Some of the best-intentioned critics are terrified by the "counterculture" which is a pandemic reaction to our society—both as a lifestyle, and as a rather amorphous set of institutions. The people I refer to are not reactionaries; they are trying to protect the sacred spaces in which they live against the sometimes brutal demystifications of the counterculture. Simultaneously, they are busy negotiating their survival in one or another bureaucratic hierarchy—the universities, the communications industry, and so on. And their selective strategy for survival clashes with the all-out assault maintained by the counterculture in the name of its own survival.

What the critics fear, of course, is that Fascism could be catalyzed by provocative countercultural behavior, leading to the increasing rigidity and repressiveness of the Establishment, in which atmosphere they would no longer prosper, even to the modest degree that they do at present. That fear, however, implies a seriously inadequate definition of Fascism, for the danger is greater, more immediate and more complex than many political liberals, or, for that matter, radicals appear to believe.

Fascism is grounded in state capitalism, bureaucratic autonomy and class collaboration; its goal is the "integration" of all into the hierarchical system, by reducing persons to integers. Racism and sexism may or may not be adopted as techniques, but they are not essential to the Fascist process. That process can be defined as the seismic, almost unconscious social movement that occurs when a population that has been regimented by bureaucracies finds distorted affective release, in turn tolerated by the Establishment which created the initial need for such expression. The emotions, being captive, become dissociated, from significant subjects, become discontinuous pseudo-experiences, and the social system in which they function becomes self-perpetuating, tautological.

Jean Genêt, who understands this perfectly, commented on his experiences in Nazi Germany, from which he fled: "If I steal here I perform no singular deed that might fulfill me. I obey the customary order. I do not destroy it. I am not committing evil. I am not upsetting anything. The outrageous is impossible. I am stealing in the void." And, as Richard Coe properly concluded, "To break a law within a society of outlaws, Genêt felt, was not only useless—since there was no sense of transgression, no satisfaction in opposing an established hierarchy and discipline— but, more serious still, the revolt would fail to produce the calculated reaction ... in Hitler's Germany, Genêt felt suddenly free, and so he ran away as fast as possible."

Fascism is epitomized in the modern fragmented individual, finding a random place in the disciplined mob, prepared to behave under command at one moment and permitted to explode in nihilistic fury the next. The goose step, the time clock, the inhuman precisions of Nazi Germany are the converse of the orgiastic behavior of the Nazi mobs roaming the streets in search of prey. They were also the converse of the clinically definable habits of the Nazi leadership (the quasi bohemian aspects of the Nazi movement are well known). One phenomenon reinforced the other—this structured and unresolved tension characterizes Fascism. In this sense, all modern state structures rooted in the Western experience, including the Soviet Union, such totalizing structures are chronically Fascist, and there is always and everywhere the danger of a flare-up of nuclear dimension, obliterating everything.

But the conventional cultural conservative does not realize that, just as he negotiates his survival within the Establishment, thus committing political suicide, so the countercultural conservative may well do the same thing and for the same apparent reason namely, to find a small sacred space in which to act out his alternate lifestyle. By abdicating politics, he mystifies the hierarchy as a community. It is interesting to realize that this potential accommodation between the collective structure and the counterculture was noted by Mayor Daley of Chicago some time ago. In defending the young, he stated that beards were a sign of spirituality, that idealism was a fine thing, that this country couldn't get along without it, and so on. He concluded that, so long as they did not attack the police, young people like those who were in Chicago during the Democratic National convention in 1968 were always welcome back. Similarly, participants in the Woodstock Festival were praised by local residents, bus companies, newspapers and international corporations for their capacity to act out their alternative lifestyles without compromising the Establishment.

What I am getting at is that the link—let us call it the Mylai link—between the bureaucratic personality and affective dissociation, the link that leads to murder at a great psychic distance no matter what the proximity of the victim, is not fortuitous, but necessary for the ultimate success of the system, even though it means the destruction of the counterculture's potential. Once the articulation between the Establishment and its apparent opposite occurs, each is sustained by the flow of energy between them; the circuit then accelerates and can be tactically manipulated to keep the system homeostatic. Thus the cultural conservative has a point in his terror of Fascism, although his sense of it as a punitive backlash is faulty; and although his preferred course of action reinforces the enemy he senses. For the cultural conservative would like to stay where he is, still able to exercise reason, still able to believe, still sensitive to the hierarchy of values which for him defines human nature. But he cannot stay where he is. By perceiving the counterculture as a threat to his living space and his values, he can hardly avoid contributing to the repressiveness of the Establishment, while he avoids reflecting on the consequences of his immediate position.

That is the existential dilemma of the cultural conservative. But if it is his dilemma, it is a dilemma for radicals also. His decisions, or lack of them, affect us all. Therefore, one asks of the cultural conservative that he concentrate his fire on the Establishment, that he understand the warning against provocation as terrorism, and the acceptance of it a sign of self-defeat. Let him attack and analyze the corporate structure he knows so well and thus help break down its potential link with the counterculture which, he should remember, is not confined to communes and campuses, but is also pursued by bank clerks after hours. Above all, what the conventional cultural conservative does not understand is that the counterculture is a deeply conservative movement precisely because it is so radical. It represents a form of neo-primitivist striving, proclaiming the sacredness of life, communal forms of society, the esthetic dimension of human nature, the continuity with nature at large and culture as ritual. Perhaps the conventional cultural conservative will listen to T.S. Eliot who, in 1939, anticipated my point in his "Conformity to Nature":

It may be observed that the natural life and the supernatural life have a conformity to each other which neither has with the mechanistic life. . . .

We are being made aware that the organization of society on the principle of private profit, as well as public destruction, is leading both to the deformation of humanity by unregulated industrialism, and to the exhaustion of natural resources, and that a good deal of our material progress is a progress for which succeeding generations may have to pay dearly. I need only mention, as an instance now very much before the public eye, the results of "soil-erosion"—the exploitation of the earth, on a vast scale for two generations, for commercial profit: immediate benefits leading to dearth and desert. I would not have it thought that I condemn a society because of its material ruin, for that would be to make its material success a sufficient test of its excellence; I mean only that a wrong attitude towards nature implies somewhere, a wrong attitude towards God, and that the consequence is an inevitable doom. For a long time we have believed in nothing but the values arising in a mechanized, commercialized, urbanized way of life: it would be as well for us to face the permanent conditions upon which God allows us to live upon this planet. And without sentimentalizing the life of the savage, we might practice the humility to observe, in some of the societies upon which we look down as primitive or backward, the operation of a social-religious-artistic complex which we should emulate upon a higher plane. We have been accustomed to regard "progress" as always integral; and have yet to learn that it is only by an effort and a discipline, greater than society has yet seen the need of imposing upon itself, that material knowledge and power is gained without loss of spiritual knowledge and power. *The struggle to recover the sense of relation to nature and to God, the recognition that even the most primitive feelings should be part of our heritage, seems to me to be the explanation and justification of the life of D.H. Lawrence, and the excuse for his aberrations.* But we need not only to learn how to look at the world with the eyes of a Mexican Indian—and I hardly think that Lawrence succeeded—and we certainly cannot afford to stop there. We need to know how to see the world as the Christian Fathers saw it; and the purpose of reascending to origins is that we should be able to return, with greater spiritual knowledge, to our own situation. We need to recover the sense of religious fear, so that it may be overcome by religious hope.

Both the cultural and countercultural conservatives are searching for sacred spaces in which to live, are trying to recreate culture as communion. If either group, as a consequence of its fear of the other, is captured by the Establishment, we will·have acute Fascism. Their sacred spaces will turn out to be interstices. But perhaps they can come to terms with each other, uniting to fight against the Establishment; the lessons of history are writ large enough for all types of conservatives to understand. In any event, the task for radicals remains the same: it is to rebuild an authentic politics—not absolutist, but dialectical, Marxist.

NOTES

1. INTRODUCTION: CIVILIZATION AND PROGRESS (1-48)

1. The economic contradictions are of course well known and have been dealt with in numerous works. See Myrdal, Baran, et al.

2. The Russian experience epitomizes the results of forced modernization on a gigantic scale. The party elites created a new society—and a modern working class—and then, became their prophet. The Soviet Union may now be ready for a socialist revolution. Several of the so-called Trotskyist critiques are relevant here.

3. ANTHROPOLOGY IN QUESTION (93-115)

1. Claude Lévi-Strauss, "Anthropology: Its Achievement and Future," *Current Anthropology*, vol. 7 (1966): 126.

2. Personal communication.

3. Claude Lévi-Strauss, *A World on the Wane (Tristes Tropiques)*, trans. John Russell (New York: Criterion 1961), p. 384 ff.

4. Ruth Benedict, Lecture at Columbia University, March 11, 1948.

5. Lévi-Strauss, *A World on the Wane*, p. 397.

6. Claude Lévi-Strauss, "A Confrontation," *New Left Review*, no. 62 (1970): 57-74.

7. Lévi-Strauss, "Anthropology," p. 126.

8. Jean Jacques Rousseau, *The First and Second Discourses*, ed. R.D. Masters (New York: St. Martin's Press, 1964), p. 114.

9. Jean Conilh, "A Confrontation," *New Left Review*, no. 62 (1970): 57-74.

10. Rousseau, *The First and Second Discourses*, p. 210.

11. Vernon Venable, *Human Nature: The Marxian View* (New York: Knopf 1946), pp. 151-71.

12. Rudi Supek, "Sociology and Marxism," *International Journal of Sociology*, vol. 1, no. 1 : 39.

13. Ibid., p. 39.

14. Supek, "Sociology and Marxism," *International Journal of Sociology*, p. 32.

15. Frederick Engels, *The Origin of the Family, Private Property and the State* (Chicago: Charles H. Kerr, 1902), pp. 117-19.

16. Karl Marx, *Pre-Capitalist Economic Formations*, ed. E.J. Hobsbawm (New York: International Publishers, 1965), p. 49. ff.

17. Paul Radin, *The Method and Theory of Ethnology (An Essay in Criticism)* (New York: Basic Books, 1966).

18. Rousseau, *The First and Second Discourses*, p. 93.

19. Robert Lowie, *Primitive Religion* (New York: Liveright, 1948), p. 335.

20. *New York Times*, April 18, 1971, p. 66.

4. THE SEARCH FOR THE PRIMITIVE (116-175)

1. Roderick Seidenberg, *Posthistoric Man* (Boston: Beacon, 1957).

2. William Morton Wheeler, *Emergent Evolution and the Development of Societies* (New York: Norton, 1928), p. 44.

3. Stanley Diamond, *Dahomey: A Proto-state in West Africa* (Ph.D. diss., Columbia University, 1951; University of Michigan Microfilms), pp. 32-76.

4. Arthur O. Lovejoy, *Essays in the History of Ideas* (New York: Putnam, 1960), pp. 29-37.

5. K. Oberg, "The Kingdom of Ankole in Uganda," in *African Political Systems*, eds. M. Fertes and F.E. Evans-Pritchard (London: Oxford University Press, 1955), pp. 121-61.

6. Marc Bloch, *Feudal Society* (Chicago: University of Chicago Press, 1961), p. 445.

7. Søren Kierkegaard, *Concluding Unscientific Postscript to the Philosophical Fragments*, ed. Walter Lowrie (Princeton: Princeton University Press and American-Scandinavian Foundation, 1941).

8. A.W. Hoernle, "The Expression of the Social Value of Water among the Naman of South-West Africa," *South African Journal of Science*, vol. 20 (1923): 514-26.

9. Frederick Engels, *The Origin of Family, Private Property and the State* (Chicago: Kerr, 1902).

10. E.E. Evans-Pritchard, *Kinship and Marriage Among the Nuer* (Oxford: The Clarendon Press, 1951), p. 3.

11. Laurens van der Post, *The Dark Eye in Africa* (New York: Morrow, 1955), pp. 115.

12. Stanley Diamond, *Dahomey*, pp. 32-76.

13. Ernest A. Moody, "Galileo and Avempace: Dynamics of the Leaning Tower Experiment," in *Roots of Scientific Thought*, eds. Philip P. Wiener and Aaron Noland. (New York: Basic Books, 1957), pp. 176-206.

14. H.G. Barnett, "The Nature of the Potlach," *American Anthropology*, no. 40, (1938): 349-58.

15. Jerome Rothenberg, ed., *Shaking the Pumpkin: Traditional Poetry of the Indians of North America* (New York: Doubleday, 1972), p. 189.

16. W.H. Rivers, *Instinct and the Unconscious* (Cambridge, England: Cambridge University Press, 1924), p. 95 ff.

17. Edward B. Tylor, *Anthropology: An Introduction to the Study of Man and Civilization* (London: Watts, 1946), p. 134.

18. Robert H. Lowie, *The Crow Indians* (New York, Holt, Rinehart & Winston, 1956), p. 5 ff.

19. S.F. Nadel, *A Black Byzantium* (London: Oxford University Press, 1942), p. 68.

20. Stanley Moore, "Marxian Theories of Law in Primitive Society," in *Culture in History*, ed. Stanley Diamond (New York: Columbia University Press, 1960), pp. 642-62.

21. Edward Sapir, "Culture, Genuine and Spurious," in *Selected Writings of Edward Sapir in Language, Culture and Personality*, ed. David G. Mandelbaum (Berkeley: University of California Press, 1951), pp. 308-31.

22. Jomo Kenyatta, *Facing Mt. Kenya* (New York: Vintage, 1962), p. 168.

23. Alexander Goldenweisser, *Robots or Gods* (New York: Knopf, 1931), pp. 108-09.

24. E. Adamson Hoebel, *Man in the Primitive World* (New York: McGraw-Hill, 1958), pp. 355-56.

25. Robert H. Lowie, *Social Organizations* (New York: Holt, Rinehart & Winston, 1956), p. 217.

26. A. Irving Hallowell, "Ojibwa Ontology, Behavior, and World View," in *Culture in History*, ed. Stanley Diamond (New York: Columbia University Press, 1960), pp. 19-52.

27. Kenyatta, *Facing Mt. Kenya*, p. 172.

28. Franz Boas, *The Mind of Primitive Man* (New York: Macmillan, 1938), pp. 216-19.

29. Dorothy Lee, "Being and Value in Primitive Culture," *Journal of Philosophy*, vol. 46, (1949), pp. 401-15.

30. In personal conversation at Arden House, Harriman, New York, November 18, 1961.

31. Paul Radin, "Religion of the North American Indians," *Journal of American Folklore*, vol. 27 (1914).

32. Rothenberg, *Shaking the Pumpkin*, pp. 278-79.

33. S.A. Barret, "The Wintun Hesi Ceremony," *American Archaeology and Ethnology*, vol. 14 (1919), pp. 437-88.

34. A.W. Hoernle, *Certain Rites of Transition and the Conception of !nau among the Hottentots*, Harvard African Studies, vol. 2 (Cambridge: Harvard University Press, 1918), pp. 65-82.

35. Peter Freuchen, *Book of the Eskimos* (Cleveland: World Publishing, 1961), p. 92.

36. J.H. Steward, *The Ceremonial Buffoon of the American Indian*, Papers of the Michigan Academy of Science, Arts and Letters, vol. 14 (1931), pp. 187-207.

37. Rothenberg, *Shaking the Pumpkin*, pp. 000.

38. Marshall Sahlin's, *Stone Age Economics* (Chicago: Aldine Atherton, 1972), p. 217.

39. Edward B. Tylor, *Researches into the Early History of Mankind* (Chicago: University of Chicago Press, 1964), p. 126-27.

40. Johann Huizinga, *Homo Ludens, A Study of the Play-Element in Culture* (Boston: Beacon, 1955), pp. 1-27.

41. George Bird Grinnell, "Coup and Scalp Among the Plains Indians," *American Anthropologist*, vol. 12 (1910), pp. 216-17.

42. Michael Harner, *The Jivaro, People of the Sacred Waterfalls* (New York: Doubleday, 1972), p. 146.

43. Meyer Fortes, "Mind," in *The Institutions of Primitive Society*, ed. E.E. Evans-Pritchard (Glencoe, N.Y.: Free Press, 1956), pp. 90-94.

44. Goldenweisser, *Robots or Gods*, pp. 130-31.

45. Paul Radin "The Concept of Right and Wrong" in *The Makings of Man*, ed. V.F. Calverton (New York: Norton, 0000).

46. Erving Goffman, *The Presentations of Self in Everyday Life* (Edinburgh: University of Edinburgh, Social Sciences Research Center, 1956), p. 47.

47. Paul Radin, *The World of Primitive Man* (New York: Abelard-Schuman, 1953), p. 152.

48. Kenyatta, *Facing Mt. Kenya*, p. 303.

49. Christopher Dawson, *The Making of Europe* (Cleveland: World Publishing, 1961), p. 75.

50. Erich Kahler, *The Tower and the Abyss* (New York: George Braziller, 1957), p. 43.

51. See Diamond, "Kibbutz and Shtetl," *Social Problems*; and "Plato and the Definition of the Primitive," in this book.

52. Leopold Sedar Senghor, "Teilhard de Chardin and African Policy," *West African Pilot*, Lago, December 12, 1961, p. 5.

53. Søren Kierkegaard, "The Present Age; A Literary Review," in *A Kierkegaard Anthology*, ed. Robert Bretall (Princeton: Princeton University Press, 1946), pp. 266-67.

54. Diamond, "Kibbutz and Shtetl."

55. Rothenberg, *Shaking the Pumpkin*, p. 274.

56. Ibid., p. 195.

57. Franz Boas, *Primitive Art* (New York: Dover, 1955), p. 356.

58. Fortes, "Mind," in *The Institutions of Primitive Society*, pp. 90-94.

59. Martin Heidegger, *Platos Lehre von der Wahrheit, Mit einem Brief uber den "Humanismus,"* (Berne: A. Francke, 1947).

60. Paul Claudel, Art Poetique: *Connaissance du Temps. Traité de la Co-naissance au Monde et de soi-même* (Paris: Mercure, 1929).

61. Gabriel Marcel, *Metaphysical Journal*, trans. Benard Wall (Chicago: Regnery, 1952; orig. publ. *Journal Métaphysique*, Paris: Gallimard, 1927); *Being and Having*, trans. Katherine Farrer (London: Dacre Press, 1949); orig. publ. *Etre et Avoir*, Paris: Ferdinand Aubier, 1935).

62. Boas, *The Mind of Primitive Man*, pp. 216-19.

63. E.A. Brest, *The Metaphysical Foundations of Modern Physical Science* (New York: Harcourt, Brace, 1925); Ernest Cassier, "Galileo's Platonism," in *Studies and Essays in the History of Science and Learning, offered in Homage to George Sarton*, ed. M.S. Ashley-Montague (New York: Schuman, 1944) pp. 279-97; Alexandre Koysé, "Galileo and Plato," in *Journal of the History of Ideas* 4 (1943):400-28; and Ernest Moody, "Galileo and Avempace", pp. 176-206.

5. PLATO AND THE DEFINITION OF THE PRIMITIVE (176-202)

1. Although Plato makes a passing reference to a kind of idyllic rusticity which some of his interpreters have called primitive life, it bears no resemblance to the latter at all and serves merely as a foil for his developing rationale of the state. See *The Republic of Plato*, trans. by B. Jowett (Oxford: Clarendon Press, 1925), p. 53.

2. Ralph Waldo Emerson, *Representative Men: Seven Lectures* (Boston: Houghton, Mifflin, 1903), pp. 39-40.

3. F.M. Cornford, *The Unwritten Philosophy and Other Essays* (Cambridge: At the University Press, 1950), p. 129.

4. J.B. Bury, *A History of Greece to the Death of Alexander the Great*, 3rd ed. (London: Macmillan, 1956), p. 56.

5. The *Dialogues of Plato*, trans. by B. Jowett (New York: Bigelow, Brown, 1914), vol. II, *The Republic*, p. 303. All citations, unless otherwise indicated, are to this edition.

6. Although the details of the chronicler's observations are, in all likelihood, distorted, his conclusion is sound. Stanley Diamond, *Dahomey: A Proto-State in West Africa* (Ph.D. dissertation, Columbia University, 1951 University of Michigan Microfilms), p. 26. This is a study of a society in transition from kin to civil structure and involved in a kin-civil conflict that ramifies throughout the culture.

7. Stanley Diamond, "Kibbutz and Shtetl: The History of an Idea," *Social Problems*, (Fall, 1957), Vol. 5, pp. 71-99.

8. *Republic*, p. 68.

9. Ibid., p. 102. Compare this with the famous passage from *As You Like It*: "And one man in his time plays many parts." Shakespeare would have been excluded from the republic on the double score of being both a tragedian and a comic dramatist.

10. Melville J. Herskovits, *Dahomey, An Ancient West African Kingdom*, Vol. 1 (Locust Valley, N.Y.: Augustin, 1938), p. 30.

11. V. Gordon Childe, *Man Makes Himself* (New York: New American Library, 1955), p. 149.

12. Cornford, *Unwritten Philosophy*, p. 134.

13. *Republic*, p. 129.

14. However, Plato's philosophy could today be characterized as both transcendental and essentialist.

15. Ibid., p. 187.

16. Ibid., pp. 191-92.

17. Ibid., p. 129.

18. Ibid., p. 128.

19. Diamond, *Dahomey*, p. 91.

20. *Republic*, p. 130.

21. Ibid., p. 128.

22. For a recent and rich analysis of the distinction between collective and community, see Erich Kahler, *The Tower and the Abyss* (New York, George Braziller, 1957).

23. Plato's educational psychology is what we would probably term "mechanically behavioristic." The attenuation of immediate kin ties among the elite and the emphasis on morality tales, would tend to diffuse emotional-intellectual growth; the tensions that provide leverage for such growth can hardly be generated by institutions and abstractions. Further, the collective rearing of élite children would probably have defeated itself in the end by not producing enough emotion to secure loyalty. See, for example, the writer's remarks on collective rearing in the Israeli Kibbutz. "Kibbutz and Shtetl," *Social Problems*, pp. 88-93.

24. A.L. Kroeber, *Anthropology: Race, Language, Culture, Psychology, Prehistory*, rev. ed. (New York: Harcourt Brace Jovanovich, 1948), p. 281.

25. *Republic*, p. 102.

26. Ibid., p. 98.

27. Ibid., p. 73.

28. Ibid., pp. 75-78.

29. Ibid., p. 86.

30. Ibid., p. 88.

31. Ibid., p. 78.

32. Ibid., p. 82.

33. Ibid., p. 91.

34. Paul Radin, *The Trickster, A Study in American Indian Mythology*, with commentaries by Karl Kerenyi and C.J. Jung (London, Routledge and Kegan Paul, 1956), p. ix.

35. *Republic*, p. 93.

36. Ibid., p. 380.

37. Ibid., p. 396.

38. As Joyce Kilmer confessed, "Poems are made by fools like me, but only God can make a tree."

39. *Republic*, p. 389.

40. Ibid.

41. Paul Radin, *Primitive Man as Philosopher* (New York, Dover, 1957).

42. Edward B. Tylor, *Researches Into the Early History of Mankind* (Chicago: University of Chicago Press, 1964) p. 000.

43. Robert Redfield, *Tepoztlan—A Mexican Village: A Study of Folk Life* (Chicago: University of Chicago Press, 1930), pp. 222-23.

44. I use the term "traumatic" here in the sense of deep, psychic trauma. This is not to deny the pain and suffering often involved in primitive rituals, but the personal and traditional meanings infusing them, the conventional structuring of the situation, strip these experiences of the unwitting and pathological ramifications of trauma.

45. Paul Radin, *Primitive Religion, Its Nature and Origin* (New York: Dover, 1957).

46. Francis Fergusson, *The Idea of a Theater* (New York: Doubleday, n.d.), p. 40.

47. J.H. Steward, "The Ceremonial Buffoon of the American Indian," in *Papers of the Michigan Academy of Science, Arts, and Letters*, Vol. 14 (1930), 187-207.

48. *The Republic of Plato*, trans. by A.D. Lindsay (New York, Dutton, 1940), p. 148.

49. *The Republic*, trans. by Jowett, p. 89.

50. Cornford, *Unwritten Philosophy*, p. 67.

6. THE USES OF THE PRIMITIVE (203-226)

1. Jean Jacques Rousseau, *On the Origins of Inequality, A Discourse on Political Economy*, (Chicago: Henry Regnery, 1949), p. 98.

2. Marc Bloch, *The Historian's Craft*, (New York: Knopf, 1953), p. 151.

3. Claude Lévi-Strauss, *World on the Wane* (New York: Criterion, 1946), p. 39.

4. Arthur O. Lovejoy, *Essays in the History of Ideas* (New York: E.P. Putnam's Sons, 1960), p. 18.

5. Ibid., p. 28.
6. Ibid.

7. SCHIZOPHRENIA AND CIVILIZATION (227-254)

1. The usual figure projected by the NIMH is more modest and less specific. About 22 million Americans are said to become mentally ill in the clinical sense at one time or another in their lives. Perhaps half of these would be identified as "schizophrenic."

2. The paper in question is "Genetic Factors in Behavior Disorders" by David Rosenthal. Related essays are those by S.S. Kety, D. Rosenthal, P.H. Wender, and F. Schulsinger in *The Transmission of Schizophrenia* ed. D. Rosenthal and S.S. Kety (London: Pergamon Press, 1968). Also, D. Rosenthal, P.H. Wender, S.S. Kety, J. Welner and F. Schulsinger, "The Adopted-Away Offspring of Schizophrenics," *American Journal of Psychiatry*, 1971.

3. Henri Michaux, *Miserable Miracle*, trans. Louise Varèse (San Francisco: City Lights Books, 1967).

4. Jean Arp, Arp on Arp: *Poems, Essays, Memories*, ed. Marcel Jean (New York: The Viking Press, 1972), p. 35.

5. Ibid., pp. 47-49.

6. George Devereaux, "A Sociological Theory of Schizophrenia," *Psychoanalytic Review* 26 (1939):317.

6. But even that integration cannot be understood in our language of ego psychology. It is, rather, as Radin puts it, "the recognition of (and insistence upon) multiple personality ... the direct consequence of aboriginal man's unconquerable and unsentimental realism and his refusal to assume fictitious and artificial unities." (This refusal, it should be added, is the result of the exploration and realization of the potential phases of the self during the course of the life cycle.) As Radin concludes: "the various elements [of the individual] become dissociated temporarily from the body and enter into relationship with the dissociated elements of other individuals. *The nature of the impingement of individual upon individual and of the individual upon the external world is, thus, utterly different from anything that a Western European can possibly imagine. The medley of combinations and permutations it would permit is quite bewildering....* [Nevertheless] what prevents anarchy, independent as they are, is that they fall into *a definite configuration* within each man's ego" (read self). *The World of the Primitive*, Paul Radin (New York: E.P. Dutton, 1971).

8. THE RULE OF LAW VERSUS THE ORDER OF CUSTOM (255-280)

1. Paul Bohannan, "Law," *International Encyclopedia of the Social Sciences*, (New York: MacMillan, 1968), pp. 73-78.

2. Paul Radin, *The World of Primitive Man*, (New York: H. Schuman, 1953), p. 223.

3. J.G. Peristiany, *The Institutions of Primitive Society* (New York: The Free Press, 1956), p. 45.

4. V.C. Uchendu, *The Igbo of Southeast Nigeria*, (New York: Holt, Reinhart and Winston, 1965), p. 46.

5. Sydney P. Simpson and Julius Stone, *Law and Society in Evolution, Book I* (St. Paul: West Publishing Co., 1942), p. 2.

6. William Seagle, *The History of Law* (New York: Tudor, 1946), p. 35.

7. Ibid., pp. 19-20.

8. Ibid.

9. Henry Maine, *Village Communities and Miscellanies*, (New York: Henry Holt and Co., 1889), p. 230.

10. George Vernadskya, *Medieval Russian Laws* (New York: Norton, 1969), pp. 26-27.

11. Quoted by Simpson and Stone, *Law and Society in Evolution*, p. 78.

12. Henry Maine, *Early History of Institutions* (New York: Kennikat Press Inc., 1966), p. 383.

13. Simpson and Stone, *Law and Society in Evolution*, p. 177.

14. Stanley Diamond, *Dahomey, a Proto-State in West Africa* (Ph.D. dissertation, Columbia, 1951; University of Michigan Microfilms), p. 109.

15. Quoted by Max Gluckman, "Studies in African Land Tenure," *African Studies*, vol. 3 (1944): 14-21.

16. Robert S. Rattray, *Ashanti, Law and Constitution* (London: Negro University Press, 1929).

17. L.P. Mair, "Baganda Land Tenure," *Africa*, vol. 6 (1933).

18. Henry Maine, *Ancient Law* (New York: Dutton, 1931), p. 140.

19. R. von Jhering, *Geist des Romischen Recht*, vol. 2 (Germany: 1866), p. 31.

20. Rattray, *Ashanti, Law and Constitution*, pp. 80, 286.

21. S.F. Nadel, "Nupe State Community," *Africa*, vol. 8 (1934), p. 303.

22. Friedrich Engels, *Origin of the Family, Private Property and the State* (Chicago: Kerr, 1902), p. 133.

23. M.J. Herskovitz, *Dahomey, an Ancient West African Kingdom* (New York: 1938), p. 73.

24. Ibid.

25. Albert Camus, *Caligula and Three Other Plays*, trans. Stuart Gilbert (New York: Knopf, 1958), p. 17.

26. Peristiany, *The Institutions of Primitive Society*, p. 42.

27. Uchendu, *The Igbo of Southeast Nigeria*, p. 43.

28. Michel de Montaigne, *The Complete Essays*, trans. Donald Frame. (Stanford: Stanford University Press, 1965), p. 197.

29. Rattray, *Ashanti*, p. 286.

30. Ibid.

31. Sir John Salmond, *Jurisprudence* (1920), p. 13.

32. Sir William Markby, *Elements of Law* (1905), p. 21.

33. William Stubbs, *The Constitutional History of England* vol. 1 (London: 1890), p. 48.

34. Richard F. Burton, *A Mission to Gelele, a King of Dahomey*, vol. 2 (London: 1864), p. 211.

35. Rattray, *Ashanti*, p. 292.

36. Ibid.

37. W. Bosman, *A New and Accurate Description of the Coast of Guinea* (London: 1705), p. 362.

38. R. Norris, *Reise nach Abomey, der Hofstadt des Koings von Dahomey an von Guinea im Jahr 1772* (Leipzig: 1790), p. 221 ff.

39. *Code of Hammurabi*, trans. (New York: Harper, 1904), p. 13, par. 6.

40. A. Le Herisse, *L'Ancien Royaume du Dahomey* (Paris, 1911), p. 72.

41. M. Quénum, *Au Pays des Fons* (Paris: 1938), pp. 7, 21, 22. Quénum had a poor opinion of the ethnographers who claimed to understand and interpret his country. They failed, he believed, because of the inadequate sources of information and ignorance of social customs. "Most of our ethnographers," he wrote "have had as collaborators princes and ex-ministers of state and have believed their tales." He adds that ignorance of the native language and deficient sympathy compounded the problem. The point to note here is that Quénum is objecting to the view from the top, which is a critical issue in the writing of all political history.

42. Norris, *Reise nach Abomey*, p. 257.

43. Skertchly, *Dahomey as it is* (London: 1874), p. 283.

44. Bosman, *A New Description of the Coast of New Guinea*, p. 361.

45. Seagle, *The History of Law*, p. 64.

46. Rattray, *Ashanti*, p. 295.

47. Radin, *The World of Primitive Man*, p. 252.

48. Peristiany, *The Institutions of Primitive Society*, p. 43.

49. Rattray, *Ashanti*, p. 286.

50. Margery Perham, *Native Administration in Nigeria* (London: 1962), pp. 229 ff. Acts of violence must be distinguished from *crimes* of violence. The incidence, occasions for, and character of violence in primitive, as opposed to civilized societies, is a subject of the utmost importance, which I have discussed elsewhere in this volume. But the question here has to do with crimes in which violence is used as means for, e.g., the theft of property. In contemporary societies unpremeditated acts of personal violence which have no ulterior motive, so-called crimes of passion, may not be penalized or carry minor degrees of guilt, that is, their status as legally defined crimes is ambiguous. This would certainly seem to reflect a historically profound

distinction between crime and certain types of violence. In primitive societies violence tends to be personally structured, nondissociative and, thereby, self-limiting.

51. Burton, *A Mission to Gelele*, p. 56.

52. A. Dalzel, *The History of Dahomey, an Inland Kingdom of Africa* (London: 1793), p. 212.

53. Rattray, *Ashanti*, p. 299.

54. Uchandu, *The Igbo of Southeast Nigeria*, pp. 42-43.

55. E.B. Tylor, *Anthropology: An Introduction to the Study of Man and Civilization* vol. 2 (London: Watts, 1946), p. 156.

56. Ibid., p. 134.

57. Montaigne, *The Complete Essays*, p. 153. In ignorance of Montaigne's contrast between primitive society and Plato's ideal Republic, I published an essay, "Plato and the Definition of the Primitive," in *Culture and History*, New York, 1960, which explicates some of the points briefly noted above, and which is included, in slightly revised form, in this volume. For a more comprehensive model of primitive society see "The Search for the Primitive" in this volume. In order to understand the functioning of custom in primitive society fully, one should have such a model in mind.

58. Paul Vinogradoff, *Outlines of Historical Jurisprudence* vol. 1 (London: A.M.S. Press, 1920), p. 93.

59. Engels, *The Origin of the Family, Private Property and the State*, p. 179, 207.

60. Ibid., p. 206.

61. S.F. Nadel, *A Black Byzantium*, (London: Oxford University Press, 1942), p. 144.

62. Nadel, "Nupe State and Community," *Africa*, p. 287.

63. Quénum, *Au Pays des Fons*, p. 22.

64. Dalzel, *The History of Dahomey*, p. 212.

65. Jhering, *Geist des Romischen Recht*, vol. 2, p. 471.

66. Seagle, *The History of Law*, p. 36.

67. Claude Lévi-Strauss, *A World on the Wane (Tristes Tropiques)* trans. John Russell (New York: Criterion, 1961), p. 390.

9. JOB AND THE TRICKSTER (281-291)

1. Paul Radin, *The World of Primitive Man* (New York: Henry Schuman, 1953); p. 47.

10. THE INAUTHENTICITY OF ANTHROPOLOGY (292-331)

1. Claude Lévi-Strauss, *L'Homme Nu* (Paris: Plen, 1971), pp. 575-77.

2. Claude Lévi-Strauss, *Structural Anthropology* (New York: Basic Books, 1963), p. 213.

3. Claude Lévi-Strauss, *The Raw and the Cooked* (London: Jonathan Cape, 1970), p. 13.

4. Ibid., p. 6.

5. Claude Lévi-Strauss, *A World on the Wane (Tristes Tropiques)* (New York: Criterion Books, 1961), p. 397.

6. Ibid., p. 396.

7. Lévi-Strauss, *The Raw and the Cooked*, pp. 17-18.

8. Ibid., p. 19.

9. Ibid., p. 18.

10. Lévi-Strauss, *Structural Anthropology*, p. 61.

11. Lévi-Strauss, *The Raw and the Cooked*, p. 20.

12. Ibid., pp. 10-11.

13. Lévi-Strauss, *Structural Anthropology*, Chapter 9.

14. Claude Lévi-Strauss, *The Elementary Structures of Kinship* (Boston: Beacon Press, 1969), p. 496.

15. Lévi-Strauss, *L'Homme Nu*, p. 616.

16. Claude Lévi-Strauss, "Structuralism and Ecology," Gildersleeve Lecture, delivered at Barnard College, March 28, 1972, in *Barnard Alumnae* (Spring, 1972), pp. 13-14.

17. Claude Lévi-Strauss, *The Savage Mind* (Chicago: University Press, 1966).

18. Lévi-Strauss, *Structural Anthropology*, p. 230.

19. Stanley Diamond, "Anaguta Cosmology: the Linguistic and Behavioral Implications," *Anthropological Linguistics*, vol. 2, no. 2, (1960).

20. Lévi-Strauss, *A World on the Wane*, p. 396.

21. It seems, in the total perspective of Lévi Strauss's work, that the dialectics between man and nature has also collapsed into a series of determined and polar responses. Interstingly enough, Lévi-Strauss makes only a couple of brief, and tendentious, references to Engels's *Dialectics of Nature*. For whatever one things of Engels's effort at a cosmology, the basic argument, in the context of the whole Marxist effort, contradicts Lévi-Strauss's boast, directed to Sartre in *L'Homme Nu*, that structuralism, unlike philosophy, is capable of accepting man's integration with nature. But that "integration" is hardly a dialectical process, as the latter has been defined by Engels:

"Natural science like philosophy *has hitherto entirely neglected the influence of men's activity on their thought*. . . . But it is precisely the *alteration of nature by men*, not solely nature as such, which is the essential and immediate basis of human thought. . . . Man . . . reacts on nature, changing it and creating new conditions of existence for himself. There is damned little left of 'nature,' as it was in Germany, at the time when the Germanic peoples emigrated into it. The earth's surface, climate, vegetation, fauna, the human beings themselves have continually changed, and all this owing to human activity, while the changes of nature in Germany which have occurred in the process of time without human interference are incalculably small (italics added)." (Friedrich Engels, *Dialectics of Nature* [New York: International Publishers, 1940], p. 172.)

This sounds precisely like Sartre's argument, which Lévi-Strauss rebuffs on p. 616 of *L'Homme Nu*. One understands, therefore, why Lévi-Strauss cannot root himself in Engels, and it reveals further the true character of the opposition between himself and Sartre. Similarly, Lévi-Strauss tends to avoid acknowledging the full range of his debt to Durkheim and Mauss, while basing himself on Jakobson and Saussure. In both instances the silence about certain aspects of the more obvious influences can only be understood by the fact that the denouement of Engels's approach, on the one hand, and of Durkheim's and Mauss's, on the other, remain unrelated to Lévi-Strauss.

22. Emile Durkheim, "The Dualism of Human Nature and Its Social Conditions," in *Emile Durkheim 1858-1917: A Collection of Essays*, ed. Kurt H. Wolf (Columbus, Ohio: Ohio State University Press, 1960), p. 330.

23. Jean-Paul Sartre, *Anti-Semite and Jew*, trans. George J. Becker (New York: Schochen Books, 1948), pp. 130-31.

24. Lévi-Strauss, *The Raw and the Cooked*, pp. 340-41.

25. Lévi-Strauss, *Structural Anthropology*, p. 224.

26. Lévi-Strauss, *The Raw and the Cooked*, p. 1.

27. Paul Radin, *Primitive Religion* (New York: Dover, 1957), p. 244.

28. Robert Lowie, *Primitive Religion* (New York: Liveright, 1948), p. 48.

29. Dorothy Lee, *Freedom and Culture* (New York: Prentice-Hall, 1959), p. 131.

30. Karl Marx and Friedrich Engels, *The German Ideology*, ed. R. Paseal, (New York: International Publishers, 1938), p. 27.

31. S. Kang, "A Model of 'Oriental' Rules in the Oriental Dualism: Structural Analysis of Chinese World View," in *Structuralism in Perspective*, ed. P. Rossi (E.P. Dutton, in press).

32. Stanley Diamond, "The Anaguta of Nigeria: Suburban Primitive," in *Contemporary Change in Traditional Societies*, vol. I: Introduction and African Tribes, ed. Julian W. Steward (Urbana, Illinois: University of Illinois, 1967).

33. Jerome Rothenberg, ed., *Shaking the Pumpkin* (New York: Doubleday, 1972), p. 262.

34. Oswald Spengler, *The Decline of the West*, vol. 1 (New York: Alfred A. Knopf, 1926), pp. 425 ff. In *The Decline of the West*, Spengler also attempted to penetrate to the ultimate western *Weltanschauung*, but without considering it ultimate for man—in this sense he was more of an anthropologist than Lévi-Strauss. He defines the view adopted by Lévi-Strauss as the inevitable outcome of our civilization, as the denouement of Faustian culture, the self-characterizing term he borrowed from Goethe. And it should

be recalled that Flaubert, in treating of the life of St. Anthony, the founder
of monasticism, was also influenced by Goethe—indeed he viewed the
Temptation of St. Anthony as Faustian. But let Spengler, uncannily
reminiscent of Lévi-Strauss, speak for himself:

> before the curtain falls, there is one more task for the historical Faustian
> spirit, a task not yet specified, hitherto not even imagined as possible.
> There has still to be written a morphology of the exact sciences, which
> shall discover how all laws, concepts and theories inwardly hang together
> as forms. . . .

> The separate sciences—epistemology, physics, chemistry, mathematics,
> astronomy—are approaching one another with acceleration, converging
> towards a complete identity of results. The issue will be a fusion of the
> form-worlds which will present on the one hand a system of numbers,
> functional in nature and reduced to a few ground-formulae, and on the
> other a small group of theories, denominators to those numerators,
> which in the end will be seen to be *myths of the springtime under
> modern veils.* . . . The aim to which all this is striving, and which in
> particular every Nature-researcher feels in himself as an impulse, is the
> achievement of a pure numerical transcendence, the complete and
> inclusive conquest of the visibly apparent and its replacement by a
> language of imagery *unintelligible to the layman and impossible of
> sensuous realization*—but a language that the great Faustian symbol of
> infinite space endows with the dignity of inward necessity. The deep
> scepticism of these final judgments links the soul anew to the forms of
> early Gothic religiousness. The inorganic, known and dissected
> world-around, the World as Nature and System, has deepened itself until
> it is a pure sphere of functional numbers. But, as we have seen, number is
> one of the most primary symbols in every Culture; and consequently the
> way to pure number is the return of the waking consciousness to its own
> secret, the revelation of its own formal necessity. The goal reached, the
> vast and ever more meaningless and threadbare fabric woven around
> natural science falls apart. It was, after all, *nothing but the inner
> structure of the "Reason," the grammar by which it believed it could
> overcome the Visible and extract therefrom the True.* But what appears
> under the fabric is once again the earliest and deepest, the Myth, the
> immediate Becoming, Life itself. *The less anthropomorphic science
> believes itself to be, the more anthropomorphic it is. One by one it gets
> rid of the separate human traits in the Nature-picture, only to find at the
> end that the supposed pure Nature which it holds in its hand
> is—humanity itself, pure and complete.* . . . The final issue to which the
> Faustian wisdom tends—though it is only in the highest moments that it
> has seen it—is the dissolution of all knowledge into a vast system of
> morphological relationships. Dynamics and Analysis are in respect of
> meaning, form-language and substance, identical with Romanesque
> ornament, Gothic cathedrals, Christian-German dogma and *the dynastic
> state.* . . . The united of several scientific aspects into one will bear all the
> marks of the great art of counterpoint. An infinitesimal music of the

boundless world-space ... is the grand legacy of the Faustian soul to the souls of Cultures yet to be, a bequest of ... forms that the heirs will possibly ignore. And then, weary after its striving, the Western science returns to its spiritual home (italics added).

35. Lévi-Strauss, *A World on the Wane*, p. 395.

36. Lévi-Strauss, *Structural Anthropology*, p. 346.

37. Lévi-Strauss, *A World on the Wane*, p. 396.

38. Ibid., pp. 397-98.

39. Lévi-Strauss, *L'Homme Nu*, p. 612.

40. Emile Durkheim and Marcel Mauss, *Primitive Classifications*, trans. Rodney Needham (London: Cohen and West, 1963), p. 84.

41. Ibid., p. 82.

42. Ibid.

43. Sartre, *Anti-Semite and Jew*, pp. 133-44.

44. Lévi-Strauss, *The Raw and the Cooked*, p. 10.

45. These quotations and parenthetical statements reproduce the sequence of Sartre's argument in *Anti-Semite and Jew*, pp. 55-138.

46. Jean-Paul Sartre, *L'Arc*, no. 30, p. 94.

11. WHAT HISTORY IS (332-351)

1. A.L. Kroeber, *The Nature of Culture* (Chicago: University of Chicago Press, 1952).

2. A.L. Kroeber, *Anthropology* (New York: Harcourt Brace Jovanovich, 1948), p. 256.

3. Rene Ahlberg, "Forgotton Philosopher, The Work of Abraham Deborin," *Survey*, vol. 37 (1961), pp. 79-89.

4. Leslie White, *The Science of Culture: A Study of Man and Civilization* (New York: Farrar, Straus, 1949).

5. Marc Bloch, *The Historian's Craft* (New York: Knopf, 1953), p. 151.

6. Karl Marx, *The Holy Family*.

7. Irving Goldman, "The Evolution of Polynesian Societies," in *Culture in History*, ed. Stanley Diamond (New York: Columbia University Press, 1960), p. 711.

8. Leslie White, "The Energy Theory of Cultural Development," in *Prof. Gherye Felicitation*, ed. K.M. Kapadie (Bombay: Popular Book Depot, 1954), pp. 1-8.

9. Paul Tillich, "Marx's View of History: A Study in the History of the Philosophy of History," in *Culture in History*, ed. Stanley Diamond (New York: Columbia University Press, 1960), pp. 631-41.

10. Vernon Venable, *Human Nature: The Marxian View* (New York: Knopf, 1946).

NOTES

11. Karl Marx, "Third Thesis on Feuerbach" *The German Ideology*, K. Marx and Friedrich Engels, ed. R. Pascal (New York: International Publishers, 1938), and Krader (unpublished manuscript, 1971), p. 8.

12. Irving Fetscher, *Marx and Marxism* (New York: Herder and Herder, 1971), p. 00.

13. Karl Marx, "Third Thesis on Feuerbach" *The German Ideology* K. Marx and Friedrich Engels, ed. R. Pascal (New York: International Publishers, 1938), p. 198.

14. Ibid., p. 198.

15. Teilhard de Chardin, *The Phenomenon of Man*, trans. Bernard Wall (New York: Harper and Row, 1959).

16. Søren Kierkegaard, *Concluding Unscientific Postscript to the Philosophical Fragments*, trans. David F. Swenson; ed. Walter Lowie (Princeton: Princeton University Press and American-Scandinavian Foundation, 1941).

17. Jose Ortega y Gassett, "In Search of Goethe from Within: Letter to a German," in *The Dehumanization of Art*, ed. Jose Ortega y Gassett (New York: Doubleday, 1969).

INDEX

375